THE AMERICAN ASCENDANCY

The American

Ascendancy

HOW THE UNITED STATES GAINED

AND WIELDED GLOBAL DOMINANCE

BY MICHAEL H. HUNT

The University of North Carolina Press

Chapel Hill

© 2007 The University of North Carolina Press
All rights reserved
Designed by Richard Hendel
Set in Scala types by Tseng Information Systems, Inc.
Manufactured in the United States of America

This book was published with the assistance of
the H. Eugene and Lillian Youngs Lehman Fund of
the University of North Carolina Press. A complete
list of books published in the Lehman Series appears
at the end of the book.

The paper in this book meets the guidelines for
permanence and durability of the Committee on
Production Guidelines for Book Longevity of the
Council on Library Resources.

Library of Congress Cataloging-in-Publication Data
Hunt, Michael H.
The American ascendancy : how the United States
gained and wielded global dominance / by Michael H.
Hunt.
    p. cm.
Includes bibliographical references and index.
ISBN 978-0-8078-3090-1 (cloth : alk. paper)
ISBN 978-0-8078-5963-6 (pbk. : alk. paper)
 1. United States—Foreign relations—19th century.
 2. United States—Foreign relations—20th century.
 3. United States—Foreign relations—2001–
 4. Hegemony—United States—History. 5. International
relations—History. 6. Geopolitics. 7. World history.
I. Title.
E183.7.H855 2007
327.73009'04—dc22   2006028185

Portions of this book were adapted from Michael H.
Hunt, *Ideology and U.S. Foreign Policy* (New Haven,
Conn.: Yale University Press, 1987). © 1987 Yale
University Press. Used with permission.

A Caravan book. For more information, visit www.
caravanbooks.org.

cloth   11 10 09 08 07 5 4 3 2 1
paper   12 11 10 09   5 4 3 2 1

To Paula—still the best of youth!

CONTENTS

FIGURES AND TABLE

THE AMERICAN ASCENDANCY

introduction

FRAMING THE QUESTION

In April 1950 President Harry Truman's advisers told him that
Americans had arrived at "the ascendancy of their strength." This memorable
phrase, from which this book takes its title, registered long-nurtured national
ambitions that had been finally realized, and it foreshadowed the widening
exercise of u.s. power that would outlast the Cold War and carry over into the
new century. The "fact" of ascendancy is today only too obvious. The United
States now occupies a global position of unusual, arguably unprecedented
dominance—what is often fashionably described as hegemony or empire.[1]

For many Americans over the last decade or so, this dominance has inspired a sense of triumph and dreams of global influence. It has also given rise
to anxiety and soul searching as the country has spun through a dizzying set
of changes since the end of the Cold War and especially since September 11,
2001. The most recent of developments—the invasion and occupation of Iraq
and the worldwide "war on terrorism"—have ignited a critical reaction abroad
and sharp disagreements at home. What is the surest path to u.s. security?
How tightly should Washington bind itself to allies and to international institutions and conventions? Do u.s. actions betray the country's own vaunted
standards or stain its international reputation? Is u.s. power on the decline or
can it significantly reshape the world?

History has occupied a problematic place in the intense, even feverish
discussion of these questions. Popular commentators, policymakers, and the
broader informed public have made relatively little use of the past to frame
the issues of the day even though history offers precisely the kind of steadying insights needed at a time of confusion and disorientation. To the extent
that commentators do invoke history, it is perfunctory, dated, or tendentious.
While historians of foreign relations, culture, and economy have much to say
one way or another about aspects of the u.s. rise to ascendancy, they have
done little to construct overarching narratives that trace the steps carrying
the United States to its current dominance while also taking into account the
dramatic developments over the last decade and a half in the u.s. relationship
to the broader world. The sad truth is that their work is largely irrelevant to

the debates playing out within the think tanks, among the pundits, and in the press. Indeed, except for Cold War studies, which command some interest as an immediate and usable past, that work is hardly even known outside the narrow confines of the academy.

How did a weak and insignificant country rise to the first place among nations and manage to remain there—a source of pride to her people, a marvel to some abroad, and a menace to others? Here is the historical puzzle at the heart of the American ascendancy—and the question that this book seeks to answer.

A good starting point is to stand back from the details of the u.s. case and consider in the abstract the qualities that can make a country preeminent. Wealth belongs at the head of the list. Only a dynamic and growing economy can create the material resources essential to realizing great international ambitions. Generation of wealth in turn depends on science and technology driving productivity and on a society attuned to innovation. Next in sequence and importance would be the promotion of national confidence—a faith or sense of mission. Ideas give purpose to people. Without a widely shared vision, no country can mobilize resources—no matter how ample—to a single end and ask citizens to endure sacrifices and potential setbacks to realize those ambitions. No less critical than wealth and purpose would be a strong, modern state. Even under the most favorable conditions, a country without a well-developed institutional apparatus to direct national affairs will go nowhere. With a strong state comes the possibility of spurring economic development, overcoming internal divisions, promoting a shared national sentiment, and securing the homeland against potentially dangerous neighbors. Succeeding in these areas, reaching the top, and then staying there depends in turn on elites serving the state and possessed of good judgment and an understanding of the world. From their ranks emerge under ideal circumstances state leaders with sound instincts and rich experience who know when to advance boldly and when to bide their time prudently and patiently, which battles to fight and which to defer, when conciliation and accommodation may win more than confrontation and violence. A union of wealth, confidence, and leadership provides the basis for sustained international success, which in turn creates a virtuous cycle, reinforcing confidence, confirming national myths, and giving rise to widely accepted policy codes.

By assembling precisely these constituents of national power, American leaders won security for their new nation, then international standing as a major power, and finally uncontested supremacy. This outcome was not predestined—or so at least the historian preoccupied with evidence will conclude.

It is not good enough to explain the U.S. rise to a leading role in the world as an inevitable step in the progress of human history or the unfolding of some divine plan. Seen from a historical perspective, the process was contingent.

The U.S. ascendancy depended in part on multiple pieces coming together in a complex mosaic. No one piece was enough. For example, a vibrant economy or nationalist confidence alone could not have propelled the country so dramatically forward. Success also depended on bringing the pieces together deliberately and in roughly the right order. In each phase of the national history, U.S. leaders matched national ambitions to material resources and made the choices that moved the country toward an ever more formidable global position. The foreshortened perspective of contemporary commentators makes U.S. success look recent and thus rapid, but the extraordinary development of U.S. power did not begin in 1945 with the onset of a policy of Cold War, nor in 1914 as Woodrow Wilson began his fateful encounter with a Europe at war. By the end of the nineteenth century Americans had already behind them a century of making choices that had brought stunning successes. By then they had put in place most of the key elements of American international power. And the missing parts (primarily a strong state) would soon follow. The United States was by the early twentieth century securely on a trajectory leading toward an ever more dominant international position.

This particular exercise in determining what made the United States strong falls short in one critical respect: it omits the world in which Americans achieved their ascendancy. Americans made their own history but within the bounds of the possible—the constraints and opportunities—defined not just by other states but also by global forces. Americans with increasingly broad ambitions and a lengthening reach had to contend with powerful pressures and trends—social, economic, technological, and cultural—that sometimes smoothed their way and at other times made it rocky, even impassable.

Fortunately, a new history is available to help fill out this global context in which Americans sought to realize their dreams and exercise their power. The work of global historians taken together offers an impressively wide angle of vision and an attractively insistent focus on issues usually lost to sight in the media and in public policy debates and even in historical controversies framed along narrowly national lines (as though what Americans wanted and did was all that mattered). In essence, global history highlights the worldwide trends that in part defined the direction and timing of the U.S. path to prominence. Global history also helps us see the ways in which the United States increasingly created and controlled those trends.

To begin with, the United States was at its inception a product of forces at play within the North Atlantic world. Americans have shared in the wealth and ambition that increasingly defined that world and that separated European peoples from others. The American nation took form as one of the neo-European settler societies that emerged in the seventeenth and eighteenth centuries as modern globalization began to take form. Already then it reflected its British origins in the worldview championed by its dominant classes, its premier political and economic institutions, and its defining social practices. Thereafter—from the early nineteenth century onward—the United States functioned within a network of increasingly intense and wide-ranging global contacts and processes centered on the North Atlantic. Like Europeans, Americans were galvanized by nationalist movements, industrialization driven by fossil fuels and a stream of new technologies, empire building, and global war. These critical features of globalization from the late nineteenth to the mid-twentieth centuries offered models of development and ways of thinking from which Americans could borrow, sometimes self-consciously. Ever more emphatically, u.s. leaders defined their future as a greater England and as a more and more senior ally of the island nation.

American ascendancy is more than a new chapter—a consequence and extension—in the history of British Empire. Seen in even longer-term perspective, the u.s. ascendancy carries forward a pattern of global dominance secured not just by Britain but also by the other great powers of the North Atlantic over several centuries. By mastering other regions, controlling the international economy, maintaining military superiority, and setting the terms for debate over such fundamentally cultural matters as human rights, gender relations, social justice, and environmental exploitation and protection, Americans have taken up the mantle borne earlier by Portugal, Spain, the Netherlands, France, and Britain.

Americans were products of global forces in a second way. They had to come to terms, however reluctantly, with the rise of the modern national state. In the course of the first half of the twentieth century, a people dedicated to the principles of liberty and suspicious of concentrated political power underwent a conversion. Their mounting sense of nationalism and their view of the broader world either as a stage for crusading or as a source of danger gradually effected that conversion. Between the 1880s and the 1940s a potent governmental apparatus took form in Washington. This institution brought the necessary resources under its control and demonstrated its ability to monitor and respond quickly to events around the world. In the thinking of those who served the burgeoning American state, global ambitions came to occupy a position of orthodoxy, in effect becoming the state ideology. Increasingly, advocates of more modest national goals—hostile to empire, averse to war, devoted to domestic priorities—fell silent or retreated to the margins of political life.

Some make the claim that the u.s. state, like its counterparts around the world, is declining in the face of global market forces. Mammoth transnational corporations, major banks, and in recent decades transnational organizations such as the World Trade Organization and the International Monetary Fund seem to some analysts to trump state sovereignty, overwhelm the popular will, and ride roughshod over communities. The long view would argue against putting the modern state, at least in the developed world, on the critical list. States have to the contrary steadily put on mass and muscle in the context of globalization even if their prime concerns have evolved. In the first phase during the late nineteenth and early twentieth centuries, they paid increasing attention to policing their borders as waves of newcomers washed across it. They gave protection to their industry and agriculture from foreign competitors, while also intervening against corporations, which grew in size and power as they pursued ever-wider markets. Government bureaucracies set up to regulate private firms and oversee multiplying state functions became an important new feature of the political scene, and state budgets rose to underwrite multiplying domestic as well as international programs.

In the second phase of globalization following World War II, states in the developed world have been more active in promoting and managing globalization. Above all others, the United States and its European associates laid down the rules and decided which agreements and institutions would come to life and which would flourish. Despite the ensuing half century of global change, states in general have remained the focus of loyalty and identity for most people around the world, and the source to which they have looked for education, health care, and other basic services. State budgets have accounted for a steadily larger proportion of national income. Recent central government spending in most developed countries amounts to an impressive 40 to 50 percent of the total annual output of goods and services.[2] To be sure, states disengaged in large measure from direct ownership of economic enterprises and from protectionist policies. But as economic forces reshaped countries, especially those most developed and tightly integrated by trade and investment into worldwide networks of exchange, states responded to greater competition by investing more in education, science and technology, job training, and maintenance of overall social welfare. Like other states in the developed world generally, the United States has maintained its central role in the lives of its citizens by securing allegiance, extracting resources, and offering public goods while also pursuing its unique, dominant role on the world stage. As self-assigned arbiter—if not master—of what transpires on that stage, the u.s. government gives its military the resources and status commensurate with the global scope of its ambitions.

Over the last two hundred years Americans have been intimately entangled in global developments in a third way—in the creation of an economic and social modernity that has left an ever-deeper imprint on peoples everywhere. The United States has benefited from markets and capital made available by globalization, pioneered a widely imitated system of mass production and consumption, suffered through the swings and disciplines of the international economy, and served as its rescuer and rule maker. Americans have thus been variously the beneficiaries, the victims, and the patrons of that highly dynamic economy. That economy has in turn had a far-reaching and complex cultural impact, altering the outlook and behavior of Americans and other peoples all around the world as they have been drawn into the flow of goods and capital.

Finally, global history reminds us of the critical role technology has played in the astonishing u.s. trajectory. New technologies were a prime source of North Atlantic wealth and power in relation to the rest of the world, an indispensable tool of the emergent nation-state, and the driver behind the relentless modernization of social and economic life. Technology's capacity to dramatically transform in each of these ways carried with it the power to destroy and control as well as create. The North Atlantic world's technological advantage gave it dominion over others. Colonial wars and colonial exploitation that technology made possible imposed death and suffering on an enormous scale. This point reminds us that the state embraced technology above all for military purposes—and thus made the twentieth century the most destructive in human history. Not least among that century's legacies was the nuclear specter still haunting humankind. Fresh technological breakthroughs also set in motion destabilizing social change. In the creative destruction that capitalism has spawned, technology has proven a powerful solvent of communal bonds and thus of a stable sense of individual identity. In all of its roles, technology features prominently in the u.s. story.

Global forces—whether strong or weak, sudden or slow, clear or obscure—play out in relation to humans. Understanding u.s. ascendancy thus in a sense involves more than tracing abstract and bloodless global processes and patterns. It means identifying the particular people who confronted and responded to those forces and making from the decisive moments in their lives a narrative that can both illuminate and instruct. Despite its commitment to democracy, the United States has pursued a role in the world guided disproportionately by elites. They appear in this account primarily in the guise of presidents and their immediate advisers acting as the political and military agents of an increasingly powerful state. Serving as a supporting cast are, on the one hand, commentators and public intellectuals who framed challenges facing the country in ways other influential people found convincing and, on the other, business leaders whose inroads in foreign markets had long-term cultural consequences but also commanded the attention of the state. Often these secondary characters operated in close collaboration with the state authorities, occasionally apart from or in opposition to them.

The agents of the state deserve the pride of place that they are traditionally accorded because they set the pace and direction and thus ultimately shaped the nature of u.s. dominance. They alone could gather the requisite material and moral resources, direct them in a concerted way, and create popular, political legitimacy for their undertakings. Their choices across three generations in effect defined the path Americans traveled toward ascendancy. William McKinley and Woodrow Wilson combined to set the agenda. The interwar Republicans cautiously explored ways of using what had by then become extraordinary, even unprecedented national resources to realize that agenda, while the third generation, dominated by the Democrats Franklin Roosevelt and Harry Truman, set about the task with a boldness that marks the mid-century as the dawn of u.s. dominance. To their successors over the balance of the century—from Richard Nixon to George W. Bush—fell the challenge of coping with the consequences of that dominance.

This claim to the state's leading role in the American ascendancy carries two major caveats. First, those leading the state could not simply will ascendancy into existence. State activity depended on a variety of prerequisites, perhaps foremost a society whose flexibility was perfectly adapted to economic development under conditions prevailing during the nineteenth century. Second, those directing the state apparatus had constantly to take into account global forces in a wide variety of forms, first by recognizing them and then by somehow exploiting, riding, mastering, defusing, or redirecting them. The formidable challenge facing state leaders is apparent for example in the post–World War II hunger worldwide for reconstruction and prosperity and in the third-world demands for decolonization and liberation. Readers will have to judge for themselves the explanatory value of emphasizing the state in a global history context and thereby integrating the national with the global. Privileging the state in turn elevates the prominence of the individuals who commanded it and thus raises afresh the tension—ideally fruitful—between structural interpretations with their emphasis on constraints and voluntaristic interpretations with their stress on contingency. Structures create preconditions and set limits; individuals have to decide what to do within those limits.

The focus here on tracing ascendancy over the long haul and in a global context is intended to be historically descriptive, not politically triumphalist, and to lay the basis for a more searching appraisal of success and failure. Misreading or mishandling global forces could bring disaster, as Lyndon Johnson discovered with regard to both Vietnam and the flight from the dollar. On the other hand, success—for example, in reconstructing the international economy and pushing it toward u.s. norms—could strengthen American dominance, with its attendant material and psychological rewards. Invariably failure and even sometimes success spelled trouble for ordinary Americans in the form of higher taxes, overseas military service, social tensions, or political repression. But American ascendancy often extracted a far higher cost from people abroad and especially from those in third-world states that dared to flout u.s. preferences.

This account draws on the themes sketched out above to answer the question of why the United States gained its ascendancy and with what consequences. In essence the story to be developed here is about the accumulation and exercise of formidable national power within a dynamic global context. The story begins with settler colonialism, rising economic productivity, and wispy notions generated by the minds of nationalists (chapter 1). It continues with the early twentieth-century demonstration of diplomatic and military prowess in which the rise of the American state figured centrally (chapter 2). By the 1920s the United States had achieved economic preeminence and a far-reaching economic and cultural presence, which together created new opportunities for u.s. leaders (chapter 3). These early twentieth-century developments figure as prologue to a time of remarkable exertions and accomplishments spanning three decades at midcentury, treated in three topically arranged chapters. The first (chapter 4) deals with the confrontations with the German and Soviet states that would establish overall u.s. preeminence beyond question. That time of sustained ideological construction, military testing, technological innovation, and institution building unfolded alongside the American attempt to give shape to the postwar international economic and cultural order and to master a restive third world (chapters 5 and 6). The achievement of ascendancy had untoward domestic and global consequences that left u.s. policymakers in the 1970s and 1980s hobbled and Americans questioning the costs and perils of their newly won dominance (chapter 7). The story ends with the campaign to organize and stabilize u.s. dominance around a neoliberal faith in the virtues of the free market, democracy, and individualism (chapter 8). The conclusion reflects on the current debates over hegemony and empire and offers an appraisal of u.s. ascendancy with an eye to the future.

Telling what is an extraordinary story of u.s. involvement in the world is critical to sorting out the empire-hegemony debate. But more practically, as the conclusion suggests, that story offers fresh ways of framing the pressing problems currently facing the United States. In order to ultimately address these matters, we need to begin at the beginning—with an examination of the ways that the u.s. ascendancy, established in the course of the twentieth century, depended heavily on the achievements of an earlier age.

Figure 1. American Progress, *chromolithograph by George A. Crofutt (1873),
after the painting of the same title by John Gast (1872). (Courtesy of the Library
of Congress, LC-DIG-ppmsca-09855.)*

1

NINETEENTH-CENTURY FOUNDATIONS

The New York–based artist John Gast completed *American Progress* in 1872, pushed by George Crofutt, the publisher of guides to the u.s. West (see fig. 1). Crofutt not only commissioned the work but also prescribed the themes Gast was to include and gave the oil painting its name.[1] This celebration of American destiny set center stage a fair-skinned woman, classic in profile, wearing a loose, flowing dress and serenely advancing with a schoolbook in hand. The star in her luxuriant hair announced her mission: to build an empire for liberty. Gast, drawing on an assemblage of images already made familiar by other u.s. artists, surrounded the woman with the players in the drama of continental transformation. From the east came farmers, prospectors, and Pony Express riders, their way lit by the rising sun. Behind them telegraph, railroad, and coach symbolized the binding together of newly won land. Before the forces of civilization, native peoples retreated in anger and disarray. Buffalo, bear, and wild horses joined the flight. They too were part of a wild but doomed world, bound to vanish into a dark and clouded west. Just as the natives would disappear in the face of civilization, so too would the gloom of barbarism be dispelled. Reproduced in inexpensive color, Gast's rendition of an emerging national mythology circulated widely.

The painting was more than the depiction of an empty myth. Gast also captured a set of real developments that had already by then readied the United States to play a role as an international force. Americans had asserted control of a continent against the presence of other peoples and the claims of foreign powers. Within the newly secured national boundaries, they were developing a flourishing economy that was rapidly climbing to the first rank. Finally, they were forging a sturdy conception of their national identity that would carry over into the following century and beyond. A verse appearing in a Kansas newspaper in 1876, the centennial of national independence, captured the sense of American power that was both real and richly imagined:

> The rudiments of Empire here,
> Are plastic yet and warm:

The chaos of a mighty world
Is rounding into form.[2]

Although Gast and other Americans may have seen their nation as the special, providentially blessed progressive force, the work of global historians suggests a more complicated and interesting point about the origins of u.s. ascendancy. The emergence of the United States as an international power was inextricably tied to processes playing out around the world: the consolidation of settler societies, the rise of global capitalism, and the tightening grip of state-dominated nationalism. These foundational elements ultimately yielded a nation of exceptional power and certitude, but this process was both in its origins and in its outcome wholly unexceptional. At every critical point Americans operated in the nexus of forces operating across the North Atlantic world.

TERRITORIAL CONTROL

The peoples of European origin depicted advancing across Gast's canvas were the spearheads of a settler colonialism increasingly commonplace from the sixteenth century onward. More and more Europeans—religious dissenters, prisoners, laborers, traders, displaced peasants, and colonial officials —left for strange lands. The United States along with other British settler enclaves—Canada, Australia, New Zealand, and South Africa—embodied one variation within the pattern of European settlement that was playing out across the world. While in the u.s. case the outcome was a dominant European population, in other cases the European presence either faded or became part of a cultural mix. Plantation societies of the sort that sprang up in the Caribbean and northeast Brazil had a few Europeans importing large numbers of laborers whose descendants would dominate demographically and create a plural society with coexisting cultures (for example, Malaysia and South Africa) or a creole society (as in Mexico). Instances of formal territorial control exercised by a handful of European administrators and soldiers (notably British India and the Dutch East Indies) or Europeans promoting trade from strategic overseas points such as Singapore or Goa left even less of a trace. The plantation society of the u.s. South with its enslaved labor represented a pattern of settlement with more in common with the Caribbean and Brazil than the rest of the United States to which it was linked politically—a useful reminder of marked variation possible even within one region.

British settlement in North America rolled forward territorially with such relentless success that it gives color to the later nationalist claim of predestination. The first settlements hugged the coast of New England, Virginia, and the Carolinas and struggled to maintain their numbers against disease, hunger, and the hostility of Native Americans. In 1700 native peoples constituted three-quarters of the population within the boundaries of what would become the United States. By 1820 Europeans were nearly 8 million out of a total of almost 10 million inhabitants, overshadowing both natives and a much expanded slave population. Demographic dominance in turn gave rise to rapid territorial growth, with the United States quadrupling in size during its first half century. The terms of the 1783 peace established control to the Mississippi River. The Louisiana Purchase of 1803 added a vast expanse west of the Mississippi. The succession of acquisitions between 1845 and 1867 rounded out the continental base. The total cost of expansion was three wars and the payment through various treaties of $55 million. Even recalculated into 2002 constant dollars, the total is just a bit over $1 billion—still a bargain![3]

But to stop with this clinical description would be to fundamentally misconstrue a process that was also prolonged, complicated, and often violent. The push that put people of British birth or descent in control had two main but chronologically overlapping facets. It involved overwhelming indigenous peoples with a mix of epidemics, arms, and sheer weight of numbers and often at the same time beating back competing territorial claims laid down by European powers through diplomacy and warfare. This transcontinental drive played out in a series of contested borderlands marked in varying degrees by cultural mixing, economic exchange, open conflict, and the politics of accommodation. One such borderland was the Great Lakes region, the target of British and French imperial pretensions. The lower Missouri Valley was another; there Spain eclipsed France. The southern Great Plains was a zone of Spanish and then Mexican influence. In these regions, indigenous peoples such as the Iroquois, Osage, and Comanche played a central role.

In one borderland after another Anglo-Americans mastered both native peoples and European rivals to gain unquestioned control. The broad reasons for this success bear noting. To begin with, British settlers benefited, as did all Europeans, from the imported microbes and better weapons that devastated the native population, first at a distance and then in face-to-face conflict. In relation to other Europeans the growing power of the British state proved a distinct plus in organizing and defending settlements. Perhaps most important of all were demographic advantages. The dispossession of roughly half of the English rural population between 1530 and 1630 together with rapid population growth (a tripling between 1500 and 1800) created a large pool of potential migrants to North America. The French and Spanish peasant majority clung to their land, and the Dutch had too small a population to make a mark abroad, so Britain won the North American demographic race. Once peopled, the areas of British settlement prospered thanks not just to the rich resources at hand but also to their connection to a thriving British commercial empire and their exploitation of slave labor. Colonial output rose at an impressive rate—from 4 percent of England's in 1700 to 40 percent seventy years later. By then colonial per capita income had surpassed that of the home island, and low taxes in North America further accentuated the difference in standard of living. Prosperity in turn ensured the resources needed to secure more North American land and support a rapidly growing and healthy population on it.[4]

Subordination of Native Americans

Gast invoked the nationalist myth of an empty continent, its original inhabitants having dwindled to a small band on its way to oblivion. Rather than a peaceful occupation, the encounter between settler and native calls to mind such brutal ethnic conflicts that have in our own time beset Israeli-occupied Palestine, the former Yugoslavia, Russia's Chechnya region, or Sudan. Claims to land are so closely tied to community identity, security, and livelihood that they seem to give rise to the most stubborn assertions of right and the cruel treatment of antagonists, including brutal enslavement and indiscriminate massacre. They also create a vicious climate of bigotry toward rivals for land.[5]

The subjugation of the Native Americans was a long-running drama of conquest. It began with their being entrenched in pockets from the Atlantic to the Pacific—at least 2 and perhaps as many as 10 million people living north of the Rio Grande before the first European settlements. On their first contact with Europeans, Indians were ravaged by diseases borne by these newcomers. Smallpox was perhaps the worst killer, racing through villages and along trade routes. Lacking immunity to maladies long endemic in Europe, Indians were especially vulnerable in time of hunger; entire groups could suffer losses as high as 90 percent over brief spans of time during the late seventeenth and early eighteenth centuries. Direct contact brought additional death and suffering as Native Americans were outmatched by European military technology, overwhelmed by the burgeoning settler population, hemmed in territorially, and thrown into competition with other similarly beleaguered peoples for the shrinking resources of the continent.

Euro-American settlers, mainly of British origin, bore down relentlessly on indigenous peoples thus weakened and thrown on the defensive. Successive generations of frontier whites had viewed Indians not just as an impediment to acquiring new land cheaply but also as dangerous barbarians, to be segregated for better supervision or altogether removed beyond range of contact. A mailed fist and a readiness to use forceful if not brutal methods were essential to keeping them in check. Colonial New Englanders and residents of Virginia and the Carolinas had set the pattern. Colonial forces and their Indian allies had surrounded a Pequot village of some four hundred in 1637 and set it aflame. One of the expedition's leaders explained that the "fiery Oven," resulting in the death of nearly all the villagers, was God's will. Two centuries later the governor of Georgia, a state synonymous among Cherokees with land grabbing, was equally ruthless in insisting that that the natives were an "ignorant, intractable, and savage people" and what they owned "civilized peoples had a right to possess." Savages would have to go, treaties or no treaties. Though their resort to fraudulent and violent methods collided with humanitarian principles and legal agreements (including formal treaties), the political authorities and most Americans endorsed or acquiesced in the practice of Indian extermination and removal.[6]

By the early nineteenth century, the transplanted Europeans were able to assert their dominance confidently and at will. The federal government failed to enforce the very treaties that it had signed guaranteeing Indians even their diminished holdings, while states asserted their right to deal with natives as they wished. Those Indians who did make substantial progress toward assimilation, such as Cherokees, found whites insatiable in their appetite for land and unstoppable in their drive to acquire it. When local conflicts over land developed between settler and Indians, state authorities predictably favored their own. Attempts by native peoples to save themselves through alliances with Britain or France against their common enemy repeatedly ended in betrayal by their putative European allies and in brutal frontier warfare that invariably brought Indian defeat and white retribution. The victors then pushed the vanquished aside. Those who regretted the violence wished the process of dispossession to proceed as painlessly as possible. Jefferson captured this humanitarian impulse in comments to a gathering of Native Americans at the end of his presidency: "We wish you to live in peace, to increase in numbers. . . . In time you will be as we are: you will become one people with us: your blood will mix with ours."[7] This pious wish collided so violently with the facts on the ground that it is hard not to see it as hypocrisy or self-deception.

Andrew Jackson, an ambitious Tennessean and inveterate land speculator, shared none of Jefferson's compassion. He embodied instead the settler drive to dominance that reached its climax in the first half of the nineteenth century. Indulging a violent streak, Jackson as general used the state militia to shatter the Creeks, Cherokees, Seminoles, and other Indians of the Southeast.

Through a series of military campaigns and imposed treaties in the 1810s, he forced open to speculation and settlement Indian land accounting for three-fourths of the territory of Florida and Alabama, one-third of Tennessee, one-fifth of Georgia and Mississippi, and smaller fractions of Kentucky and North Carolina. Later, in the 1830s, Jackson as president set in motion the policy—described by him as "not only liberal, but generous"—of removing some sixty thousand Indians from their land. He articulated what had become the standard rationale for the looming extinction of the Indian. "What good man would prefer a country covered with forests and ranged by a few thousand savages to our extensive Republic, studded with cities, towns, and prosperous farms, embellished with all the improvements which art can devise or industry execute, occupied by more than 12,000,000 happy people, and filled with all the blessings of liberty, civilization, and religion?"[8] By the 1840s the Indian question east of the Mississippi had been "solved" to settler satisfaction even if the eviction of native peoples and the possession of their land had involved fraud and force on a massive scale.

The process of subjugation was repeated west of the Mississippi in the latter half of the nineteenth century. Thanks to new technology in settler hands, especially rapid-fire guns, railroads, and telegraphs, the next round in the destruction of the American Indian proceeded just as inexorably and even more swiftly. Tribes long resident in the West and some ninety thousand Indians driven there from the East signed treaties with the federal government guaranteeing their land "as long as the waters run and the grass shall grow." These treaties were then universally and systematically violated. The U.S. Army protected settlers and put down resistance. It dealt with Indians according to the principles of group responsibility, expected treachery and bad faith from them as a matter of course, and anticipated their ultimate extermination.

No strategy could blunt the settler demand for land backed by military might. Some tribes offered no resistance. Such was the case with the California Indians, who numbered one hundred thousand in 1848. In eleven years barbarous treatment reduced them to thirty thousand; by 1900 only fifteen thousand were left. Other tribes prudently retreated, seeking in renegotiated treaties to preserve some part of their ever-dwindling patrimony. Some, such as the Sioux, fought back, but even their small and temporary victories were purchased at the price of severe reprisals. The Nez Percé, successful livestock breeders living in the area of modern-day Idaho, tried a bit of all these coping mechanisms—to no avail. Chief Joseph explained to a congressional committee in 1879 how his people had cooperated with the u.s. government and sought to accommodate the growing press of settlers until the 1870s. But settlers with their insatiable greed stole land, horses, and cattle, and finally government officials announced the tribe was to be moved to a reservation in Oklahoma. When Chief Joseph attempted to lead the Nez Percé to refuge in Canada, u.s. forces followed in hot pursuit. In 1877 he struck a deal, surrendering on the condition that his people could return to Idaho. Betrayed, they were instead forced to go to Oklahoma, where many encountered disease and starvation. "When I think of our condition my heart is heavy," he told the Congressmen. "I see men of my race treated as outlaws and driven from country to country, or shot down like animals."[9]

By the 1870s an American policy of continental expansion had run full course so far as the Indian was concerned. In 1871 (just as Gast was rendering his own version of this doleful drama) Congress stopped making new treaties, and old treaties, the Supreme Court had ruled the year before, were no longer binding. Whatever formal concessions Native Americans had negotiated would now depend on the pleasure of the u.s. government. Even cultural autonomy was denied to the Indian as the federal government extended its control over reservation life. The Dawes Act of 1887 completed the process of distributing tribal lands and undermining tribal power. In the 1890s the last spark of native resistance flickered out among a defeated, dispirited remnant. The massacre at Wounded Knee on 29 December 1890 conventionally and appropriately marks the end. A band of Lakota Sioux led by Big Foot were rounded up by a cavalry force with simple orders: "If he fights, destroy him." Fearful Indians surrounded by impatient troopers on South Dakota's Pine Ridge Reservation proved a volatile mix. What was to have been a peaceful surrender of weapons suddenly erupted in gunshots and then turned into a prolonged massacre. Nearly three hundred Sioux died, two-thirds of them women and children.[10]

Warfare, starvation, and exposure reduced the number of Indians living in the continental United States to about 600,000 in 1800, already then outnumbered by 5 million Euro-Americans and 1 million slaves brought from Africa. By 1930 Native American numbers had fallen still further—to roughly half the 1800 figure. White Americans had not inherited the fabled empty continent. Rather, by their presence and policies, they had substantially emptied it.[11] The survivors subsisted on fragments of their former territory or were forced onto reservations, confined patches of marginal land, to live under governmental protection and supervision. While Indians sought to salvage the last shreds of their cultural autonomy, their white overseers labored to eradicate the old "savage," nomadic patterns and to settle their charges into a new civilized, Christian way of life.

No longer a troublesome foreign policy problem, Native Americans could now be quietly set aside as wards of the federal government and missionary organizations. Gast's *American Progress* captured precisely this comforting nationalist notion of barbaric peoples erased by the inexorable advance of civilization. It stripped away the violence and double dealing that characterized the abasement of the Indian in real life. In this humanitarian gloss on an ethnically cleansed continent, the Indian stood as a melancholy, even tragic figure, the victim not of land grabbing but of an abstraction, the inexorable pressure of human progress. The sacrifice of this people had been necessary, noted one school text as early as 1813, "for the increase of mankind, and for the promotion of the world's glory and happiness."[12] A child of the wilderness — simple, brave, enduring, and dignified — the native had proven constitutionally deficient in those qualities of industry and self-discipline essential to getting on in a world being rapidly transformed by the forces of civilization. So, like the wilderness, the noble savage in this Anglo racial myth would simply have to fade away, thereby confirming that general law of nature: where two races meet, the inferior yields inevitably to the superior.

Expulsion of the European Powers

Sorting out competing European claims to land that would come to constitute the United States began later but proceeded more rapidly than the campaigns against the Native Americans. Indigenous peoples had the misfortune of having nowhere to get permanently out of harm's way, so they either resisted or fell back in hopes of mounting a successful resistance another day. The European powers had the option of shifting to other points for colonial settlement and conquest after encountering so pugnacious, increasingly powerful, and rapidly multiplying a people as they faced in the United States.

From the very inception of their independence, the citizens of the new state proved their skill in driving fellow Europeans from the continent. They were able (in the memorable and telling phrase of one diplomatic historian) "to draw advantage from Europe's distress."[13] Locked in competition with each other, the European powers were constrained in their dealings with the u.s. upstart by the broad Atlantic, limited budgets, and war-weary populations. If American policymakers exercised patience, they would find the moment when those powers, distracted by problems close to home, could be driven to settle on terms advantageous to the United States. Where diplomacy failed, even when backed by a growing population of Americans in disputed territories, policymakers could try stronger medicine: threatening an alliance with one European power against its rival, grabbing weakly defended territories of distant European antagonists, or in extremity resorting to armed force—with the marked advantage of fighting on home ground.

The major American achievement was forcing the British to give way. London had to concede independence in 1783 after discovering that their rebellious subjects, backed by the French, were difficult to defeat on their own soil. The fallback British position was to contain the United States within a narrow coastal strip, keep the new country commercially dependent on the British Isles, and monopolize American maritime and natural resources during wartime. This strategy gave rise to intractable maritime issues, created intense economic and nationalist resentments on the part of the Americans, and finally led to a second round of fighting between 1812 and 1815. This time the British were forced to recognize that even their vaunted sea power was not enough to tame an ever stronger United States. They would have to accept the dominance of the American republic on the continent and thus by extension Canada's status as a hostage to good Anglo-American relations.

British leaders grudgingly came to terms with the empire's growing military vulnerability in North America. They began to see the wisdom of cultivating good relations with Washington if it wished to keep Canada and avoid a war that European rivals were sure to exploit. In 1846 London accepted a compromise division of the Pacific Northwest (the Oregon territory) and showed a growing deference through the balance of the century in handling a series of potentially explosive maritime cases and disputes over the u.s.-Canadian border. Lord Palmerston (Henry John Temple), who served as foreign minister or prime minister much of the time between 1830 and 1865, provided the rationale for the reluctant retreat based on sound experience. "These Yankees are most disagreeable Fellows to have to do with about any American question: They are on the Spot, strong, deeply interested in the matter, totally unscrupulous and dishonest and determined somehow or other to carry their Point; We are far away, weak from Distance, controlled, by the Indifference of the Nation as to the Question discussed, and by its Strong Commercial Interest in maintaining Peace with the United States."[14] His government fantasized that the Civil War would reduce the North American giant to a set of powers of pygmy proportions, but it hesitated even at this moment of u.s. internal crisis to take action that might bring on war. The Americans were formidable rogues indeed!

What the powerful British had to grudgingly accept other lesser powers conceded more swiftly. Napoleon liquidated France's Louisiana territory in 1803 to make ready for a renewal of his struggle against Britain. A weakened Spain, bullied by Andrew Jackson's forces, gave up Florida in 1819. Madrid lived in fear of the rampaging Jackson, dubbed "the Napoleon of the woods."[15] Retreat seemed the wiser course, it being better to concentrate on holding on to Cuba in the face of U.S. threats and pacifying Latin American colonies agitating for independence. Tangling with the United States at this point might result in a total rout.

The high point of this territorial drive came at midcentury with the seizure of a vast expanse of land first staked out as part of Spain's empire in the New World. The chief agents were Jackson's Tennessee protégés—Sam Houston and James K. Polk—whose sights were trained on Texas and land west to the Pacific. With its independence in 1821, Mexico had inherited claims to territory running from the California coast to tropical Central America. The northern portions of the Spanish legacy were thinly populated and by the early nineteenth century the destination of growing numbers of U.S. expatriates. In 1836 these Americans revolted and in 1845 under Houston's leadership joined Mexico's province of Texas to the United States. The Mexican failure to accept this fait accompli provided President James K. Polk an opening for a war that would sheer Mexico of more land. With the American army occupying its capital in 1848, Mexico again had to submit, this time surrendering almost half of its territory as the price of peace. In 1853 a cash-strapped Mexican government surrendered an additional slice of land (the Gadsden Purchase) part of present-day New Mexico and Arizona. Rounding out the continental holdings, Secretary of State William Seward—prominent among an impressive line of nineteenth-century expansionists—gained Alaska in 1867 from a Russia eager to shed the last of its holdings in the Americas.

The priority given to continental control was reflected in a U.S. foreign policy devoted to keeping Europe at bay while also avoiding entanglements in European quarrels that bore little if any relevance to pressing tasks at home. The fundamental proposition on which policy rested was the notion of two geographic spheres dividing European countries from the lands settled by Europeans in the Americas. In this two-sphere conception widely embraced by U.S. commentators, the characteristic of the Old World that most fundamentally distinguished it from the newly settled lands on the other side of the Atlantic was its despotism, a natural outcome of the survival of monarchy and nobility. This aristocratic political culture in turn created a proclivity to militarism, aggression, and war. It also bred popular discontent with political subjugation and social injustice. The resulting unrest occasionally exploded into spasms of revolution that confirmed these perceptions of Europe. In 1789, just as Americans were bringing their own seminal struggle for liberty to a successful constitutional conclusion, France embarked on a revolution that turned alarmingly radical and violent. Revolutions struck again in Europe in 1848 (with monarchies tottering but most surviving) and in 1871 (as anarchic Paris mobs confirmed a deep-seated belief among Americans in a badly flawed European order).

The propensity of Americans to stay clear of Europe's politics and wars followed not just from notions of difference but also from practical lessons learned in the course of their colonial experience. They recalled how Anglo-French imperial rivalry had repeatedly disrupted their lives between 1688 and 1763. In the course of this prolonged European quarrel, Americans not only had suffered the trauma of war but had also been deprived of a voice in the critical questions of when and how to fight, and they were often forgotten when the spoils were divided. Once independent, Americans searched for a policy that would remove them as far as possible from the European maelstrom generated by the French Revolution and then Napoleon's grand ambitions pursued across the face of Europe. In 1796, on the eve of his retirement from the presidency, George Washington urged on his countrymen the wisdom of maintaining a "detached and distant situation"—a safe distance from these dangerous European quarrels.[16]

Washington's successors in the White House consistently echoed his sentiments throughout the nineteenth century in what became a basic doctrine of early U.S. policy—that of nonentanglement (or isolation). The difference between Europe's political and diplomatic interests and those of the American hemisphere created effectively two distinct realms—so the prevailing view went. The United States as a peaceful republic epitomized the bright prospects for one side of the Atlantic, while dominant on the other side were monarchies that were rapacious, war prone, and oppressive. Thus just as European interference on this side of the Atlantic was to be resisted, so too was the temptation to get caught up in European alliances and wars. Nonentanglement was a doctrine of denial that applied to only one region—Europe—and only to political and military ties, and so isolationism, a term that has come to be associated with this approach, does not accurately apply. Americans could still trade avidly with the Old World, borrow large amounts of its capital, travel to look with awe on its monuments, read its literature and philosophy,

accept its poor, and mix socially with its prominent families. Nonentanglement was thus narrowly construed and in any case would barely outlive the
continental phase of u.s. development. By the early twentieth century, u.s.
policymakers were becoming more deeply engaged in European politics and
colonial questions. Intervention in World War I would deal political and military nonentanglement a grievous wound from which it would not recover.

Alongside nonentanglement grew up a second doctrine—that of Monroe.
It emerged as an offshoot of Washington's doctrine of nonentanglement but
proved far longer lived. Just as Americans should resist any temptation to get
pulled into Europe's alliances and wars, so too should they commit themselves
to resisting European interference on their side of the Atlantic. This line of
thinking received its first formal expression under President James Monroe in
1823 when the European monarchies seemed ready to act in unison to restore
Spanish colonial dominion in Latin America. Monroe responded by asserting
that because Europe and the Americas had distinct interests and different
destinies, the United States would not countenance European interference.
Monroe's threat of resistance was empty at that time, but it did establish a
basis for a u.s. claim as the leader and protector of this hemisphere. The Monroe Doctrine began to acquire teeth soon after the Civil War when Secretary
of State Seward used Monroe's doctrine to justify a successful drive against a
French presence in Mexico. The doctrine made an even more impressive appearance in 1895 when Secretary of State Richard Olney restrained Britain in
a boundary dispute with Venezuela. He announced, "To-day the United States
is practically sovereign on this continent," and he underscored for the benefit
of his British counterpart the simple fact that his country stood "practically invulnerable as against any or all other powers." London gulped, stepped back,
and came to definitive terms with the Monroe Doctrine. The United States
was indeed, as Olney put it, "master of the situation."[17]

The rapid u.s. continental drive came to a successful conclusion in the second half of the nineteenth century. The United States passed through its moment of maximum danger as a sectional dispute over slavery in new territories degenerated into political paralysis by the 1850s and thence into civil war.
The post–Civil War decades brought no significant territorial extensions; the
financial burden of the Civil War together with unabated sectional animosity
made expansionist projects politically unpalatable. But those decades did see a
consolidation of continental control. Americans peopled their newly acquired
lands thanks to a high natural birthrate and a heavy influx of immigrants. A
population of only 10 million in 1820 quadrupled to 40 million by 1870 and
then more than doubled to 98 million by 1913.[18] The burgeoning nation was

increasingly integrated administratively and tied together by transport and communications. A European outpost was turning into a formidable territorial giant.

THE PREMIER ECONOMY

Conquering and securing a continent was an essential but hardly in itself sufficient condition to moving toward ascendancy. Americans needed to develop wealth if they were to cut a larger figure on the world stage. This they did with astonishing success over the course of the nineteenth century. Gast's *American Progress* captures that achievement with its imagery of a wilderness turning into productive farms, bustling cities, and webs of commerce spanning land and sea. By century's end the United States was firmly established as the world's leading economy.

The commerce and agriculture that Gast had extending across a continent was an expression of a global capitalism that had been deepening its hold on the North Atlantic world for several centuries and that flourished in the nineteenth century. Nowhere were capitalist forces more transformative than in settler societies like the United States. Recently arrived Europeans exploited natural resources, above all productive land, timber, and minerals, to generate wealth at an impressive pace, and by their initial success attracted a continuing stream of European goods, capital, and migrants critical to even greater success at economic development.

To the Head of the Pack

Every available yardstick shows the U.S. economy outstripping the rest of the world between 1820 and 1913, itself a remarkable time of growing global trade and investment. Perhaps the prime yardstick of growth is gross domestic product (or GDP), the value of all goods and services produced by a country in a given year. The United States had achieved exceptional, sustained growth to judge from a GDP that was forty times greater by the early twentieth century than it had been a century earlier. By 1919 the United States was firmly established as the world's largest economy, accounting for nearly a fifth of all global production. Per capita GDP is another revealing yardstick. By taking population into account, this measurement tells us what each person within an economy would receive were the value of the output divided evenly. That figure grew fourfold between 1820 and 1913 even though there were ever more Americans to claim a share of the total output. They had become the wealthiest people on earth.

This high level of economic performance pushed the United States past

TABLE I. *Forging ahead: Yardsticks of U.S. economic expansion*

	1820	1870	1913
total GDP (billions of 1990$)[a]	13	98	517
U.S. share of total world GDP (%)	2	9	19
per capita GDP (1990$)	1,257	2,445	5,301
population (millions)	10	40	98
exports (billions of 1990$)	.3	2.5	19.2

Source: Angus Maddison, *The World Economy: A Millennial Perspective* (Paris: Development Centre of the Organisation for Economic Co-operation and Development, 2001), 183, 185, 261, 263, 361.

[a]Expressing dollar figures in terms of the value of 1990 dollars creates what economists call "constant dollars" that can be compared across time. Otherwise, the effects of inflation would put the value of one year's GDP beyond comparison with that of another year, especially over long periods of time.

Britain, the leading power of the day. As early as 1870 the United States had caught up in total output and by 1913 dwarfed the British economy by a margin greater than two to one. By that latter date, Americans had also surpassed British per capita income, which was the highest in Europe. Germany and France lagged behind at about two-thirds of the U.S. figure. In terms of manufacturing, a defining feature of advanced economic development at the time, Americans could boast special success. In 1860 they stood behind the leaders, Britain and France. By 1913 the U.S. manufacturing output was far in the lead; indeed it exceeded the combined output of the two industrial powerhouses of the day, Germany and Britain, and accounted for a third of the total world production.[19]

This stunning material leap forward was the product of an economic expansion the likes of which had never before been seen anywhere in the North Atlantic world. Long-term growth rates in Europe between 1000 and 1820 averaged below half a percent a year, and even in the lands that would become the United States the rates in the seventeenth and eighteenth centuries were higher but still below 1 percent during this early settlement phase. During the nineteenth century and into the early twentieth, the European rate moved up moderately (to 1.65 percent per annum from 1820 to 1870 and then to 2.10 percent from 1870 to 1913). The U.S. economy did even better, achieving rates that hovered around 4 percent annually on average for the period 1820–1913.

The 2 percent annual u.s. advantage may seem small, but it translates into impressive overall gains if sustained over time.[20]

Foreign commentators and visitors at the end of the nineteenth century noted the striking if predictable results of relatively high levels of steady growth. Their accounts made the u.s. economy a byword around the world for speedy economic development, steady technological achievement, and rapidly rising affluence. That the country was already in the 1880s "a vast hive of industry" that had arrived at an "advanced position as a leader of nations" was a point that visitor after visitor repeated, no matter how otherwise critical they were of this bland, crass, soulless civilization without modesty or redeeming social or moral ideals. H. G. Wells came away from turn-of-the-century America convinced that "nowhere now is growth still so certainly and confidently *going on* as here. Nowhere is it upon so great a scale as here, and with so confident an outlook towards the things to come." A French visitor marveled at the "extraordinary intensity" that Americans devoted to their work, yielding them "great riches" and swiftly transforming open land into "populous and industrious districts."[21]

What was true of European visitors was also true of East Asians on the lookout for models for their own development. A Japanese elite bent on making their country strong and modern looked with ill-concealed admiration at u.s. achievements, especially its devotion to technology and practical education. A Japanese who studied in the United States in the decade after the Civil War found Americans "a nervous, energetic, enterprising people" and their development of the continent a "stupendous undertaking." One of the leading intellectuals of that generation of dramatic change, Fukuzawa Yukichi, expressed amazement in 1884 at "America's richness. . . . As the population grew, wealth increased. As wealth increased, the population swelled. The pace of progress quickened. It continued, day and night, swiftly and without letup, until eventually, all Europe, hitherto the center of civilization, stood astounded. This can only be termed an unprecedented phenomenon." The influential Chinese reformer and journalist, Liang Qichao, was equally impressed but also alarmed by his encounter in 1903 with what he described for readers at home as "the premier capitalist nation in the world." Another prominent reformer, Tan Hualong, expressed fifteen years later a now fixed fascination with the u.s. economic drive: "What was a bleak and barren wilderness a hundred and some years ago has quickly become this splendid and magnificent new world."[22]

Explaining Success

How did the United States manage this rapid and widely recognized economic ascent to a position of agricultural and industrial preeminence? An explanation begins with natural endowments—abundant fertile land and rich timber and mineral resources that accrued to settler societies as a prerogative of conquest. Americans, like South Africans and Australians, seized these valuable assets with little or no recompense (as we have seen). They provided the bedrock for the u.s. economy well into the twentieth century, and even as late as 1914 nonindustrial goods were the main u.s. export.

To abundant, cheap resources must be added fortunate location and timing. The United States as a settler society was able to bring an entire continent rapidly into production and lay the enduring economic basis for u.s. global power because nineteenth-century Americans occupied a privileged place within a dynamic North Atlantic economy. They enjoyed a prolonged peace—a century of freedom from major conflict running from the end of the Napoleonic wars in 1815 to the onset of World War I in 1914. During that time liberal notions of free trade gained wide currency. They exercised especially strong appeal during the middle decades of the nineteenth century as Britain led in removing barriers to trade. The free-trade gospel spread to Europe and the United States and with the backing of gunboats to China and Japan. A backlash against free trade and toward stronger national protection from foreign competition took hold from the 1870s onward, driven by economic downturns, social unrest, and revived great-power rivalry. Even so, this trend did not erase the earlier gains toward greater international economic openness and specialization. Measured as a percentage of total world GDP, total world exports rose from 1 percent in 1820 to 5 percent in 1870 to 8.7 by 1913.[23]

More than anything else, new technology drove economic integration in a calm, outward-looking North Atlantic world. New forms of transport and communication—trains and steamships as well as telegraph cables across land and under the ocean—deepened and tightened the connections among the parts of the international economy. The first cable crossed the North Atlantic in 1869. Freight costs on land and sea fell dramatically, while speed and convenience increased no less dramatically. Refrigeration, introduced in the late 1870s and early 1880s, made possible long-distance shipment of goods such as meat, dairy products, and fruit. Taken together, the machines exploiting steam and electricity had revolutionary implications perhaps greater than more recent and familiar innovations such as the telephone, the airplane, and the computer. Ingenious mechanical contraptions were critical to pushing world trade to a level in 1913 that would not be matched relative to total world output until several decades after World War II.

No one within that North Atlantic world would reap the benefits of peace and technological innovation better than the European Americans. During the Napoleonic wars the u.s. government had struggled with mixed success to hold the Old World at a safe political and military distance while claiming unimpeded access to that most important market. American officials demanded freedom of the seas so that as a neutral in wartime the country's ships and goods could travel safe from harassment, seizure, or interference and take advantage of skyrocketing prices. This attempt to keep the Atlantic an open highway for American commerce collided with Britain's determination to give its well-endowed navy full rein to control commerce. Repeated Anglo-American crises punctuated the first decades of the new u.s. government, divided the country along sectional lines, and finally led to war in 1812. The post-1815 peace among the European powers proved a godsend. With no serious threats at sea or along the borders, the u.s. government could dispense with a large standing armed force and focus national energies and resources on economic development.

Federal, state, and local government made signal contributions to the ensuing economic drive. Foremost were policies meant to shape a single national market. This effort began with the building of canals and roads early in the nineteenth century and continued into the age of steam and electricity. Railroads crisscrossed the country and by 1866 spanned the continent. Telegraph lines paralleled the tracks, creating what one inventor at the time described as "the nervous system of this nation and of modern society."[24] These developments laid the basis for the continent-wide network of mass production and mass marketing that would soon establish the United States as the international economic leader.

Government policies contributed to economic growth in other ways. Taxes were low, with spending directed at critical infrastructure such as public education and transport. Regulations on economic activity stayed minimal. Resources in the public domain—whether land, mineral deposits, grazing rights, or timber—were available to exploit on attractive terms, including land grants to encourage westward settlement. Businesses gained the right to incorporate and thus to act freely as a kind of superindividual—accumulating resources under no more restraint than any real person and shedding employees during economic downturns without a second thought, all the while wielding political influence that no individual alone could match. Beyond all this, the federal government provided patent protection to inventors and tariff protection to rising industries. To ensure an ample labor force, Washington followed a pro-immigration policy. Finally, a point easy to overlook, the federal government maintained political stability and national unity that allowed entrepreneurs to work in a predictable, stable setting. It resolutely crushed the southern attempt to destroy that unity.

Government measures themselves reflected the preferences of a settler society oriented toward growth. That society encouraged innovation and risk and chafed against the constraints imposed by informal social structures or formal political regulations common in Europe. Individuals shed local attachments that limited geographic mobility, rejected arrangements such as guilds that obstructed technological innovation and market access, and shook free from rigid class identities that put a brake on individual initiative. An inspired breed of independent inventors such as Alexander Graham Bell, Thomas A. Edison, and the Wright brothers epitomized the country's bias toward material creativity. Their labs set off what *Scientific American* in 1896 called "a gigantic tidal wave of human ingenuity and resource, so stupendous in its magnitude, so complex in its diversity, so profound in its thought, so fruitful in its wealth, so beneficent in its results, that the mind is strained and embarrassed in its effort to expand to a full appreciation of it."[25] From those labs came not only the telephone and the radio but also the phonograph, the incandescent lamp, motion pictures, power transmission, the engine-driven airplane, the gyroscope, and the machine gun. New technologies made the u.s. economy steadily more productive and left international competitors ever farther behind.

A long peace, new technology, and an integrated, rapidly developing continental market not only accounted for the striking u.s. economic growth rates but also raised the u.s. profile in international trade. Both the farmer and the industrialist took advantage of the North Atlantic's dynamic markets with their remarkable capacity to distribute goods, generate capital and technology, quicken the flow of immigrant labor, and raise living standards. The degree of economic and social dynamism was unprecedented in human history. As goods became cheaper and easier to ship through the nineteenth century, u.s. exports rose, prompting talk in turn-of-the-century Europe of an "American invasion." Between 1870 and 1913, exports increased at an annual average of 4.9 percent. By the eve of World War I, they were seventy-six times higher than in 1820, and only Britain and Germany were more heavily dependent on exports.[26] Unlike these and other trading powerhouses, the u.s. output was still primarily oriented toward a large and rapidly growing home market. External commerce was relatively marginal. Exports from the 1870s to the eve of World War I—a time of burgeoning international trade—held steady at 6–7 percent of gross national product (GNP).[27]

The core of U.S. foreign trade was unprocessed goods sent to Europe. Britain was especially dependent on food imports and industrial raw materials. The British embrace of sweeping free trade principles in the latter half of the 1840s meant the island nation would specialize in industry where its comparative advantage rested, push labor from rural production to urban workplaces, and look overseas for food stuffs and the inputs such as cotton for its manufactures. American farmers with their expanding acreage and increasingly productive technology along with mining and timber interests were well placed to meet this demand from the other side of the Atlantic.

Industrial exports began to loom larger in the course of the nineteenth century, raising the U.S. great-power profile. This shift was in part due to the relative decline of agriculture, which had fallen from 41 percent of GNP in 1840 to 18 percent by 1900. Manufacturing together with mining and hand trades rose between those same dates from 17 to 31 percent. In absolute terms, agricultural productivity remained high even though the proportion of workers in that sector dropped from three-quarters in 1800 to less than a third in 1910. Farms were operating with growing efficiency. Mechanization, improved transport for crops, and fertilizers all made possible higher output with fewer hands. This shift in the domestic economy away from agriculture was mirrored in exports. Around 80 percent through much of the nineteenth century, agricultural products fell rapidly to just over half of total U.S. exports by the first years of the new century. By then manufacturing had risen rapidly so that it accounted for a quarter of the whole. Agricultural goods dependent on foreign demand were especially hurt by rising international competition as lowered transport costs opened new regions of the global economy to production. American wheat producers watched prices fall as new acreage appeared in Australia, New Zealand, Argentina, Canada, and South Africa. Similarly, another mainstay of U.S. agriculture, cotton, faced competition in export markets from India, Brazil, and Egypt.[28]

The rise in industrial activity during the late nineteenth century can also be explained in terms of firms exploiting new technology and organizational strategies to make the most of the continental market. So large was that market that most emerging industrial corporations such as Otis Elevator, National Cash Register, and Edison Electric (later General Electric) derived a relatively small part of their overall earnings from sales overseas. In the face of the boom and bust conditions of the late nineteenth century, many firms sought to control output and price by resorting to gentlemen's agreements, pools, trusts, holding companies, and eventually mergers. These arrangements helped the strong survive and consolidate through hard times and laid the groundwork for some to emerge as formidable competitors in overseas markets.

A few firms began already in the 1850s to carve out a significant international position for themselves. The earliest overseas pioneers specialized in mass-produced machine tools, guns, reapers, and sewing machines. The Singer Manufacturing Company led the way by taking its patented sewing machine technology to European markets and creating an efficient system of general agents. They established offices first in London and then Hamburg, publicized the marvels of u.s. machinery, trained and supervised a local force, promoted installment purchases, and stayed in close touch with the home office. By 1874 more than half of Singer's total machine sales were abroad. To keep prices low and to circumvent national tariffs, Singer moved some of its production overseas. By the 1890s this multinational production, sales, and marketing system constituted (in the words of one of the company's pioneer executives) "a living moving army of irresistible power, peacefully working to conquer the world."[29]

Like most other u.s. firms heavily committed abroad (notably Standard Oil of New Jersey, International Harvester, and New York Life), Singer's strength lay in technical sophistication and organization. Those advantages translated into competitive prices, good marketing, and innovative advertising. Like the others, it looked first to Europe and Canada as high per capita income regions that would repay effort with high sales. Only after its footing in these rich markets was firm did Singer and the others begin to look to Latin America, China, and Russia. Finally, Singer and the other pioneers were short of capital and made only those overseas investments deemed critical (such as Singer's European production facilities).

The relative decline of agriculture in favor of industry transformed the labor force, shifting dependence from the African born and African descended to Europeans. In the early stages of American economic development, unfree labor—approximately 400,000 slaves introduced over the course of the eighteenth century—played a critical role in expanding production. Agricultural output in the South was heavily dependent on workers of African descent, 1.7 million by 1820 or nearly one in five of the total u.s. population.[30] Industrialization created a fresh demand for labor that was only partially met by workers thrown out of the agricultural sector. Many new hands came from overseas. The railways and steamships that carried goods quickly and cheaply and the telegraph that supplied timely information for business also facilitated a major labor migration out of the European, Russian, and Asian country-side—in sum about 150 million people on the move in three great streams over long distances between the 1840s and the 1930s. Of the nearly 50 million Europeans who left their homeland between the 1840s and the onset of World War I, most headed toward the Americas—Argentina, Brazil, Canada, and above all the United States (the destination for two-thirds of these transplants). The net migration to the United States alone between 1870 and 1913 came to 15.8 million. The peak year was 1907 with 1.3 million arrivals. This influx, which made possible an extraordinary economic expansion, helped push the total work force from 14.7 million in 1870 to 38.3 million in 1913. It also raised the percentage of foreign born in the total population to just below 15 percent in the decades around the turn of the century (well above the figure of nearly 10 percent in 1997). American labor and thus American society were more intimately tied to the world than they would ever subsequently be, even during the post–World War II phase of globalization.[31]

The migration networks that led to u.s. farms, mines, and factories had their origins within Europe—in the movement of people from poorer rural regions to richer, industrializing ones either within the same country or in neighboring Britain and France. As the demand for labor in the United States increased, the network spread across the Atlantic. Drawing workers onward were newspaper accounts, promotional material from steamship companies and land agents, and direct testimony in the form of letters and remittances from kin and neighbors. This network bore traffic both ways depending on the opportunities that opened or closed on one or the other side of the North Atlantic labor market. Serious downswings in the u.s. economy, as for example in the 1890s, could give prospective immigrants pause. But they still had to consider the dismal prospects at home: slow economic growth, a rising population, a rigid class system, sometimes virulent ethnic and religious prejudice, and relentless consolidation of land holdings. These difficult Old World conditions created an avid audience for recruitment literature such as the 1878 pamphlet issued by the state of Minnesota addressed "to Labouring Men, who earn a livelihood by honest toil; to Landless Men, who aspire to the dignity and independence which comes from possession in God's free earth, to All Men of moderate means, and men of wealth, who will accept homes in a beautiful and prosperous country."[32]

The hard-headed calculations that drove the extraordinary population shift from Europe to North America are evident in the testimony of ordinary Germans. Immigrants faced in the United States serious challenges posed by cultural adjustment, ethnic prejudice, and material sacrifice, but leaving lands of constricted economic and social opportunities still made sense. Their letters home were eloquent on both the difficulties and the opportunities. "The streets aren't paved with gold here like people always write," Matthias Dorgathen confessed in 1881 during his first year in the United States. On the other side of the balance sheet, Christian Kirst, writing from Pittsburgh in 1882, celebrated the sense of liberation that he felt: "Here it doesn't matter who you are, here everybody's equal, here the banker knows the beggar." A person who had a trade, stayed healthy, and worked hard could (as Kirst explained) "save more money in a short time than he could in a lifetime in Germany." Kirst lamented that he had not made the decision to emigrate until his midfifties. "I spent the best years of my life in the German land of Egypt so miserably and painfully, for nothing." Ludwig Dilger writing from his home in St. Louis in 1907 could, despite several bruising decades of boom and bust conditions and labor union struggles, still offer an emphatically positive verdict: "America, I love you, no longing for Germany at all. It's the richest country in the world. It's the best country for the poor man."[33]

Foreign capital as well as foreign labor fueled U.S. economic growth. But overall funds from overseas were less important to U.S. dynamism than repeated infusions of fresh labor. A high and increasing savings rate among Americans over the course of the nineteenth century made it possible to meet much of the demand for fresh investment from domestic sources. Gross savings climbed from about 14 percent in the 1840s to 23 percent in the years around 1890. European money did, however, make an important contribution, particularly in facilitating railway construction and economic restructuring during the 1830s and 1880–1896 when demand for fresh capital surged. London banks were especially important. About half of all British savings were directed abroad. Sophisticated British investors understood the U.S. market, kept close tabs on it thanks to the telegraph, and could move their funds unimpeded by state controls. As a result about three-quarters of all long-term monies entering the United States at the end of the nineteenth century came from Britain.[34]

What dependence there had been on foreign investors began to diminish around the turn of the century as U.S. money moving overseas began to exceed incoming foreign funds. By 1914 U.S. direct investments overseas had risen to $2.65 billion, with nearly one-half directed at extracting raw materials (mining or oil operations). Canada and Mexico were the favored destinations as U.S. investors helped integrate these neighbors into the U.S. economy. By 1914 65 percent of U.S. investments were to be found in the Western Hemisphere.

Europe was next (the destination for about 20 percent) thanks largely to the commitment of companies like Singer, General Electric, Westinghouse, and Standard Oil to creating marketing networks there. While even as late as 1914 the United States was on balance still a net debtor on international accounts to the tune of about $2.5 billion, the trend line pointed to a reversal of that position in the near term. It was already easy to glimpse a financial colossus in the making.

A SENSE OF MASTERY

Animating Gast's imagery of the American continent was a powerful nationalism. Gast represented national superiority and destiny by juxtaposing light that went with the settlers' advance against the gloom enveloping Native Americans and untamed nature. This righteous sense of historical destiny was not unique to the United States; it found its counterpart in many lands where people increasingly defined themselves in national terms. Like the elites in other countries engaged in this ideological enterprise, their American counterparts (predominantly of English descent) constructed elaborate explanations for their country's dominion and created glowing images of its destiny. Their constructs drew from European sources, especially from Britain, but had to accommodate to the peculiar circumstances of a settler society. The resulting nationalist notions came to circulate widely thanks to publicly funded education, public celebrations, religious sermons, memorials and monuments, and the propaganda of political parties. And as they gained in reach, they were to prove important—as a force for creating cultural coherence out of a multiplicity of ethnic identities, as a response to a world of jostling European nationalisms, and as both a justification and tool for a central government devoted to an ambitious agenda.

Nationalism in the u.s. case developed a special intensity as a result of its relationship to an ethnically diverse society created by early settlement patterns and subsequently maintained by repeated waves of labor migration. That society consisted notably of peoples from Africa forced into economic service, free labor drawn from an increasingly wide swath of Europe, and vestiges of a native population. Leading intellectuals and politicians in the Anglo community set about establishing their dominion. They created and propagated a definition of the nation that entirely excluded blacks (as well as women) from citizenship, incorporated Europeans in relation to their perceived whiteness (a standard that became more inclusive over time, beginning with Scots and Germans), and banished Indians to the realm of myths and to remote reservations. In the process, these lords of North America practiced what has come to be called "orientalism"—expressing their own sense of superiority by diminishing others as infantile, feminine, and barbarous.[35]

Legitimizing Dominance

"Manifest destiny" was the mid-nineteenth century encapsulation of an emerging u.s. nationalism. John L. O'Sullivan, an influential New York City magazine and newspaper editor and supporter of the Democratic Party and its expansionist policies, coined the term in an article published in 1839. "Our national birth was the beginning of a new history, the formation and progress of an untried political system, which separates us from the past and connects us with the future only; and so far as regards the entire development of the natural rights of man, in moral, political, and national life, we may confidently assume that our country is destined to be the great nation of futurity."[36] In the 1840s proponents of the nation's "manifest destiny" such as President James K. Polk echoed O'Sullivan's formulation, contending that the addition of new territories was consistent with the u.s. role as a special agent of freedom and progress and as a special country with boundless possibilities. This settler society had a right, even an obligation to master nature no less than other peoples making a claim to the continent.

This faith in a progressive human drama to be played out on the North American continent was strongly tinctured by a British and above all Anglo identity. This particular ethnic bias reflected the distribution of power within the u.s. settler population. An Anglo elite that dominated business, politics, education, and the church maintained their culture preferences in the New World setting. Even their rejection of British rule came straight from British political philosophers. An imagined link to England or Anglo-Saxonism—the belief that Americans and the English were one people united by uncommon qualities and common interests—came to occupy a central position in elite circles.

By the first half of the nineteenth century influential Americans began proclaiming their proud place in a transatlantic community of English-speaking people. Howard Bushnell, an influential Connecticut minister, boasted in 1837, "Out of all the inhabitants of the world . . . a select stock, the Saxon, and of this the British family, the noblest of the stock, was chosen to people our country." In 1836 Sam Houston characterized the victors in the war for Texas independence from Mexico as "the Anglo-Saxon race" devoted to liberty's advance. By the end of the century the Anglo-Saxon spell had further strengthened its hold. The predominant racial characteristics of both peoples, as they were now defined, included industry, intelligence, a keen sense of moral purpose, and a talent for government. The English with their admirable record of industrial, colonial, and cultural achievement were close relatives, even family. The affirmation of this point came back to Americans from across the Atlantic in what became a cultural and political echo chamber of fraternal goodwill. Bram Stoker, best known as the author of *Dracula*, reported in 1885 on how a visit to the United States had underlined the new racial brotherhood: "Our history is their history—our fame is their pride—their progress is our glory. They are bound to us, and we to them, by every tie of love and sympathy."[37]

Confidant Anglos led the drive for cultural homogenization, taking aim at Spanish, Dutch, French, Swedes, and Germans, not to mention Native Americans and Africans, each with identities as diverse as those of Europeans. Some members of this multicultural, multinational population were part of the new U.S. state at the outset, while others arrived as part of the annexationist packages gathered through the first half of the nineteenth century. For example, the drive against Mexico from the 1830s to the early 1850s incorporated 75,000 Spanish-speaking subjects and 150,000 Indians. Yet others arrived in the millions on the waves of emigration from Europe. Faced with this great ethnic diversity, those with a sturdy sense of their own Anglo background were determined that the continent would have one unquestioned value system defining its politics, education, economy, and society. Their effort—properly deemed nationalist—gave rise to a sustained cultural campaign over the course of the nineteenth century.

Supporting that campaign was a collection of images with potent, long-term implications for shaping the view of policymakers and the influential public. Americans who identified themselves as Anglo viewed the peoples around them in terms that might best be described as racial. Skin color was the surface marker, closely related to innate worth, whether measured in terms of individual virtue or the capacity of a people to find freedom, achieve economic growth, or mount a colonial campaign. Taken all together, this Anglo view of others assumed the form of a racial hierarchy in which whites in general and Protestants of English descent in particular were at the top. Predictably, on the lowest rung of the ladder were the peoples of Africa, a continent that, above all others, invited white dominion. Other peoples were arrayed at intermediate and sometimes changing points between the highs of civilization and progress and the lows of barbarism and backwardness. There was to be no doubt who owned the national idea and would give it definition.

Northern Europeans occupied a fairly exalted position in this Anglo cultural construct. Germans stood just behind the Anglo-Saxon family. They had the same qualities as their racial cousins save one—they had lost their love of liberty. This single serious defect meant that the Germans as a formidable people and a threatening global competitor would have to be watched closely. By the turn of the century, American commentators increasingly pictured them as latter-day Huns, prone to the aggressive, even brutal behavior characteristic of a militaristic and autocratic system. The Slavs, depicted as half European and half Asiatic, were also seen as formidable racial competitors on the international stage. Highly regimented and of rugged peasant stock, they had displayed great endurance, patience, and strength (but not intelligence or a knack for innovation) as they had slowly but irresistibly extended their control over much of the Eurasian land mass.

Lower down in the hierarchy were the Latin peoples of Europe (defined to include the French as well as Italians and Spaniards). They lacked vigor; they were sentimental, undisciplined, and superstitious; consequently they were of small account in international affairs. Their defects carried over to the colonies, most notably Latin America, whose peoples figured prominently as somewhat childlike or brutish inferiors in need of the benevolent hand of the more mature. Latin America's struggle for freedom from Spanish control early in the nineteenth century revealed that peoples long oppressed by foreign rule might want liberty, but the conditions that had held them down, including the burden of race, might also leave them incapable of either winning or maintaining it. The Spanish legacy of misrule, superstition, and cruelty (the elements of what is known as the "black legend") did much to explain why Latin Americans were ill suited to liberty. "You cannot make liberty out of Spanish matter," observed a prominent Virginia congressman in 1816. They were, Jefferson declared in 1813, "a priest-ridden people," while John Quincy Adams summed up their flaws in 1821 (having helped Jackson seize Spain's Florida holdings): "Arbitrary power, military and ecclesiastical, was stamped upon their education, upon their habits, and upon all their institutions." Mexicans as competitors for the lands of the Southwest could only be considered (in the view of Polk's secretary of state, James Buchanan) "imbecile and indolent." This "mongrel race" therefore had an inferior claim to lands that Anglo-Saxons could put to better use. With the war for control of northern Mexico under way, the poet and editor Walt Whitman in September 1847 described the people of that country as "ignorant, prejudiced, and perfectly faithless."[38]

The peoples of East Asia, sometimes designated "the Mongolian race" but more popularly referred to as "orientals," also stood somewhere near the middle of the racial ladder. They emerged from the accounts of merchants, missionaries, and diplomats from the 1780s onward as a disturbing, even dangerous, bundle of contradictions. Inscrutable and somnolent, they were also a people of promise, on the verge of shaking off a stagnant cultural tradition and improving their position in the hierarchy of race. They were subhuman, yet cunning; unfeeling, yet boiling inwardly with rage; cowardly and decadent, yet capable of great conquests. A 1784 geography captured the negative side of this appraisal when it described the Chinese as "the most dishonest, low, thieving people in the world." Reflecting that other more hopeful side, a Massachusetts politician about to set off on a diplomatic mission to China shared with a Boston audience in 1843 his dreams of rejuvenating a once glorious culture. "We have become the teachers of our teachers."[39]

As in other settler societies, the struggle for land was the fuel that first brought the nationalist imagination to a boil. The claim of Anglo settlers to dominance on the continent depended on putting the other peoples sharing that continent with them in their proper, subordinate place. This impulse toward control was as much figurative as literal. Out of the physical struggle with other ethnic groups would emerge an outlook of racial dominance, one that sought cultural differences and extracted from them signs of settler superiority that made "manifest" the reasons for domination over these "lesser others." In dialectical fashion, the more the conflict with these others, the sharper became the Anglo sense of difference and superiority. In other words, the struggle to subjugate ethnic competitors for control of the continent served to consolidate Anglo identity. Nowhere was the process of negative stereotyping more evident than in the practice of extermination and the policy of removal practiced toward Native Americans (treated earlier in this chapter). Only in the latter half of the nineteenth century, with the land issue basically resolved, did the image of the Indian begin to take a positive turn—toward that of the noble savage.

By contrast, Anglos' perspectives on Africans in their midst—whether enslaved or nominally free descendants—remained resolutely harsh and strikingly color-conscious. Colonists carried with them prejudices common in Elizabethan England that associated the color black and by extension the dark-skinned peoples of Africa with baseness and evil. White stood as the moral and aesthetic opposite, the symbol of virtue, beauty, and purity. An English poem of 1620 played on this contrast by describing the African as "a black deformed Elfe" while picturing the white Englishman as "like unto God himselfe."[40] By the early eighteenth century Euro-Americans were applying explicitly racial formulations to blacks. In the South this intellectual legacy combined with economic self-interest to produce the most extreme views. There exploitation of blacks had become a way of life, and their submission essential to the prosperity of a tobacco- and cotton-export economy and to a sense of security among often-outnumbered whites. The black was first abased in the Southern slave codes, while the folklore of the region stigmatized slaves as incipient insurrectionists and brooding rapists. Close supervision and control and the threat of severe punishment, including lynching and castration, were thought essential to keep them in check. Abolitionist agitation early in the nineteenth century and the North's post–Civil War intervention on behalf of emancipated blacks failed to dislodge long-propagated views on racial difference and racial danger.

Though whites often disagreed on aspects of the "Negro question," sometimes emotionally so, they nonetheless agreed almost universally on the fundamental issue of white supremacy and black inferiority. By the beginning of the twentieth century, the issue of the place of blacks in American society rested on the foundation laid three centuries earlier—the protean association of inferiority with darkness of skin color. This strikingly persistent consensus on race was evident in scholarly works, but even more to the point it suffused the popular literature of the time. School texts, for example, consistently conveyed from decade to decade the same essential message: blacks occupied the bottom rung in the hierarchy of race dominated by whites. Blacks were "destitute of intelligence." A geography of 1789 delicately explained, "They are a brutish people, having little more of humanity but the form." At best these texts presented blacks as victims of slavery, incapable of climbing higher on their own, possibly educable as dependents of paternalistic whites, but also perhaps irremediably backward. A 1900 account probably reflected mainstream white attitudes when it glumly concluded, "In spite of the efforts to educate them . . . many [blacks] still remain densely ignorant." These attitudes translated into a system of Jim Crow segregation and disenfranchisement that had dehumanizing effects all too evident from the other side of the racial divide. Black men "just weren't counted to be no more than a dog."[41]

Views that took shape through the subjugation of Native Americans and the enslavement and repression of African Americans gained additional form and force in reaction to the late nineteenth-century surge of immigrants threatening Anglo cultural hegemony. In the 1880s and 1890s both Democratic and Republican parties moved toward a more restrictive position on immigration. The threat new arrivals posed to the established work force was one issue, but the overriding concern was the threat "alien types"—paupers, illiterates, and criminals—posed to the social, political, and religious traditions that the old English stock embodied.

The West Coast was one front in the battle to contain culturally as well as demographically the new immigrants arriving to work mines and rail lines. Between 1860 and 1900 some half a million Chinese arrived. Just as the Chinese stream slowed, Japanese immigration picked up—200,000 came to the West Coast between 1890 and 1924, when blanket federal restrictions took effect. Both groups of newcomers faced charges that their presence threatened free labor as well as social decency. In the words of San Francisco's mayor, who was at the forefront of labor's "anti-oriental" campaign, the Chinese and Japanese were "not the stuff of which American citizens can be made." This apparent invasion of cheap, immoral labor converted Irish and Cornish workers at the forefront of agitation into honorary Anglos. Regional resistance found expression in discriminatory measures (such as miscegenation laws and restrictions on work and landholding) as well as physical harassment. In 1882, with the support of both major parties, Congress made the cause national by voting to end Chinese immigration. This policy was sustained and strengthened on the grounds articulated by Theodore Roosevelt in 1895: the presence of the "Chinaman" is "ruinous to the white race." By 1905 agitators on the West Coast were demanding Congress call a halt to Japanese immigration as well. Within two decades they would have their way.[42]

The East Coast was the other front in the battle for Anglo cultural dominance over newcomers. Despite decades of rising immigration, calls for exclusion did not become strong until the 1890s. A string of economic depressions, culminating in the severe downturn of 1893–97, had put a question mark over the need for adding to a labor force that was showing signs of revolutionary agitation. At the same time, the increasing proportion of newcomers from southern and eastern Europe sparked discussion of whether they were as culturally digestible as the northern Europeans who had previously dominated the immigrant ranks.

The campaign for exclusion began in earnest in 1894 with the creation of the Immigration Restriction League. Based in the northeast, it was headed by a Boston Brahmin, Henry Cabot Lodge. The League attracted leaders like Lodge in education, culture, and politics. Its arguments reflected fears that newcomers threatened domestic peace and racial purity. They worked for a pittance, imported dangerous socialist and anarchist ideas, lapsed into poverty and dependence, and threw support to urban political machines. Lodge saw the new type of immigrant threatening "a great and perilous change in the very fabric of our race." The artist best known for his images of the frontier struggle, Frederic Remington, lumped "Jews, Injuns, Chinamen, Italians, and Huns" all together as "the rubbish of the earth I hate." He professed himself ready to turn his rifle on them. The historian Frederick Jackson Turner was repelled by the "brutal and degraded life" of these undesirable races. Henry James, the novelist, found the Italians in Boston "gross aliens to a man." By keeping out what the League's constitution described as "elements undesirable for citizenship or injurious to our national character," exclusionists hoped to preserve the Anglo makeup of the country. Frustrated for a time, they would finally get Congress to impose restrictions in the early 1920s in the wake of war and postwar economic strains.[43]

Visions of a Dynamic Republic

The Anglo elite that had dominated American politics and foreign policy since the founding of the new state agreed on two basic points critical to their sense of national identity. They took for granted the superiority of their kind. Their dominance over other peoples—whether competitors for territorial control, newcomers to a burgeoning labor market, or descendants of enslaved Africans—was natural and right. This elite, moreover, saw their country engaged in an experiment of historical and global significance. As the patriot and pamphleteer Thomas Paine declared at the outset of the struggle for independence, Americans had it in their power "to begin the world over again."[44] The phrase captured a widely accepted truth about national uniqueness and destiny.

But this Anglo elite repeatedly divided over the best path of political and social development of the continent, and those differences were in turn tied to questions of how the New World would relate to the Old and even in time how an ascendant America would play its role in the world. This divergence came into sharp focus in the 1790s even as Americans sought to consolidate their newly won independence against a still powerful Europe. In a heated and far-ranging exchange the ruling Federalists engaged the emergent opposition party, the Republicans. That debate brought into the open an enduring tension within American nationalism over which of the values Anglos prized would receive preference and what consequences would flow from political and military commitments abroad.

Alexander Hamilton, the first treasury secretary and the animating force within the Washington administration, was the leading Federalist voice in that first debate. This man of huge talent and no less huge ambition imagined the United States as a dynamic republic. He embraced the British model of promoting commerce and industry, a strong central government, and rule by the best men. By extension, he regarded Britain as the natural partner for the rising American nation. Overshadowed for the moment, Americans as "the embryo of a great empire" (as Hamilton phrased it in 1795) should bide their time, suffer the occasionally overbearing behavior of London, build national wealth and power, and in time achieve eminence. The first step, he had suggested in the debate over the Constitution in 1787, was to create "one great American system, superior to the controul of all trans-atlantic force or influence, and able to dictate the terms of the connections between the old and the new world!" But the ultimate goal was to equal or even eclipse the British.[45]

As Washington's secretary of state and then as leader of the political opposition, Thomas Jefferson articulated a competing vision of his country. It was rooted in his fundamental conviction (captured in his famous observation from the early 1780s) that "cultivators of the earth are the most virtuous and independent citizens."[46] His goal was to create and preserve for these cultivators a freeholder democracy. Success in his estimate depended on breaking the constraints on foreign trade that an overbearing Britain sought to impose. Agricultural goods moving freely to overseas markets would help sustain the prosperity that kept independent yeoman farming viable. Success also depended on securing land—whether from the Europeans or the natives—for a growing population. By thus preserving the basis for an agriculturalist world, Jefferson hoped to maintain a rough equality essential to his notion of a good society.

Perhaps most challenging of all, republican success depended on fending off commercial development that had brought Europe overcrowded cities and degrading factory work. If the European model took hold on this side of the Atlantic (as Hamilton seemed to wish), the American republican experiment would not survive. Jefferson imagined the citizenry losing their virtue as they fell prey to avarice and a taste for luxury. As the European model took hold, the country would come under the sway of a social aristocracy and a powerful central government controlled by a corrupt elite. Jefferson's anxiety was rooted in his classical education that highlighted the vulnerability of earlier republics. Athens, Rome, and the Renaissance city-states all succumbed to strongmen and military adventures. The commitment of Jefferson and his political allies to free trade and their antipathy to aristocratic society and politics left them deeply suspicious of any suggestion of subordination to Britain. Jefferson's fellow republican, James Madison, had warned in the mid-1790s that such a tie would pose a profound threat to "our taste, our manners, and our form of Government itself."[47]

The Hamilton-Jefferson exchange proved only the first round in a match that repeatedly and deeply divided Americans over the course of the nineteenth century and persisted into the twentieth. Jefferson's disciples with their cautious, populist vision of the future knew that in the continental phase of the nation's development new land was essential to sustaining an agricultural society with a growing population. The vitality of the republic depended heavily, Jefferson wrote in 1817, "on the enlargement of the resources of life going hand in hand with the enlargement of territory."[48] But those sharing Jefferson's views also worried that land grabbing and other foreign adventures would have an insidious effect at home, just as they had had in leading to the collapse of past republics. During the Mexican War in the late 1840s and again following the war with Spain in 1898, these critics decried imperial conquests that posed a danger to liberty and to republican virtue. In the twentieth century the advocates of the Jeffersonian position came to be dubbed "isolationists" as a result of their opposition to involvement in European rivalries. Such involvement, they contended, made the United States hostage to developments beyond its control, and the resulting wars imposed real domestic costs: increased national debt, lives lost and disrupted, and the dangerous concentration of power in the hands of the president. Better that the country stand aloof from a world prone to despotism and violence and instead attend to its primary obligation, advancing the welfare of its own people and protecting a fragile experiment in democracy. The United States might thus serve as a model for others, whereas foreign entanglements would set that model at risk.

Those who shared Hamilton's confidence in pursuing a bold policy of strength and influence responded that passivity would doom the American experiment to stagnation and ultimate failure, while the acquisition of wider influence in the world would revitalize the American spirit and make liberty generally more secure. With this vision went a commitment to a strong central government. Only a strong executive could assert international influence while also encouraging the economic development at home essential to that influence. Increasingly over the nineteenth century, the edge in this debate went to the Hamiltonians with their confidence in the national future. The United States was exempt from the historical laws of decline that had destroyed other republics; it was insulated against the perils of contact with a benighted Europe; and it could perhaps even exercise dominion over other, lesser peoples.

It might be tempting to see this ideological contest epitomized by Hamilton and Jefferson as a peculiarly American drama. Their respective views resonate powerfully in a national narrative in which a people devoted to freedom and self-advancement struggle to come to terms with a state powerful enough to promote domestic development and assert national interests abroad. But this tension was in fact playing out across the North Atlantic world. It was already evident in the 1790s in the British state, which had a growing administrative capacity as attractive to Hamilton as it was repulsive to Jefferson. Over the course of the eighteenth century it had demonstrated its ability to raise taxes, manage public credit, fund a formidable armed force, repress political discontent, protect land and financial interests, and promote taxable economic activity.[49] The French state was also launched along this course, and during the nineteenth century other states would develop similarly in response to industrial growth, rapid technological innovation, military insecurity, and colonial rivalries. It is easy to imagine Hamilton conversing knowingly not just with Britain's Pitt (father or son) but also France's Colbert, the leaders of Japan's Meiji Restoration, or Germany's Bismarck. It is equally easy to imagine Jefferson exchanging confidences with those in other countries who shared his anxieties about the relentless centralization of political power. How really different were the Americans as they felt their way into the modern world?

The forces shaping the United States were global in nature. Settlers in Australia and South Africa could boast similar conquests of land. Global capitalism was having a no less profound impact throughout Europe and in its colonies. Elites elsewhere were, like Americans, seeking to define and propagate a sense of national identity the better to strengthen the state and cope with rival powers and economic change. But the consequences of these global forces were proving in the u.s. case, however unexceptional in their nature, exceptional in their impact. What began as scattered and struggling outposts of Europeans in the seventeenth century had already by the late nineteenth century become a country secure, wealthy, and self-confident. Standing on strong foundations, Americans were ready for a burst of international activity between 1898 and 1920 that would mark the first overt step toward global ascendancy.

Figure 2. McKinley's war room, pictured in McClure's Magazine, July 1898, 209.

2

GRAND PROJECTS

1898★1920

What President William McKinley's staff called the war room (fig. 2) tells a lot about a major turn in the u.s. relationship with the broader world—from continental mastery to grand overseas projects. In 1898, at the outset of the war with Spain, McKinley outfitted this room on the second floor of the White House with telegraph lines and maps and placed it under the direction of Capt. B. Montgomery (seated left).[1] Thanks to this facility, the president could direct first his armed forces operating in the Caribbean and the Pacific and then the diplomats assigned the task of extending u.s. holdings in both those regions. Like other empire builders of the day, McKinley was exploiting the new globe-shrinking technologies of cable and steam transport.

Having potential—whether technological or military and economic—is one thing; making use of it as McKinley did is another. He saw a decrepit Spain barely clinging to the remnants of empire against restive subjects. The Philippines as well as Cuba were in revolt. McKinley exploited this vulnerability to aggrandize the United States. His initial boldness carried him and the country in unexpected directions. The war with Spain whetted the national appetite for wider influence in regions under the imperialist onslaught and even for colonies. It proved a short step from joining in the European rivalries on the colonial periphery to intervening in Europe's first great war. Intervention in that war in turn gave rise to a plan, firmly linked to Woodrow Wilson's name, to replace the system of rival imperial states with one of American design—democratic, peaceful, and commercial. This succession of grand projects in turn helped launch the modern American state. Whether these developments of such signal importance would have happened without McKinley is beyond knowing.

What is certain is that the drama on which McKinley raised the curtain was not uniquely American. Fighting wars, occupying colonies, superintending dependencies, securing far-flung diplomatic interests, and monitoring rivals not only raised the government in Washington to a level with the European states but reflected patterns playing out in the capitals of the major North Atlantic states as well as in Japan. Americans assumed a place among the leading powers of the day precisely because they were feeling a pervasive set of pressures and responding to them in altogether unexceptional ways.

MCKINLEY'S IMPERIAL IMPULSE

If we could pass through the large door visible at the back of McKinley's war room, we might encounter down one of the corridors the man who to the surprise of many launched this dramatic reorientation of the u.s. place in the world. McKinley was an Ohio lawyer with a reputation as a straight arrow. He worked hard and behaved properly in public. He never swore and discouraged those who did, attended church regularly, and gave his invalid wife devoted care. A conservative, conciliatory Republican, his political career took him first to the u.s. House of Representatives, to the Ohio governorship, and finally to the White House in the election of 1896. Despite having scant prior international background and having never ventured beyond his country's borders, McKinley proved a strong, shrewd, skillful policymaker with a broad view of American interests overseas. It would not be the last time that a president unburdened by knowledge of and experience in foreign affairs would boldly reorient u.s. foreign policy.

Defining Decisions

A simmering Cuban independence movement set the stage for McKinley's great imperial initiative. The independence struggle against Spain erupted in 1895 in a well-organized, sustained military drive. During his first year in office, McKinley tried to end what had become a bloody contest between the Spanish colonial army and Cuban insurgents. By February 1898 he had clearly failed, consigning u.s. investment and trade to continued danger and throwing into doubt u.s. claims to supervise the hemisphere. Spain's brutal pacification campaign got dramatic play in the u.s. press, more popular than ever thanks to low-cost offset printing and lively on-the-scene accounts sent in by cable. Public and congressional pressure for action mounted. An explosion that sank the u.s. battleship *Maine* while anchored in Havana harbor added to the outrage. But McKinley hesitated to go to war, perhaps remembering the bloody losses that he had personally witnessed on the front lines of the Civil War. "I have been through one war; I have seen the dead piled up, and I do not want to see another."[2] He tried to buy time by appointing a commission to investigate the cause of the *Maine*'s destruction. Finally in April, facing a Congress near revolt and himself feeling intense personal strain, he acquiesced in a declaration of war.

Now in a major reversal, McKinley moved aggressively to make the most of the opportunities afforded by a vulnerable foe. Spain's economy was a tenth that of the United States, its political class was divided, and its imperial remnants easy pickings. The president personally directed the assault. The u.s. Army and Navy moved against Spanish forces in Cuba with the help of the insurgents and occupied Puerto Rico, while the navy attacked the Spanish fleet in the Philippines, a step first contemplated by naval planners several years earlier, and scored a resounding victory in Manila Bay on 1 May. By month's end 20,000 u.s. soldiers had orders for the Philippines. In July the president pushed the annexation of Hawaii through Congress by joint resolution. U.S. settlers had gained cultural and economic control over the course of the nineteenth century and in 1893 seized political power and waited for Washington to come to terms with annexation. McKinley correctly counted on war fever to break the long-standing impasse. In August, with Madrid's surrender in hand, McKinley began inching his way toward a decision on acquiring all of the Philippines. Under his guidance the American delegation negotiated peace terms with the Spanish in Paris and signed a treaty of peace in December providing for the transfer of the Philippines as well as Puerto Rico and Guam. McKinley proceeded to push the treaty through a Senate sharply divided over taking the Philippines. In early February 1899 he made full use of presidential persuasion and patronage to hold his majority Republicans together and secure enough defections from Democrats and independents. With fifty-seven votes, the president had one more than the bare two-thirds needed to ratify the treaty. The Philippines bases together with those on Guam and Hawaii established the United States as a commercial and strategic presence all the way across the Pacific.

Having swept up the spoils of war against Spain, McKinley pressed fresh initiatives in the Pacific. In December 1899 he agreed with Germany to partition Samoa. The next year his secretary of state, John Hay, issued the first of two open-door notes that sought to assure Americans access to China on a basis of equality with the other powers and prevent a formal colonial division of the faltering Chinese empire. The first note claimed equal treatment for American commerce vying for a place in a market supposedly of enormous potential but seemingly threatened by European territorial partition. Concern about access to markets and competition on equal terms had been a consistent element of U.S. Pacific policy, prompting naval expeditions to break down barriers to trade in Japan in the 1850s and Korea in the 1870s.

Hardly had Washington articulated this open-door doctrine than a challenge emerged from a completely unexpected quarter—a popular insurgency known as the Boxers that sprang up in North China's Shandong province. In 1900 Washington watched incredulously and helplessly as U.S. and other foreign missionaries and their converts came under attack and the diplomatic quarter in Beijing fell under siege. McKinley's response was to launch his second major American military intervention in eastern Asia. Some four thousand U.S. soldiers joined other foreign troops in North China in a mission of rescue and punishment. They fought their way to Beijing, scoured the countryside of all resistance, and brought to account officials as well as commoners implicated in the outrage. At the same time, Hay issued his second note, interpreting the open door in broader terms. To the previous concern with access to China's market, he now added a commitment to safeguarding China's independence. If the rival powers were to partition China, U.S. business prospects and missionary interests were sure to suffer. The open door thus linked equal trade opportunity (central to the first Hay note) to long-term American political and cultural influences (the emphasis of the second). It also elevated China, the weak Asian giant whose future development seemed to hold the key to long-term American influence throughout the region, to a place of importance in U.S. policy.

Far-reaching technological advances that made possible both globalization and imperialism help explain this sudden stirring of U.S. power. Technology was raising industrial and agricultural productivity in national markets, nowhere more dramatically than in McKinley's America. New technology was also boosting the destructive potential of warfare on land and at sea as well as the costs of preparing for war. The Civil War had already demonstrated how telegraph, train, and steamships together made possible the rapid movement, dependable supply, and easy coordination of large, far-flung forces. More sophisticated armaments were coming in a rush—smokeless powder, torpedoes, mines, and breach-loading cannon with rifled barrels for greater long-range accuracy. Warships grew ever larger with bigger, more accurate guns and heavier armor. The war against Spain confirmed both the complexity of modern warfare and the advantages that went with better guns, logistics, and communications. Technology delivered economic and political elites more information faster, and gave them direct control over events thousands of miles away. McKinley's reliance on a war room testifies to the importance of this longer, firmer reach.

Finally, technology was broadening the vistas of ordinary people. In the United States cheap newspapers ("penny press") reached the mass market with sensational international reports of yesterday's Spanish military outrage in Cuba or the slaughter of American innocents doing God's work in China. Thanks to the convenience and speed of new transport and communications, transatlantic tourist travel became cheaper and faster, attracting growing numbers of the middle class along with the wealthy. A safe guess would put the number at a hundred thousand tourists a year by the turn of the century. These travelers eagerly retailed their impressions of the Old World both in their communities and in major national publications. Travel was edifying for the American, the *New York Times* editorialized in 1908. "It broadens his vision, increases his knowledge, and improves his taste." This enhanced accessibility of the broader world through news and travel was reflected in a revitalized overseas missionary movement, the activism of philanthropic organizations, and a burst of interest in overseas exploration promoted by the National Geographic Society (founded in 1888); it even could be seen in a taste for the exotic in home furnishings.[3]

This worldwide technological shakeup in the decades around the turn of the century gave rise to concerns that made McKinley's circle and his supporters receptive to the idea of an American empire. Taken together, these concerns looked strikingly similar to those gripping colonially minded Europeans. Little wonder: American advocates of empire were fascinated witnesses to the new wave of European colonialism in Africa and Asia in the 1880s and 1890s, and they were especially influenced by the British example and British imperial ideology. The views of the prominent British colonial secretary, Joseph Chamberlain, carried widely. So too though to a lesser degree did statements by France's Jules Ferry, Germany's Otto von Bismarck, and Belgium's Leopold II. That a nation barely a century away from its own break with British control should contemplate emulating British colonialism may seem surprising—unless one considers the growing sense of Anglo-Saxon solidarity among the small but influential segment of the American public interested in foreign affairs. The Spanish-American War stimulated an outpouring of talk about the vigor and manhood of the two "kindred peoples," and inspired leading figures in the United States to join with counterparts in Britain in organizing an Anglo-American League (with branches in New York and London) to celebrate a common heritage and an enduring friendship.

From their observations American imperialists extracted four simple propositions to justify overseas conquest. First, empire would make Americans feel good about doing their duty. British commentators described formal colonial holdings as the ornaments of a modern, powerful state and the test-ing grounds of civilized peoples. If Britain could claim a quarter of the world as its domain and even tiny Belgium could boast a major African kingdom, why should Americans not share in the glory? As a superior people in com-mand of an advanced civilization, Americans were no less suited to exercise dominion over peoples unfit to direct their own affairs. The United States was in the words of one of the most fervent supporters of McKinley's em-pire, Indiana senator Albert J. Beveridge, "a greater England with a nobler destiny." That meant, according to the u.s. military governor of an occupied Cuba, taking "a race that has steadily been going down for a hundred years" and infusing it with "new life, new principles and new methods of doing things." The same message came from the military governor in the Philip-pines: Americans were molding "essentially plastic" people into republicans, thus opening "a magnificent and mighty destiny" for themselves in Asia. A Princeton professor bound for the highest political office agreed on the need to help "undeveloped peoples, still in the childhood of their political growth," as the first step toward u.s. leadership "in the opening and transformation of the East." Theodore Roosevelt returned from fighting in Cuba a convinced imperialist: "It is our duty to the people living in barbarism to see that they are freed from their chains, and we can free them only by destroying barba-rism itself. . . . Throughout all history the advance of civilization has been of incalculable benefit to mankind, and those through whom it has advanced deserve the highest honor." Once president, he contended that the u.s. cause in the Philippines represented nothing less than "the triumph of civilization over the black chaos of savagery and barbarianism." In pursuing their colonial enterprise, Americans could show the "manly resolve" that figured promi-nently in an increasingly assertive, even martial u.s. nationalism.[4]

Second, empire looked easy. Advances in military technology had lowered the costs of fixing control over peripheral peoples. Europeans had already demonstrated how gunboats, well-organized logistical trains linking colony to metropole, and rapid-fire guns could subdue even the most distant and hostile lands. Small French forces had extinguished repeated outbreaks of resistance in Vietnam, while equally limited application of British power had quelled opposition in India and at a variety of points in Africa. Surely Ameri-cans, tested in a running battle with Native Americans across the continent, knew how to coerce obedience as well as Europeans. When Filipinos failed to acquiesce to the claims of a superior people, imperialists predictably looked to a familiar past—the pacification of Native Americans—for a solution. Most of the u.s. generals serving in the Philippines had been schooled in Indian warfare early in their careers, and the American troops came primarily from the western states, where that warfare had most recently been conducted.

Third, empire also seemed to serve security. Cable and steam had made the world smaller, while an increasingly colonized periphery—Africa carved up, the Middle East staked out, the independent states of Southeast Asia gobbled up, China threatened on all sides, and Pacific islands annexed—hemmed Americans in. From the perspective of u.s. strategists these same developments provided potential foes, now possessed of greater mobility and firepower than ever, with bases to launch an attack across the once secure ocean approaches to North America. Fending off this danger required defense in depth—the control of Pacific and Caribbean outposts. These same outposts could also serve as coaling stations and bases of operation if the United States wished to enforce the Monroe Doctrine in Latin America and have a say in the future of a China undergoing a slow-motion collapse.

Finally, empire promised domestic benefits—something for everyone. Empire seemed an answer to the needs of a dynamic economy suffering from bouts of overproduction that plunged the country into painful economic downswings in the 1870s, in the 1880s, and with special severity in the 1890s. To provide an outlet for the increasing output of American farm and factory, so one popular argument went, the government would have to help open and protect foreign markets. This might mean gaining access to Europe, the richest of the foreign markets, but it also entailed asserting American interests in regions under colonial pressure where investments were substantial (such as Cuba) or where future prospects seemed bright (China). Industry and trade groups, diplomats, and even missionaries rhapsodized over the nearly boundless prospects for u.s. products in a gigantic China market but worried about Europeans barring the way. One business journal warned in late 1897 that "we stand at the dividing of the ways between gaining or losing the greatest market which awaits exploitation." Empire promised in addition to promote national unity. Americans were badly divided by the 1890s by the socially disruptive effects of rapid industrialization and urbanization, the disaffection created by gyrations in the economy, the political insurgency in the rural heartland ignited by low farm prices, the reaction against a rising tide of immigrants that made the country worrisomely heterogeneous, and the sectional bitterness left over from the Civil War. A single, unifying, stabilizing civic religion that made all Americans agents of progress abroad could help bridge or obscure these divisions.[5]

The Limits of Empire

Of all his achievements, McKinley's decision to establish advanced positions on the western side of the Pacific was the most remarkable. The earlier acquisition of coaling stations (Midway in 1867, Pago Pago in 1878, and Pearl Harbor in 1887) foreshadowed and facilitated but did not in themselves constitute a major Asian commitment. U.S. naval expeditions had prowled the western Pacific but accomplished little aside from opening Japan and Korea to outside contact so that other powers could go rushing in. American diplomats in Asia tried to keep up with their European colleagues but were regularly muscled aside. While businessmen and missionaries called for a more activist policy, others dismissed closer contacts with Asia as a source not of benefit but of danger. McKinley's drive to acquire territory spanning the Pacific and to secure an influence equal to the already well-entrenched Europeans proved the skeptics right. Deeper u.s. political and military involvement in the region would lead in time to an all-out war with Japan, a four-decade confrontation with China, and limited wars in Korea and Vietnam. A more consequential decision than McKinley's is hard to imagine. Given the stakes, it is little wonder that these Pacific initiatives undertaken in a rush and with such élan were dogged by controversy.

The Philippines, the centerpiece of the u.s. initiative in Asia, became almost at once a bone of contention. McKinley's move toward annexation in the fall of 1898 sparked a protest movement consisting of a diverse coalition with a strongly Jeffersonian hue. Southern Democrats recoiled before Republican initiatives that strengthened the federal government relative to the states and that might bring more people of color within the union. Fiscal conservatives and defenders of simple republican government feared costly, corrupting foreign adventures sure to invite abuses of power, while defenders of liberty rallied against the betrayal of fundamental values. Women's organizations denounced colonial oppression of a foreign people. The leading opposition group, the American Anti-Imperialist League (created in November 1898), proclaimed the incompatibility of liberty with the exercise of dominion over others. The League charged that "the subjugation of any people is 'criminal aggression' and open disloyalty to the distinctive principles of our government."[6]

These objections took on greater force beginning in early 1899 when Filipino resistance, led by Emilio Aguinaldo, gave the lie to American notions of "native" plasticity and gratitude. Though ill armed, poorly coordinated, and lacking a mass base, regional guerrilla forces frustrated American soldiers, who quickly adopted the dehumanizing language of "nigger" and "goo-goo" to refer to the enemy. Torture and atrocities soon followed. Congress, the public, and those in charge in the archipelago found that pacification was costly. Expenditures eventually climbed to $10.5 billion in 2000 dollars ($600 million in contemporary dollars); the conflict would take the lives of 4,234 U.S. soldiers; and excesses by the military provoked public outrage and congressional demands for an accounting. To calls to take up the white man's burden, sarcastic anti-imperialists responded in 1899:

> Pile on the brown man's burden,
> And if his cry be sore,
> That surely need not irk you—
> Ye've driven slaves before.[7]

For some Americans the difficulties of uplift became evident for the first time and others were confirmed in their belief in McKinley's shocking betrayal of national ideals.

Mark Twain offers a sensitive barometer of the rising pressure for Americans to compete in a world of rival nation-states. In 1900 he had reacted against McKinley's overseas projects after reading about atrocities and looting associated with the "pacification" of the Philippines and the American role in the international occupation of North China. In an October interview he contemplated with distaste Americans "spreading themselves over the face of the globe." Early the next year Twain published his first sustained reflection on these developments, the sardonic "To the Person Sitting in Darkness." There he asked: "Shall we go on conferring our Civilization upon the peoples that sit in darkness, or shall we give those poor things a rest?" Widely circulated, Twain's piece of corrosive humor proved a smashing success for the Anti-Imperialist League. The debate over the Philippines and China faded, but Twain continued to brood over a popular, self-righteous nationalism with its crusading spirit and its imagined divine sanction. In "The War Prayer," a parable from March 1905, he conjured up a country that had caught this "holy fire of patriotism" and that dismissed as "lunatic" those who pointed to the havoc patriotism created. Publishers confirmed Twain's pessimistic reading of the national mood by rejecting this and other iconoclastic assaults of his on what he took to be the new national arrogance.[8]

Although McKinley's critics hoped to make the presidential election of 1900 a referendum on imperialism, the president won handily after a campaign governed largely by other issues closer to home. But by then the agents of empire had already gotten the message sent by guerrillas in the Philippines and dissenters at home. The American empire builders did not decamp, but they did scale back their goals and struck a tacit bargain with Filipino leaders who were themselves unhappy with the immediate costs and doubtful of the long-term viability of resistance to u.s. rule. At least 20,000 Filipinos were killed in action, and at least another 200,000 died from war-related famine and disease. A recent demographic study suggests an even higher human cost for this war. Between 1899 and 1903 the death rate exceeded normal mortality by 775,000 (out of a population of about 7 million). The accommodation between Filipino landed elites and American authorities brought the war to a formal end in 1903, though resistance continued to sputter for years. The elites conceded to the United States immediate colonial control and in return won a promise of independence within the foreseeable future and in the interim their own increasing participation in the running of the country.

While this bargain preserved the form of American tutelage, it proved in practice a retreat from the dreams of uplift and advantage that had inspired the colonial decision in the first place. American proconsuls arrived with dreams of making the islands an advanced base for free men and free markets but quickly found themselves bogged down in the wearisome details of administration. In the end they were unable to deliver on the u.s. commitment to develop the economy, upgrade basic education, and democratize the political system in preparation for independence. The elite that u.s. authorities had embraced operated from family-dominated regional bases, with each family seeking to capture the benefits of controlling the government in Manila while neglecting public goods. The resulting social and economic order was marked by yawning gaps between the privileged and the poor. While the American performance at nation building fell far short of the promise, the Philippines itself turned into a point of strategic vulnerability for u.s. forces in the Pacific and a source of competition for American farmers.

McKinley's successors struggled to find a workable policy for handling the expanded u.s. role as a Pacific power. That arch-expansionist, Theodore Roosevelt brought to the problem experience in the Navy Department and a keen interest in great-power politics. As president, he saw that the best way to rationalize the gains of the McKinley era was to scale back along the exposed western Pacific salient. He recognized that Japanese naval power had made the Philippines a strategic liability ("our heel of Achilles" in his memorable phrase), so he cultivated good relations with Tokyo by acknowledging Japan's leading role in Northeast Asia.[9] A China in disarray and a strong Japan with regional ambitions did not make the western Pacific an inviting place in Roosevelt's judgment.

William Howard Taft, the third in this string of activist Republican presidents, rejected this scaled-down version of America's Pacific destiny. His secretary of state, Philander C. Knox, pressed instead for a greater stake in China's political and economic future. The approach known as dollar diplomacy was based on the conviction (as Knox phrased it) that "today diplomacy works for trade, and the Foreign Offices of the world are powerful engines for the promotion of the commerce of each country."[10] Taft and Knox expected that in China as elsewhere on the global periphery foreign trade and investment would promote prosperity and peace, and thus private u.s. interests deserved resolute official support. Roosevelt had doubts. In 1909 he warned Taft against trying to defend the open door in China at the risk of war with Japan. The reply prepared by Knox indicated a determination to contest Japanese pretensions to regional hegemony, to promote American influence in China, and even to vindicate Hay's commitment to defend China's political integrity. Knox indicated that he would not renounce the "traditional" open-door policy or even rule out war with Japan in defense of that policy. But this policy of bravado was soon in trouble. The businessmen and bankers critical to the conduct of dollar diplomacy did not see their role as Washington did. They trimmed their expectations for the China market and looked instead to Japan as the most promising market and the strongest force for regional economic development.

Once in the White House in 1913, the Democratic Woodrow Wilson followed a policy that reflected both the ambition and the hesitation that had come to characterize the Republican approach. He favored an early but orderly exit from the Philippines. He sympathized with China's attempt at reform and resistance to Japanese control and felt a special u.s. obligation to help. But he could do little except offer the new Chinese republic the cold comfort of verbal support, especially after the war in Europe claimed Wilson's full attention.

In contrast to what he tried to accomplish in the Pacific, McKinley's achievements in the Caribbean were less controversial at the time and more enduring—nothing less than staking it out as an American lake. His humbling of Spain, military occupation of Cuba, and annexation of Puerto Rico underlined the new forceful u.s. position in the hemisphere sounded by Secretary of State Richard Olney in 1895. Though there was talk of statehood for both islands, McKinley operated under restrictions imposed by congressional Democrats allergic to the notion of more nonwhite citizens. Puerto Rico was left in limbo—not a normal territory bound for statehood but a protectorate whose inhabitants received from Congress citizenship in 1917 and then in 1952 themselves adopted "commonwealth" status (somewhere between a state and a colony). Cuba got its independence but on a highly restricted basis.

After Congress ruled out annexation on the eve of war in April 1898 in the Teller amendment, the McKinley administration secured Cuba's effective dependency. Three years later the Platt amendment, drafted by Secretary of the Army Elihu Root, demanded the right to send U.S. troops into Cuba, provided for the grant of a naval base (Guantanamo), and limited Cuba in the conduct of its foreign relations. Washington's price for the grant of Cuba's independence was incorporating these terms into the new country's constitution. The U.S. Army ended its occupation in May 1902, but thenceforth the survival of Cuban governments depended on U.S. approval, and the Cuban economy fell under the dominance of U.S. capital and functioned as an appendage of the larger mainland market. Thus was Cuba linked to the United States, as McKinley had envisioned in late 1899, by "ties of singular intimacy."[11]

With the entire Caribbean region sealed off from interlopers, McKinley's successors would watch over it like hawks. Theodore Roosevelt gave doctrinal voice to this expanded U.S. position in 1904 when he formally arrogated to the United States the role of policeman duty bound "to see the neighboring countries stable, orderly, and prosperous."[12] Under this extension of the Monroe Doctrine, the American cop would impose good behavior on the "natives" while blocking European interlopers. The Germans were the prime suspects. Influential Americans promoted an image of them as naval rivals eager for empire and led by an impulsive, sometimes belligerent kaiser.

Roosevelt's doctrine served as the underpinning for a string of interventions spanning two decades. Roosevelt helped wrench from Colombia its Panama territory in 1903 with an eye to building a transisthmian canal that would allow the U.S. fleet to shift rapidly between the Atlantic and the Pacific. Panama became the second U.S. protectorate in the Caribbean. He sent troops and advisers into the Dominican Republic in 1905 to assure political stability and effect fiscal reforms. By deploying marines and New York bankers in tandem, Roosevelt incorporated a tried-and-true European imperial strategy into the U.S. policy repertoire. Frustrated by disorder in Cuba, he exploded that he "would like to wipe its people off the face of the earth" but instead dispatched U.S. forces, which stayed from 1906 to 1909.[13] Taft made Nicaragua the target of intervention and occupation, first ousting a defiant dictator in 1910 and then using loans and financial supervision to shape the political aftermath. In frustration he sent in the marines in 1912, and there they stayed until 1925.

Wilson proved the most enthusiastic practitioner of gunboat diplomacy — and Mexico his greatest challenge. There as elsewhere in Latin America, a leader intent on economic development and state building had borrowed heavily on international markets. U.S. investments alone climbed from $200 million in 1897 to $672 million in 1908.[14] The result had not been prosperity and peace but rural discontent and a nationalist backlash. The revolution that broke out in 1910 and consumed the country for a decade was fought over deeply divisive issues of land reform, restrictions on foreign economic control, labor rights, and social equality. Wilson, however, saw primarily a people with disorderly tendencies that had to be curbed by putting constitutional procedures in place under U.S. guidance. In 1914 and again in 1916 he sent in U.S. forces, privately explaining that as a neighbor he wanted to help Mexico "adjust her unruly household."[15] This "assistance" sent anti-American sentiment soaring and left U.S. forces confronting serious resistance. The outbreak of the European war turned the Wilson administration's attention to cleaning up and fencing off the Caribbean. U.S. troops took over Haiti in 1915 and the Dominican Republic in 1916. Wilson compelled the sale of the Danish Virgin Islands in 1916 to keep them out of German hands. U.S. policymakers—whether Republican or Democratic—were leaving nothing in the region to chance. They had in the span of two decades made a colony of Puerto Rico, imposed protectorates on Cuba and Panama, and converted into fiscal dependencies Haiti, Nicaragua, and the Dominican Republic.

WILSON AND A WORLD REMADE

On the morning of Saturday, 5 January 1918, Wilson met with Edward House, an independently wealthy power broker in Texas politics. The president and his confidante and alter ego wanted simply to figure out how to put international relations on an entirely new basis. After a two-hour meeting in the White House, they had (so House recorded in his diary) "finished remaking the map of the world, as we would have it." Wilson's next step was to inform Congress of his fourteen-point program and thus assume the role (as House put it to the president) of "the spokesman for the liberals of the world." Content with their labors, this audacious pair rested on Sunday. On Monday Wilson belatedly gave his secretary of state, Robert Lansing, his first look at these plans. When Wilson formally unveiled them on Tuesday, 8 January, they came as a surprise to all the rest of Wilson's cabinet, to Congress, to the diplomatic corps, and to the American press and public.[16]

In ambition, Wilson's project for reconstructing the international order made McKinley's Pacific and Caribbean initiatives look timid. The speech called for what both House and Wilson devoutly believed in—the transformation of a fundamentally flawed international system that the Europeans had made and dominated. That system was ruled by power, prone to violence, devoted to expansion abroad and repression at home. World War I highlighted the system's flaws while also creating an opening for u.s. action guided by the conviction that u.s. efforts might save the Old World from itself. Wilson's plan was supposed to usher in an age of international peace under the auspices of a community of nations dedicated to democracy and economic development.

The Grand Plan Takes Shape

While Wilson's grand plan was the product of a two-hour meeting, the impulse behind its formulation arose from a long-gestating combination of personal faith, conviction, and experience. This son of a Presbyterian minister carried in his head a voice that made service to humanity an inescapable duty. Growing up in a southern and genteel middle-class milieu left Wilson with a strong Anglo ethnic identity. It was reinforced by the circles in which he moved, first as a student at Princeton, Virginia, and Johns Hopkins (where he took a Ph.D. in politics), then as a professor, and finally as an administrator at Princeton. He deeply admired British political values and institutions. Indeed, he thought them models that Americans might copy with profit. His academic writings as well as his personal life reflected his admiration for British literature, philosophy, and manners. He was also animated by a belief that carefully trained, rational experts could resolve social problems and thus promote progress. Wilson's brief stint as a reform governor of New Jersey before his 1912 run for president allowed him to act on this commitment to enlightened political action while confirming his taste for public service and the public stage.

The European war provided the primary impetus behind Wilson's famous, wide-ranging plan for reforming the world as well as the indispensable setting. At first, the president responded to the war gingerly, going no farther than his Republican predecessors might have. They had shown some willingness to play on the field of European politics—but only within carefully circumscribed limits set by Washington's injunction against entangling alliances and the hardy notion of the United States and Europe as two distinct spheres. The seizure of colonies and the creation of dependencies had begun to tangle Americans in European colonial rivalries, most notably in China and Samoa. President Theodore Roosevelt had ventured a more direct but nominally neutral role in 1905—as a mediator first in a French-German dispute over Morocco and then in Russia's losing war against Japan. But none of these steps directly challenged the sanctity of the two-spheres dictum.

When fighting broke out in August 1914, Wilson promptly declared his country's neutrality, assuming along with many on both sides of the Atlantic that the war would not last long. In any case, he did not want the United States with its multiethnic population to become a battleground for partisans of the Entente (Britain, France, and Russia) or the Central Powers (Germany and Austria-Hungary). Preferences for one side or the other were evident from the outset. The political, business, and cultural elites were on the whole pro-British, a bias evident in the editorial policy of the national press. In the fall of 1914, even before British propaganda and the controversy over submarine warfare had poisoned American views of Germany, 189 editors favored the Entente, only 38 Germany, with 140 not yet clearly committed.[17] The Central Powers found strong sympathy among the 15 percent of the population that was Irish American or German American. American Jews also strongly favored Germany either because of warm cultural ties to that country or hostility toward Russia with its starkly anti-Semitic record.

Despite his public call for neutrality, Wilson fell emphatically on the pro-British side of this divide. He accepted the notion of an Anglo-American family relationship that made the Germans distant relatives at best. The president's sentimental entanglement with Britain and corresponding antipathy toward the Central Powers showed up in the first months of the fighting. In a revealing moment in late August 1914 he privately offered his "condemnation of Germany's part in this war" and predicted dire consequences to civilization and to u.s. security if Germany won. On the other hand, he thought a serious falling out between the United States and Britain "would be the crowning calamity" (as he told the British ambassador in early September). In mid-December he offered his candid views on the European conflict to a reporter for the *New York Times.* "The Government of Germany must be profoundly changed," while Austria-Hungary's collapse would serve "the welfare of Europe." By contrast, Britain figured in his estimate as a status quo imperial power that might be trusted along with its allies to respect u.s. interests. Wilson's pro-English bias was reinforced by his advisers—most notably House who served as Wilson's informal emissary to European capitals during wartime and the subsequent peace negotiations.[18]

This preference for the British shaped Wilson's early policy response to the conflict. On the face of it, his course seemed consistent with the long-established u.s. policy of keeping a distance from Old World quarrels while also preserving the rights of Americans as neutrals to continue to trade as expressed in the freedom of the seas doctrine. His interpretation of neutral rights and obligations, however, soon had him tilting toward the British cause. While threatening Germany with "strict accountability" for use of its submarine fleet, Wilson couched warnings against equally serious British violations of neutral rights in less belligerent terms sprinkled with expressions of cordial friendship and a promise to delay the accounting for any British violations of u.s. rights. A German submarine's sinking of the British passenger liner *Lusitania* in June 1915 with heavy loss of life confirmed Wilson's pro-British reading of neutral rights and deepened his conviction of German barbarity. Public shock and outrage reinforced the view preponderant among elites that Britain was the civilized combatant in a war increasingly seen as good against evil. British propaganda played to a receptive u.s. audience stories of Belgium's "rape" by the German occupation army as well as images of innocent women and children going down with torpedoed passenger liners.

However questionable his policy was under international law, Wilson had by mid-1915 served notice on Berlin that unleashing its submarine weapon might well push the United States into the war. German policymakers teetered between diplomatic caution and desperation to bring the bloody military deadlock to an end. By early 1916 high-ranking government officials were describing the Wilson administration as nominally neutral but in fact "a direct enemy of Germany" as a result of economic and racial ties binding influential Americans to Britain.[19] By the fall the kaiser's military advisers were wearing down the German chancellor, Theobald von Bethmann Hollweg, who stood as the main obstacle to unrestricted submarine warfare. Such a step, he warned, would bring the powerful Americans into the war against Germany.

While Berlin wrestled with how to use its submarines, Wilson gave increasing thought to ending the carnage and to formulating a program that would ensure there would be no repetition. In January 1917 he laid out his ideas in broad outline in an address to the Senate. By then Berlin had already reached a decision to unleash German submarines. The announcement of that decision early the next month pushed a reluctant Wilson toward war and impelled him to consider further how to redeem the sacrifices he was about to ask Americans to make. Distracted for a time with the details of economic and military mobilization, the president finally returned in September 1917 to thinking about the postwar world. He assembled a group of American international affairs specialists to prepare guidelines for peace making. Those guidelines added flesh to the bones of Wilson's fourteen-point program, the subject of the speech that Wilson and House finalized on that Saturday morning in early January 1918.

When he spoke to members of Congress and other dignitaries gathered in the Capitol on 8 January, Wilson explained that his principles reflected "nothing peculiar to ourselves" but were rather universal in their origins and application. His was not, in other words, a program of national aggrandizement. His aim was altruistic—to make the world "safe for every peace-loving nation which, like our own, wishes to live its own life, determine its own institutions, be assured of justice and fair dealing by the other peoples of the world as against force and selfish aggression." At the heart of Wilson's conception of the world made new was the promotion of the values of freedom. Those principles assumed a variety of guises in the address: proposals for unhindered trade on the high seas and "the removal of all economic barriers" (implicitly including the opening of colonies to commerce); the application of self-determination to contested lands in Europe, to Russia in revolutionary ferment, and to the dissolving Ottoman Empire; and most prominently a call for popular political control within all states. Because democracies were not warlike, their displacement of monarchies and militarism would make disarmament a practical matter (thus its appearance as one of the Fourteen Points). Capping Wilson's conception of a new world order was the League of Nations, an institution to serve as the parliament for the international community, a forum for a new style of public diplomacy accountable to the people, and the embodiment of enlightened rules of international conduct.[20]

The Fourteen Points emerged from Wilson's vision of a world in fundamental conflict. On the one side were the rising forces of the future: self-determination, democracy, and the will of the people. On the other were the retrograde survivals from the past: imperialism, militarism, and autocracy. Wilson was heartened by the breaking up of empires. The Russian empire had collapsed the year before; the German, Austro-Hungarian, and Ottoman empires were about to go. Building on these positive developments, he sought to create an international environment more conducive to democracy and progress. That meant eliminating international power rivalries and all that went with them—naval and arms races, secret diplomacy, alliances and secret agreements, cynical balance of power politics, and wars. In their place he sought to put a community of nations whose solidarity and cooperation was made possible by a shared commitment to democratic government and peaceful commerce.

An address long in the making and audacious in its goals not surprisingly served multiple purposes. In the most immediate and practical sense it was a piece of wartime propaganda broadcast live to Europe as well as East Asia and Latin America. German forces had pushed to the outskirts of Paris, had the Russians reeling, and scored a major victory over the Italians. But the arrival of u.s. troops offset these German gains and accentuated the vulnerability of an already overstretched empire. Wilson wanted to invest the Entente cause with high purpose, not just to highlight the moral distinction between the two warring camps but also to drive a wedge between German and Austrian rulers and their people and persuade the new Bolshevik government in Russia not to conclude a separate peace with the Central Powers. Wilson was, moreover, looking ahead to the end of the war. Generating public demands in France, Italy, and Britain for an enlightened peace would strengthen Wilson's leverage over their leaders and signal that they could not conduct business as usual at the upcoming international conference.

Wilson also spoke to Americans whose sense of national crusading the war had sharpened. The self-righteousness and self-confidence that marked the national mood and informed his Fourteen Points had the same source—the belief that the United States was (in John O'Sullivan's phrase) "the great nation of futurity." This national vision embodied a deep-seated belief in progress, in the perfectibility of the human condition, and in the pivotal u.s. role in creating a better world. Wilson's long-time hero, Jefferson, had imagined that leadership through example. But Wilson had swung around to the alternative Hamiltonian notion of active engagement of u.s. power and influence. Wilson had found the country already dominant on the continent and in the Caribbean and newly assertive in the Pacific. He had plunged into European diplomacy and warfare. And now he imagined the entire world his stage.

Finally, Wilson's address gave voice to the dreams of a global community that had taken hold among a wide range of Anglo-American scholars, commentators, and political leaders. The League of Nations Society had sprung up in Britain in 1915. Its u.s. counterpart was the League to Enforce Peace, which was dominated by prominent Republicans such as Taft and Senator Henry Cabot Lodge reinforced by northeastern influentials from the press, the universities, and legal circles. Anticipating Wilson, they called for setting international relations on a new basis—a cooperative community of nations bound by mutually beneficial trade and investment, resistant to arms races, committed to diplomacy and arbitration of disputes rather than war, respectful of small as well as large states, and supportive of the principle of popular self-determination with its natural instinct toward national autonomy and political democracy. Their hopes for global progress under Anglo-American auspices came to life in Wilson's bold program.

Shattering Blows
Wilson the global reformer quickly ran into trouble. He indulged in what the ancient Greeks called hubris or excessive pride and predictably suffered terrible retribution, including a stinging political defeat and his own personal destruction. But Wilson's problems were more than personal. His guiding vision was drawn from a rapidly fading global age—an open, commercial,

peaceful world—under assault from Europe's narrow nationalisms, colonial appetites, and social tensions accentuated by war. This vision was so out of season that it was doomed.

The Russian revolutions of 1917 provided the first indication of trouble. Wilson had initially welcomed the overthrow of the monarchy in March 1917 as confirmation of his faith in the democratic instincts of the Russian people. He used the welcome event to bolster his case for intervening in the war in the name of democracy. The president was the first to recognize the new regime, and he sent Elihu Root to help shore it up. Wilson remained hopeful even after the triumph of Vladimir Lenin's Bolshevik party in November 1917 in a war-weary country whose army was on the verge of mutiny. He framed his fourteen-point program two months later in part as a counter to the Bolshevik program of capitulation and class conflict—but in vain. Lenin concluded an armistice with Germany in December, followed in March 1918 by a peace agreement (the Treaty of Brest-Litovsk) secured at the price of Russian imperial territory out of which Poland, Finland, and the Baltic states (Latvia, Lithuania, and Estonia) were to emerge. Lenin also fanned revolutionary sentiments in Germany, Poland, and Hungary, and Communist parties sprang up all across a war-ravaged region. London and Paris responded with military incursions into Russia; they called on Wilson to lend the anti-Bolshevik cause a hand. In July 1918 Wilson agreed and dispatched a force of 15,500 to bolster Anglo-French forces in northwest Russia as well 20,000 men to join (and keep an eye on) Japanese troops operating along the trans-Siberian railway. Though relatively small—and withdrawn by early 1920—this U.S. deployment revealed that Wilson's initial hopes for democracy had given way to a system that stood in his view for the "negation of everything that is American." The president firmly rejected any diplomatic contact with the Bolshevik government. All that he could do now was to express his sympathy for the suffering of the Russian people, offer to mediate an end to the civil war between the "Reds" and their "White" opponents, and send humanitarian relief under the direction of Herbert Hoover.[21]

Wilson's allies would prove nearly as much an obstacle to an enlightened postwar order as the Bolsheviks, as he began to realize in October 1918. He offered peace negotiations to Germany on the basis of his Fourteen Points. When Wilson asked London and Paris to agree to those terms, his allies issued reservations on two critical points, freedom of the seas and reparations by Germany. With good reason, he suspected their motives. Those suspicions had led him to insist on calling the United States an "associate" rather than a full-fledged ally in the war effort and to keep U.S. forces under his own command. His suspicions had been confirmed by his discovery of secret agreements made in 1915 by Britain, Italy, and Japan at odds with his own vision of the peace. Now in October 1918 at the critical point of transition from war to peace, Wilson tried and failed to get the Entente powers to put aside these damaging reservations. His wartime associates were now proving tenacious in defense of their interests even as Wilson was losing with the silencing of the guns his most important leverage—American troops and supplies to throw into the battle against Germany. At the Paris peace conference his appeals to goodwill and high ideals and even the promise of collaboration in postwar reconstruction carried considerably less weight than European publics clamoring for revenge and compensation and strategists anticipating another test of arms. A sharp-eyed member of the British delegation blamed Wilson for acting like a "blind and deaf Don Quixote" in the face of formidable resistance to his basic principles. He arrived knowing little of Europe and then floundered amid the thrust and parry of prolonged, complex negotiations.[22]

The u.s. electorate delivered the third blow in November 1918, when the midterm elections handed Republicans control of the House and the Senate. This outcome not only alerted Entente leaders to Wilson's weakening position at home but placed the treaty process in the hands of his Republican opponents, foremost Senator Lodge. Wilson had refused to make Lodge or other influential Republicans part of his negotiating team or take them into his confidence. As the new head of the Senate Foreign Relations Committee, Lodge promptly repaid the slight by packing the committee against Wilson.

Once in Paris for the peace talks, Wilson had to confront a string of demands from the Entente leaders—Britain's David Lloyd George, France's Georges Clemenceau, and Italy's Vittorio Orlando. As they negotiated peace terms intermittently from December 1918 to July 1919, the Europeans stripped one provision after another from Wilson's enlightened peace plan. The French wanted an absolute and crippling victory over Germany, especially the return of Alsace-Lorraine (lost in 1871 as a result of the Franco-Prussian War), a large punitive indemnity, and enforced disarmament. The British wanted latitude to exercise their naval supremacy and thus rejected freedom of the seas. Both the French and the British, together with the Japanese, sought to make spoils of German colonies. Finally, the victors wanted to redraw European boundaries without regard to popular wishes, at least where the Central Powers were concerned. German territory would pass not only to France but also to the new state of Poland. Austria would emerge as a troubled state, bereft of a strong national identity, denied union with Germany by a jealous France, and shorn of border lands by Italy. Wilson made repeated concessions on these points in order to save what he saw as the element essential to creating an enlightened postwar world, his League of Nations.

Those same talks had resulted in another setback for Wilson, though he was barely aware of it. His talk of national self-determination had roused considerable excitement in the colonial world. An Egyptian nationalist exclaimed, "This is it! We have the right to self-determination, and therefore the English will leave Egypt." Delegations from China, Vietnam, the Middle East, Africa, and even U.S. Caribbean dependencies had flocked to Paris in 1919. When asked to make good on his talk of liberation, Wilson sided with the Europeans. Britain and France were far from ready to surrender their colonies, and indeed were intent on laying their hands on new ones taken from Germany and the Ottoman Empire under the guise of "mandates" held with nominal oversight by the League of Nations. Wilson in any case agreed with them that only mature peoples on the upper rungs of the racial hierarchy deserved the chance to decide their own future. Would not independence prematurely granted (mused Secretary of State Lansing) "breed discontent, disorder and rebellion?" Peoples awakening to their rights would have to pay tuition under foreign control (whether old-style colonies or new-style League mandates) and learn civilized standards. A young Mao Zedong searching for a political path followed the Paris peace conference with interest—and came away convinced that Wilson's call for self-determination was empty and that the Bolshevik Revolution, not a counterrevolutionary United States, pointed the most hopeful way forward. Nationalists elsewhere could also see the limits of Wilson's liberalism, and they too began to eye Washington with greater suspicion and to look to a revolutionary Moscow for support for their liberation struggles.[23]

Arriving home in the summer of 1919 with a peace treaty loaded with compromises, Wilson had to have it approved, as per the Constitution, by two-thirds of the Senate, yet that body was simmering with discontent. Some Republicans wanted to cut down a strong Democratic president, who also seemed obnoxiously arrogant. Some in both parties carped that Wilson had traded away too much of his program or endorsed an unjust peace, including the maintenance of the colonial system and the burdening of Germany with moral responsibility for the war and with punitive indemnities. Others—again on both sides of the aisle—charged that the League of Nations would violate U.S. sovereignty and interests by interfering in domestic questions such as the tariff and immigration and by ignoring the Monroe Doctrine. But above all, the opposition focused on the obligations under Article X of the proposed League. That article required that member states "undertake to respect and preserve as against external aggression the territorial integrity and existing independence of all Members of the League" and that the League Council "shall advise upon the means by which this obligation shall be fulfilled."[24] Critics saw in this language a violation of congressional prerogatives under the Constitution. Some also feared Article X was a step toward permanent entanglement in European rivalries and conflicts, while others—notably senior Republican senators Lodge and Knox as well as party elders Taft and Root—wanted entanglement but in the more limited and practical form of a security commitment to France against renewed German aggression.

Wilson steadfastly refused the compromises needed to construct a winning coalition. He had a solid base of Democratic loyalists. But he would not horse-trade with the Republicans in favor of mild reservations, and even less was he willing to deal with the senators, mostly Republicans, with strong reservations limiting the application of Article X and excluding from League jurisdiction domestic issues and the Monroe Doctrine. Thus rather than isolating the so-called Irreconcilables (mostly Republicans including William E. Borah, Robert LaFollette, and George E. Norris), who were determined to defeat the treaty in any form, an unbending Wilson handed them victory.

In the midst of the treaty battle, Wilson's body delivered a crushing blow. He had already suffered mini-strokes in 1896 and 1906 and perhaps also once in the White House, as a result of untreated hypertension. In September 1919 he was three weeks into a strenuous national speaking tour of the Middle and Far West that was meant to persuade the public and thus bring the Senate opposition around. Feeling ill, he hurried his train back to Washington. On 2 October the president suffered a massive stroke that immobilized his left side. His estrangement from House and dismissal of Lansing left him isolated. Edith Galt Wilson assumed the role of gatekeeper and interpreter for her invalid husband, whose true condition was kept from the public.

The Senate now formally defied Wilson. In November 1919 the peace treaty twice fell short of the necessary two-thirds. The first time the strong reservations favored by Lodge were on the table; 39 mild and strong reservationists said yes, while 55 Democrats loyal to Wilson joined the irreconcilable camp to vote no. On the second attempt the treaty in the form favored by Wilson (unencumbered by reservations) won the support of 38 loyal Democrats, far short of the required two-thirds and even fewer than the combined 53 votes mustered by the mild and strong reservationists and the Irreconcilables. In March 1920 the treaty with reservations was again put to a vote and once more suffered defeated by a 49 to 35 margin, seven short of two-thirds. Insistent on all or nothing, an enfeebled Wilson had gotten nothing.

While his dreams for the postwar period dissolved on the floor of the Senate, Wilson watched his own country slide into the Red Scare of 1919–20 with its suspicion, fear, and repression. His own administration's strident wartime propaganda and its passage of sedition and espionage legislation had paved the way. What began as an effort to stifle any German American and Irish American disloyalty and to silence pacifist voices turned into a broader attack on radical ideas and disloyal immigrants. Groups dedicated to ethnic purity, patriotism, and union busting exploited the anxieties created by alarming reports of Bolshevik excesses—political purges and class dictatorship, forced collectivization, atheistic and materialistic doctrines, free love, and pervasive terror. As the Bolshevik "infection" spread into the heart of Europe and American workers challenged their bosses, the reaction in the United States intensified with the main targets labor unions, public schools, universities, churches, and the press. Wilson's own attorney general, A. Mitchell Palmer, put himself at the front of the anti-Red campaign. Working closely with J. Edgar Hoover (head of the embryonic Federal Bureau of Investigation), Palmer staged nationwide raids on suspect individuals and organizations, deported radicals, and generally violated civil liberties. State governments joined the assault on unpopular or unorthodox ideas, while the courts failed to protect basic civil rights.

As his term drew to a close in 1920, a still frail president devised impossible schemes to revive his treaty. One was to ask his opponents in the Senate to resign and to take their case to the electorate of their home states. If they were defeated, he expected their successors to pass his treaty. If the opponent were reelected, Wilson would have his vice president and secretary of state (next in line to the presidency) resign, and he would appoint a leading Republican as secretary of state and then himself promptly resign, making the new secretary of state president. Another possibility Wilson contemplated was running for a third term so that he could personally make the 1920 election "a great and solemn referendum" on the League.[25] Democratic presidential candidate James Cox and his running mate, Franklin D. Roosevelt, did endorse Wilson's plans, while the Republican candidate, Warren G. Harding, hedged and won decisively (16 million to 9 million in the popular vote). The sixty-four-year-old visionary in the White House could take scant solace from this outcome even though it had more to do with a weak economy following a wartime boom than with popular attitudes toward the League or the general peace settlement. Wilson would die in early 1924, having endured a political and personal defeat as complete as can be imagined.

Yet that defeat should not obscure Wilson's profound impact on the subsequent u.s. path to ascendancy. To begin with, he contributed signally to an emerging Anglo-American relationship. Currents of Anglo-Saxonism in late nineteenth-century America had helped prepare the way as had the realization on the part of British elites that it had across the Atlantic a potential partner to shore up its declining imperial position. A member of the British cabinet put the matter tersely in September 1917 with the Americans finally in the war: "Though the American people are very largely foreign, both in origin and in modes of thought, their rulers are almost exclusively Anglo-Saxons, and share our political ideals."[26] Wilson's pro-British interpretation of neutrality, his dispatch of u.s. troops to fight alongside the British against the Germans, and his formulation of a progressive peace plan fully consonant with an influential body of thought in Britain eased the passing of global power from one side of the North Atlantic to the other and strengthened an ideological, political, and military partnership that would prove an enduring feature of u.s. foreign relations through the rest of the twentieth century and beyond. The United States would make Britain its main partner in interwar attempts to maintain peace and prosperity just as it would be the chief ally in the world war and the Cold War that followed. This junior partnership allowed Britain to salvage something of past imperial glories and cut an international figure far beyond its material means.

Wilson, moreover, articulated more clearly than any of his contemporaries an insight increasingly taken for granted by his successors in the White House—that global integration, prosperity, and cooperation depended on u.s. leadership, above all in Europe itself. His attempts to preserve the peaceful world that he had grown up in failed not merely because he was inflexible but more fundamentally because he faced powerful nationalist and imperial forces that had in August 1914 sparked a prolonged European crisis. They would continue to destroy hopes, lives, cities, and entire economies until finally in the late 1940s and early 1950s European and American elites were ready to pursue together the Wilsonian goals of peace, order, and prosperity. Wilson's understanding that World War I was only the rehearsal for a greater European disaster and that u.s. involvement was critical to breaking the cycle of devastation made him the prophet of an assertive, global policy.

Wilson's was a call not simply for u.s. action but for action guided by a particular set of principles. His claim to fame rests above all on his authorship of the fourteen-point program—the most important statement in the history of twentieth-century u.s. foreign relations. The principles he laid out would serve as a blueprint for u.s. leaders intent on constructing a new world order and projecting their values abroad. They would also serve as a bridge between the pre–World War I globalized world Wilson had tried to sustain and the post–World War II global economy over which his successors would preside. Even today his fundamental faith in freedom as a universal right and his distinction between "bad rulers" and "good people" oppressed by autocratic, dictatorial, and totalitarian regimes together set the broad conceptual parameters for u.s. foreign policy. No one can have an informed opinion about the American role in the world without considering the assumptions and beliefs embodied in Wilson's seminal January 1918 address.

STATE BUILDING

The empire building, war fighting, and peacemaking that marked the McKinley-Wilson years spurred a dramatic growth in the power of the American state. The state as an abstraction is easily overshadowed by striking personalities and ambitious policies. But neither leadership nor achievement was possible without some state power—the institutions and resources to make things happen. And once state initiatives were set in motion, admirals, generals, diplomats, and colonial agents lobbied for further strengthening the state so that they could more effectively do their job of making a mark on the world. By the time Wilson left the White House, the American state stood on a par with those of the Europeans. To be sure, the three major departments of foreign affairs—State, War, and Navy—still all fit in a single building next to the White House. But all three had become more effective tools of presidential will on the international stage. What scholars would call "the imperial presidency" with its sprawling, physically dominant institutional presence in the capital and its claim to domestic deference as the embodiment of the national will was beginning to take form. The United States was not yet the dominant world power, but its leaders were laying the institutional basis for the exercise of dominance.

State building in the United States was part of a trend around the turn of the century playing out elsewhere in the North Atlantic world as well as in Japan. The technological innovations in communications and transport that propelled globalization also helped government bureaucracies and political leaders to monitor their people's lives and economic activity, deliver social services, mobilize political support, levy armies, pursue international ambitions, and command a growing share of expanding national output. The drive to possess colonies and secure markets, the competition to produce behemoth warships and field well-trained, well-armed ground forces, and the concerted celebration of the nation with its special identity and mission—none of this was possible without this florescence of state power. However suspicious they might be of centralized power, Americans were making their peace with this countervailing trend with surprising ease. They were not the exceptions that their nationalist mythology suggested but rather marching in a direction that Japanese, Germans, British, French, and Italians were also headed.

Marshaling Resources

McKinley's war room, gathering into a single place the lines of communications for a far-flung war effort, hints at far-reaching changes in the American state. That state was employing more and better people to attend to policies and programs at home and overseas. The number of civilian employees rose from 50,000 in 1871 to 231,000 in 1901 to 645,000 in 1920. Those employees were becoming more professional, less tied to political patrons, and thus more effective servants of the state. A campaign for putting civil servants under a merit system began in the 1870s, just as similar systems were starting up in Britain and other centralizing states, and by 1920 the one in the United States covered 70 percent of executive branch employees. At the same time, the federal government siphoned off more economic resources from an increasing national output. From the 1890s to the eve of World War I, Washington claimed about 3 percent of GDP, considerably less than was the case among the other major powers. But u.s. GDP was itself so much higher—more than twice that of Britain and Germany and nearly four times that of France by 1913—and it was growing so rapidly that the gap between Washington's actual budget and that of the others was quickly closing.[27]

This trend toward a larger, more skilled, and better financed executive branch was especially evident in the State Department. Growing u.s. overseas interests had helped expand the foreign affairs bureaucracy. The State Department staff in Washington, a mere eight in 1790, had grown to seventy-six in 1890 and then to 708 by 1920. The end of the war found some 514 foreign service personnel serving in legations and consulates overseas.[28] Despite the expansion, an amateur ethic prevailed through the nineteenth century and carried over into the twentieth, in part the product of the populist conviction that diplomats should embody the values of ordinary Americans. It mattered less that they lacked diplomatic polish and an understanding of the situation abroad. Also sustaining the amateur ethic was a spoils system that made diplomatic appointments a way for presidents to reward party service, dump political foes, or banish embarrassing allies.

Proponents of higher professional standards called for reform, pointing to the record of fumbling amateurs and unreliable politicos in posts of responsibility at a time of increasing international involvement. Elihu Root, a New

York corporate lawyer who became secretary of state in 1904, began in earnest putting the foreign service on a more professional footing. He raised salaries, made appointments and promotions on the basis of merit, and created regional desks within the department itself to serve as repositories of international expertise. These changes, sustained by Knox during his tenure as secretary of state, became so deeply entrenched that they survived the Democrats' taking the White House in 1914.

Like the State Department, the army was undergoing its own slow but steady transformation. From 1871 until the late 1890s the force never exceeded 30,000 men, sufficient to wage the mopping up campaigns against Indians and to break labor protests but not to meet the demand for expeditionary and occupation forces that could be deployed to Cuba, the Philippines, China, or Mexico. War with Spain entailed a rapid increase of the army to 210,000. The commitment in the Philippines alone required 70,000 troops at the height of pacification, and thereafter down to u.s. entry into World War I the standing army's overall strength ranged between 64,000 and 108,000 men (backed by a marine force of 5,000–10,000 for use primarily in the Caribbean region). In the wake of the war with Spain, the army gave increasing attention to professional standards and a central staff to plan and direct operations. The growing complexity and scale of industrial warfare—the number of men to be mobilized, trained, transported, and supported on the battlefield—put a premium on thorough advanced preparation by skilled personnel engaged in careful coordination.[29]

Professionalizing the army required the attention of a strong secretary of war. Here too Elihu Root took the lead during his five-year tenure. In 1899 McKinley assigned him the task of dealing with scandals and administrative snafus that plagued the conduct of the recent war. Though lacking military experience, Root became a convert to the views of Emory Upton, a distinguished Civil War commander and postwar military intellectual, and other reformers impressed by the central staff system of the Prussian army. That army had scored impressive victories over Denmark, Austria, and France on the way to German unification thanks to its staff system. The staff, operating free of civilian interference, directed a skeleton regular army and oversaw the training of a large reserve force. In an emergency the staff would rapidly mobilize the regulars and reserves and coordinate their actions. Arrayed against reform of the u.s. Army were conservative, long-entrenched senior officers defending their bureaucratic fiefdoms and congressional sentiment favorable to the militia system (the state-controlled National Guard) and opposed to replacing the citizen-soldiers of earlier u.s. wars with a large, standing army.

While managing the occupation of Cuba, Puerto Rico, and the Philippines, Root also pressed for greater professionalism. He developed the educational system for officers and got congressional approval for an increase in the regular army. The militia system was too entrenched to be abolished, but Root was able to apply federal standards to the National Guard and link it more closely to the regular army so that it would function in effect as the reserve force the reformers had wanted. The most urgent of the professional changes was the creation of a central staff. As Root told the Senate in March 1902, "Neither law nor custom places the preparation of plans for national defense in the hands of any particular officer or body of officers, and what is everybody's business is nobody's business."[30] The new staff, created in 1903, would take that responsibility, with its military chief reporting directly to the civilian secretary of war and working with his navy counterpart on interservice issues.

U.S. participation in World War I swept away the last serious resistance that senior officers and Congress posed to a staff system. The army faced its toughest expeditionary challenge to date—getting some 2 million American troops, along with a swelling stream of supplies, across the Atlantic and ready to engage experienced German forces. Planning and directing this feat finally made the army more like its European counterparts. When World War I had begun, the u.s. staff was limited to 19 officers, a puny figure compared to 600-plus in Germany and France and over 200 in Britain at that same time. By war's end the army's brain had accumulated gray matter; the staff had grown to 1,000 and it exercised real authority over a force that had grown by 1918 to 2.4 million men.[31]

The navy pushed ahead faster and farther than either the foreign service or the army. The post–Civil War navy had fallen into such a state of neglect that a future secretary of the navy derided it in 1885 as "an alphabet of floating wash-tubs."[32] Big-navy advocates began making the case for a buildup, none more effectively than the navy's leading strategist and publicist, Alfred Thayer Mahan. He based his case on the British navy, which had made possible (so he argued) the very things that outward-looking Americans wanted—colonial assets and a flourishing worldwide trade. The British experience supported the call for abandoning the old strategy of passive coastal defense and raiding enemy commerce in time of war. In the place of these outmoded doctrines, Mahan and others called for a massed, offensive, up-to-date seagoing battle fleet. It would block the ocean approaches to the American continent by the new navies being built in Europe (and soon in Japan), destroy the enemy's main fleet, and protect u.s. commerce. To those tasks would be added in the era of grand projects a supporting role in the new expeditionary strategy in the Pacific and the Caribbean and finally even across the Atlantic.

In the 1880s Congress began appropriating funds for a modern naval force that would easily defeat a dilapidated Spanish fleet in 1898. The navy continued to grow under Theodore Roosevelt, a friend of Mahan's and a convert to his offensive battle-fleet concept. By the outbreak of war in Europe the U.S. Navy had achieved world-class status with 25 capital ships (including 10 major battleships called dreadnoughts) compared to Britain's 46 (including 33 dreadnoughts) and Germany's 30 (including 22 dreadnoughts). Wilson's wartime construction program made the U.S. Navy second to none.

Operating thick-plated steamships armed with heavy guns over long distances in a variety of missions put a premium on high professional standards. Beginning in the 1880s, a string of effective secretaries of the navy pressed internal reforms in tandem with the building program. They put in place an extensive system of schooling, emphasized merit in making promotions, and eradicated the political spoils system that was still dogging the foreign service and the army. The Naval War College started offering professional training in 1884. The creation of a general board in 1900 gave senior officers a mechanism to direct this fast-moving, technologically complex organization and to provide strategic advice directly to the navy secretary. The chief of naval operations, a position put in place in 1915, further strengthened the navy's capacity to function professionally. The American state had generated a sophisticated strike force consistent with its expanding overseas ambitions.

The Power to Control and Persuade

Along with better tools to conduct foreign policy, presidents at the turn of the century were gaining greater power to harness the resources of the executive branch and to persuade the people and Congress. Military commitments—first against Spain in the Caribbean, then in the Philippines, next in interventions elsewhere in the hemisphere, and above all in Europe—gave prominence to the president in his easily aggrandized constitutional role of commander in chief. World War I demonstrated how the White House could take charge of a diverse and bustling country effectively and on a broad front. The Wilson administration directed the manpower needed for a mass army (having implemented the Selective Service System in May 1917). It extracted from the national output vital production as well as the requisite funding for war (in the form of both increased income taxes and heavy borrowing). It safeguarded the home front (with the all-purpose Espionage Act of June 1917 and the barrage of nationalist propaganda from George Creel's Committee on Public Information). And it coordinated a complex of public organizations that had corporate leaders working alongside professional societies and the military (most notably the War Industries Board). The presidency had by 1918 demonstrated a capacity for concentrated action unimagined twenty years earlier.

The most obvious index of this trend toward broader presidential power was the White House staff. George B. Cortelyou helped McKinley give the presidency a modern cast. Already experienced from working for McKinley's predecessor, Cortelyou emerged as chief of staff as well as presidential confidante. He brought the increasing flow of paper under control, monitored major departments within the executive branch, cultivated the press so that the president's views reached the public loud and clear, tracked newspaper opinion around the country as a surrogate for polling, managed the legislative agenda, and upgraded the White House communications links within Washington and far beyond. By March 1901 he had expanded the staff of clerks from six to thirty. By the time Roosevelt handed the White House to Taft in 1909, the staff had grown to about eighty.[33]

As international issues loomed larger, presidents asserted their control over the State Department. The White House could no longer let that department function as the fiefdom of a politically independent figure. McKinley was from the outset of his presidency his own secretary of state. He made his loyal lieutenant, William Day, the second in command charged with keeping an eye on the secretary, the aging and politically worthy John Sherman. The president closely followed department business and freely intervened to bring decisions into line with his preferences. In late April 1898 he secured Sherman's resignation, leaving Day in control through year's end when McKinley brought in the able and like-minded John Hay. Once in the White House, Roosevelt eventually turned to a close ally, Elihu Root, who had proven his mettle as McKinley's man running the War Department. Taft brought in as department head a corporate lawyer (Knox), who enjoyed the greatest latitude of any of the occupants in the early twentieth century. In a shift back to the predominant pattern, Wilson more and more consigned his secretaries of state to handmaiden roles. Prominence in the Democratic Party won William Jennings Bryan his appointment to that post, and Wilson at first handled him gingerly. But once war began, the president so tightly controlled foreign affairs that Bryan resigned, and Wilson thereafter worked only with political nonentities entirely dependent on his pleasure, first Lansing and then Bainbridge Colby.

Swaying Congress on foreign affairs proved a more formidable task, especially under a constitution constructed to balance the legislative branch against the executive. Congress and presidents began their struggle for influence in the 1790s with the ink barely dry on the Constitution, and they maintained a rough balance through the nineteenth century. The Senate had the power to ratify treaties and approve appointments by the president; the House and the Senate shared the war-making power and the power of the purse (denial of funds constituted a virtual veto on executive action). The president for his part exercised command of the armed forces and conducted relations with other countries, though the agents he dispatched abroad needed Senate approval.

Both McKinley and Roosevelt shifted the balance in favor of the president. As with Polk during the Mexican War and Lincoln during the Civil War, McKinley used his powers as commander in chief during the war with Spain to set in motion his expansionist initiatives in the Caribbean and the Pacific, and after the war he held the reins of military governments in Cuba and the Philippines without congressional oversight. Moreover, he directed u.s. forces to fight in both the Philippines and China without asking for a congressional declaration of war. Roosevelt added to presidential latitude by punching a hole in the Senate's power to ratify treaties. He relied on executive agreements with other states, sanctioned by the Constitution, but brought them into play on major issues in place of a treaty so that he avoided the annoyance of Senate involvement. The resort to executive agreements was most helpful in adjusting politically sensitive relations with Japan in 1905 and 1908 on immigration to the United States and influence in the western Pacific. Wilson also resorted to executive agreements in his own, equally sensitive dealings with Japan in 1917.

These developments weakened but did not break constitutional checks and balances in foreign affairs. McKinley had had to listen to a Congress clamoring for war in 1898, and in early 1899 he went to great efforts to get his peace treaty (including the controversial Philippines annexation) through the Senate. Similarly, Wilson dutifully went to Congress for a war declaration in 1917. So sharp was the friction with Germany by then that only a handful of senators and representatives voted in opposition. In peacemaking, however, Wilson found himself at loggerheads with the Senate and failed despite strenuous efforts to get around senatorial opposition. This failure stands out in an era marked in the main by augmented presidential power.

No less important than the president's growing advantage over Congress was the rising interest in the White House at the turn of the century in shaping public opinion. The voting population was small, limited to adult white males and thus perhaps about 20 percent of the total population. Some three-quarters of the electorate were uninformed or barely informed. These voters tended to be rural and working class with limited access to communications channels that would allow the president to speak directly to them. The remaining quarter of the electorate (perhaps as many as 3 million men at the end of the century) were better informed. They were urban and educated, had higher incomes, and could for the most part be identified as Protestant and Anglo. Within this informed segment could be found the foreign policy influentials who could shape opinion within their communities as well as within business and professional circles. Some derived special authority from having served in Washington or from having lived or traveled abroad. To reach the voting public the president had to speak through these local elites (at least until radio and television technology gave his voice a national and instantaneous reach).

In an environment in which public opinion was segmented and locally generated, presidents had to win converts one locale at a time. McKinley demonstrated the president's power to persuade when in October 1898 he took advantage of the speed and convenience of rail travel to tour the Midwest and discuss the future of the Philippines. As he went from city to city, he spoke of the obligations of empire, gauged the response of audiences, newspapers, and local people of influence, and then expressed himself in ever bolder terms as the responses came back positive. By the end, McKinley stood four square behind retention of the entire archipelago, and he thought that he had the public with him. As early as 1908, Wilson had recognized the growing power of the president to persuade the nation and "form it to his own views."[34] His most ambitious attempt to replicate McKinley's exercise in persuasion at the retail level came in the fall of 1919. Determined to address the electorate over the heads of an uncooperative Senate, he jumped on a train to take his message from one whistle stop to another.

Neither McKinley's successful bid to win the public nor Wilson's failed attempt can be imagined without the president's emergence as the spokesman and embodiment of the national will. This symbolic role was closely connected to the rising influence of the vision of a strong, activist state around the turn of the century. Increasingly the new orthodoxy of national greatness threw on the defensive those with a mistrust of concentrated power in the hands of the executive and a fear of overseas entanglements and a large standing army. This version of u.s. nationalism had become an impatient steed, and an increasingly strong American state would both encourage and harness it.

The debate over annexation of the Philippines revealed the growing advantage of the state builders. McKinley spoke ever more emphatically about the duties awaiting the nation on the other side of the Pacific. In a speech in Iowa in October 1898 he observed cautiously, "Territory sometimes comes to us when we go to war in a holy cause, and whenever it does the banner of liberty will float over it and bring, I trust, the blessings and benefits to all peoples." Two months later speaking publicly in Atlanta, he announced the planting of the American flag "in two hemispheres" in the name "of liberty and law, of peace and progress." Defiant, he asked, "Who will haul it down?" Finally, before an enthusiastic Boston audience in February 1899 following the successful Senate treaty fight, the president spoke as the advocate of "benevolent assimilation" and predicted that Filipinos "shall for ages hence bless the American republic because it emancipated and redeemed their fatherland, and set them in the pathway of the world's best civilization."[35] He was thus echoing the liturgy of earlier foreign policy activists by claiming for the United States a right and duty to establish colonies, help "oppressed peoples," and generally project its power and influence into the world. Americans would benefit, and so would all humanity. Having taken his stand, McKinley prevailed against his critics in two revealing referenda, first winning the Senate over to his treaty in 1899 and then securing a popular endorsement in the election of 1900.

The debate over entry into war in 1914–17 and over American participation in a League of Nations in 1919–20 found the president once again in the position of claiming to represent the spirit of a country ready for a global role. Wilson steered the country toward ever deeper involvement in a Europe at war. He drove from his cabinet William Jennings Bryan, who challenged the wisdom of this involvement. He committed the country to war over the objections of a remaining handful who feared the costs to republican ideals and to the welfare of the common man. He created a wartime propaganda agency (the Committee on Public Information or Creel Committee) that exploited new communications technologies to marshal support at home as well as abroad. Only in the battle over the peace treaty did Wilson come up short. He had the votes to prevail against critics fundamentally opposed to what they saw as his costly and delusive attempt to remake a dangerous world. But his own rigidity cost him victory by driving away Republicans whose disagreement with Wilson was over how, not whether, the United States should vigorously engage the world. During the course of two decades the political elite had undergone a fateful ideological shift even if Wilson could not fully exploit it.

The cumulative effect of the initiatives launched around the turn of the century was astonishing. A string of policymakers pulled the Caribbean tightly into the u.s. orbit, extended military and diplomatic influence across the Pacific, made Europe's business their own, altered the ideological balance of opinion on matters of foreign relations, gained a rich and varied experience in international affairs, and laid the foundations for the modern presidency with the tools to conduct an ambitious and increasingly far-flung foreign policy. Wilson acted on an acute, far-sighted understanding of the mounting global crisis. His desperate attempt to head off deeper disaster miscarried, but both his insight and his program would in time become a defining feature of u.s. policy.

This remarkable range of achievements between 1898 and 1920 has made the following decade look to some like an "isolationist" retreat. But this view fails to recognize the way that the u.s. role in the world had fundamentally and unalterably changed. Americans had won prominence on a broad international front that put them in a strikingly strong international position. A peripheral power had established its centrality in world affairs, and it would remain a central actor after World War I. What had become the world's leading economy already by 1900 emerged from the European war as the world's prime source of capital and a steamroller in trade competition. Having demonstrated their prowess by taking colonies and staking out a sphere of influence, Americans in the interwar period gave no sign of retreat. They had, moreover, embraced Britain as an informal ally based on a shared sense of kinship, and that close relationship would remain a defining feature of great-power politics through the balance of the century. Contrary to conventional charges of isolationism, the strong u.s. position would survive the interwar decades and emerge from another world war by any measure greater still.

3

THE AMERICAN WAY IN A FRAGMENTING WORLD

1921★1940

In early 1923 the popular German satirical weekly *Simplicissimus* featured a cover (fig. 3) by the Norwegian cartoonist Olaf Gulbransson, one of the regular contributors to this gadfly of the German social and political establishment. His sketch captured an important truth about newly won U.S. dominance. Europe in the person of the French leader, Raymond Poincaré, appeared as a supplicant before J. P. Morgan, the U.S. banker represented in the popular stereotype of the capitalist (top hat and mustache) but with a twist. In place of the usual tuxedo, cigar, cane, and domineering gaze, Gulbransson featured a loosely draped, corpulent figure, lofty and indifferent. The European on bended knee prayed for even the slightest sign of recognition and support.

Gulbransson was right—the Europeans were in the position of supplicants in the wake of World War I. That conflict had caused the death of some 8.5 million combatants and 6.5 million civilians as modern warfare took a terrible turn toward the unrelenting and indiscriminate. The major powers had spent billions trying to destroy each other and in the bargain managed to sap their own economies. The sorry result, one contemporary observed, was "a Europe devastated, bled white, convulsed and impoverished." The nationalist rivalries that had precipitated World War I continued to fester. Germany had heavy punitive reparations to discharge as the party judged by the victors guilty of starting the war. (In 1921 a commission arrived at the figure due: $33 billion.) Germany also lost its colonies to those same victors, returned Alsace-Lorraine to France, and surrendered territory to the new state of Poland. Postwar German leaders rejected this crippling peace as fundamentally illegitimate and schemed to undo it, while French nationalists felt it did not go far enough to guarantee security. The new states carved out of the Austro-Hungarian Em-

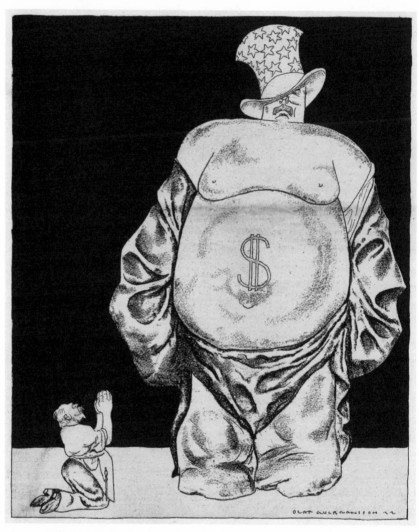

Figure 3. "The Almighty Gold," by Olaf Gulbransson,
cover illustration for Simplicissimus, *10 January 1923.*

pire were hotbeds of competing nationalists groups. The Bolshevik regime in Russia survived to act as a magnet for social revolutionaries in Europe as well as a champion for anti-imperialists on the periphery.[1]

The global economic collapse of the 1930s intensified nationalist and social discontents and bolstered a trend toward populist and authoritarian politics across the region, but especially in Germany and Italy. Out of this accumulated hatred and hardship would come World War II—and with it an orgy of devastation that would scramble the political map, once more extinguish lives by the millions, spawn a vast stream of refugees all across Europe, and pound some of the world's leading economies to rubble. As Europe imploded, rising discontents on the periphery—in the colonies across Africa, the Middle East, and Asia—foreshadowed the end of Europe's overseas imperium.

Those at the head of the American colossus understood their limits—and their opportunities. While gloom gathered over Europe, a booming u.s. economy created the first mass consumer society, winning worldwide admiration and envy that would survive the Great Depression of the 1930s. A British diplomat summed up the u.s. advantage by measuring it against his homeland. U.S. leaders were at the head of "a State twenty-five times as large, five times as wealthy, three times as populous, twice as ambitious, almost invulnerable, and at least our equal in prosperity, vital energy, technical equipment and industrial science."[2] At the top of their agenda was promoting peace and stability in Europe, but they also had the good sense to know that they could not impose solutions on that once proud, privileged center of global power. In the other two regions of top concern—Latin America and East Asia—they worked to consolidate recent gains in influence rather than to extend it. The giant was feeling its way cautiously toward global dominance.

ECONOMIC AND CULTURAL PRIMACY

Economic vitality remained the bedrock of u.s. strength. The war years had brought the economy out of recession and pushed GDP in 1918 to twice the figure at the end of McKinley's war with Spain ($639 billion in constant 2000 dollars). The return to peace plunged the country back into recession. Unions that had deferred their demands during the war turned militant. Demobilized troops competed with recently fired wartime workers for scarce jobs. The growing strains were evident in a string of strikes, bombings, and race riots. Then, however, the economy rallied, with output reaching a new high in 1923 ($713 billion) and then climbing steadily until 1929 ($865 billion). The Great Depression at its worst in 1933 had shaved off a quarter of the GDP (down to

$636 billion), but by 1939 production had rebounded to a new high ($951 billion), well over three times the 1898 figure.[3]

This continued growth in an already enormous economy was globally significant in two ways. By the end of the interwar period the United States more then ever eclipsed the other major powers. In 1938 the Soviet Union and Germany, the closest competitors, each had less than half the u.s. output, Britain and France had between a quarter and a third, while Japan and Italy had around a fifth. Of the total GDP produced by the great powers that year, the United States accounted for a third.[4] But the United States was more than a giant to the pygmy economies of the world. As more and more Americans moved into a new realm of abundance during the first decades of the twentieth century, the products that they exported and the lifestyle they represented forced peoples in other lands to grapple with their own identity.

The First Modern Nation

Americans pioneered a modernity that promised abundance and ease to ordinary people to a degree never before known. It realized that promise through a system of mass production and mass consumption with pervasive economic, social, and cultural consequences. By the 1920s those consequences were playing out in the United States on an impressively wide scale before a transfixed world audience.

This American-style modernity existed at base because of the rapid and enthusiastic embrace of new industrial technology (noted in chapter 1). That technology in turn multiplied productivity many times what had earlier been possible. Fossil fuels, primarily coal and oil, delivered this miracle by providing energy on a scale that human and animal power had never been able to match. Coal production increased one-hundred-fold during the nineteenth century, and by 1900 oil was becoming part of the fossil fuel mix. The world was by then set to establish some extraordinary records for energy use. Global energy consumption jumped sixteenfold over the course of the twentieth century and cumulatively surpassed the totals for the previous thousand years by an amazing factor of ten. Almost all of that increase was limited to North America, western Europe, and Japan.[5] The abundance of power had effects that trickled down from production into other areas. Transportation and communications became faster, cheaper, and more convenient. Widespread electrification put radios in every home and created a national audience for advertisers. Energy abundance together with mass production heralded the age of the automobile, linking home, work, shopping, and leisure.

The changes in production, transportation, and communications transformed U.S. society. Americans had smaller families and lived longer lives. Urban residents overtook the rural population in the 1920s as employment steadily shifted away from agriculture to the industrial and service sectors of the economy. The shrinking minority who stayed behind on the land were themselves caught up in the trends evident in the urban, industrial part of the economy: farms became larger to sustain mass production, more capital intensive as machinery and fertilizer played a greater role, and more scientific as agricultural extension services disseminated new techniques, seed strains, herbicides, and insecticides. Thanks to these improvements in productivity, a smaller labor force was able to keep the United States an agricultural powerhouse.

Machines and electricity functioning within an extraordinarily productive carbon-based economy had a profound impact on everyday life. Literacy and technical skills required at the workplace put a growing premium on education. Apprenticeship and other informal ways of learning gave way to a variety of formal educational programs. High school, college, and advanced degrees became not only credentials for employment but also markers of social status. Scientific and materialistic outlooks on the world fueled a faith in the power of human rationality and ever-improving technology as engines of historical progress. Americans were more than ever a mobile people on whom the constraints of community and kinship networks rested lightly. Americans began rethinking gender roles, which would in time open the way for significant numbers of women to move into higher education and the workforce.

There was one additional feature implied by all the others—the emergence in the 1920s of a full-fledged consumer society. At the start of the nineteenth century most Americans lived on the land and were preoccupied with producing enough to sustain themselves. By the end of the century rising incomes, especially in cities, were creating a new society edging toward mass consumption. Providing the critical element in this transformation, U.S. industry took the pioneering steps toward mass-produced goods. By keeping output high, industry could keep the price of each unit of output low—within the purchasing power of a growing number of ordinary Americans. The productivity of this economy rewarded workers with an increasing income that exceeded the costs of essential food and housing and thus brought more and more within the charmed circle of abundance. Fordism became the shorthand for this emerging system of mass production plus common prosperity. Henry Ford's workers earned enough to purchase the very cars that they manufactured. Per capita income, which provides a crude sense of increasing affluence, doubled between 1850 and 1898, and then doubled again between 1898 and 1940, even though the total population was almost six times greater in 1940 than it had been in 1850.[6] Rising incomes allowed Americans to make discretionary purchases of consumer goods and services to a degree undreamt of a century earlier. Family budgets grew to include such new items as household appliances, automobiles, public entertainment, and vacations.

The consumer society that emerged in the 1920s rested on an intricate set of arrangements. Industrial production for mass consumption had multiplied the range of standardized, brand-name goods available to a national market. To supply this sprawling continental market cheaply and quickly, producers had to construct an elaborate system of distribution and field a large sales force. Supporting production and distribution was the job of the new business of advertising. Described by its proponents as a "science," its task was to discover consumer preferences, then stimulate and channel them, and ultimately to create loyalty to particular brand names so that firms producing in high volume would have some assurance that their ever-expanding output would in fact find purchasers waiting at the other end of the distribution system.

Advertisers had already early in the century begun to frame the popular understanding of this new culture. Print advertising and movies defined the lifestyle to which the new consumers aspired. Advertisements spoke to Americans in a rich and appealing variety of marketing voices, telling them "how to dress, what to buy, and what to value in life" (as it was put by someone who labored for a publishing empire built on advertising revenue). But advertisers self-consciously promoted a broader message loaded with political meaning. Consumption was a duty of the citizen, and material abundance a sign of national grace. Purchasing goods and services was like voting. Every day the consumer could cast ballots for the best products, and these ongoing elections raised to prominence those products and corporations best able to serve the public good. Advertisers thus imagined themselves like statesmen, their activities served (in the words of one) to "increase the wealth and happiness of society." All Americans had a right of access to the most goods at the lowest possible price. This idealized consumer society was classless ("a democracy of goods") but also strikingly gendered. Advertisers knew full well that women did the bulk of the buying, and so they peopled their advertisements with sleek, domestic women from the upper and middle classes.[7]

This burgeoning culture of consumption helped reshape popular aspirations. Early twentieth-century Americans began to define themselves in terms of what they consumed rather than, as they had formerly, in terms of what they produced. Self-gratification became the new touchstone for the good life, in place of thrift, social virtue, or religious morality. Going into debt to enjoy the present took precedence over savings for future benefits. A system of consumer credit enabled even the cash poor to purchase new consumer products such as telephones, radios, phonographs, and automobiles and to afford various forms of entertainment such as movies and vacations. These goods and diversions were coming to define the prime aspirations of substantial numbers of Americans even below the middle class.

This consumer culture acquired a distinct political dimension during the Great Depression. The state expanded its purview to include the protection of the new consumer-oriented society. Democrats running the New Deal promoted the notion that consumers were a distinct entity within the national economy alongside business, labor, and agriculture and as such deserved (in President Franklin Roosevelt's own words) "to have their interests represented in the formulation of government policy."[8] This meant specifically provisions for information and protection that were indispensable to making good, safe consumer choices. Moreover, consumer behavior loomed ever larger in the thinking of those within the administration who saw underconsumption as the root cause of American economic woes and stimulating consumer spending as the most effective way to revive economic activity and restore prosperity. In what was to amount to the triumph of Keynesian economics, these New Dealers began asserting that government should fulfill its responsibility to the consumer through fiscal and monetary policy that kept demand high and production lines humming. Programs such as Social Security and public works could also help sustain consumer spending and thus combat economic downturns.

Exporting Modernity

It is no surprise given the size and success of the u.s. economy that it registered its presence around the world in a variety of ways. Most obviously it had attractive goods to sell, but it also had banks and corporations flush with capital to underwrite foreign operations. Beyond that, it propagated dreams so powerful that they forced other peoples to reflect on both their personal and their national identity and consider whether to accommodate the newly demarcated American way, to resist its influences, or to chart some middle path of selective adaptation.

The United States emerged from World War I as the new center of global capitalism. The transition had begun around 1900. Americans were still then on balance a debtor nation. But their foreign investments were beginning to rise, and loans made in the course of the European conflict completed the transition to net creditor. During the twenties investment overseas more than doubled, and the u.s. dollar and New York began to replace the British pound and London as the pivot of international finance. At the same time American corporations were venturing abroad with growing confidence. The late nineteenth century had seen the rise of pioneering u.s.-based multinational corporations such as Singer Sewing Machine, which made substantial overseas investments in factories and distribution systems to win foreign customers. Increasingly u.s. firms invested abroad to ensure access to natural resources critical to the home market or to production lines and distribution networks they were operating elsewhere in the world. U.S. direct investment jumped from $.6 billion in 1897 to $2.7 billion in 1914. The interwar export drive with autos, electrical products, farm machinery, and oil in the lead pushed direct investment even higher—from $3.9 billion in 1919 to $8.0 billion in 1930. Total u.s. holdings abroad rose from $12.2 billion in 1919 to $35.1 billion in 1929.[9]

Hollywood films figured particularly prominently among the u.s. goods flooding foreign markets. The export of movies, which would spearhead the twentieth-century American entertainment juggernaut, gained headway during World War I. Foreign competitors, especially in France and Italy, had been hobbled by wartime restrictions and shortages. After the war u.s. inroads continued at the expense of Pathé and the other leading French producers, which had dominated prewar international markets. U.S. companies were well funded. Their technologically innovative assembly-line products were resolutely commercial in their attention to mass tastes. The film industry, concentrated in a few well-capitalized companies, had learned that simple plots were the secret to capturing a large, diverse home audience. Control of that home market in turn gave them a competitive edge abroad, made even sharper by strong government backing, especially from the Department of Commerce. A good show at home could cover the costs of production, leaving earnings on exports pure profit.

Hollywood quickly became a major international presence. By 1928 it claimed a quarter of the film market in Japan, almost a half in Germany, roughly two-thirds in France and Italy. The figure was higher still—between 80 and 95 percent—in Anglophone Britain and Canada as well as in Mexico and Brazil. U.S. films remained prominent into the late 1930s (despite the depression-induced trend toward economic and cultural protectionism). An overseas audience that was disproportionately younger, more female, and more working class found the fast-paced, varied u.s. fare more appealing than European films influenced by an older, more sedate theatrical style. This exposure to a world conceived by Hollywood had an impact on audiences. According to a London paper, "They talk American, think American, dream American; we have several million people, mostly women, who, to all intents and purposes, are temporary American citizens." More prosaically the head of the association representing the leading Hollywood firms described their products as "silent salesmen of American goods." What audiences saw on the screen—especially the cars, furniture, and fashion—they would want for themselves. Films became more broadly an advertisement for the opportunity and wealth generated by the American way.[10]

The success of the u.s. model commanded widespread attention. Americans overwhelmingly took pride in their modernity, reveled in their wealth and comfort, and found their success confirmation of their special standing in the world. The response of European observers to this rising presence across the Atlantic was more complicated. They had long followed the American political and social experiment. Their impressions came from diverse sources—reports of immigrants, accounts of travelers, touring Wild West shows, and encounters with the growing numbers of well-heeled American visitors. In the 1920s with the continent awash in American goods, commercial ideas, entertainment, and tourists (some quarter of a million a year by 1929), fascination with the American experiment reached a peak.[11] Outward-looking Europeans—from businessmen to labor leaders, from social reformers to social conservatives—repaid in kind the ambivalence that Americans had long felt toward the Old World. Some on the receiving end who had once been full of praise for the u.s. commitment to self-determination and democracy had by the early twentieth century developed doubts. The United States was in the grip of a capitalist system that inculcated mass material delusions. Others who had no sympathy for the American commitment to equality and freedom from class restraints and authoritarian politics avidly celebrated its economic achievements and studied its methods of production and consumption. Still others regarded the United States as an expression of modern life that Europe could not escape or had somehow to avoid. These reactions, which would anticipate in broad terms that of other regions, tended to reveal more about the respondent's identity and hopes than any special insight into the United States. In other words the appearance of an American economic and cultural dynamo made Europeans reflect on who they were and what they wanted of their societies.

Notable on the positive side of this European reaction was admiration for the broad opportunity and technological efficiency on display in the United States. For example, German trade unionists praised the u.s. success at securing higher wages and thus abundance for many at a time when roughly three-quarters of German workers had income just sufficient for the bare necessities of food, rent, and clothing, with little left for discretionary spending. So far were most Germans from the income levels of Americans that it was hard for them to imagine precisely what a consumer society was and how it operated. One commentator went farther and pronounced the life of the middle-class German compared to his American counterpart "highly primitive, uncomfortable, unhygienic, and often downright unworthy." Peasants in remote, poverty-stricken parts of southern Italy in the mid-1930s supply another example of this positive engagement with the American model. Thanks to immigrant ties, they knew more about New York than they did about Rome and imagined the United States as a dream world offering escape from hope-killing, grinding deprivation. Its bounty made it possible to work and save, at first for remittances to lift living standards at home and ultimately enough to return and buy land or set oneself up in business. Peasants paid tribute to this distant utopia. They placed images of a hearty President Franklin Roosevelt on their walls alongside pictures of the Madonna; they figured weights and measures in pounds and inches; and they treasured the workaday artifacts obtained in the United States—scissors, knives, razors, hammers, and farm tools.[12]

On the negative side, a diverse group of European cultural and political elites—some Catholics, others Marxists, some on the Left, others on the Right—worried about the "American invasion." They expressed their fear of becoming, like the United States, a mass society, bereft of spirituality and driven by a heartless and unchecked capitalism. If the market rather than the intellectually cultivated were to decide what had value, then Europe too would drift toward a materialistic, violent, and vulgar way of life directly at odds with traditional, refined Europeans ways. German critics, for example, disparaged the American home as a soulless place and the American woman as a cold, neutered figure more engaged in work, entertainment, and consumption than her proper domestic duties. The United States lacked high culture of the sort that flourished in Europe, and life there in general seemed marked by a "gray, monotone, mechanistic uniformity."[13]

These elite anxieties about the pernicious effects of the American way were particularly pronounced in France. A French chef in the interwar period denounced u.s. food as "doctored, thermochemical, and dreadful," and suggested that the loud bands in American restaurants were there to drown out "the cries of despair emitted by the unfortunate diners." The prominent and prolific literary figure Georges Duhamel unleashed a widely read and controversial diatribe in 1930. As a surgeon during War World I, he had witnessed industrial killing and come away with a powerful aversion toward any civilization dominated by the machine. A brief U.S. visit on the eve of the Wall Street crash evoked his antipathy. He found Americans hurried, distracted, soulless. Their machine culture had robbed them of their individuality while despoiling their rich environment because of what Duhamel saw as their compulsion to "grasp" and "plunder." Alienated from nature, Americans devoted themselves to an endless and meaningless quest for material goods. "They desperately yearn for phonographs, radios, illustrated magazines, 'movies,' elevators, electric refrigerators, and automobiles, automobiles, and, once again, automobiles." The comfortable bathroom was the epitome of American civilization, so it struck Duhamel, while the cinema that Americans loved to attend was "stupefying and destroying the mind." These people were, to judge from their faces, "uniformly dejected."[14]

The participants in this running European debate divided over what the American model said about Europe's future. Duhamel, for example, announced the rise of a dread new empire to challenge a superior European civilization. The encroachment of the "American system" could be seen everywhere, so that it "now has the whole world for its field." Americans were sure to press their advantage, he warned. The United States had "had two centuries of success, a constant rise; few wars, all of happy issue; it has kept its many problems at a safe distance; it feels the pride of being a numerous people, rich, feared, admired." The editor of the German newspaper *Frankfurter Zeitung* expressed the sanguine alternative to Duhamel's dread. He came away from a visit in the mid-1920s impressed by a prosperous, optimistic, restless, technology-obsessed, spiritually empty people. But he was not alarmed. Though the United States might influence Europe at points, on the whole Americans and Europeans had distinct roads to travel. The Americans were a colonial offshoot heavily influenced by life in a vast land of plenty and only now finding their own way. For better or for worse, Europeans had to traverse a land of scarcity, guided by old values, divided nationally, and subject of late to punishing conflict. "It is our destiny to live in meagerness and narrowness."[15]

Contrasting appraisals of the American experiment persisted into the 1930s. Some of the elite European critics continued to see the United States in the grip of the Great Depression as a prime exhibit for capitalism's worst excesses. Others noted that the American economic model was weathering this test and increasingly represented the bastion for liberal democrats no longer at home in an intolerant Europe edging toward war. The flight across the Atlantic of prominent artists, writers, and academics—the continent's best and brightest—testified to the standing of the United States as a place of political hope and economic opportunity.

The crosscurrents attending interwar Americanization were becoming evident in regions beyond Europe. The experience of the future head of Sony, Akio Morita, is revealing about the impact American products were already having in Japan. His well-to-do family acquired a Ford car to take Sunday drives along narrow, bumpy cart roads as well as a GE washing machine and a Westinghouse refrigerator. The father loved Hollywood movies such as *King Kong,* and his mother had a taste for Western classical music, which prompted the purchase of a crank Victrola and then an electric phonograph. Akio recalls that hearing the sound quality of the new phonograph left him "absolutely astounded," inspiring a scientific interest that would years later bear fruit in a host of Sony consumer products.[16] But along with this interest in foreign goods and culture went an unabated devotion to the family's venerable sake-brewing business, a keen sense of social obligation toward the family village, and a strong national pride.

Assessing this emergence of the United States as the first modern nation— the exemplar and vanguard of a way of life—requires some care. The features that developed first and most fully in the United States would soon emerge in other developed countries and even such cities of the developing world as Shanghai and Havana. Indulging national pride, Americans felt they were generating the trends that induced others to move toward modernity, and critics paid the United States a compliment by expressing their fear of an American economic and cultural invasion. But both boosterism and disdain may miss the mark by assuming a U.S. cause for every foreign effect. It might be more revealing to think of the U.S. relationship to modernity in a more complex way.

The United States was in part a leading indicator of where other advanced industrial countries exploiting the same technological opportunities for wealth and convenience were likely to go. Already by the late nineteenth century, others in the developed world were also exploring the implications of industrialization, moving toward greater urbanization, and undergoing the breakdown of older social and cultural patterns. In this sense the United States, western Europe, and Japan were following roughly parallel trajectories, and each was moving toward a modernity that would look largely but not entirely like that of the others. Transnational economic and technological trends were felt by all but expressed in different regional and national ways.

At the same time, by its products and presence Americans did influence the path others took toward modernity. None had moved as fast or gotten as far as the United States had by the 1920s. The United States thus represented for foreign observers a laboratory of possibilities, experiments from which they might learn. Some gravitated to aspects of the American model, while others were dismayed and fought back. Either way, the u.s. example forced others to reflect on what they personally and collectively valued and wanted to become. A more powerful symbolic role is hard to imagine.

NO END OF EUROPEAN TROUBLES

In matters of state as in economics and culture, the interwar years had the United States and Europe locked in a close relationship. Europe stood at the very center of u.s. policymakers' concerns. Above all else, they understood that the tensions spawned by the First World War could erupt in a second, even more horrific conflict. The Republicans confronted this problem from the time Warren G. Harding took the helm in 1921. He and his successors, first Calvin Coolidge and then Herbert Hoover for a single term that ended in 1933, took advantage of their country's considerable economic power and cultural confidence to promote international peace and prosperity as the most effective antidote to the dangers haunting Europe. The harsh peace ending World War I was at the heart of the continent's continuing tensions, with the French clinging to any advantage over a defeated and resentful Germany. By the time the Democrats took control of the White House in 1933, mounting European troubles dictated greater caution, an attitude emphatically reinforced by the Great Depression's blow to the livelihood of Americans. The administration of Franklin Roosevelt watched in shock and bewilderment as Europe drifted toward war—and for the moment kept a safe distance.

Republicans to the Rescue

Dominating policy during the Republican resurgence between 1921 and 1933 was an elite born, bred, and educated in the urban Northeast. Elihu Root, Theodore Roosevelt, and Henry Cabot Lodge were charter members of this establishment club. Its most prominent interwar representatives were Charles Evans Hughes and Henry L. Stimson. Members of the club shared a strikingly similar background. They came from prominent, often wealthy families. They were brought up Episcopalian or Presbyterian and got the best education. After attending private prep schools, they enrolled at Yale or Harvard and then a prominent law school before entering lucrative corporate law practice with a prestigious firm. Their gathering place was the Council on Foreign Relations, a New York–based organization that originated during the war as an elite Anglo-American initiative and then split in 1921 into distinct

American and British organizations. The u.s. side devoted itself to the emerging orthodoxy of serious and sustained u.s. involvement in the world. The part of that world that its members knew best was Europe, especially Britain. There they conducted business, vacationed, and cultivated friendships.

Stimson was a model northeastern establishment figure—good New York family, good schools (Phillips Academy, Yale College, and Harvard Law), good record in New York's best law office, and good connections (Root headed his law firm and Theodore Roosevelt was his political mentor). More drawn to public service than the petty claims his clients brought him, Stimson signed up as William Howard Taft's secretary of war to carry forward Root's reform of the army. Trim, hair close cropped, strong willed, and short tempered, he had been even more in his element during World War I as an artillery officer in France.

Hughes, Stimson, and their kind were closely tied to earlier Republican policy. In their time of apprenticeship to power they had worked with such prominent midwestern Republicans as William McKinley and Taft. The years of empire building as well as war and peacemaking gave them considerable experience that they could apply to interwar issues. They had supported acquiring the Philippines and tightening the u.s. grip on the Caribbean. They called for intervention in the European war well before President Woodrow Wilson and followed the lead of Lodge in favoring modification, not outright rejection, of the treaty of peace that Wilson presented the Senate. They were hardly isolationists. For example, a majority of Republicans in the Senate had called for a treaty of alliance with France as insurance against a resurgent Germany.

In this stable of Republic leaders, Herbert Hoover was a notable exception to the establishment pattern. He was neither a lawyer nor a privileged northeasterner. Born in Iowa and raised in Oregon, Hoover came from a working-class family with a Quaker faith. He had attended the newly opened Stanford University, trained as an engineer, and made his fortune and reputation in the mining business (including a stint in China around the time of the Boxer uprising). His initiation into the policy world came at the end of World War I when he ran the u.s. humanitarian food aid program in Europe and Russia. He headed the Commerce Department under Harding and then Coolidge, involving it deeply in foreign policy. He capped his rapid political rise by making a successful bid for the presidency in 1928. His concerns were shaped by an almost religious faith in the u.s. economic system: "Our processes of production and distribution, the outgrowth of a hundred generations, in the stimulation to individual initiative, the large equality of opportunity and infinite development of mind and body, while not perfect, come about as near perfection as is possible."[17]

The Republican approach reflected a conviction that knowledge rationally applied could resolve international disputes, promote prosperity, and banish war. This conviction assumed the special role of Britain and the United States on the world stage as guides toward a better world and of those of British background as the brains behind u.s. policy. The appeal of using disinterested experts was already evident in shaping colonial policy in the Philippines and in fleshing out Wilson's Fourteen Points, but in the postwar period it would take on far greater prominence with the rise of experts on international affairs claiming insights important to policymakers. Professionals devoted to state making and state reforming were carving out for themselves a place in universities such as Harvard, Georgetown, Johns Hopkins, and Tufts. They populated the think tanks, such as the Brookings Institution, that began to spring up in Washington. And they looked to new internationally minded institutions such as the Carnegie Endowment for International Peace (founded 1913), the Rockefeller Foundation (1914), the Foreign Policy Association (1918), the Council on Foreign Relations (1921), and the Institute of Pacific Relations (1925) for help with educating the public and swaying policymakers.

The Republicans approached Europe's problems with a mix of confidence and caution. They had faith in rationality, technical competence, and prosperity as the most potent counters to the old scourge of militarism and imperialism no less than the new danger of Bolshevism and class warfare. From the White House Republicans pursued policies on a strikingly broad front that put into deeper question the old two-spheres injunction against entanglement in European affairs that Theodore Roosevelt had encroached upon and Wilson had boldly set aside. But Republican leadership was limited by an assertive Congress and a cautious public. U.S. intervention in World War I looked more and more like a failure, a conclusion that argued against any new steps likely to result in a repeat performance. U.S. policymakers themselves recognized the limits of their influence over a Europe burdened by bitterness and frustrated national ambition. The peace settlement had left a score of places such as the Rhineland, the Saar, Fiume, and Danzig territorial hotspots. New regimes, especially those arising from the debris of the Austro-Hungarian Empire, were dangerously unstable. The League of Nations was too much under the control of Britain and France to serve as a helpful forum for resolving these problems.

Republican leaders pursued their carefully calibrated policy along two main lines, each marked off by their predecessors. One relied on international agreements to promote peace and limit the destructive effects of war. The late nineteenth century had brought a burst of enthusiasm among the great powers, Americans included, for conferences on facilitating international commerce and limiting warfare. Well over two hundred agreements emerged between 1850 and 1910. Those on the commercial side dealt with a host of practical matters such as global time zones, property rights, weights and measures, sea and rail transport, and postal service. U.S. policymakers were equally enthusiastic about mechanisms to head off international conflict and to make warfare on land and at sea more humane when it was unavoidable. Formal commitments to take great-power disputes to arbitration had special appeal. McKinley had championed an arbitration treaty with Britain in 1897. Though it had failed to win Senate approval, his successors pressed ahead with their own accords. As Roosevelt's secretary of state, Root had negotiated and secured Senate approval for twenty-five of these agreements. During his tenure in that post, William Jennings Bryan had renewed some of these agreements and concluded new ones, raising the total number.[18]

Hughes as secretary of state under both Harding and Coolidge (1921–25) carried forward the campaign for international cooperation. He brought to this task a sharp mind that had enabled him at the ripe age of nineteen to graduate from Brown with honors. After legal training at Columbia, he built up a high-powered law practice and then moved into politics—first as the governor of New York, then as a Supreme Court justice, and finally as a presidential candidate in a failed bid against Wilson in 1916. During the fight over the League of Nations, he had emerged as a mild reservationist. The Washington naval conference of 1921–22 was Hughes's greatest contribution to the campaign to promote peace. He called the major powers together, drew up the agenda, and orchestrated a set of agreements that contributed to calming the international environment during the 1920s. The most important of those agreements averted a costly naval arms race. It fixed a ratio of 5:5:3 among the large, so-called capital warships (battleships, heavy cruisers, and aircraft carriers) of the United States, Britain, and Japan. This bargain assured u.s. parity with Britain. At the same time by bringing an end to a two-decade-old alliance between Britain and Japan, the conference guaranteed that no naval combination could threaten the American hemisphere. Follow-up conferences in Geneva in 1927 and in London in 1930 sought to extend naval limits to lesser warships (light cruisers, destroyers, and submarines), though with little success.

Efforts to avert an arms race did not prevent the u.s. armed forces from innovating in ways that would help them to mobilize on a massive scale and to strike in a decisive way when war did come. Reforms continued to promote the professionalism of the army. Its skilled, core cadre had the capacity to train and field a large force in short order. Technological advances were high on the agenda of all the services. Developments on this front would push the army's air force to world status (third largest by the early 1930s), lay the basis for amphibious operations that were to prove so critical in the Pacific during World War II, and make the aircraft carrier the new embodiment of naval power.

Republicans made another notable contribution to interwar harmony with the Kellogg-Briand Pact of 1928 outlawing war. The main author was Secretary of State Frank Kellogg, a Minnesota corporate lawyer who had cut his foreign policy teeth in the Senate (he had been a mild reservationist) and as ambassador to Britain before following Hughes in the Coolidge cabinet (1925–1929). The calculations behind this seemingly naïve agreement were distinctly hard headed. French foreign minister Aristide Briand had pressed in 1927 for a bilateral agreement committing the United States to France's security. Kellogg deflected the proposal, which had Germany as its target and would have generated a firestorm of controversy in the United States. He got Briand to accept a bland counterproposal for a Franco-American commitment to avoid war supplemented by an invitation to other powers to join in the accord. The initiative proved popular with the powerful American peace movement. Most countries quickly lined up in mid-1928 to renounce war "as an instrument of national policy," and the u.s. Senate approved overwhelmingly. Knowing full well that the accord did not exclude war in self-defense made the treaty easy to embrace all around.[19]

The influential journalist Walter Lippmann sarcastically summed up what he thought had been a basic fallacy behind this Republican quest for international cooperation: "Big warships meant big wars. Smaller warships meant smaller wars. No warships might eventually mean no wars."[20] This verdict is unfair. U.S. leaders embraced arms control agreements and the Kellogg-Briand Pact not because they were utopian but because they were convinced that international accords might in some small way make war less likely. Naval limits and peace agreements were for them practical measures to promote confidence among leaders and define clear lines that any troublemakers would have to cross at the price of serving timely notice on the world community of their malign intent. In these ways u.s. policy served to slow if not arrest the downward plunge of the Old World to self-destruction.

The League of Nations figured a distant third in the Republican policy of peace through international cooperation. Though that organization was poison in some quarters, both the Harding and Coolidge administrations maintained a discreet presence at its meetings. U.S. diplomats in Geneva served as "observers" to proceedings of the League Council and of affiliated bodies dealing with critical international issues such as reparations, drug control, world health, and human trafficking. Leading Republicans strongly favored joining the World Court, affiliated with the League of Nations, as a way to promote the rule of international law, but this step proved too politically controversial at home to press to conclusion.

The other main line of interwar Republican policy, also building on precedent, was to promote and harness growing u.s. economic muscle. This course was to add further to the power wielded by the executive branch. In 1890 Congress for the first time conceded to the president authority to negotiate for lower foreign tariffs (so-called bargaining tariffs) without congressional review of the results. The White House further strengthened its position in international economic matters through the creation of new agencies to manage the country's considerable economic clout, such as the Tariff Commission, the Federal Trade Commission, and the Federal Reserve. Perhaps the most important was the Department of Commerce, created in 1903. Its Bureau of Foreign and Domestic Commerce and its commercial attachés posted around the world were soon intruding on State Department turf in the name of promoting u.s. business abroad. World War I accelerated this trend toward greater executive power in economic matters. These developments foreshadowed the prominent foreign affairs role played by Commerce and Treasury in the 1920s. In an attempt to keep up, the State Department began reviewing overseas loans made by private Americans with an eye to keeping bondholders out of risky situations and extracting concessions from cash-strapped governments.

Where the president lacked authority to act, he teamed up with corporate leaders. The most dramatic breakthrough had occurred when the Taft administration turned to New York banks to serve as the chosen instruments of its policy in China and the Caribbean. Interwar Republicans pressed further with this strategy of collaboration between Washington and Wall Street—between the corporations that were creating such wealth and the state which could protect, encourage, and occasionally guide corporate activities overseas. This collaborative relationship between public and private interests including labor, humanitarian, and philanthropic organizations with an international agenda has been fittingly named corporatism. Like the rest of the Republican interwar policy, it combined confidence in private enterprise to serve the public good with a cautious sense of the limits of the u.s. government's power to set the world right. Corporations backed by Washington were the most potent and efficient agents of progress, so the Republicans held with an almost missionary fervor.

A corporatist approach was critical to coping with the debt problem left over from World War I. Washington policymakers combined with New York bankers and the best brains in the new international affairs establishment to manage this tangle. The Entente had over the course of the war accumulated $10.3 billion in debt to u.s. bondholders. (Of that $4.3 billion was British, $3.4 billion was French, and $1.6 billion Italian.) Resolving the problem simply by canceling this debt was one solution that Washington firmly rejected. As Coolidge is supposed to have observed of the Entente, "They hired the money, didn't they?" Why should u.s. investors sacrifice for European mismanagement of its own affairs? It was even harder to imagine asking the taxpayer to assume the costs of the cancellation at a time when annual federal revenue was $4 billion, less than half the total Entente debt. The alternative solution was for Britain and France to cover payments owed u.s. bondholders by squeezing from Germany the $33 billion in reparations imposed as part of the peace settlement. But the Germans, politically resentful and economically stressed, were dragging their heels. France tried to forcibly extract its share by occupying the Ruhr in 1923, an action that left the Germans even less cooperative.

To resolve the standoff, the Coolidge administration intervened in 1924. Hughes was certain that "there could be no economic recuperation in Europe unless Germany recuperates."[21] And without the return of prosperity, Europe would remain in the grip of dangerous political tensions and popular discontents. Acting on a set of propositions widely accepted in the United States, the secretary of state behaved in a predictably corporatist fashion. He appointed the Chicago banker Charles G. Dawes and the chief of General Electric and RCA, Owen D. Young, to head a commission to tackle the debt-reparations tangle.

Young epitomized the elite collaboration at the heart of Republican foreign policy during the 1920s. This New York farm boy made good had joined GE as its legal counsel in 1913 and led the company between 1922 and 1945 to a dominant position in the new field of consumer electronics. Young came into the orbit of u.s. policy in 1919 when he established the Radio Corporation of America, prompted by the Wilson administration's determination that foreigners not gain control of the emerging, strategically important radio industry. The German debt issue was his next political challenge. Meanwhile he oversaw GE's expansion into a major player overseas with important production facilities and markets (with investments over $100 million by 1930), while also serving on the boards of leading European firms, cultivating major figures in international business and finance, and advocating an enlightened, cooperative form of capitalism. He was as cosmopolitan in his outlook and contacts as GE was in its business.[22]

Dawes and Young worked closely with the Senate and State Department to devise a debt solution. One part was a loan of $110 million arranged by the banking house of J. P. Morgan to ease the German financial situation and send an encouraging signal to U.S. capital markets. The other part of the solution was to scale down German reparations payments to more manageable levels. The so-called Dawes plan seemed to work. Between 1925 and 1930 U.S. capital markets supplied $2.3 billion to German borrowers, while the former Entente powers were able in turn to send $2.6 billion back to the United States. But the German economy continued to sputter, so in 1929, with default of the debt looming, the Hoover administration predictably turned to Young for help. A new agreement, implemented in 1930 after considerable wrangling among the concerned powers, lowered the German debt from $33 billion to $9 billion and pushed debt payments below the point set in the Dawes plan. As part of the Young plan, the Hoover administration agreed to participate in a new Bank for International Settlement to help central banks coordinate reparations transfers. Despite these efforts, Germany moved toward default in 1932 having paid only $5 billion in reparations.

Republican economic policy has come in for as much criticism as its approach to national security. The critics charge that tariff increases in 1922 (Fordney-McCumber) and again in 1930 (Smoot-Hawley) obstructed European exports to the large and prosperous U.S. market and thus frustrated European efforts to put their accounts in order, regain prosperity, and settle their debts. Such short-sighted protectionism contributed to the 1929 financial crisis, which in turn spawned the Great Depression, widespread material privation, political discontent, and ultimately war. This charge of economic incompetence is simplistic if not wrong. U.S. tariffs were at best a marginal part of the difficulties plaguing the postwar European economies. Their exports generally suffered from a lack of competitiveness on international markets that rendered tariff barriers largely irrelevant, while U.S. firms enjoyed at home as well as overseas a distinct advantage—in technology that raised worker productivity, in easy access to abundant raw materials, and in the availability of an enormous, integrated, and fairly homogeneous home market that kept production runs long and the cost of goods low. Only in small-scale, handicraft-type production was Europe competitive, but in this case the opening of the u.s. market would not have resulted in sales great enough to stimulate the European economy and generate the income for debt repayment. That economy was burdened by a second problem also beyond Washington's control—pervasive underconsumption. Workers on low wages could not purchase the goods and services on a scale to spur European production. Other internal causes for economic stagnation included a continental market fragmented into national pieces, underinvestment in new technology and in industry, and infrastructure devoured by the war. These structural problems in the economy were in turn compounded by political problems. Germans resented heavy reparations and used u.s. loans to maintain social welfare rather than invest in production that might have helped to pay the debt. The French for their part were ready to see Germany default in order to retain control of strategic parts of their intensely contested frontier (the Rhineland, the Saar, and the Ruhr). It was no more within the u.s. power to tamp down smoldering nationalist rivalry than to remake a struggling European economy.

The critics of Republican economic policy contend that Hoover might have done more to arrest the downward spiral by intervening in the financial markets following the 1929 crash. Prompt government intervention in the markets and strong deficit spending would arguably have slowed plummeting stock values, contained the panic, and arrested the demoralizing deflation in the value of goods and income. These steps might well have spared the world much material suffering and perhaps ultimately the disaster of another war. The only problem is that this critique is anachronistic. The notion that markets would not self-correct and that government should bail out business on a massive scale was anathema at the time. Bold state intervention in the economy would have to wait for fresh insight from economists like John Maynard Keynes who in the 1930s were only beginning to figure out the reasons for market failure. It would also have to wait for a more permissive political attitude toward broad state powers as a result of economic depression, world war, and cold war.

Guided by their commitment to stabilize Europe and their corporate values, the interwar Republicans continued Wilson's stoutly anti-Bolshevik policy. They too regarded the Soviet state as illegitimate—a pernicious threat to private property and social order—and sought to isolate it internationally. Also like Wilson, they expressed their solicitude for the Russian people's welfare and the hope that Russia would in time get back on track and (in Coolidge's telling phrase) "take up the burden of civilization with the rest of us." Their confidence in capitalism led Washington to turn a blind eye to technology transfers, which were high on the Soviet agenda and profitable for General

Electric and Ford. Droves of u.s. engineers and other industrial specialists went to work in the Soviet Union and might, some hoped, demonstrate that Bolshevism was an inefficient dead end. Even Soviet leader Joseph Stalin was willing to single out for public praise "American efficiency [as] that indomitable force . . . without which serious constructive work is inconceivable."[23]

While waiting for the ultimate demise of communism, Republican administrations focused on making sure that communist agitators did not make inroads in Europe and complicate the tasks of stabilization. Conservative American observers felt anxiety about the Bolshevik specter hanging over industrial Europe that was the counterpoint to European nationalists and traditionalists alarmed by the inroads of consumer culture. To contain the Bolshevik danger, u.s. policymakers in the 1920s turned to strongmen. The State Department accordingly favored General Francisco Franco in his destruction of the left-leaning Spanish Republic in the late 1930s and approved of the Greek dictatorship set up by General John Metaxas in 1936. The official u.s. response to the rise of Italy's Benito Mussolini stands as the most striking example of this approach. Italy figured as one of those countries vulnerable to subversion because the people "had undertaken to govern themselves without quite having learned the hang of it" (as Root, the Republican elder statesman, observed in 1926). Treasury Secretary Andrew Mellon was so impressed by Mussolini's success at bringing order that he orchestrated a debt settlement that in turn opened u.s. capital markets. By 1930 Americans had invested almost $900 million in Italy, and a senior partner at J. P. Morgan could boast that the investment bank had become the dictator's "loyal and disinterested counselors on all external finance problems." The Republicans regretted the excesses committed by the ruling Fascists—political repression and destruction of the constitution—while insisting that order was essential to creating prosperity and holding Bolshevism at bay.[24]

The Republicans were no less active in promoting u.s. corporate advantage overseas. They sought to pry open countries containing essential commodities such as nitrate, rubber, and oil. In the major case of oil, Washington worked with Jersey Standard and other u.s. firms, in some cases to gain access to European-controlled territory and in others to win over wary Latin American governments. U.S. firms scored major successes, gaining concessions in Venezuela, the Dutch East Indies, and Iraq and other parts of the defunct Ottoman Empire that had passed into British hands. While the oil companies got production critical to servicing their global distribution networks, Republican policymakers prided themselves on vindicating the open-door principle important to u.s. economic expansion. Those policymakers also encouraged private enterprise to build strategic communications links. The British had a stranglehold on the strategically sensitive long-distance cable business, but American companies with strong backing from Washington exploited new technology to nullify the British cable advantage, especially in Latin America. Pan American emerged as a leader in international aviation, while RCA proved the commercial possibilities of radio.

The valiant Republican effort to promote global integration and coopera-tion had had the support of an increasing number of internationally engaged nongovernmental organizations. By 1930, according to one estimate, some 375 were operating, three times their pre–World War I numbers.[25] These groups were part of a lively and increasingly dense traffic across the North Atlantic. Among the travelers were political and social reformers eager to learn from the variety of experiments being conducted in other countries. Also going abroad were economic and legal technicians and natural and social scientists convinced that knowledge as a progressive force knew no boundaries. Making the transatlantic passage, too, were tourists, peace activists representing such groups as the American Friends Service Committee (established in 1917), and athletes (some to participate in the quadrennial Olympic Games revived in 1896). This traffic was made possible—and sometimes was occasioned by—discussions among governments concerning the rules meant to govern global contact. These discussions, commonplace during the decades before World War I, resumed after the war and led to international rules for aviation, radio broadcasting, shipping, and wildlife protection.

But the Republicans and their internationally minded allies faced destruc-tive forces already gathering strength and well beyond their power to control. Nationalist ideologies and economic instability frayed the fabric of global inte-gration and then shredded it altogether. The damage began even before World War I with reactions on the European continent against the social costs of free market policies. Cries for protection were getting ever louder and more politi-cally potent. The war itself dealt even more damage and marked the real on-slaught against the global connections created over the previous half century as states began channeling trade along regional lines to national advantage and as borders hardened against the movement of people and ideas as well as goods. The pressure continued with the rising economic imbalances and political grievances among the North Atlantic states after the war, and came to a climax during the Great Depression, which drove higher already substan-tial state controls on capital movement, trade, and migration. The deepening

European loss of faith in a future of peace and prosperity helped create a global climate of insecurity toxic to cultivating ties among states and peoples. A 1931 League of Nations report clearly articulated the profound nature of the mounting crisis: "The operation of the world's economic organization rests on confidence; as soon as this disappears it undergoes profound disturbances and the evil spreads rapidly." Ahead lay an industrial war of global scale that would take some 60 million lives. The slaughter would prompt one war correspondent to describe what he saw as "dead men by mass production . . . in one country after another—month after month and year after year. Dead men in winter. Dead men in summer. Dead men in such familiar promiscuity that they become monotonous. Dead men in such monstrous infinity that you come almost to hate them." The Republicans had with good reason sought to hold the mayhem at bay![26]

FDR's Odyssey

The downward economic spiral from 1929 to 1933 brought hard times. Franco-German friction intensified. Beggar-thy-neighbor protectionist policies and restrictive trading blocs were the order of the day as international trade fell, investment capital dried up, and currency suffered from instability. The resulting popular suffering smoothed Hitler's way to power in Germany and facilitated Japan's assault on China. No less significant, the u.s. public lost confidence in Republican rule, and in 1932 the Democratic presidential candidate, Franklin Roosevelt, handily defeated Hoover's reelection bid.

Roosevelt brought to office familiar northeastern establishment traits. His was a wealthy, socially prominent New York family of Dutch stock. He was well schooled (Hotchkiss and Harvard), pro-British, and internationally minded. Modeling himself on his cousin, Theodore Roosevelt, he had retraced that worthy's path to the presidency, serving as the assistant secretary of the navy under Wilson, then running as the Democrats' candidate for vice president in 1920, and finally securing the New York governorship in 1928. The younger Roosevelt had launched his political career as a staunch Wilsonian. He had strongly backed the president's decision for war in 1917 and championed his peace plan during the 1920 election.

During his first two terms Roosevelt acted out of the same sense of caution that had guided the Republicans—and with good reason. The world economy was firmly in the grip of depression, accentuating social and interstate tensions in Europe. At home unemployment was the fate of a quarter of all workers and nearly two out of five workers in the industrial sector in

Roosevelt's first year in office. Social suffering and political discontent was rife. Under the circumstances Congress and public opinion became strongly averse to foreign adventures.

A group of midwestern progressives within the Republican party were the most outspoken advocates of restraint. The leading voice was William E. Borah, an Idaho senator and staunch ("Irreconcilable") opponent of Wilson's peace terms. As chair of the foreign relations committee from 1925 to 1933, he argued for keeping a distance from Europe with its nationalist quarrels, its imperialist instincts, and its militarist traditions. The loss of life and treasure and of domestic liberty as a result of World War I had confirmed for him the dangers of political or military entanglement. Americans could not put back together the European Humpty Dumpty that had shattered in 1914 and would suffer themselves in any attempt. Senator Gerald Nye, a Borah-style Republican progressive from North Dakota, helped crystallize the deepening disillusionment with Wilson's crusade. Hearings he conducted in 1935 blamed bankers and munitions-makers. These "merchants of death" had together with propagandists for the British cause aroused the public and maneuvered the Wilson administration into war.

These findings supported congressional efforts to constrain the president. Neutrality legislation passed in 1935 sought to avoid a repeat of Wilson's mishandled neutrality policy by restricting wartime arms sales, loans to belligerents, and travel by Americans on the high seas. Congress then took up a measure (the Ludlow amendment), calling for a public referendum on any presidential recommendation for war. This notion of giving the public as well as Congress a say had the support of 73 percent of the public in fall 1937. Seven of ten Americans had already in an earlier poll flatly pronounced entering World War I a mistake.[27] Multiplying evils overseas fed this public resistance to fresh involvement. Italy had invaded Ethiopia; Germany had reoccupied the Rhineland; Spain had erupted into civil war, with Germany, Italy, and the Soviet Union intervening on opposing sides; and Japan had seized control of China's northeast provinces (known as Manchuria) and then embarked on its invasion of the rest of China.

Roosevelt knew that any meddling in Europe would engulf him in controversy at a time when he needed to focus on the depression. In 1933 at the very start of his administration he wiggled out of an international conference in London called to address the lingering debt issue, now compounded by widespread default. He saw greater promise in promoting free trade agreements. They would not only relieve the glut at home and restart the engine of global

commerce but also counter the pervasive trend toward economic bloc building on the part of the great powers—Britain and France within their imperial
domains, Germany in eastern and southeastern Europe (Hungary, Rumania,
Bulgaria, Yugoslavia, Greece, and Turkey), and Japan in East Asia. Secretary
of State Cordell Hull, who led the campaign, believed even more devoutly
than the president in the dream of a revived, integrated global system. He regarded removing obstacles to commerce as economically beneficial but also as
conducive to international peace and understanding. Privation was bound to
foment popular discontent, international tensions, and ultimately interstate
conflict. Congress went along with Hull in 1934, giving the executive branch
power to negotiate bilateral agreements cutting tariffs. By 1940 he had in
hand twenty-two such agreements. To further facilitate trade deals for u.s.
goods, the administration created the Export-Import Bank in 1934. The bank
began as an ad hoc instrument for the president's policies toward the Soviet
Union and Cuba, but it became a permanent part of the Washington bureaucracy because it gave the executive a mechanism to promote trade through
loans, insurance, or other assistance comparable to the tools available to European and Japanese officials.

This commitment to expanded trade led Roosevelt to break with his predecessors on handling the Soviets. Rather than containing Moscow, he was ready
to engage it in hopes of gaining access to an untapped outlet for u.s. goods.
Roosevelt may have also seen the Soviet Union as a potential strategic counter
to Japan's advance into Manchuria. Bypassing a resistant, conservative State
Department, the president himself took charge of negotiations and established formal diplomatic ties in 1933. The relationship failed to develop further. With neither the United States nor Britain willing to coordinate security
policy, Stalin finally entered into nonaggression pacts, first with Germany in
August 1939 and then with Japan in April 1941. A disappointed Soviet leader
also held back on the other parts of his deal with Roosevelt, including the
final settlement of debts contracted by the Czarist government and an end
to communist subversion in the United States. This unsatisfactory outcome
confirmed skeptics of Roosevelt's overtures in their belief that the Bolshevik
contagion was in remission, nothing more.

Roosevelt began his second term still wary in the face of rising international tensions. During his campaign for reelection he expressed a disillusionment with the World War I crusade that roughly paralleled the public's.
An August 1936 speech recalled a litany of horrors from a tour of the western
front in 1918: "Blood running from the wounded. . . . men coughing out their
gassed lungs. . . . the dead in the mud. . . . children starving. . . . the agony

of mothers and wives."[28] Though reelected handily, Roosevelt still responded tentatively to Japan's invasion of China and German remilitarization. In a speech delivered in Chicago in October 1937 in the wake of these events, he strongly condemned outlaw states, a transparent reference to Germany and Italy as well as Japan, and warned of the peril they posed. But his call for an international "quarantine" of aggressors was vague and was in any case softened by his pious wish to preserve peace. Facing the prospect of a German invasion of Poland in 1939, he made an international appeal for peace—an initiative that one u.s. diplomat compared to "a valentine sent to somebody's mother-in-law out of season." When Britain and France responded to the invasion with a declaration of war, Roosevelt still took a cautious public stance and maintained it through most of 1940 as he focused on his bid for a third term in the White House. Though the Wilsonian in Roosevelt was beginning to stir beneath the surface (as we'll see in the next chapter), he was careful to conceal it.[29]

UNREST ON THE PERIPHERY

Interwar leaders confronted a mounting crisis not only in Europe, the old core of global politics and economy, but also in two other regions in which the United States had recently staked out a presence. In Latin America and East Asia as in other places under the North Atlantic sway—in countries that would soon be classified third world—the status quo was breaking down. Nationalist ideas were one of the solvents. In achieving their dominance, Europeans had demonstrated nationalism's potency, and through the schooling they supplied to indigenous peoples, they made normative the notion of self-contained, culturally distinct, and politically sovereign communities. The lesson was that everyone had an inherent right to nationhood, and once in possession of state power, national communities could achieve great things. The brutal bloodletting Europeans inflicted on themselves between 1914 and 1918 deepened doubts about their claims to represent civilizational superiority and hence their right to control the lives of the "less advanced." The Bolsheviks accepted and exploited the lesson. Their revolutionary government in Moscow held itself up as an example and an ally for struggling nationalist elites in lands all along the periphery and in 1919 it created the Communist International to demonstrate that it alone among the centers of world power was genuinely committed to a new international order. As the prospects for revolution in Europe receded, Moscow began scanning the periphery with greater interest.

Between the wars u.s. policymakers reacted to these two ideologies of liberation with considerable concern. Toward Bolshevism they expressed an un-ambiguous hostility. Nationalism posed a more complicated challenge. Colonial peoples deserved independence—but only when they were ready. Thus Wilson's successors fundamentally agreed with him on the third world's incapacity even if they preferred to deal with its tendency toward instability—particularly in Latin America and East Asia—with a greater mix of caution and sophistication than Wilson had shown.

Be Nice to the Neighbors

Latin America was the main troubled point on the periphery commanding the attention of postwar U.S. policymakers. The mastery of the region—initiated by Republican presidents and then pressed aggressively by Wilson—was stronger than ever. This U.S. sphere of influence was safe from European powers weakened by war. At the same time the U.S. economic stake in the region had grown larger. Investments tripled between 1914 and 1929 when they reached $5.4 billion. The rising tide of U.S. enterprise and goods spurred Americanization trends similar to those in Europe. Consumer products from the United States had a popular allure, and travelers and commentators stood in awe of the wealth generated and distributed by the technologically advanced U.S. economy.[30]

But mastery—strategic, financial, and commercial—came at a cost, as Republicans returning to office in 1921 recognized. Frequent armed intervention had created a self-reinforcing cycle of hostility, instability, and more intervention. Communist parties took root, and nationalist politicians, military officers, and government bureaucrats took aim at Yankee imperialism. They made respect for national sovereignty against meddling U.S. diplomats a rallying cry. They asserted ownership of natural resources such as oil controlled by foreign investors. They denounced U.S. firms grabbing those resources as "boa constrictors" that could swallow small countries whole and squeeze large ones to death. These intrusive Americans, so cultural critics reminded their compatriots, were all the more contemptible because they were shaped by a spiritually empty civilization.[31]

Republican policymakers shifted to a more restrained strategy, convinced that it might not only work better but also cost less. The Republicans began liquidating the occupations carried over from the Wilson years confident that economic penetration and cultural suasion rather than armed intervention would bring both stability and development. This adjustment of Latin American policy would change the form but not the substance of U.S. domination. In the face of resistance or unrest, Republican policymakers relied on strongmen who could do the job that earlier required the u.s. Marines. Washington embraced wealthy landed interests and ambitious military leaders who saw their self-interest well served by close collaboration.

President Coolidge and Secretary of State Hughes cautiously began the shift toward a kinder, gentler application of the Monroe Doctrine. Coolidge's view was that it was best to "leave those countries as undisturbed as possible to work out their own salvation."[32] While Hughes affirmed the right of armed intervention (what he characterized in lawyer talk as "nonbelligerent inter-position") and rejected Latin American proposals making nonintervention the law of the hemisphere, he also called for carefully limiting that right. To underline his doubts about the utility of force, he refused to intervene in Cuba during a period of unrest in 1923 and then withdrew troops from the Domini-can Republic in 1924 and Nicaragua in 1925. In keeping with the emerging new outlook, he arranged for a $25 million payment to Colombia—in effect compensation for Theodore Roosevelt's role in prying loose that country's Panama territory two decades earlier. The State Department took a step back from bankers recruited during the dollar diplomacy era to help underwrite the goals of u.s. Latin American policy.

Hoover carried the Republican policy of restraint to the next step. He intro-duced the rhetoric of good neighborliness, and in 1930 he publicly separated the Roosevelt corollary (with its sweeping claim to police powers) from the original Monroe Doctrine (with its emphasis on the distinction between the Old World and the New World). He withdrew the marines from Nicaragua in 1933 and prepared to pull them out of Haiti. He committed the United States to recognizing de facto governments, in effect reversing Wilson's position of dealing only with those that met his moral standard.

What began as a trend under the Republicans came to a consummation under the Democratic Roosevelt. On coming into the White House in March 1933, he borrowed Hoover's language and announced his desire to make the United States a "good neighbor." The depression encouraged Roosevelt to fol-low the Republican path and eschew the crusading spirit so characteristic of his old boss and idol, Woodrow Wilson. Good relations were more likely to secure for u.s. products access to Latin American markets. War clouds gather-ing in Europe by the late 1930s provided another reason for cooperation. Build-ing regional solidarity behind u.s. leadership seemed the best way to contain German influence. At a series of conferences from 1933 onward Roosevelt and Hull responded to continued Latin American calls for nonintervention with their own formal declarations of the new policy of good neighborliness and with public renunciation of armed intervention as a tool of u.s. policy. Like the Republicans, they were careful to make none of these pledges absolute or legally binding.

Nowhere did the new interwar approach face a greater challenge than in Mexico. Its revolution had from its start in 1911 a distinctly anti-American turn that grew stronger following Wilson's interventions of 1914 and 1917. The constitution of 1917 reflected the revolution's economic nationalism stimulated by an influx of foreign capital. The resulting restrictions on the rights of foreign investors and the nationalization of subsoil rights to mine and drill alarmed Republicans at the helm of u.s. policy. Hughes feared Mexico was launched on a "socialist experiment," while the u.s. ambassador in Mexico lapsed into crude stereotyping in his assessment of the Mexican revolution. He concluded that its leaders had "very little white blood"—and fumed that the "Latin-Indians" who made up the country's population "in the final analysis recognize no arguments but force."[33] Policymakers in Washington, however, also recognized that Wilson's militant response had already proven barren of results—and indeed made a bad situation worse. They sought instead to smooth relations by recognizing the Mexican government (as Wilson had not), negotiating a compromise on the contentious issue of economic rights, and in general expressing tolerance for differences and keeping channels of diplomacy open.

Mexico again tested good neighbor intentions when in 1938 the government expropriated u.s. and other foreign oil properties. Hull wanted to back the foreign owners in part because he saw the hand of "communists down there" and in part because he felt principles of international law and the sanctity of private property were at stake.[34] Roosevelt, however, sided with the advocates of accommodation, notably Ambassador Josephus Daniels in Mexico and Secretary of the Treasury Henry Morgenthau. Washington accepted the legality of this expropriation and brokered a settlement between Mexico and the oil companies just as the United States was drifting into war.

In Nicaragua, another proving ground for the good neighbor policy, a bankrupt intervention strategy gave way to what seemed like a successful reliance on strongman rule. U.S. troops had gone into the country in 1912 and left in 1925, only to return the next year to pull apart quarreling political parties. In 1927 Coolidge and Kellogg sent Henry L. Stimson south as a troubleshooter with instructions to extricate u.s. forces from this quagmire while somehow maintaining order among a politically volatile people. Stimson set in motion a strongman strategy. He cultivated Anastasio Somoza, a fluent English-speaker with pro-u.s. and pro-business views, and placed him at the head of the u.s.-trained military force. The marines were able to pull out in 1933, and the next year Somoza's force confirmed its worth by capturing and killing Augusto Sandino, the internationally celebrated symbol of resistance to U.S. imperialism. Somoza took the presidency in 1936. His family dynasty controlled the country until 1979 and delivered the stability Washington perennially craved.

As Hoover's secretary of state, Stimson again confirmed the utility of military strongmen. In El Salvador political activism by students, peasants, and trade unions as well as the Communist party had led to violence and raised before Stimson's eyes the specter of "a rather nasty proletarian revolution."[35] In early 1932 the military saved the day by seizing power and crushing the leftist opposition. The Hoover administration gave its quiet blessings, and the next year the incoming Roosevelt administration publicly endorsed the new military dictatorship as one more welcome force for order in Central America.

Cuba soon offered yet another demonstration of how the good neighbor approach combined with strongman rule. During the twenties Cuba had become more and more an appendage of the U.S. economy. U.S. investments had grown from less than $50 million in 1897 to about $1.7 billion in 1929.[36] American-owned firms dominated the island's economy and U.S.-made goods flooded its markets. When a government headed by Ramón Grau San Martín came to power in 1933, Hull feared communist inroads. To head off trouble, Roosevelt dispatched Sumner Welles, an old schoolmate and career diplomat, to Havana. Welles, too, decided that the Grau government was under "frankly communistic" influence and called for U.S. troops to set things right. Roosevelt rejected overt intervention as a gross affront to good neighborliness. But his sense of paternalism was still strong. He felt a "duty to do what we could so that there should be no starvation or chaos among the Cuban people." He thus backed Welles in his confrontation with the new government by withholding diplomatic recognition and sending warships in a display of force. Taking a page from Stimson's book, Welles found in Fulgencio Batista someone willing to impose order and respect U.S. preferences. This army sergeant emerged as the new kingmaker in Cuban politics. In January 1934 Batista deposed Grau, and in May Washington indicated confidence in the new Batista-backed government by increasing the quota of Cuban sugar allowed into the U.S. market, making loans to promote the purchase of U.S. goods, and abrogating the Platt amendment (the legal basis for U.S. military intervention in Cuba). In the close relationship with Washington that would last until 1959, the authoritarian Batista made the island a safe haven for U.S. firms, off limits to troublemaking radicals, and a strong point in U.S. hemispheric defenses.[37]

An East Asia in Ferment

In an increasingly global U.S. policy, East Asia posed a puzzle. Officials in Washington lacked the leverage they could exercise in the other two critical regions, Europe and Latin America. They were also ambivalent about the region's importance. It did not compare strategically or economically with either Europe or Latin America, but they could not turn their back on the western Pacific where U.S. prestige was invested in the Philippines and the open-door policy applied to China's trade and territorial integrity.

The appeal of nationalism and communism across interwar East Asia compounded the difficulties for U.S. policymakers and raised the risks of involvement. The Chinese and Japanese were not only at odds with each other, but the antagonism felt by both toward the United States would generate conflict that would persist into the 1970s. In both countries "wealth and power" figured prominently as the prime national goals, and both prized the state as the indispensable agent for realizing those goals. Neither saw the United States as a political model, and neither could easily accommodate U.S. dreams of influence in the region. An increasingly intrusive U.S. presence disillusioned some regional elites and deepened the hostility of others. A pattern already in play in Latin America, it would in time regulate U.S. relations with virtually the entire third world.

Among Chinese officials and intellectuals, hopes that the United States might serve as a diplomatic counterweight against the more aggressive powers and as a developmental model were strongest at the end of the nineteenth century but thereafter steadily dwindled. Chinese visitors to the United States reported mistreatment of their immigrant countrymen and of African Americans. They viewed the American electoral system as a crude, contentious, and tumultuous process in which unprincipled factions wrangled, bought their way to power, and distributed the spoils of office. The U.S. conquest of the Philippines, a small weak neighbor whose plight Chinese observers identified with, carried a particularly strong symbolic charge. More and more, politically engaged Chinese such as Liang Qichao worried that the broader American expansion across the Pacific at the turn of the century would turn aggressive, driven by a maturing capitalist system with an insatiable appetite for overseas markets.

The collapse of the last imperial dynasty (the Qing) in 1912 and its replacement by a weak republican government accentuated a radical drift in elite political views and with it an intensified animus toward the United States. Chinese nationalists denounced U.S. and other missionaries as part of a "Christian invasion," demanded an end to the special privileges foreigners of all stripes claimed through treaties imposed on China at gunpoint, and occasionally resorted to antiforeigner violence. In 1927 the Nationalist Party of Chiang Kai-shek established the closest thing to a central government that interwar China would have. His party-state sought to secure greater respect for China's sovereignty, which had been massively compromised by the major powers and would be directly threatened by the late 1930s by Japanese aggression. The Chinese Communist Party, Chiang's most dangerous domestic challenger, espoused a strong anti-imperialist program that had much in common with the outlook of the rival Nationalist Party. The Communists took the position—also not so different from Chiang's—that only a strong, centralized state could transform China's foreign relations and create the unity and wealth necessary to achieve national security and independence.

Through the 1920s Republican policymakers sought to appease the increasingly nationalist sentiment in China even while they worried about the spread of what was loosely characterized as "Bolshevik activities and propaganda."[38] Whatever the threat to u.s. interests, Washington did not see intervention as an option and indeed recognized that it would intensify nationalist resentments to u.s. disadvantage. Washington instead offered support (tepid to be sure) for revision of the much-hated unequal treaties and otherwise looked to Chiang's authoritarian Nationalist Party to maintain order, contain the Communists, and keep the door open to American businessmen and missionaries. Once more a military strongman seemed the most effective available ally.

Japanese nationalists with their great-power goals posed a challenge that Washington could less easily sidestep. Beginning in 1868, reformers acting in the name of the Meiji emperor had laid the foundations for realizing those goals. They replaced a feudal political system with a centralized bureaucratic state, propagated a nationalist ideology, created a professional armed force, promoted economic development and mass education, and identified the imperial institution as the soul of the new nation-state. That this Japanese version of modernity diverged from the u.s. model was a matter of considered choice. Much like Chinese who mused on the American way, Japanese inspecting the United States for lessons had come away uncomfortable. They found a society shockingly at odds with core Confucian values; they noted the chaos of democracy, unrestrained individualism, an indifference to social ritual, and gender roles that gave women far too public a place. The American initiatives of 1898 raised new concerns. The acquisition of Hawaii and the Philippines and enthusiastic declarations on American destiny in the Pacific collided with Japanese aspirations to become a regional power. Restrictions on Japanese immigration to the West Coast and the Taft-Knox opposition to Tokyo's growing influence in Northeast China in the wake of the Russo-Japanese War accentuated the rivalry and resentment. When the Japanese delegation to the Paris peace conference asked for a formal statement on racial equality, the European and American refusal spoke volumes. One member of the Japanese delegation with a bright political future warned that the postwar Anglo-American dominance threatened Japanese with "rampant economic imperialism" and the humiliation of racial discrimination.[39]

Increasingly u.s. observers and policymakers reciprocated Japanese resentments and suspicions. The sweeping reforms launched in 1868 seemed to place Japan on the proper (Western) path of development. But already by the late 1890s, Japan's assertive regional role put in question the prospects for its development along peaceful, civilized lines. Following the thrashing of China in 1894–95, Japan took Taiwan and demanded a sphere of influence in the adjacent mainland province of Fujian. "Oriental" Japan's dramatic victory over "European" Russia in 1905 did as much to shake Americans as Japan's ensuing takeover of Korea and its consolidation of control in the southern part of Manchuria. Japan appeared increasingly like a deviant: Westernization was bringing industry, education, and even multiparty politics yet not eradicating the country's feudal, militaristic outlook. Lodge echoed a widespread view when in 1919 he characterized Japan as "the Prussia of the East," with its overriding goal "to get control of China."[40]

Through the 1920s the Republicans struggled to maintain good relations with Japan. They rejected the belligerent policy that Taft and Knox had earlier advocated and sided instead with Roosevelt's policy of accommodation. The payoff came at the Washington conference in 1921–22. Treaties concluded there headed off a Pacific naval race and enshrined in international law the open-door commitment to the preservation of China as a political entity. These broad agreements facilitated cooperation between Washington and Tokyo through the balance of the decade despite friction over China, over relative naval strength in the Pacific, and over Congress's termination of Japanese immigration in 1924.

This rough working relationship collapsed in 1931 when the Japanese army went on its rampage in Manchuria. Provoked by Chinese nationalists, the army violently asserted formal control. The government in Tokyo bowed to this fait accompli even though it knew the high cost it would pay in u.s. ill will. Finding a way to express that ill will fell primarily to Stimson. After service in Nicaragua, he had become governor-general of the Philippines (1927–29) and then Hoover's secretary of state (1929–33). Stimson soon concluded that Japan's conquest directly challenged the carefully worked-out agreements of the 1920s and with them the open door and the American claim to be a major voice in the future of the region. Japan's disregard of its treaty obligations pained but did not surprise him. He mused at a cabinet meeting in early October 1931 that these Western-style international agreements fit the Japanese as "a stovepipe hat would fit an African savage."[41] He favored threatening Tokyo with a naval race, confident that a far superior u.s. economy was bound to win. Hoover demurred. In the midst of the depression, he had neither the public support nor the funds to pursue such a course, and so he settled for a half measure: a formal and emphatic refusal to recognize Japan's Manchurian conquest but backed by no meaningful action.

When Roosevelt and Hull came into office in 1933, they sympathized emotionally with Stimson's hard-line response but in fact followed the hesitant course set by Hoover. Even the outbreak of war between China and Japan in July 1937 did not alter the public stance of the Roosevelt administration. But in the poisoned international atmosphere of the late 1930s Roosevelt was privately at least beginning to question whether half measures were enough. Leaders in Tokyo for their part were ever more resolutely asserting themselves against the threat posed by hostile Chinese nationalists, pro-Soviet Chinese Communists, and colonies and naval bases belonging to the United States and Britain. They were alternately irritated and perplexed by u.s. criticism of Japan for carving out Japan's proper Asian sphere of influence, while Washington took as a natural right American dominance in Latin America. Prospects for accommodation looked steadily dimmer; war seemed ever more likely.

In the 1940s and 1950s policy intellectuals would ridicule interwar leaders as wrongheaded "isolationists" who failed to prevent things from going disastrously wrong first in Europe and ultimately on a global scale. In 1914 a world at peace amid a rising tide of wealth stumbled into a thirty-year military and economic catastrophe. By 1945 millions upon millions lay dead, many of the world's leading cities were in rubble, starvation was widespread, and hope was shattered. This outcome was, at least according to what became orthodox Cold War era thinking, the result of a naïve dedication to peace and disarmament.

This critique, which has hardened into a widely accepted myth, obscures the achievements of the interwar period and misreads its place in the broad sweep of u.s. foreign relations. Policymakers and commentators refined attitudes and practices devised during the McKinley-Wilson era. They found new ways to sustain u.s. dominance in Latin America, while handling Europe and East Asia with a shrewd caution appropriate to regions too important to neglect but too dangerous to embrace. At the same time the policy elite presided over a vital, resilient economy, a maturing consumer model, and a large accumulation of capital that taken together gave the country unrivaled economic and cultural clout. Far from a time of lost opportunities and naïve miscalculations, the interwar period had prepared the American state to meet the challenges posed first by World War II and then by the Cold War. Americans could boast an unmatched capacity to wage war on a global scale, a strong sense of national mission, and a rich and dynamic economy. It was time to bid for ascendancy.

4

REACHING FOR GEOPOLITICAL DOMINANCE

1941★1968

Adolf Hitler appeared on the cover of *Time* in April 1941, a brooding, composed, flesh-and-blood figure, his preoccupied gaze directed into the distance (fig. 4). The accompanying article informed readers that he had asserted total control in Germany and then embarked on continental conquest. He had shattered Czechoslovakia, Poland, Austria, Norway, Belgium, and Denmark; he had reduced France and Italy to fawning dependencies; his forces were bearing down on Yugoslavia and Greece; and Britain lay vulnerable to attack from air and sea. Even as the article appeared, the German army was preparing its plunge deep into the Soviet Union. Hitler now stood on the brink, *Time* warned, of making himself "master of at least half the world" and then (still more ominously) of reconstructing "mankind in his image."[1]

Time's dark appraisal reflected the views of its founder and hands-on editor, Henry Luce. This hard-driving, chain-smoking, intellectually intense, emotionally introspective media mogul had concluded that Hitler was a deadly peril not because his regime was internally repressive but because it was territorially aggressive. As late as the summer of 1938 during a trip through Europe, he had praised the German leader's achievements and excused his excesses. German annexation of a great chunk of Czechoslovakia in the fall finally set off alarm bells at the top of Time, Inc.'s New York headquarters. Early the next year Hitler appeared on *Time*'s cover as man of the year, now depicted in caricature as an "unholy organist" playing "a hymn of hate." During 1940 Luce began rehearsing in radio addresses as well as talks to select audiences the proper u.s. response to German aggression. The upshot was a carefully considered essay, published in February 1941 in his popular *Life* magazine, heralding "the American Century." He called on Americans "as the most powerful and vital nation in the world" to assert themselves as interna-

Figure 4. "HITLER: *Spring is here. (World War),*" *cover of* Time, *14 April 1941.*
(TIME *Magazine © 1941 Time Inc. Reprinted by permission.*)

tional champions of "the triumphal purpose of freedom." Their most immediate task was stopping the German bid to dominate Europe. But beyond that, Luce saw great and enduring global obligations to assume. Thanks to his sway over the Republican Party and his editorial control of widely read journals, Luce's voice mattered more than most any other American's at that time, and his views continued to resonate through the coming war and beyond.[2]

Luce's manifesto omitted one critical element—a discussion of the heavy tasks that fell to the American state if it were to stop aggression and go on to wield the international military and political dominance equal to the economic and cultural primacy already established in the 1920s. One of those tasks was ideological: determining the source of the European crisis and devising a conceptually compelling u.s. response. Hitler's Germany got the process going, and under the postwar Soviet shadow a powerful state orthodoxy took form. The second was a dexterity in war making. U.S. advantages, especially in technological innovation and economic mobilization, contributed to decisive victories on two fronts in World War II and gave Washington a distinct advantage in its prolonged confrontation with the Soviet Union. The final task was institutional—the creation of a full-blown imperial presidency devoted above all to matters of "national security." What William McKinley, Woodrow Wilson, and the interwar Republicans had begun in making the White House the nerve center of the nation, Roosevelt and Truman completed in the course of waging the conflicts of the 1940s. Regarded by Congress and the public as the country's embodiment and voice, the president gained broad latitude to identify threats to national security and direct the full range of governmental resources around the globe. Thanks to these developments, the American state would not only help master Europe's thirty-year crisis but also emerge as the new, undisputed power center of the North Atlantic world.

AN EDUCATION IN AGGRESSION

Challengers to the international status quo at midcentury provided u.s. leaders a kind of education. The schooling began under Franklin D. Roosevelt in the face of German and Japanese expansion, and it continued under Harry S. Truman as he assessed the postwar gains and intentions of the Soviet Union. Experience with challengers seen as "aggressive" helped fuse nationalist ideas already in play into a foreign policy orthodoxy. The prime u.s. obligation was to put an end to aggression and create a world of peace and prosperity. Perfectly in line with the views Luce had propounded in 1941, this new ideological construct had a firm grip on the thinking of the foreign policy establishment and the advisers to the president by the late 1940s and reached its high point of influence in the 1950s and early 1960s. As the fundamental proposition sustaining U.S. Cold War policy, it would influence every facet of American society, for a time silence skeptics, and maintain at least residual influence well into the 1980s.

A Wilsonian with a Difference

When he looked abroad, President Roosevelt was, much like Luce, less interested in a state's internal makeup than in its international behavior. He had demonstrated early in his presidency that he could live with states that practiced economic autarky, authoritarian politics, class warfare, and even persecution of minorities and dissidents. He did not take a stand against Joseph Stalin's bloody purges of the 1930s. While he condemned the German persecution of the Jews, he took no significant action, not even after 1941, when the Holocaust began and the United States formally joined the war. Congress, the public, labor unions, and the State Department were equally passive and at times even overtly anti-Semitic. Polls done in the late 1930s found two-thirds of the public opposed to admitting any Jewish refugees, and this sentiment may have intensified during the war years. In his nonchalance the president was in line with if not constrained by the views of Congress and most of the public.

It was, rather, great power aggression that gradually forced Roosevelt, the lapsed Wilsonian, back to his faith. Japan's takeover of Manchuria in 1931–32, its renunciation of naval limits in 1935, and Mussolini's move into Ethiopia were troubling, as was Japan's invasion of China in 1937. But none of these developments had altered the priority he gave to battling hard times at home or dispelled the widespread aversion to another entanglement in European rivalries. What it took to shake his sense of security and push him to serious resistance was a militantly expansionist Germany asserting its dominance over the European heartland. Hitler's incorporation of Austria in March 1938 followed by the Munich settlement partitioning Czechoslovakia in September began to arouse Roosevelt. Munich had him reflecting gloomily on the coming European conflict and the prospect that the United States might have "to pick up the pieces of European civilization and help them save what remains of the wreck." By November he was ready to pronounce Hitler "a pure unadulterated devil." The following March he clarified the grounds for his hostility; the issue was "a policy of military domination" and not "the form of government which European people should have."[3] Hitler's invasion of Poland in September 1939 and the declarations of war that immediately followed confirmed his worst fears. The fall of France less than a year later left Britain isolated and under threat of invasion and defeat. With Europe in security free fall, the conclusion of the Tripartite Pact in September 1940 qualitatively altered the president's sense of danger. He faced a united front of aggressor states (the Axis). In the context of this genuinely internationalized European crisis, Japan ceased to be a peripheral threat to regional order; it emerged as one piece in a broader pattern of aggression threatening from east and west.

Roosevelt interpreted these events in a way reminiscent of Woodrow Wilson. He saw German and Japanese aggression arising from deeply flawed, nondemocratic political systems and posing a challenge to Western civilization. Like his predecessors, Roosevelt thought of the British as kin in this time of crisis, but not in the intimate sense that Wilson had. The young Roosevelt had felt flashes of resentment over domineering British ways and cultivated a keen and proud sense of his Dutch heritage. The influence of geopolitics further muddied Roosevelt's Wilsonian outlook and contributed to the pain and alarm he felt as Britain fell into deeper and deeper peril and left the United States ever more strategically exposed.

German and British geographers had been contending that new technology was shrinking the globe and thus made imperative a rethinking of the relationship among major regions. For example, a conventional Mercator map of the world usually placed the Western Hemisphere squarely in the middle and made the Atlantic and Pacific look like moats securing the approaches to the continental United States, while a map drawn from a fresh polar perspective put the homeland only a short flight from Berlin or Tokyo or Buenos Aires. In a world more closely drawn together, Fortress America was an illusion and isolation an impossibility. Strategic vulnerability was a new fact of life for Americans.

Roosevelt's long-standing interest in the navy predisposed him to accept the new geopolitical insights that had begun circulating in u.s. policy circles for the first time in the late 1930s. The oceans were becoming highways quickly crossed by powerful battle fleets. The looming importance of long-range aircraft added to the danger and made security a global problem that had to be considered in truly global terms. As Roosevelt wrote privately to the u.s. ambassador in Tokyo in January 1941, "The problems which we face are so vast and so interrelated that any attempts even to state them compels one to think in terms of five continents and seven seas."[4]

Whatever the calculations, Roosevelt still arrived at a distinctly Wilsonian conclusion. His task was to defeat aggression now and ensure that it did not arise again. To create an international community committed to peace would require, as he told the nation on 9 December 1941 following the Pearl Harbor attack, that "the sources of international brutality, wherever they exist, must be absolutely and finally broken." The Atlantic Charter, an encapsulation of postwar goals issued at a summit meeting with British prime minister Winston Churchill the previous August, invoked a familiar program even if it took the form of eight points rather than Wilson's fourteen. The charter's British and American authors declared the goal of their common Anglo-American struggle an enlightened peace. The president and the prime minister foreswore territorial ambitions and committed themselves to postwar reconstruction guided by the principles of self-determination, free trade and economic development, freedom of the seas, collective security, and disarmament. Occupation and reform was to be the fate of the most egregious offenders against international order, Germany and Japan. By eliminating the blatant impulse to aggression, so much woven into the fiber of their national life, the Allies could ensure that bad leaders should never again be able to corrupt the good instincts of their people and implicate them in international misbehavior.[5]

Gripped by the growing sense of insecurity, Roosevelt began to respond in ways that had already by early 1941 put him well ahead of Luce. He had resisted congressional initiatives in the mid-1930s to tie the president's hands in case of renewed war in Europe. He went all-out to kill the Ludlow amendment requiring a public referendum to declare war, finally defeating it in January 1938 by a vote of 209 to 188 in the House. By watering down neutrality legislation, first in 1937 and again in 1939, he was able to regain some latitude for presidential action at a time of danger. Beginning in 1938, he got Congress to support his plans for a two-ocean navy, directed aid to Britain and China, and applied economic and military pressure on Japan. In September 1940, in the boldest gesture to date, he handed u.s. destroyers over to Britain in exchange for access to British bases on the Canadian coast and in the Caribbean.

With reelection behind him in November 1940, Roosevelt took even more dramatic steps that were to deeply entangle the United States in the European and Pacific struggles and foreshadow war. In December 1940 he declared that the u.s. economy would serve as the "arsenal of democracy" and the following March announced aid to Britain on a nominal "lend-lease" basis. In May he put the country on an emergency footing in the face of a Nazi war machine now seemingly threatening the Western Hemisphere. The German invasion of the Soviet Union in June intensified Roosevelt's alarm but also created a fresh opportunity to expand the coalition against the Axis powers. He pledged help for the embattled Soviets. In July he made the fateful decision to cut off Japan's supply of oil with the hope of immobilizing this threat to both European colonies in Southeast Asia and the eastern flank of his new Soviet ally. In September 1941, following his summit with Churchill, he had the u.s. Navy join the British in protecting convoys against the German submarines threatening the flow of desperately needed supplies across the North Atlantic. Roosevelt had gone to war in all but name well in advance of the Japanese attack on Pearl Harbor in December. Before the month was out the United States was formally at war with all three Axis powers—Japan, Germany, and Italy.

During wartime Roosevelt continued to pay public homage to Wilsonian principles but proved a lukewarm practitioner. Eight years in the White House had taught this astute observer two lessons Wilson had overlooked. One was the need to accommodate the requirements of other powers. The second was the importance of taking into account the public's reluctance to sacrifice on distant battlefields if he were to maintain a base of domestic support for an active u.s. postwar role. While he reiterated publicly his commitment to the high ideals of the Atlantic Charter and mobilized support for the United Nations as the successor to the League of Nations, his conduct of the war and plans for the postwar settlement showed considerable caution. Roosevelt supplied the aid that helped keep his British and Soviet allies afloat, but he also let Soviet forces bear the brunt of the fighting in Europe and brought American troops into combat only when the prospect of rapid victory and minimal casualties was good. He was, moreover, intent in having the Soviets share in the heavy losses that planners expected from the invasion of the Japanese home islands (slated to begin in late 1945, with fighting expected to continue well into 1946). In the final reckoning, Roosevelt's strategic caution limited total u.s. deaths to 400,000—far short of the price paid by the other powers. Here was compelling testimony to the success of Roosevelt's strategy.

But this approach carried a postwar price that Roosevelt willingly paid. Stalin's forces had had to withstand the worst of the struggle against Germany, suffering losses fifteen times that of the Americans, and Stalin had agreed to have these forces make further sacrifices in the final, brutal phase of the Pacific War. In return he expected his allies to accept his claim to influence over the European real estate that his army had occupied and to give him a voice in the overall postwar arrangements. Accommodation with the Soviets, whatever their domestic failings, was one of Roosevelt's central postwar goals and highlights his selective commitment to Wilsonian orthodoxy. By giving the Soviets their sphere of influence, he would also provide the u.s. public peace and prosperity not seen since the 1920s. The full realization of the Wilsonian world would have to wait at least until after a period of stability and recovery overseen by the United States working with the Soviet Union and

Britain. Just days before the president's death the influential commentator Walter Lippmann paid tribute to Roosevelt's policy of realpolitik. "He has led this country out of the greatest peril in which it has ever been to the highest point of security, influence, and respect which it has ever attained."[6]

Truman and the Cold War Orthodoxy

On 12 April 1945, with the German Third Reich in ruins and Japan under aerial bombardment, Vice President Truman got a summons to go immediately to the White House. There he heard from Eleanor Roosevelt, "Harry, the president is dead." The news left Truman feeling "like the moon, the stars, and all the planets had fallen on me."[7] Roosevelt was a hard act to follow, and Truman was a poorly prepared understudy—and he knew it. Born just two years after Roosevelt and raised in small-town Missouri, he had had none of the advantages of family wealth and little formal education. After fighting in France during World War I and then struggling in business when the war was over, Truman joined the Missouri Democratic political machine and in 1934 won election to the Senate. In 1944 Roosevelt turned to Truman for the bland vice-presidential candidate then needed on the Democratic ticket. Truman had scant foreign policy background and in the months before Roosevelt's death gained little sense of the president's postwar strategy.

Suddenly faced with issues both complex and unfamiliar, Truman fell back on Wilson as his inspiration and guide. Truman had lamented the rejection of Wilson's peace plan as a blow to "our responsibility as a world power" (as he put it publicly in March 1938). World War II offered a second chance to honor that responsibility, which consisted fundamentally of the defense of freedom as the bedrock of civilization. He stressed in a speech in November 1942 that "the war we are fighting is a continuation of the one we fought in 1917 and 1918." Burdened with few of the reservations and caveats that Roosevelt had developed, this Wilsonian outlook fit with the new president's personal tendency to reduce problems to moral, black-and-white terms.[8]

During his first year in his new job, Truman grew convinced that the Soviets posed a new danger of aggression. Even as he was settling in the White House in April 1945 his advisers were warning him that Poland was a litmus test of Soviet intentions in eastern Europe. Truman vowed to be tough but waffled for a time over how to read the Soviets. After meeting Stalin at an Allied summit in Potsdam (outside Berlin) in July 1945, Truman sized him up as someone smart and tough that he could do business with. He compared Stalin's police state to that of the czars and the Soviet dictator himself to a city boss of the sort that he had worked with in Kansas City. By early 1946 his patience with Moscow was growing thin. Apparent probes in Iran and China combined with an implacable grip on eastern Europe left the president fuming that he was "tired babying the Soviets." In August he announced to his advisers that "we might as well find out whether the Russians were bent on world conquest now as in five or ten years."[9]

Another year would pass before Truman's increasingly emphatic private concerns received public expression in the famous Truman Doctrine. The president addressed Congress in March 1947 with a request for aid for Greece and Turkey so that they could better resist communist threats. The speech echoed Wilson: the entire world was caught up in a struggle between two different ways of life—one free and one slave. The United States had a moral imperative "to support free peoples who are resisting attempted subjugation by armed minorities or by outside pressures." Truman's policy was thus "containment"—putting most of the world off limits to the Soviet Union and the international communist movement. But there was also room in his policy for gingerly probing the Soviet bloc using covert operations and propaganda conveyed in conventional publications, through the airwaves, and by air-dropped leaflets in hopes of shaking the Kremlin's grip on conquered countries and even on Russia itself. The Voice of America, Radio Liberty, the u.s. Information Agency, and the Psychological Strategy Board mounted an impressive operation to win the hearts and minds of ordinary people on the other side of the Iron Curtain. The emerging Cold War policy brought together two competing, even contradictory strategies—alongside containment a hope for rollback (or liberation).[10]

Inspiring these polices in 1947 and ultimately rationalizing the entire u.s. Cold War effort was an official orthodoxy. The bedrock and most familiar element of that orthodoxy was the Wilsonian faith brought back to prominence by Roosevelt's public wartime pronouncements. Hitler's attempt to reshape the face of Europe had failed, but the man who would take his own life amid the rubble of his endangered capital would haunt an entire generation of American leaders. Hitler taught them that the only proper response to territorial aggression was immediate, resolute resistance. This insight was codified in the so-called lesson of Munich, which condemned the democracies for attempting to appease Hitler in 1938. Their failure to create the collective security structure of the sort that Wilson had proposed and then to stand up to the forces of tyranny and aggression in Germany and Japan not only made war more likely but doomed them to enter it on disadvantageous terms. "Munich" and the "appeasement" that it represented became highly resonant code words in the u.s. foreign affairs lexicon, each a standing rebuke to "isolationists" who failed to grasp that U.S. security required a brave, decisive, wide-ranging international program in defense of democracy and civilized values.

In the emerging postwar orthodoxy, geopolitical insights sharpened Wilsonian anxieties. The war had confirmed Roosevelt's view that armed forces could strike over great distances—whether in land offensives, naval operations, or bombing campaigns. Fortress America was truly outmoded; the frontiers of security now lay on the distant shores of the Atlantic and Pacific. This keen new sense of vulnerability and regional connections came to be expressed in the idea of dominoes. A defeat at some distant and once insignificant point could now affect adjacent areas and ramify outward in a way that could ultimately and fundamentally threaten the United States. Thus a defeat in Greece, so the State Department's Dean Acheson explained to congressional leaders on the eve of the Truman Doctrine speech, "might open three continents to Soviet penetration."[11] Security for Americans had ceased to be hemispheric or transatlantic; it had become global. To maintain that security their country would need forces at the ready operating out of forward bases along the distant shores of the Atlantic and Pacific as well as across the Middle East and South Asia. The days of a small peacetime military and hemispheric defense were gone.

The third galvanizing element in the new orthodoxy was totalitarianism. It gave focus and energy to otherwise diffuse Wilsonian and geopolitical concerns by identifying a fearsome political mutant threatening U.S. security and values around the world. The term "totalitarian" came into usage in Italy and Germany in the 1920s and early 1930s, and it made its way into English by the mid-1930s. Journalists, academics, and even politicians began to take up the idea of a new, ruthless kind of regime that was far more dangerous and dynamic than the old authoritarian governments represented by the German kaisers or the Russian czars. As the term gained currency in the interwar years, Hitler's Nazi government in Germany, Mussolini's fascist regime in Italy, and the Soviet Union under Communist control were the examples usually cited, but some writers suggested that even democracies were not immune to totalitarian trends. Those who then employed the term worried about the rise of modern mass society, whose popular political passivity created a special vulnerability to manipulation by malign leaders. Once in power, those leaders could exploit the technological and communications tools available to the modern state to penetrate the private lives of citizens, control both family and civil society, and eliminate the least sign of resistance. With total, enduring control at home went a powerful and relentless ideological drive to eliminate external opposition and thus a powerful impulse toward brutal aggression. The antidote to totalitarianism involved more than removing the all-powerful leader presiding over this frightful system and dismantling the system itself. Only a far-reaching program in favor of freedom could neutralize the dangerous currents running just below the surface of modern life. A free press, multiple parties, constitutional checks on political power, and defense of individual rights were essential to saving countries and preserving peace among them.[12]

This totalitarian line of analysis exercised growing influence among u.s. commentators and policymakers. The mid-1939 pact between Moscow and Berlin dividing Poland led some journalists to conclude that both powers were in equal measure totalitarian and at odds with democracy. Roosevelt made limited use of the term, most notably during the 1940 election, and he mainly had Germany in mind, especially after June 1941 when the Soviets became an ally. As World War II drew to a close and military dependence on the Soviet Union waned, long-time critics of Roosevelt's accommodation of Moscow, such as Soviet specialists within foreign service and shapers of opinion such as Luce, began recasting Stalin as a new Hitler and the Soviet Union as a dangerous expansionist force resembling Germany. By Truman's first years in the White House, proponents of the totalitarian interpretation were beginning to integrate it into the conceptual armory of u.s. policy. Hitler became the widely understood template for the totalitarian condition—the cruel denial of freedom, individuality, prosperity, and peace. Influential u.s. observers and policymakers imagined Stalin stepping into his place almost at once. The equation between the two involved a simple syllogism: Hitler the totalitarian had been aggressive; Stalin was a totalitarian; therefore Stalin would be aggressive. His policies in eastern Europe and especially Poland confirmed suspicions about the nature of the Soviet regime and the external threat that it posed. So strong was the appeal of the totalitarian interpretation that other ways of thinking about the Soviet system and explaining Soviet behavior fell to the margins.

Truman offers a revealing example of the appeal of the totalitarian interpretation. In 1939, in what was probably his first use of the term, he characterized totalitarians as people who had taken their countries "back to a code little short of the cave-man." As Cold War tensions rose, Truman invoked the term regularly. It played a featured role in his March 1947 address to Congress as the general enemy against which all free peoples were arrayed and as a direct threat to u.s. security. Truman's understanding of the term remained loose, serving more as an epithet than a sharply defined concept. In his mind, a totalitarian regime was on the same plane as a dictatorship, police state, or even a monarchy. Thus he equated the Soviet system with the rule of Hitler, Mussolini, the Czars, Louis XIV, Napoleon, Charles I, and Cromwell. "A totalitarian state is no different whether you call it Nazi, Fascist, Communist or Franco Spain," he wrote to his daughter in March 1948. The Soviet version of totalitarianism represented a fundamental threat because in Truman's estimate it negated precisely what the United States stood for and what good people everywhere valued—liberty, religious faith, and civilization.[13]

The totalitarian model may have served well as a simplifying and clarifying notion amid the confusion and pressure of the late 1940s. But as one historian has suggested, it was conceptually shallow, "with little or no explanatory power." To be sure, the German and Soviet regimes emerged from similar national backgrounds—in countries with authoritarian monarchies that had strong bureaucracies and militaries supported by a landowning class and that were in the midst of intense industrialization and empire building. Both had suffered traumatic defeats in the course of World War I. But the similarities disappeared when the respective mechanisms of rule by indoctrination, repression, manipulation, and mobilization come under close examination. The charismatic Hitler was the creator and basis for his one-party state, while a highly bureaucratized and indoctrinated Leninist party served as the foundation for the Soviet state that Stalin inherited and passed on to his successors. The Stalin cult served as an ornament—not as the essence—of the Soviet system. Without Hitler, the German system dissolved. One operated on the basis of a stark nationalism, while the other leaned heavily on notions of class identity transcending the nation-state. Ethnic exclusivity predominated in the Germany case, a striking contrast to the strong strain of Soviet internationalism arising from a belief in transnational class interests and loyalties. Finally, one focused resolutely on territorial conquest, while the other gave priority to state-directed economic development and security from attack. By eliding important differences between two supposedly similar regimes, the totalitarian model ignored the diverse effects of the strains imposed by the thirty-year crisis of war and deprivation, not just in these two cases but also in Italy, Spain, Portugal, and Japan. The model created instead a single, easily grasped class of enemies. They not only stood as the antithesis of the u.s. core value of freedom but also directly challenged the faith that freedom and modernity were bound to advance together.[14]

The new state ideology—Wilsonian, geopolitical, and antitotalitarian—took its most stark, authoritative form in April 1950 in a secret Truman administration policy review known as nsc-68 (short for National Security Council study number 68). The study came in the wake of two alarming events in the latter half of 1949, the Soviet atomic bomb test breaking the u.s. nuclear monopoly and the victory of Communist forces in China. In emphatically ideological terms NSC-68 called for a vigorous and wide-ranging response: "The assault on free institutions is world-wide now, and in the context of the present polarization of power a defeat of free institutions anywhere is a defeat everywhere." This all-or-nothing logic dictated protecting freedom wherever it was threatened; not to do so would be to risk freedom's total collapse as demoralized peoples fell like dominoes one by one. It was not enough to safeguard western Europe and Japan; the United States would also have to take a stand within the emerging third world wherever communism seemed to threaten. Thus thrown into a global contest, the United States faced potentially vast claims on determination and resources. Truman endorsed at once the study's dire findings, and following the outbreak of war in Korea two months later he adopted NSC-68's recommendation for a dramatic increase in military spending. By 1953 that funding had tripled.

The new orthodoxy ramified through the Truman administration. If it is true that "jobs come equipped with their own ideologies," then the emerging Cold War state had found the credo that would give the official mind and the minds of those yearning for induction into government service a common sense of urgency and direction.[15] There was now no room for compromise and no place for doubt or dissent. The result was a narrowing of debate within the executive branch. Foreign affairs specialists who were at odds with the new premises of u.s. policy risked investigation, loss of employment, and personal harassment. The chill took institutional form when in March 1947 the president launched an internal security program. It would steadily broaden its reach and tighten its net so that loyalty boards operating throughout the federal government fired employees for disloyalty based on past beliefs and affiliations (including excess enthusiasm for the Soviets during wartime or affiliation with the u.s. Communist Party), possession of suspect reading materials, and the suspicion of homosexuality.

While government officials policed their own, the Truman administration sought to secure American society against the formidable Soviet threat and to educate the public to that threat. "Communists are everywhere," Truman's attorney general declared in 1946—"in factories, offices, butcher shops, on street corners, in private business." The administration singled out for special attention the groups that had yet to embrace the new orthodoxy or who might betray it—fellow travelers and Communist Party members, sexual deviants vulnerable to blackmail, naïve intellectuals, isolationists with their heads in the sand, and "maladjusted groups," such as Jews, African Americans, and immigrants. In a rare public appearance in March 1947 before the revealingly named House Un-American Activities Committee, FBI head J. Edgar Hoover described communism by using a metaphor that was becoming commonplace. He compared it to a "disease that spreads like an epidemic[,] and like an epidemic a quarantine is necessary to keep it from infecting the nation." To effect that quarantine the FBI created a long list of subversive organizations and deported aliens with communist ties. Truman himself took up anticommunist themes during his 1948 reelection campaign. His emphasis on the dangers lurking at home no less than abroad was meant to rally public support, neutralize Republican attacks, and quiet dissent against his Cold War policies coming from the Left led by Henry Wallace.[16]

The administration's effort to promote the new orthodoxy was part of a new Red Scare whose grip on American society proved broader and longer lasting than the one of 1919–20. Though commonly called McCarthyism, the winds of anticommunist crusading began to blow well before Senator Joseph McCarthy appeared on the scene. Even as the war was ending, business leaders and Republicans—Henry Luce was one of the most prominent and influential—began a campaign to end the Democratic control of the White House and undercut the New Deal. They wanted in particular to roll back government regulation in the name of political freedom and free enterprise and to weaken labor unions that had grown strong in the 1930s and had embraced the ideals of social and economic democracy. Those worried by "socialist" inroads at home found allies among other conservatives who identified attacks on racial segregation with communism and feared that gender roles disrupted by the war were weakening American society and laying it open to subversion.

Senator McCarthy gained prominence in February 1950 with a widely noticed speech on traitors in the State Department. The Cold War consensus, which was by then taking shape, facilitated his highly publicized search for subversives through press conferences and congressional hearings. Intimidation and official investigations had already spread a pall of fear over schools and universities, labor unions, the entertainment industry, publishing, and churches. One by one elites in culture, business, and politics either adopted the new anticommunist ethos or assumed a prudent public silence if they doubted the official line on the Soviet threat or opposed the violation of civil liberties. With the terms of political discourse narrowing, the United States would emerge as unique among the industrial democracies for its lack of an influential socialist party and a legal communist party. The Wilsonian persuasion in its anxious Cold War incarnation had triumphed—and in the process

confirmed the fear that insidious totalitarian trends could be found everywhere.

TECHNO-WAR AND MASS DESTRUCTION

The midcentury evolution of Wilsonian ideas into a durable Cold War
orthodoxy was accompanied by an astonishing expansion of u.s. military
power. With an increasing range and mounting capacity to destroy, the United
States was riding a technological trend going back to the nineteenth century.
Larger and more powerful warships represented the beginning of that trend.
By World War I the introduction of tanks, machine guns, massed artillery, gas,
and warplanes to strafe and bomb was making ground combat more lethal.
The interwar period saw the continued development of long-range aircraft,
aircraft carriers, and submarines that made the once broad and secure Atlantic and Pacific into easy avenues of attack. While these advances generated
geopolitical anxiety about u.s. vulnerability, they also spurred the national
spirit of inventiveness and technological virtuosity, which in turn gave the
American war machine a marked edge well beyond any overseas rival.

This technological response to insecurity had a paradoxical effect. American strategists went into World War II thinking in terms of annihilating
enemy forces, while Roosevelt demanded as a concomitant the uncondi-
tional surrender of the Axis powers. The American advantage in devising new
and massively destructive kinds of warfare made these absolutist positions
possible. Yet that very power to destroy boomeranged after the war, leaving
Americans themselves more exposed to risk than they had been for at least a
century. Technology as a source of insecurity formed a closed loop in which
all powers sought more and better weapons that steadily fed general anxiety
and perpetuated the cycle of fear and rising destructive power. Technology
confronted policymakers with the choice of either accepting and managing
vulnerability or continuing to seek new technological antidotes to danger.

A Military-Industrial Complex

The United States became in the course of World War II the world's leading war machine. A larger and growing economy was the precondition for
the miracle of mobilization. Already in 1938 it accounted for a third of the
total GDP of the great powers—only slightly smaller than the combined GDP
of its allies and 20 percent larger than the combined Axis GDP. Roosevelt and
his senior commanders skillfully exploited that economic advantage to encompass the simultaneous defeat of Germany and Japan on two distinct and
widely separated fronts with a loss of life lower than that of any other major

combatant. An army and a navy totaling a third of a million in 1939 grew to 12.1 million by war's end. They were supported by massive agricultural and industrial output; facilities slack during the depression expanded rapidly and made heavy claims on a work force diminished by the departure of men for military service. U.S. industry produced half of the munitions used against the Axis, massive quantities of war matériel (some 2.7 million machine guns and 2.4 million trucks, for example), and ships in dazzling numbers (nearly 6,000 tankers and cargo vessels to keep the supplies moving). In the apt characterization by one historian, "The United States was not only the arsenal of democracy; it was the factory, the breadbasket, the warehouse, and the delivery truck."[17]

Hitler made the mistake of discounting the American advantage. Like Georges Duhamel and other interwar European observers, he was convinced he was dealing with an enervated, degenerate people. Hitler's racial preoccupations led him to believe that that mongrel society was incapable of fighting in a united, resolute fashion. "America is not dangerous to us," he asserted in November 1939.[18] He confirmed that dismissive assessment in January 1942, having just formally embarked on war with the United States. He would soon find himself arrayed against the combined might of the United States and the Soviet Union. Strained to the utmost on the eastern front, German defenses were overwhelmed by the arrival of American troops and supplies in the west in mid-1944.

Japanese leaders contemplating a collision were generally more acute in their appraisals. They understood that u.s. strength—vast resources, superior industry, and an impregnable territorial position—would more and more come into play the longer any war lasted. Going to war was thus a throw of the dice. Drawing on his long military experience, Prime Minister Tojo Hideki conceded with delicate understatement in early November 1941, "If we enter into a protracted war, there will be difficulties."[19] The war that his government launched the next month went even less well than expected. Japanese forces were on the defensive sooner than either they or the Americans had imagined possible. Defeat quickly became a foregone conclusion as mobile, lavishly supplied u.s. forces jumped from island to island across the Pacific, cut off maritime contact with Japan, and freely bombed Japanese cities.

In addition to impressive output, the United States brought to war technical and scientific virtuosity. Scientists and engineers produced a string of innovations that gave u.s. forces a significant advantage. These included radar, gunsights and bombsights, long-distance bombers, amphibious vessels, code-breaking techniques, proximity fuses, and electronic countermeasures to blind enemy radar. Above all, the development of the first atomic bombs epitomized the u.s. lead in high-tech warfare.

By the late 1930s physicists around the world understood that splitting the nucleus of an atom could release considerable power. Prompted by worries about Germany's producing the first atomic weapons and by a British call to invest resources not available to them, Roosevelt had by October 1941, alone among wartime leaders, decided on a serious exploration of the potential for atomic weapons. The top-secret program (given the code-name the "Manhattan Project") enjoyed generous funding, received priority in the face of competing wartime demands for matériel, and commanded a large proportion of the nation's scientific and engineering talent, including, notably, scientists who had fled Hitler's persecution of Jews. Despite the enormous technical challenges, the Manhattan team succeeded on 16 July 1945 with the first test, illuminating the desert sky near Alamogordo, New Mexico. With the two bombs remaining in the arsenal, the u.s. Air Force reduced to wastelands first Hiroshima on 6 August and then Nagasaki three days later. These two devastating strikes, together with the Soviet entry into the Pacific war, forced Japan to surrender on 14 August.

While u.s. forces quickly demobilized, the economy proved that it could shift to civilian production as rapidly as it had tooled up for war and embarked in the postwar decades on a period of growth that was the fastest in u.s. history. This unmatched capacity for mass production made it possible to wage the Cold War and at the same time accommodate the preferences of a public that did not want guns (military spending) to crowd out butter (cheap, plentiful consumer goods). Having endured economic depression and wartime sacrifice, many Americans hankered after rising disposable income and a rich array of products to spend it on, not higher taxes and government controls. A robust economy was the critical ingredient in what would become a tacit bargain between the public and its Cold War leaders. Generous Cold War spending did not significantly crimp output or harm overall productivity. In absolute terms the military budget tripled between 1950 and 1953 (in the wake of nsc-68 and the Korean emergency), declined under Eisenhower (from $442 billion to $344 billion in constant 2002 dollars), and then returned to Korean War levels by the end of the Johnson years. But that budget took an ever smaller share of an impressively expanding economy, shrinking from 13 percent of GDP in 1953 to 9 percent in 1968. Thanks to a growing federal revenue stream, Washington could funnel more and more monies into education, health, housing, conservation, and economic infrastructure. A budget that in the early postwar decades devoted seven or eight of every ten dollars to the military, international programs, veterans benefits, and payment of World War II debt was by 1968 down to six of ten despite the war in Vietnam.[20]

A large standing military, substantial and sustained military spending, and an increasingly active research program gave rise to a "military-industrial complex." Already taking shape by the end of World War II, it was fully formed by the early decades of the Cold War. The term came into common usage after Eisenhower invoked it in his farewell address in 1960. He expressed long-held fears that a prolonged Cold War struggle might result in a "garrison state" in which the influence of the military establishment and the arms industry would erode the democratic system that Americans were fighting to defend. Recent scholarly appraisals see something broader at work: a military-industrial-congressional-university complex. Alongside the arms makers and the armed services that they sold to stood shoulder to shoulder the elected politicians in Washington who shaped the military budget to suit their constituents' interests (especially southern congressmen), the lobbyists who worked the halls of Congress, and the broader population in regions where military bases, rates of enlistment in the military, and military manufacturing were concentrated (once more disproportionately the South as well as the West Coast). This far-reaching set of interests had an inherent bias to keep defense spending high if not progressively rising and to resist presidential efforts to make cuts. Military spending had, in other words, become a form of pork barrel on a huge scale rather than a reflection of some considered grand strategy. Monies flowed into a hybrid public-private system of research and development with multiple sponsors and scattered centers of research. A coalition of Republicans, southern Democrats, leaders of big business, and top scientists preferred this decentralized, loosely coordinated research program proceeding on multiple fronts. Each group for its own reasons stoutly opposed bureaucratic control vested in one office or work centered on one laboratory or arsenal. Collectively they ensured that federal spending on research and development moved sharply upward. By 1968 it was nineteen times higher than in 1947, with about four-fifths—roughly $14 billion (or $54 billion in 2000 constant dollars)—devoted to the military, atomic energy, and space exploration. Federal spending, only a fraction of total research and development in the 1930s, had become the dominant share, and it had shifted dramatically from agricultural to military ends.[21]

Government agencies took the lead in keeping the u.s. military on the technological cutting edge. The pioneer was the National Defense Research Committee, created in 1939 and transformed in 1941 into the Office of Scientific Research and Development headed by Vannevar Bush (a former MIT engineering dean). It recruited scientists and engineers to conduct research but, rejecting the World War I practice, left them to work at their home institutions. It also ran government arsenals such as Los Alamos (heart of the Manhattan Project) as separate research centers. These government research agencies proliferated after World War II. The Office of Naval Research served as the prototype between 1946 and 1950, to be followed by the National Science Foundation, the National Institutes of Health, the Atomic Energy Commission, the National Aeronautics and Space Administration, and the Advanced Research Project Agency (under the control of the Department of Defense). These agencies spent some of the growing stream of appropriations on in-house projects. But three-quarters of the federal spending on research over the course of the Cold War went through administrative research contracts concluded with industry, universities, and quasi-public laboratories. They emerged as essential parts of a decentralized u.s.-style research network.

University empire builders seized on this government largesse to fatten their budgets and boost their institutional standing, all while demonstrating their patriotism. The Massachusetts Institute of Technology, Stanford, and Johns Hopkins led the way in building physics, electronics, and aeronautics programs, with wartime research usually serving as the foundation for post-war expansion. This university-based, government-funded research and development not only created innovative tools of warfare but also stimulated the economy by spinning out new products and technologies for civilian use. For example, MIT's work on air defense in the early 1950s paved the way for the computer industry, while Stanford's work on microwave technology and then semiconductors gave rise to the Silicon Valley electronics industry.

Preparing for the Unthinkable

World War II left a terrible legacy: a barbaric doctrine of mass destruction. The practice of annihilating cities from the air had become an accepted strategy in the course of the war. German, Japanese, British, and u.s. airmen had demonstrated ever more dramatically that massed aircraft carrying conventional bombs could rain down destruction, terrorizing the civilian population in fire bombings and destroying industry and transport. The climax came in 1945, beginning with the firestorm created by waves of bombers over Dresden and Tokyo early that year. In Tokyo alone on the single night of 9–10 March a u.s. raid resulted in 80,000 to 100,000 deaths and left more than a million people homeless.[22] The following August a single aircraft carrying a single atomic bomb proved it could instantaneously inflict Tokyo-like damage, first on Hiroshima and then on Nagasaki. The capacity for long-range (even intercontinental) bombing, the difficulty of defense, and the growing accuracy of the bombs would deeply worry postwar strategists and statesmen.

Some scientists intimately involved in the development of the atomic bomb understood their work as contributing to this terrible trend. One response was to try to alert Roosevelt and Churchill to the alarming implications of a successful bomb project. Another was to question work on the bomb once it was clear Germany was out of the race. In July 1945 on the eve of the first test the skeptics warned Truman that this new weapon was "primarily a means for the annihilation of cities" and urged him to find a way to avoid "opening the door to an era of devastation on an unimaginable scale."[23] One proposal envisioned a mid-Pacific demonstration for Japanese observers in hopes of forcing surrender without recourse to bombing actual cities filled with real people. But military and civilian leaders were not at first responsive to warnings of this sort. Only slowly did they grasp the implications of the dawning age of nuclear destruction.

Truman is a revealing case in point. He came to the nuclear project late and with no preparation. He adopted the views of his advisers that the new atomic weapon was a club like any other to beat Tokyo into surrender and save American forces a costly invasion of the Japanese home islands. Those advisers acted not on race hatred but on a faith in technology and the justice of their cause. They had firebombed German cities and would have dropped the atomic bomb on anyone standing in the way of u.s. forces. Only slowly did the president begin to understand the terrible destructive power now in his hands. To news of the first nuclear test, he had responded that the atomic bomb "seems to be the most terrible thing ever discovered, but it can be made the most useful." With virtually no hesitation, Truman authorized the use of the two remaining atomic bombs in the u.s. arsenal on Japan. In his own mind at least he was exercising restraint. "Even if the Japs are savages, ruthless, merciless and fanatic," the United States could not make a target of "women and children." In the immediate aftermath of Hiroshima, he became more conflicted as he realized that it was not a purely military target. After the Nagasaki bombing he told his cabinet that he could not countenance the further killing of "all those kids." In September with the war over and tensions with the Soviets rising, Secretary of War Henry L. Stimson urged the president to explore some kind of deal with the Soviets. This Republican influential who had enlisted in the war effort as Roosevelt's secretary of war and overseen the Manhattan Project was worried that merely carrying "this weapon rather ostentatiously on our hip" would result in a dangerous arms race unprecedented in the history of international relations. But Truman with his growing distrust of the Soviets rejected any attempt at negotiating limits on u.s. nuclear development, and he accepted atomic bombing as the prime weapon in case of war with the Soviet Union even as he described the atomic bomb as a terrible weapon that would (as he put it in 1948) "wipe out women and children and unarmed people."[24]

For a time the u.s. monopoly held up. During the war Germany and Japan had worked in a desultory fashion, but neither made significant progress. British scientists participated in the Manhattan Project but then had to take a slower, more costly independent path after Truman decided not to continue the nuclear collaboration into the postwar period. Only the Soviet Union made a sustained effort to follow the Americans in developing strategic nuclear weapons (in other words, those delivered over long range by bombers and later ballistic missiles and submarine-launched missiles). Although Roosevelt had kept Stalin in the dark about the Manhattan Project, the Soviet leader nonetheless knew about it and launched his own bomb-building program in 1942. Right after Truman personally informed him during the Potsdam conference of the first successful test, he ordered the Soviet nuclear effort intensified. He grumbled that "Truman is trying to exert pressure, to dominate" but that the Soviet Union "should not allow any other country to have a decisive superiority over us." Soviet scientists worked with the same dedication as their American counterparts—and harbored some of the same doubts about nuclear war. In July 1949 they successfully tested the first device and proudly reported to Moscow that they had broken the American monopoly.[25]

Thus was set the stage for a new and terrifying arms race. Ever more powerful bombs as well as longer-range, more accurate, and faster delivery systems proved irresistible to policymakers on both sides of the Cold War. Each hoped to gain an advantage over the other and conversely feared that hesitation might let the enemy gain the upper hand. This slavish devotion to exploiting new technologies, already apparent in the Manhattan Project, shaped the u.s. decision in 1950 to work on a vastly more powerful "super" or hydrogen bomb. While Truman's advisers were divided over whether the project would keep the United States in the lead or make mass destruction more likely, Truman decided that the country could not afford to settle for second best. Seven minutes into a meeting on 31 January 1950 to discuss the pros and cons, he ordered work begun. The result was a device tested in November 1952 that was over 700 times more destructive than the Hiroshima bomb. Between 1953 and 1955 the Soviets matched the u.s. achievement on this new nuclear front.

Thanks to technological proficiency the United States kept the lead in the emerging arms race. The u.s. Air Force deployed its first intercontinental bombers in 1948, seven years ahead of the Soviets. The pattern held as well for jet bombers (1951 versus 1954), satellite photo reconnaissance (1960 versus 1962), submarine-launched ballistic missiles (1960 versus 1964), and anti-satellite weapons (1963 versus 1968). The only notable exception to this pattern was the Soviets' head start in developing intercontinental ballistic missiles (ICBMS) in 1957. But U.S. engineers matched the feat a year later and then in 1962 improved on the design by replacing liquid with more stable, reliable solid fuel. The comparable Soviet version did not appear until 1966.[26]

In the nuclear arms race as in the Cold War contest more generally the United States enjoyed a marked advantage. While the United States had escaped the direct effects of World War II, the Soviet Union had been devastated. It suffered over 20 million dead; the most populous and industrialized part of the Soviet Union was in ruins; along with peace came widespread starvation. Preoccupied with Soviet security and great-power standing, Stalin continued to emphasize industrial development, presenting to a weary population the prospect of more sacrifice and hardship. In its new areas of control along its western frontier, Moscow faced nationalist resentment and in places open guerrilla resistance. The economic balance remained overwhelmingly in the U.S. favor. For example, in 1953 even after the Soviets had recovered from the wartime losses, the United States had four times the manufacturing output of the Soviets and three times the GDP.[27] Already far ahead after World War II, the U.S. economic lead widened in the following decades both in gross output and in new technologies such as computers and microelectronics. The U.S. Army, if not Soviet in size, was ready and global in its reach. The navy was dominant everywhere on the high seas with a capability in its marine forces to intervene quickly at distant points. The air force, a strenuous advocate for strategic airpower as the key to containment, built its mission around nuclear weapons and global basing. The total U.S. stock of nuclear weapons reached some 200 strategic warheads in 1949 (when the Soviets were just breaking into the nuclear club) and would rise to 7,000 in 1960 (with the Soviet badly lagging with about 400 warheads). Finally, the Soviet Union suffered from a vulnerable strategic location. It was flanked by West Germany and Japan, both sites of U.S. bases. Its own attempt at creating a defensive system was hobbled by a troubled relationship with coalition partners. Yugoslavia strayed from the Soviet bloc in 1948. In 1956 the Hungarians literally fought to get the Soviets out of their country while the Chinese were by the end of the decade ready to bolt from their alliance with Moscow. The Sino-Soviet split would be attended by embarrassing public acrimony and in time border clashes.

Soviet leaders understood more clearly than had the Germans and the Japanese the need for caution with a country that could outproduce and outgun them. However paranoid, Stalin recognized his vulnerability and curbed his goals and rhetoric accordingly. He coped with u.s. superiority by squeezing more from an exhausted postwar society and by clinging to his belief in the ultimate triumph of socialism over an inwardly decaying, strife-prone capitalism. Coping with the United States grew more difficult once Stalin's death brought to the fore a new generation of leaders less prepared to give priority to heavy industry and the military at the expense of general living standards. Nikita Khrushchev sought accommodation with the United States so that he could trim the military budget and shift resources to the consumer sector. Khrushchev was also influenced by Soviet scientists, who had finally convinced him that nuclear war carried unthinkable consequences. These concerns with domestic welfare and nuclear danger resulted in his calling in 1956 for "peaceful coexistence" between the socialist and capitalist camps.

Washington held a marked overall military advantage that gave it the confidence to confront the Soviet Union—even to probe at the Soviet periphery. Foremost among u.s. advantages was a secure lead in nuclear weapons, an unmatched strategic bombing capability, and an impressively productive economy. To these was added in 1949 the North Atlantic Treaty Organization (NATO). This first formal u.s. alliance since the French connection during the Revolutionary War proved a formidable, durable anticommunist bulwark in the region deemed more important than any other to u.s. security. The twelve charter members included Britain, France, Italy, Belgium, the Netherlands, Denmark, Norway, Portugal, and Canada. Greece and Turkey joined in 1951, followed by West Germany in 1955. The treaty served as more than merely insurance against a Soviet attack; it was in an often invoked formulation "to keep the Russians out, the Germans down, and the Americans in." These and other alliances put in the hands of u.s. strategists hundreds of bases scattered around the world. Only on land along Europe's Iron Curtain was the u.s. alliance perhaps at some disadvantage. In early 1948 the Soviet Union had 2.9 million men under arms, down from 11.3 million at the end of World War II, well below contemporary u.s. intelligence estimates and close to the combined American-British total of 2.8 million. To be sure, many British contingents were scattered overseas, but at the same time much of the Red Army was at a low state of readiness.[28]

Given the disproportion in strength, war was unlikely. But what if the two nuclear powers stumbled into a confrontation? Truman left office reflecting on the dangers. "The weapons of destruction have become so powerful and so terrible that we can't even think of another all-out war." Indeed, Truman did precisely that—refused to think through the military use of atomic weapons—while also insisting for himself the ultimate decision on their use. Trapped with the responsibility without a plan, Truman had good reason to feel the burden. The Eisenhower administration's first full-fledged assessment of security, completed in October 1953, offered the sobering conclusion that the substantial and growing Soviet nuclear arsenal could "inflict serious damage on the United States." The situation looked even grimmer according to a report the president received two and a half years later. In his diary he laconically noted its prediction that nuclear war, whether it began with a surprise Soviet attack or with advanced warning, would bring the country to "practically total economic collapse" for at least six months. While trying to restore government functions, u.s. leaders would also have to care for a population, two-thirds of whom would be casualties, with limited medical facilities. Eisenhower later confessed privately that nuclear weapons "frighten the devil out of me." He moved to the conclusion that the u.s. arsenal had only one sane role—to deter the Soviets from using their nuclear weapons (the basis for the doctrine appropriately named MAD or Mutually Assured Destruction). The arsenal's prime function was, in other words, not to win wars or resolve crises but rather to induce such fear that neither Soviet nor American leaders would launch an attack, knowing full well that they were likely to suffer a terrible counterattack.[29]

A broad consensus gradually formed on the wisdom of some sort of limits on the nuclear arms race. In the late 1950s, Eisenhower sought to brake the expansion of the u.s. arsenal. He knew from U-2 reconnaissance aircraft flying high over the Soviet Union that Khrushchev's boasts of major advances in ballistics missiles were hollow. He thus ignored Democratic politicians' calls for more money to overcome what they charged had become a Soviet lead, and he gingerly explored an understanding with Moscow on nuclear weapons. The president's impulse to talk rather than engage in a race was reinforced by popular alarm over fallout from nuclear tests. The resulting public protests against the threat radioactivity posed to humans would prove one of the first ruptures in the Cold War consensus.

The Cuban missile crisis in October 1962 gave the new Kennedy administration a crash course in the nuclear peril. That sobering confrontation together with continuing protest against nuclear testing finally provided the impetus to action on arms control. As a presidential candidate, John Kennedy had charged Eisenhower with letting a missile gap develop to Soviet advantage and once in office dramatically ramped up u.s. nuclear programs, even though he then had access to the very data made available to Eisenhower that undercut claims of a u.s. lag. The United States in fact enjoyed a marked superiority, perhaps even a first-strike capability (meaning possession of weaponry sufficient to destroy so much of an opponent's nuclear force so quickly that it would forestall a serious counterblow). The missile crisis scared the public but also drove home to the Kennedy administration that it was walking on the edge of disaster. Secretary of Defense Robert McNamara recalled going to the office on 27 October at the height of the crisis and thinking, "I might never live to see another Saturday night." After bargaining his way out of the crisis, Kennedy finally embraced the goal of actively working to avoid nuclear war. In a statesmanlike address at the American University in June 1963, the president himself confronted the alternative. "All we have built, all we have worked for, would be destroyed in the first 24 hours." In his last months in office a chastened Kennedy joined with Khrushchev in taking some small but symbolically important steps, agreeing in June to install a hotline to facilitate rapid, direct communications between Washington and Moscow in future crises and in August to ban tests in the atmosphere (but not underground). Johnson followed in 1968 with an international nonproliferation treaty, worked out with the Soviets, to stop the spread of nuclear weapons.[30]

Even so, the situation became more, not less dangerous. The number of nuclear warheads on bombs, missiles, and submarines kept rising. By 1970 the United States had 12,223 strategic warheads and the Soviet Union 2,443. The superpowers' mutual suspicions still obstructed far-reaching, effective arms control. Americans worried that the Soviets would cheat, while insecure Soviets did not want Americans snooping around their secret facilities. Even with the best of wills, leaders still faced the difficulty of striking a balance between differently constituted u.s. and Soviet strategic systems and the technical problems of verification. And even then, as Washington and Moscow would learn, the most carefully worked out agreement might soon be undercut by new technologies that would open fresh fronts in the arms race. The Soviets introduced into the equation in 1966 antiballistic missile defenses (placed around Moscow to make the capital a tougher target for the superior u.s. missile force). Washington began debating how to respond (and in 1974 finally installed the first u.s. antiballistic missile system). More dangerous still, the United States introduced in 1970 multiple independent reentry vehicles. What came to be known as MIRVs consisted of a single missile carrying more than one warhead, each with an independent target to hit once the missile neared the end of its flight. The Soviets matched the u.s. innovation in 1975. Thus had the technology of warfare come increasingly to haunt the Cold War rivals. Each advance was supposed to bring at least a brief reprieve from vulnerability, but it tended instead to raise the level of strategic anxiety and the potential destructiveness of any nuclear war.

THE IMPERIAL PRESIDENCY

The midcentury American crusade against aggression and totalitarianism accelerated the trend toward a stronger state. As under McKinley and Wilson, war proved a potent stimulant to concentrating power in the hands of the president. What began on an emergency basis and in a helter-skelter fashion during World War II assumed more systematic form immediately thereafter as the Cold War took shape. By 1950 a full-fledged "imperial presidency" had arrived.[31] Thanks to the accumulation of power over a half century, the White House could now assume the role (in the words of one presidential historian) of "a kind of de facto command center for the Free World in the struggle with Communism."[32] Devoted above all else to the management of global dominion, the office of the president had acquired vast and varied resources. The White House commanded an enormous national security bureaucracy whose spending consumed much of the federal budget and whose buildings were coming to dominate the Washington-area landscape. The claims on ordinary Americans went beyond taxes to support this bureaucracy to include the first peacetime draft. Increasingly, Congress took a back seat to the person of the president, who commanded general deference as the embodiment of the nation in a semipermanent state of war. Though the strong presidency would come under attack in the late 1960s and 1970s, it would survive as a defining feature of u.s. political life.

Expansion of Bureaucratic Capacity

The best yardstick for measuring presidential dominance can be found in increasing personnel, expanding functions, and much enhanced funding. The mobilization required for two world wars and the global anticommunist campaign along with domestic programs prompted by the Great Depression pushed federal government spending as a share of GDP dramatically upward. Around 3 percent before World War I, it jumped to nearly 20 percent in the course of that conflict. Though it fell during the interwar period, it remained above the prewar level. World War II sent the figure skyward again (to 43 percent in 1944, the last full year of the war). Again in the postwar era the figure declined, but Cold War costs as well as rising social spending kept it well above the interwar level (13 percent in 1950, 18 percent in 1960, and 20 percent in 1968). Greater federal resources disproportionately benefited the executive branch. The number of civilian employees jumped from just below a million in 1939 to a high of 3.8 million in 1945 and then stayed between roughly two and three million until 1968. The active duty military underwent a no less dramatic expansion—from a third of a million in 1939 to over 12 million in 1945, then down to a postwar low of 1.5 million in 1950 before settling between roughly 2.5 million (the low in 1960) and 3.5 million (the high in 1968). Similarly, World War II and the early Cold War gave rise to a tangle of new agencies with at least some international involvement.[33]

The expansion of the executive branch during World War II was rapid and ad hoc. As the end of fighting gave way not to peace but rising tensions with the Soviet Union, voices within the Pentagon began calling for creating some order within a sprawling military and foreign affairs bureaucracy. After sorting through competing proposals from the army and navy, Congress in July 1947 passed the National Security Act. That act together with an amendment two years later effected structural changes in the executive branch that largely survive today.

One major objective of these reforms was to promote cooperation among the military branches and greater coherence in overall planning and operations. The War Department was split to create an air force independent of the army, and they together with the Navy Department came under the new Department of Defense, headed by a civilian, cabinet-level secretary possessed of real authority over the entire military and the civilian secretaries heading up the three main departments. The uniformed heads of the army, navy, marines, and air force came together for the first time as members of the Joint Chiefs of Staff. The chair of the Joint Chiefs was to be a senior military officer appointed by the president. As the ranking officer, he would serve as the principal adviser to the president and the secretary of defense. Ultimate authority remained in civilian hands.

The National Security Act made no less dramatic changes in nonmilitary areas of policymaking. The Central Intelligence Agency (CIA) emerged as the first permanent organization with the responsibility to gather and assess intelligence and with an implied mandate to conduct covert operations. The origins of the modern intelligence establishment can be traced back to activities undertaken around the turn of the century by the army, the navy, and the FBI (established in embryo in 1908). In 1942 Roosevelt created the Office of Strategic Services under the leadership of William Donovan to serve as a single center for gathering and evaluating wartime intelligence but also for carrying out covert operations. Truman abolished the OSS at war's end, but fragments survived as part of the War and State Departments and provided the core around which the CIA formed in 1947. The agency's annual appropriations were kept secret but appear to have amounted to about half a percent of the total federal budget at least in its early years.[34]

Most important of all in the long term, the 1947 act created the National Security Council (NSC) to function as the central coordinating body under the president's control. It built on the State-War-Navy Coordinating Committee, improvised in 1944 to give some coherence to wartime planning. The NSC staff, located in the White House complex, had the task of formulating national policy, assuring the president a wide range of advice, and seeing to the implementation of his decisions. Its statutory members consisted of the secretaries of state and defense and the vice president, while the head of the CIA and the chair of the Joint Chiefs of Staff were included in advisory roles. Representatives from other parts of the executive branch could attend as the president saw appropriate. Reflecting the NSC's importance, the president (or his designee) was to chair its meetings.

The National Security Act reflected a quest for policy coordination and coherence that remained more of an ideal than a reality. The CIA faced competition from multiplying intelligence agencies. The State Department's Bureau of Intelligence and Research emerged in 1946. The National Security Agency, with a specialty in spying on communications, appeared in 1952, followed the next year by the Defense Department's own Defense Intelligence Agency. The National Reconnaissance Office—a centralization of aerial reconnaissance functions—was created in 1961. The CIA had a brief golden age of dominance over its competitors in the 1950s thanks to Eisenhower's good relations with its head, Allen Dulles, and to its versatility and effectiveness. Its coups in Iran and Guatemala demonstrated right at the start of the Eisenhower administration a cheap, quick, quiet, effective response to problems in the third world. The agency also demonstrated its value in secretly funneling funds to anticommunist political groups and developing aerial reconnaissance (first the U-2 and then satellites). The CIA spent more time in the doghouse in the 1960s, having botched the Bay of Pigs invasion of Cuba for Kennedy in 1961 and delivered a steady stream of bad news to Johnson on the progress of his war in Vietnam. (This U.S. involvement in Iran, Guatemala, Cuba, Vietnam, and elsewhere in the third world is covered in chapter 6.)

On the military side, the creation of the Defense Department did not inaugurate an era of interservice harmony and acceptance of civilian-imposed spending limits. Guided by parochial interests, each of the services battled for key defense missions and a slice of the budget, mobilized supporters in Congress, veterans groups, and civilian contractors, and sometimes challenged the president's directives. Even the major boost in resources along the lines recommended by NSC-68 did not calm the tensions within the Pentagon or between it and the White House. Thus, for example, it was not possible to end the overlap in combat functions (such as air support or the delivery of nuclear weapons) or the duplication of types of equipment (each service wanted its own airplanes, helicopters, and radio transmitters). It proved no less difficult to arrive at a coherent, integrated strategic plan. Keeping all the parts of the Pentagon on the same page remained a persistent headache for a long string of defense secretaries and presidents. Its byzantine politics exhausted James V. Forrestal, the first secretary of defense and one of the authors of the 1947 reform, and drove him to suicide. The 1947 reorganization had not ended the armed services' unseemly scramble for advantage in which according to a recent close historical examination "each of the services tried to maximize its share of the defense budget, each identified its mission with the nation's security, and each wanted economies to come at the others' expense."[35]

While the CIA coped with competitors and the armed services with each other, the State Department suffered a steady decline of influence. Until the interwar years, State had occupied the dominant position within the executive bureaucracy on matters of foreign affairs, and the secretary of state had been the chief adviser to the president. The intrusion of the Commerce and Treasury Departments in the 1920s marked the beginning of the end of that dominance. Henry Morgenthau's Treasury enjoyed considerable clout in the 1930s, while the wartime saw Army Chief of Staff George C. Marshall, Secretary of War Stimson, and Secretary of Treasury Morgenthau overshadow Cordell Hull's State Department. No less threatening to State's standing was Roosevelt's growing tendency, following McKinley and Wilson, to pull critical policy issues into his personal purview.

The State Department's slide slowed in the late 1940s and 1950s thanks to a series of strong secretaries. George Marshall, who took charge in 1947, had easy access to Truman. The president was awestruck by generals and duly respectful of Marshall's experience and prestige. Hoping to stimulate in the department a sense of vision that might give it more policy clout, Marshall created a Policy Planning Staff in 1947 and brought the suddenly famous Soviet specialist George Kennan back from Moscow to serve as its first head. When Dean Acheson took Marshall's place in 1949, he was able to maintain a close if formal relationship to Truman. John Foster Dulles, who became Eisenhower's secretary of state in 1953, was equally influential, at least one-on-one with the president. But by then the overseas expansion of other agencies such as the Voice of America, the Agency for International Development, and the United States Information Agency was cutting into the State Department's role, while loyalty probes by congressional committees and the executive branch were damaging morale. Beginning with Dean Rusk's tenure in the 1960s, secretaries of state had to fight other cabinet secretaries and circles of White House advisers to be heard. The department's growing reputation for being both ponderous and unresponsive, already a problem by the 1930s, did nothing to endear it to presidents wanting quick answers and rapid action.

An increasingly militarized Cold War enhanced the generals' influence, even in nonmilitary areas. Marshall himself began the trend. After serving as the architect of victory in Europe and the Pacific, he retired, only to be recalled to duty, first as Truman's envoy to avert civil war in China, then as head of the State Department, and finally as secretary of defense in the midst of the Korean War. His World War II subordinate, Dwight Eisenhower, enjoyed postwar prominence as president of Columbia University and then commander of NATO before becoming a two-term president. Other officers tested in wartime who came to the fore in postwar policymaking included the proconsuls who oversaw the occupation of Japan (Douglas MacArthur and Matthew Ridgway), the first two heads of the CIA, the manager of Eisenhower's daily national security business between 1954 and 1960 (Andrew Goodpaster), and an influential Kennedy adviser (Maxwell Taylor).

The generals' civilian partners in running the burgeoning bureaucracy had a familiar northeastern establishment profile. Like the influential interwar Republicans with their commitment to a prudent but broad global engagement, the new generation tended to have privileged backgrounds. They had attended Ivy League schools, gravitated toward the law, and possessed a sense of public service (as long as it did not involve standing for election). Stimson was a transitional figure. After his own distinguished interwar career, he loyally worked for the Democrats Roosevelt and Truman. Acheson, the quintessential northeasterner in the postwar years, got his start in Roosevelt's State Department before becoming Truman's secretary of state. The Dulles brothers (John Foster and Allen), both at the front rank of the Eisenhower administration, carried the establishment flag into the 1950s. McGeorge Bundy, who played an important behind-the-scenes role in the 1960s as Kennedy's and Johnson's NSC head, fit the profile save for an academic background substituting for the standard legal training. His father, Harvey, had been a close Stimson aide, while his brother William held posts in the CIA and the State Department.

To control the proliferating and competing foreign policy agencies, presidents turned more and more to the NSC. Each proceeded in ways that reflected his personal style and priorities. Uncomfortable in formal settings, the insecure Truman at first held the NSC at arm's length, attending only twelve of fifty-seven meetings up to the outbreak of the Korean War in June 1950. Even after the crisis in Korea made him into a fairly regular attendee at NSC meetings, he continued to rely heavily on private consultations with his favored senior advisers, such as Acheson and Marshall. Eisenhower, who had a commander's respect for good staff work and formal lines of authority, made the NSC the prime forum for setting policy. He took an active role in its meetings, created the position of special assistant to the president for national security affairs to run the NSC, and increased the staff to about thirty.[36] In contrast to Eisenhower, Kennedy opted for the same free-wheeling style that he brought to his private life. While giving the NSC more resources, he looked less to NSC meetings than to close advisers—above all McGeorge Bundy as his special assistant for national security affairs, his brother Robert Kennedy, and his speechwriter Theodore Sorenson—to resolve policy issues. Tellingly, during the Cuban missile crisis, the president asked the Executive Committee (Ex-Comm) of the NSC for guidance while also consulting with trusted advisers behind closed doors. Johnson preferred informal meetings with the NSC principals (Bundy and his successor Walt Rostow as well as Secretary of Defense McNamara and Secretary of State Dean Rusk). He used formal NSC meetings to rubber stamp the conclusions reached by the senior inner circle.

The thread running through this shifting presidential relationship to the NSC was the growth in the clout of the special assistant for national security affairs. Increasingly a major policy player in his own right, he was also a gatekeeper for those wanting access to the president and the head of a growing NSC staff with intelligence, diplomatic, and military expertise. Presidents appreciated having their own in-house bureaucracy, which was answerable only to them and not subject to congressional review and appointment. Presidents also hoped that the NSC would smooth decision making, prevent the divisiveness and leaks likely to attend formal meetings with external agencies, and keep the bureaucracy behind the White House line. McKinley's one-room command post had come a long way.

Commanding Deference

An institutionally strengthened president exercised greater command over the public and Congress and increasingly claimed to speak for the nation. The president's views carried special weight because they reflected the best up-to-date information and the considered judgment afforded by the newly accumulated expertise at his disposal. Adding to that weight was the multiplication of international issues to address as the U.S. reach extended to a wide range of points around the globe. The complexity of international issues and their distance from the concerns of most Americans magnified the president's standing as the single guiding intelligence able to formulate a coherent response to pressing problems.

The president's rising status as a celebrity added a fresh dimension to his public appeal and gave additional force to his foreign policy preferences. Harding and Coolidge had cultivated the press and made themselves and their families available to the media, including radio and motion pictures. Roosevelt continued this media-savvy way of doing things. He charmed the press at regular conferences and demonstrated that radio addresses and motion picture news were especially effective means of making the president a familiar figure, whether speaking from the White House or traveling to wartime summits overseas. The trend toward giving the president, along with his family, a public persona culminated with the bustling, photogenic Kennedy clan. The rising celebrity status of the first family dominated the news and commanded public attention. A White House staff that had grown to more than four hundred members by the mid-1960s took charge of managing not just policy and politics but also the presidential image.[37]

This growing deference to White House leadership entailed a fundamental reworking of the Constitution. Congress had already early in the century acquiesced in the use of executive agreements to circumvent its treaty-making powers. While exploiting this opening to the full, Cold War presidents eroded the congressional role in going to war. Entry into both World War I and World War II followed the formal constitutional provisions, which vested in the House and Senate the power to approve a war declaration on the initiative of the president, even if in both cases a string of decisions made by the president had made war virtually inevitable. Thereafter, beginning with the Korean conflict in June 1950 and again the large-scale commitment of u.s. troops to Vietnam in July 1965, Congress surrendered its formal role in authorizing a declaration of war. Truman disguised the departure from standard practice by naming his war a "police action" while Lyndon Johnson could point to the Tonkin Gulf resolution, a vague 1964 congressional authorization for him to use force in Southeast Asia following putative attacks on u.s. naval vessels. Leaders on Capitol Hill tried to regain influence by creating, for example, their own staff of specialists on committees such as foreign affairs and in the offices of individual members and by asserting oversight on executive activities as sensitive as intelligence gathering and covert operations. Even so, the House and Senate fell ever farther behind an ever more imperial presidency.

Franklin Roosevelt demonstrated that a skilled president could also command substantial deference from a public increasingly responsive to cues coming out of the White House on potential foreign threats. He proved himself generally shrewd and selectively aggressive in shaping the national debate over how far the United States should get involved in renewed European conflict. Before the election of 1940, he had resolutely refused in his public comments to get ahead of public opinion, about which he systematically gathered information. Thus his public statements between 1937 and 1939 were cautious (as noted in chapter 3). He condemned aggression while offering reassuring comments on his commitment to peace. In 1940 and 1941 as arguments raged in the press, over radio, through films, in public rallies and speaking tours, and in letter-writing campaigns and lobbying in Congress, he shifted toward a bolder strategy that played out on three related fronts.

Roosevelt sought out allies among those who regarded British survival as critical to U.S. security and U.S. participation in the war essential to building a better world. The Committee to Defend America by Aiding the Allies, which had a nationwide membership, and the Century Group, composed of prominent, Anglophilic northeasterners, agreed with the president that inaction was foolhardy while disagreeing with him and among themselves on whether the country should plunge at once into war or settle for support of Britain short of war. Roosevelt had taken a hand in pressing for the organization of the Committee to Defend America and consulted with both its leaders and the Century Group's prominent northeasterners, who were like the president wealthy, Ivy League types. At times he let the interventionist committees make his case; at other times he echoed their arguments in virtuoso performances for the media; and sometimes he used them to launch trial balloons so that he might gauge public reaction before openly advocating a policy himself.

The president sought on a second front to discredit the opposition. The main organization arrayed against him was America First, which was based in the Midwest and enjoyed the support of progressives such as William E. Borah as well as conservatives fearful of mounting government power under Roosevelt's New Deal. Its leading voice was Charles Lindbergh, a celebrity after completing the first Atlantic solo flight. He argued for hemispheric defense as the best way to safeguard U.S. security and preserve a fragile democratic experiment. Influenced by his father's midwestern agrarian populism, Lindbergh rejected the new totalitarian interpretation of events in Europe in favor of an older racial one. He saw Germans as a virile people blocking the advance of a brutal, barbaric, godless, semi-Asiatic Soviet Union. Roosevelt's response was to discredit Lindbergh and other America Firsters by publicly impugning their character and describing them as Nazis, traitors, and fifth columnists. These Americans had not only "shut their eyes to the ugly reality of international banditry"; they were echoing the message of "the Axis bureaus of propaganda."[38] The president encouraged his political allies to speak out in similarly forceful terms. In private he repeatedly pressed for FBI investigations of Lindbergh and other critics on the grounds that national security justified violation of civil rights. To their credit, his attorney general and the FBI's Hoover refused.

An increasingly permissive domestic environment opened up opportunities on a third front. Roosevelt began to maneuver the country to the brink of war. He and Hull quietly applied increasing pressure on Japan. The president won public and congressional support for programs of aid to Britain such as the destroyers-for-bases deal and the lend-lease program. Finally, he manipulated the news concerning the battle for the Atlantic, which he as commander in chief had the U.S. Navy join in the fall of 1941. While Roosevelt restricted information in press conferences and press releases, the media on the whole proved acquiescent. The leaders of the movie and radio industries feared that Washington would turn its regulatory power against any naysayers and were in any case themselves predominantly Anglo or Jewish and thus personally inclined to back the interventionist cause. Serious newspapers managed to remain an open forum for a diversity of views. But even they were flooded with material from interventionist groups and government press offices.

Presidential sway over the public was considerable but not unlimited. A poll in early November 1941 revealed that over half (57 percent) of the country thought Roosevelt's steps to aid Britain "just right"; 27 percent thought he had done "too much"; and 16 percent "too little." But the public also expressed emphatic opposition to a war with Germany (by a 63 to 26 percent margin). In the confrontation with Japan, the public showed more belligerence. Asked by pollsters in November, 64 percent of respondents said they were ready to risk war and only 25 percent disagreed. For the public Pearl Harbor proved a shock because it gave the lie to the widely shared perception that the Japanese were a less advanced people and hence a less formidable foe. For Roosevelt that surprise attack proved a blessing because it is not at all clear otherwise whether or when he would have finally gotten over the considerable hump of public resistance to formal entry into the European conflict.[39]

During the late 1940s Truman offered a no less impressive demonstration of presidential persuasion. His first task was to get a war-weary public behind his policy of confrontation and containment. Polls suggested that Americans needed convincing, at least on the fundamental issue of a Soviet threat. In March 1945, as the war in Europe was drawing to a close and frictions over the peace were coming into the open, a majority (55 percent) thought Russia could be trusted to cooperate in the postwar period and 33 percent thought not. A year later (in March 1946), following Washington's complaints about Soviet troops in Iran and a speech by Stalin depicted in the u.s. media as hard line, Americans seemed to reverse their view, with 35 percent saying "yes" and 52 percent "no." Polling in January 1947 revealed one more shift, with the public now splitting evenly over whether the Soviets were trustworthy (43 percent "yes" and 40 percent "no"). After hesitating in 1946 about taking a forceful public stance, Truman finally turned to the task of selling his policy in March 1947 by rolling out what would become known as the Truman Doctrine. He followed with an attack on subversives in government and communist sympathizers in u.s. political life—a tack that helped him win reelection in 1948 and silence critics of his hard-line approach to the Soviet Union, including the third-party candidate, Henry Wallace. By February 1949 (following a Communist coup in Czechoslovakia and with Berlin under Soviet blockade), the public had settled into a decidedly Cold War mood: only 16 percent thought that "the Russian government sincerely desires peace," and 72 percent firmly embraced the contrary view espoused by Truman and his advisers.[40] This strong support was reinforced in the course of 1949 by the shock of Communist victory in China and the even more disturbing news of the first Soviet nuclear tests. This atmosphere of public alarm made it possible for Truman to go to war in Korea without asking for congressional approval.

Truman's use of the presidential bully pulpit had done a great deal to create a durable Cold War consensus. The Truman team had tackled the task out of a deep conviction that the public needed strong leadership. The president himself contended at the time, "We elect men to use their best judgment for the public interest." Looking back, Dean Acheson seconded the view that policymakers needed to lead: "If you truly had a democracy and did what the people wanted, you'd go wrong every time."[41] The 1930s served as an object lesson for both men. They saw public division and doubt giving rise to a policy of drift that made aggression easier and democracy less safe. They would not repeat that mistake.

A strong activist president—embodying an imperial presidency—was integral to the global role that the United States was assuming at midcentury. American ascendancy would become difficult to imagine and impossible to manage without the president's being able to command the power of the state and to serve as a voice for those national values that u.s. policy was supposed to preserve and advance. The office was now something like a combination of prime minister and king, even if it was sometimes hamstrung by the country's plural, interest-group politics; by a foreign policy machinery subject to breakdown, division, and leaks; and by a world sometimes stubbornly resistant to U.S. power and U.S. values.

At midcentury the American state had amid renewed conflict in Europe taken the mantle of transatlantic leadership. Europe's eclipse was long in the making. Between the sixteenth and nineteenth centuries its leading states had climbed to the commanding heights of world power, with its economies and armies unmatched and its influence extending to virtually every outlying region. The United States, itself a product of that global influence, followed the European playbook. European Americans seized land from indigenous peoples, built an advanced economy, developed military might, took colonies, and finally even plunged into European wars, which had been anathema to earlier generations of Americans. World War II and the early Cold War were the culmination of a long, steady trend toward matching and then surpassing the might of the other states of the developed world. As American leaders quickly realized, newly won dominance carried with it obligations greater than merely winning friends and defeating foes. It also meant creating the conditions conducive to international peace and prosperity. Global crusades of one sort entailed no less global crusades of other kinds.

5

IN THE AMERICAN IMAGE

1941★1968

In 1959 the u.s. government staged an exhibition in Sokolniki Park in Moscow. It was notable for its display of American goods carrying a consumer message whose appeal reached back to the 1920s and was now especially strong among peoples around the world with fresh memories of grueling depression and war years of material sacrifice, personal loss, and guttering hope. This appeal reached even into the capital of the Cold War foe. The exhibit's display of Detroit's finest—a big, sleek, finned model—was perhaps the most wondrous example of consumer extravagance (fig. 5). The car commanded rapt attention from Muscovites still living in communal apartments and queuing for food. Soviet apparatchiks sought to quiet the buzz, but the large crowds and intense interest carried a clear message about material abundance distinctly to u.s. advantage. On a visit to the exhibit in July Vice President Richard Nixon boasted of a system that supplied homes, cars, televisions, and radios to millions of American families. Soviet premier Nikita Khrushchev dismissed the u.s. fixation on "fancy gadgets" that were either useless or beyond the reach of ordinary Americans, but he knew from the crush of interested Muscovites that the Soviet system had to compete.[1]

Consumerism was itself part of an economic and cultural bundle of influences that made a wide range of Americans—policymakers surveying the world, businessmen carving out foreign markets, and ordinary families savoring abundance—allies in a concerted effort to put an American stamp on the postwar world. In 1941 Henry Luce's seminal "The American Century" had linked stopping Hitler to promoting a powerful and attractive American way. He had in mind "a sharing with all peoples of our Bill of Rights, our Declaration of Independence, our Constitution, our magnificent industrial products, our technical skills." His argument was especially perceptive in pointing to

Figure 5. "Moscow Gets a Glimpse of America,"
New York Times Magazine, 2 August 1959, 7.

the broad impact of American music, movies, slang, and inventions that had already established the United States as "the intellectual, scientific, and artistic capital of the world." Luce imagined the international appeal of this vital and prosperous society growing still greater in the postwar period.[2]

U.S. leaders in the decades after World War II shared this nationalist vision and moved confidently to exploit their country's economic preeminence and cultural clout. They set about creating an international regime—organizations and agreements—congruent with U.S. values. They resuscitated the old centers of the international economy devastated by depression and war and provided the structure to integrate their production and markets. Finally, they promoted a consumer model with broad appeal. In all these ways the American state set the terms, just as Luce wanted, for how the world should operate. This economic and cultural drive would establish U.S. ascendancy on a second front parallel to the political-military struggle for Cold War dominance.

A NEW INTERNATIONAL ORDER

The Roosevelt administration approached the end of the war possessed of enormous leverage. Part was from the prestige of leading a global coalition to victory. Part was the result of holding two-thirds of the world's gold reserves and accounting for half of the world's industrial output in 1946.[3] Wartime destruction had spared none of the other economic powers. Franklin Roosevelt and like-minded interventionists also possessed a firm, clear resolve. They regarded victory over the Axis as a second chance to build a world of peace and bounty. Narrow-minded "isolationists" at home and short-sighted leaders abroad had frustrated Woodrow Wilson's program and put the world in deep peril. They would not spoil the prospects for global reform this time. While Roosevelt's short-term goal was to accommodate his allies even if it meant accepting British colonies and a Soviet sphere of influence, his long-term preoccupations were distinctly Wilsonian and reflected in the Atlantic Charter of 1941. He wanted a new League of Nations—the United Nations—to guarantee the security of the international community. To shore up this revamped international institution, the Roosevelt and Truman administrations launched a path-breaking campaign to establish international norms. They would hold to account leaders who abused state power at the expense of either their own people or their neighbors, and they would at the same time promote the rights of individuals, especially against totalitarian abuse. No less important in this mix of initiatives was the creation of a free-market world. Roosevelt gave high priority to the drive to revive and reform the international economy.

Collectively these initiatives formed the bedrock for the postwar international order.

The Foundations for Global Governance

The United Nations stood at the center of Roosevelt's long-term hopes for a prosperous and peaceful world. Sponsors of u.s. membership in such a body held that the failure of the United States to join the League accounted for that body's ineffective response to the rising tide of aggression in the 1930s. However desirable a new League of Nations might be, Roosevelt had omitted any reference to it in the Atlantic Charter. He wanted to create greater national unity in 1941, not to ignite controversy. But it was hard to imagine achieving the goals that the charter explicitly laid down—shedding costly armaments, abandoning force as an instrument of policy, collaborating on economic issues, promoting self determination and territorial security, and ultimately establishing "a wider system of general security"—without a new league. A peaceful, democratic, free-trade world had to have some sort of forum. Even in the short term, Roosevelt needed that forum as a place where the great powers could regularly gather to resolve their practical differences over whatever problems the postwar years presented them.

While directing American forces on two fronts and keeping his allies placated and supplied, Roosevelt somehow found time to create the domestic consensus for the establishment of the United Nations. He started with some advantages. The public was in broad terms favorable to u.s. membership in a postwar international security organization, and Republican leaders such as Wendell Wilkie and John Foster Dulles were also supportive and eager to avoid a repeat of the destructive partisan collision of 1919–20. The potential sources of opposition were die-hard critics (most Republicans) of any Wilsonian measures that might entangle the United States in foreign conflict and diminish u.s. sovereignty and, at the other extreme, global federalists, who saw the only possibility for peace in the creation of a super state. In the course of 1943 Roosevelt set to work with Cordell Hull to broaden public support, create bipartisan political backing, and win over major media pundits such as the hard-headed Walter Lippmann. The leitmotiv of the presidential message was that failure was unthinkable and that perfection was impossible. Americans had to bear their "responsibilities in an admittedly imperfect world" or accept the prospect of "follow[ing] the same tragic road again—the road to a third world war."[4]

In 1943 Roosevelt also went to work to line up his British and Soviet allies. He began at the Tehran summit late that year, let Allied ministers hash out some details (most notably at Dumbarton Oaks in Washington between August and October 1944), and then took up especially knotty matters himself at the Yalta conference in early 1945. He had to bring around Churchill, who was primarily interested in a regional approach to security, and Stalin, who was focused on retaining a firm hold on his eastern European trophies. Roosevelt's own conception of a postwar world dominated by the "four policemen" made it easy in principle to reassure Stalin, though such concessions sent shivers up the spine of those both in the u.s. government and out who were deeply suspicious of Soviet postwar goals. Roosevelt appears to have been unshakable in his view that peace depended on continued collaboration among the leading Allied powers and that the UN had to embody that system of collaboration if it were to work and survive.

In late April 1945, just weeks after Roosevelt's death, delegates from forty-six nations then enlisted in the anti-Axis struggle met in San Francisco to form the new international organization. Their handiwork, completed in June, proceeded within the framework that Roosevelt had devised. They divided the UN into two main bodies. A security council was to consist of the big-five states of the time (the United States, the Soviet Union, France, Britain, and China), together with a rotating group of six other states. Each of the big five was to have veto power over substantive matters coming to the UN for action. Matters of war and peace were to be the exclusive domain of this body. The General Assembly was to contain all member states, to make its decisions by majority vote, and to concern itself primarily with nonsecurity issues, notably economic and social matters. On questions relating to the internal UN budget and administration, the General Assembly had the power to dictate, but its votes on resolutions deemed substantive (in other words, primarily within the purview of the Security Council) were nonbinding. Strikingly deliberations leading up to the creation of the UN had consistently emphasized security concerns—measures to keep the peace and defeat any aggression—and neglected other ways in which the UN could promote global integration and human welfare. Truman's address at the closing session at San Francisco sounded the familiar concerns with security going back to Wilson: "Let us not fail to grasp this supreme chance to establish a world-wide rule of reason—to create an enduring peace under the guidance of God."[5] The Senate in a bipartisan mood gave its overwhelming support for u.s. membership in this new league. That the vote was 89 to 2 was a tribute to the care that the Roosevelt and the Truman administrations had taken to avoid a repeat of the Wilson-Senate fiasco.

U.S. leaders had a good claim to paternity. They had not only set the tempo and agenda in discussions among the Allies but also devoted the most resources to planning for the new organization. The U.S. delegations to the two main conferences—at Dumbarton Oaks and in San Francisco—were the largest and best prepared. The host country ran both meetings and stood at the center of the negotiations over virtually every one of the hard issues that arose. Appropriately, the UN headquarters was on land in New York donated by the Rockefeller family, and the organization bore a name first coined by Roosevelt shortly after Pearl Harbor. He had used "United Nations" to describe the twenty-six powers then waging war together to create a just peace.

The UN proved in its early years a useful creation. With U.S. encouragement it went to work at once on reconstruction and relief programs in China and Europe. These were the beginnings of a far-reaching effort to deal with practical international problems through specialized agencies functioning under UN auspices. Notable among the agencies that sprang up during the UN's first two decades were the UN International Children's Emergency Fund, the International Labor Organization, the World Health Organization, the UN High Commissioner for Refugees, the Food and Agricultural Organization, and the UN Educational, Scientific, and Cultural Organization. The UN, moreover, quickly demonstrated that it could act as a peacekeeper cooling down disputes where the interests of the Soviets and Americans were not directly engaged, especially in smoothing the process of decolonization. In 1947 the Security Council involved itself in the Dutch retreat from the East Indies and the partition of British Palestine. The next year the General Assembly was central in securing the independence of the former Italian colonies of Eritrea, Somalia, and Libya. In 1948 and 1949 the Security Council took the precedent-making step of authorizing forces acting under UN auspices to establish a buffer between warring parties in Palestine and in Kashmir. UN "blue helmets" figured prominently again in 1956 after the British-French-Israeli invasion of Egypt and in the early 1960s amid conflict in the former Belgian Congo colony. In all the Security Council would authorize thirteen such operations during the UN's first forty years and set the stage for more frequent intervention once the Cold War was over.

In the most surprising turn, the UN proved that it could also play a role in the Cold War. The Truman administration turned to the Security Council in 1946 as a forum to air complaints about Soviet troops that had stayed in northern Iran beyond the war. Stalin withdrew them. In 1950 the Security Council proved even more important in securing UN backing for resistance to the North Korean invasion. Thanks to a temporary Soviet boycott of the Security Council, no Soviet delegation was present to wield the veto against the U.S. call for action. The council gave its blessings and with it international legitimacy to the u.s.-led coalition defending South Korea. Once more during the Cuban missile crisis in October 1962 the UN figured prominently. The Security Council initially provided a forum for the Kennedy administration to publicize charges against the clandestine Soviet placement of missiles. As the crisis reached its climax, UN secretary general U Thant provided President Kennedy a confidential channel for devising a peaceful settlement.

With Cold War rivalry short-circuiting great-power collaboration on the Security Council, Washington looked to the General Assembly. There no one had a veto. The one-nation, one-vote procedure gave the United States and its allies a majority that lasted into the 1960s. Then the arrival of new states created by decolonization not only dramatically expanded membership—from the fifty-one charter members in 1945 to 127 by 1970, with more waiting in the wings—but also deprived the United States of its safe majority in the General Assembly. Outspoken and impatient, the newcomers tended to take a neutral stance on Cold War issues while championing other priorities. They wanted UN programs funded by the rich countries to spur economic development, and they sought a voice in the administration of headquarters in New York and in the various constituent organizations. With the Security Council immobilized and control of the General Assembly slipping away, u.s. officials and other prominent Americans began in the late 1960s to raise doubts about the utility of the UN. The American creation was beginning to prove a disappointment.

Alongside the UN, the Roosevelt and Truman administrations fashioned a second major support for the postwar international order. Their goal was to tame the power of states. Over three centuries—since the Peace of Westphalia in 1648—states had managed to establish themselves as the basic sovereign unit of international society. Individuals figured as the subjects of state authority with no recourse against immoral or illegitimate domestic acts. The first hints of a postwar program to hold states accountable appeared in Roosevelt's Atlantic Charter. While it affirmed the Wilsonian goal consistent with the Westphalian order of preserving states against aggression, it also promised people everywhere "freedom from fear and want" and the right "to choose the form of government under which they will live." These notions marked the beginning of a revolutionary shift in thinking. The needs and interests of individuals, collectives such as ethnic and racial minorities, and even entire broad categories of people such as women, children, and migrants would weigh against the interests of states.

The trial of German leaders was the first step toward holding states accountable to international norms. Secretary of War Henry L. Stimson championed this course against a formidable array of opposition. Publics in the United States, Britain, and France all favored summary punishment, a view that was shared by the Churchill government in Britain, by the Soviet government, and within the Roosevelt cabinet by Secretary of the Treasury Henry Morgenthau, Secretary of State Cordell Hull, and the president himself. Stimson argued that leaders charged with misconduct should answer to the international community in formal proceedings in which they received minimum due process. In April 1945 in one of his first decisions as president, Harry Truman backed Stimson. The British and the Soviets quickly fell into line.

Washington took the lead in designing and conducting the trial. The chief prosecutor was the Supreme Court justice Robert H. Jackson. In a report to Truman in June 1945 on preparatory work for the trial, he spelled out his goal of clarifying and expanding the international code: "Out of this war should come unmistakable rules and workable machinery from which any who might contemplate another era of brigandage would know that they would be held personally responsible and would be personally punished." Jackson formulated three basic charges applicable now to the German leadership and in the future to anyone who followed in their footsteps. One was conspiracy by criminal organizations to commit aggression against peace. The notion of conspiracy by criminal organizations was unique to U.S. law, but the underlying charge of aggression against peace built on the Kellogg-Briand Pact of 1928 outlawing war. Germany as well as Japan had been signatories. One of Roberts's British associates noted at the opening of the trial his wish that henceforth leaders who "plunge their own countries and other countries into aggressive war should do so with a halter around their necks." A second set of charges related to the civilized conduct of war and drew on conventions going back to 1864 protecting wounded combatants and prisoners of war. "Crimes against humanity" (including forced labor, deportation, extermination, and execution of hostages) constituted the third and most innovative set of charges. These were mainly intended to cover the German assault on religious or racial groups in Germany and occupied countries unconnected to the conduct of war itself. Though the notion of crimes against humanity had come into circulation in the early decades of the twentieth century, it had not produced an international consensus or been incorporated into treaties. This new standard was thus vulnerable to criticism for imposing an unfair, retroactive rule of conduct on leaders.[6]

The proceedings began formally in November 1945 in Nuremberg, chosen not only because it had been a stronghold of the Nazi movement but also because it had one of the few courthouses that had survived the Allied bombing. The renovated courtroom was outfitted with a new IBM simultaneous translation system that left the floor crisscrossed with wires. Judges representing the United States, Britain, the Soviet Union, and France presided. The trial, which produced a voluminous historical record, continued until October 1946, when the presiding judges handed down against the Germans sitting in the dock twelve verdicts of death by hanging, seven of imprisonment for periods ranging from ten years to life, and three acquittals.

Nuremberg paved the way and in large measure provided the template for the centerpiece trial of Japanese leaders, held in Tokyo between May 1946 and November 1948. Here too Americans took the lead in devising the ground rules and running the actual trial, even though eleven nations formally participated. Prominent Japanese faced charges of atrocities against civilians, destruction of cities from the air and ground, fatally harsh treatment of prisoners of war, and—most sensationally of all—conspiracy to commit aggression. The prosecution placed on Japan's leaders blame for "wholesale destruction of human lives, not alone on the field of battle . . . but in the homes, hospitals, and orphanages, in factories and fields; and the victims would be the young and the old, the well and the infirm—men, women and children alike."[7] As at Nuremberg, the Tokyo court found clear-cut guilt. For their brutal course of conquest, seven of the defendants were condemned to hang, and the remaining eighteen received prison sentences of varying lengths, most for life. The high-profile proceedings not only generated another rich documentary record but also functioned as part of a region-wide attempt to gain a measure of justice. Some fifty trials of lesser figures were held outside Japan—at points all around Asia that had been subject to Japanese aggression and brutality.

Running parallel with these dramatic trials was a drive to give human rights greater prominence in international law and discourse. The notion of rights was rooted in the eighteenth-century Enlightenment concepts of respect for human dignity and reason. As the language of rights became commonplace, it gave rise to political battles, nowhere more dramatically than in the French and American revolutions. Natural rights had had from the outset critics who found them dangerous to political stability and social cohesion, and skeptics were unconvinced that natural rights were either natural or self-evident. One unfriendly observer memorably derided them as "rhetorical nonsense, nonsense on stilts."[8] On the defensive in the course of the nineteenth and early twentieth centuries, rights were now to enjoy a revival marked by repeated rounds of international negotiation and codification within a far larger, more diverse, and closely bound global community than had existed in the eighteenth century.

Franklin Roosevelt played a particularly crucial role as a bridge between u.s. policy and the renewed concern with rights percolating among academics and intellectuals during the interwar years. One of the prime influences on his thinking was a group of scholars in Paris, most prominently the Russian émigré jurist André Mandelstam. The Bolshevik revolution and the massacre of Armenians in Turkey in 1915 had quickened the Paris group's commitment to going beyond the protection of minorities, which was espoused by a variety of interwar agreements. The Paris group wanted to extend safeguards to include individual human rights. Another key influence on Roosevelt was the British author H. G. Wells. In 1939–40 he had conducted a public crusade to make human rights a respected part of any postwar arrangements. Roosevelt not only knew Wells personally but also received a copy of his draft declaration of rights. From these and perhaps other sources Roosevelt got the idea for the Four Freedoms, laid out in his January 1941 State of the Union address and reiterated in comments during the rest of the year. His notion of a world free from the fear of want, repression, religious persecution, and international conflict helped stimulate a flood of documents and discussions, both in public and within official circles, supporting a human rights agenda.

As the war drew to a close, nongovernmental organizations worked at making sure that human rights did not drop from sight. A u.s. proposal to include some statement on human rights failed to obtain support from the other delegations at the Dumbarton Oaks conference in Washington in 1944. Following that failure, nongovernmental organizations flocked to the formal UN conference in San Francisco in April 1945 to stiffen the resolve of the official u.s. delegation, which in turn overcame reluctance on the part of the British, the Soviets, and the Chinese. As a result, the UN charter featured prominently—in the preamble itself—a commitment "to reaffirm faith in fundamental human rights, in the dignity and worth of the human person, in the equal rights of men and women and of nations large and small."[9] To ensure that these words did not become dead letters, the conferees established a human rights commission operating under the UN's Social and Economic Council.

The international norms that u.s. leaders had promoted in the heady days of victory over Germany and Japan seemed all the more important as the grim details of the Holocaust emerged. The most consequential effort in that direction, the Universal Declaration of Human Rights, made direct reference in its prologue to the "barbarous acts which have outraged the conscience of mankind."[10] Once more the UN had served as the locus of initiative as delegates from around the world had assembled to discuss, draft, and finalize what would prove to be the foundational human rights document. Eleanor Roosevelt, the widow of Franklin Roosevelt, played a pivotal role in constructing a consensus among the delegates despite their ethical, cultural, philosophical, and political differences. In the words of one of the planning documents penned in early 1947, the delegates came to agree that "the world of man is at a critical stage in its political, social, and economic evolution. If it is to proceed further on the path towards unity, it must develop a common set of ideas and principles."[11] Put to a formal vote in the General Assembly in late December 1948, the declaration won broad support. No country opposed it, and only South Africa, Saudi Arabia, the Soviet Union, and its eastern European allies abstained.

The declaration's broad definition of political and economic rights directly challenged the view that the treatment of individuals was a matter of concern only for the states in which they lived. Global society could set standards that signatories were obliged to honor. These included guarantees of civic and political participation and protections such as freedom of speech, conscience, thought, and assembly as well as the right to vote, to receive fair legal treatment, to enjoy privacy, and, with regard to dissidents, to receive asylum in other countries. But the declaration also extended its concerns to such social and economic issues as the right to basic education, to work, to receive a living wage, and to enjoy rest and leisure. It broke new ground in other ways. For example, its concerns for women's rights were evident in provisions for nondiscriminatory employment, universal suffrage and education, and marriage with consent and with the right to initiate divorce.

The United Nations bolstered the u.s.-initiated new order through a variety of other measures. In 1946, following the conclusion of the Nuremburg trial, the General Assembly gave its imprimatur to the legal principles on which the court had proceeded, and in 1948 a convention negotiated under UN auspices dealt specifically with the prevention and punishment of genocide. In 1949 an international conference held apart from the UN reaffirmed earlier agreements on humane treatment of combatants and extended protection to civilians (the so-called fourth Geneva convention). Through the 1950s a series of UN-sponsored conventions threw the mantle of protection over refugees and the stateless and put a halt to slavery, other trafficking in persons, and forced labor. A convention concluded in 1965 committed signatories to the elimination of all forms of racial discrimination. The next year a pair of covenants provided a systematic, broad-gauge definition of rights—economic, social, cultural, civil, and political. The process of restricting the state and protecting the individual had just begun.

But already in this its early phase, the human rights movement was generating controversy. The foremost issue reflected Cold War divisions between Marxist and non-Marxist conceptions of a good society and thus over whether to put the emphasis on individual and political rights or on collective, economic rights. Were human rights primarily, if not exclusively, civil and political (as the Anglo-American view had it)? If so, then protecting free speech and voting, as well as preventing arbitrary arrest and censorship, were the most pressing matters. But what if rights were broader, including foremost economic and social provisions? If that were the case, then economic development and matters of material welfare such as health care, unionization, and minimum income could claim a prominent, even prior place in the human rights agenda, and the state could claim an important role, not as a threat to but as an essential promoter of rights.

A Framework for Prosperity

Well before World War II had ended, the Roosevelt administration turned to the problems of reconstructing a devastated international economy. Hopes for a new era of international cooperation and personal freedom would prove empty without a revival of a market-oriented system of global trade and finance. Secretary of State Cordell Hull, Secretary of the Treasury Henry Morgenthau, and the president himself became the main sponsors of that system.

A set of clear historical lessons guided them. The late nineteenth-century international economy had created prosperity and peace, a point Wilson had grasped. But the failure of his fourteen-point program (including notably free trade) had had in the view of Roosevelt and his associates doleful consequences: depression, protectionism, and the struggle for resources and markets, which in turn had fueled national rivalry and aggression. Already in the 1930s the Roosevelt administration had begun translating its vision of an open world into action. Hull with Roosevelt's backing had championed free-trade agreements as a practical response to a world under stress. On the eve of war Roosevelt had included in the Atlantic Charter provisions for free trade and access to raw materials and for international collaboration on economic issues. In mid-1944, with the end of the war in sight and with the u.s. economic advantage overwhelming, the Roosevelt administration sponsored a conference in Bretton Woods, New Hampshire. The conference supplied a durable framework for the postwar international economy (virtually unchanged into the early 1970s), and its dedication to free trade and its institutional offspring would give rise to a powerful international consensus operating into the next century and reaching into the daily lives of individuals all around the world.

In effecting this far-reaching design the Roosevelt administration worked closely with British bankers and bureaucrats. They had been partners in efforts to manage the interwar economy and then to guide wartime mobilization, and they were like-minded on most fundamental economic and political issues. Leading the u.s. delegation at Bretton Woods was Harry Dexter White of the Treasury Department, an effective economic bureaucrat whose reputation later suffered from allegations that he spied for the Soviet Union. Representing the British was the redoubtable John Maynard Keynes, economic theorist, policy adviser, and sophisticated man of the world. A bit of doggerel penned at the time revealed one distinctly pro-British estimate of what the two sides brought to this meeting: "It's true *they* have the money bags / But *we* have all the brains." The obvious riposte, offered by a u.s. official, was that in this alliance, as in all others, "one party wears boots and spurs while the other wears a saddle."[12] Out of this rough-edged but fruitful transatlantic collaboration came three major initiatives endorsed by representatives of the other allied powers at the conference.

The longest lived of the conference's inventions was the International Monetary Fund (IMF) and the World Bank (initially named the International Bank for Reconstruction and Development). The role of the IMF was to promote financial stability by helping countries short of foreign exchange to keep their international accounts solvent. The IMF would make a loan to prevent the system of exchange from freezing up as it had in the 1930s, and the recipient country would repay the emergency funding as production and sales recovered. The World Bank took development as its brief. It initially made European reconstruction its main concern but through the 1950s steadily shifted its focus to the emerging third world. Both institutions were formally part of the United Nations, though in fact each was a creature of the United States and its Cold War allies by virtue of a weighted voting system that effectively excluded poor countries from their councils and explicitly excluded nonmarket, socialist states. The countries with big, advanced economies guided IMF and World Bank operations and selected their leaders. As the most powerful economy and the main source of start-up funds, the United States exercised virtual veto power.

Bretton Woods' second major decision was to recognize the centrality of u.s. capital as New York completed its eclipse of London as the center of international finance. The conference made the new pivotal currency the dollar valued in terms of a fixed amount of gold. This fixed ratio created international monetary stability, which in turn made commerce easier because it eliminated uncertainty associated with fluctuating exchange rates.

Rather than returning to the free movement of capital characteristic of the pre-1914 period, Bretton Woods sanctioned restrictions on the import and export of capital of the sort that had developed after 1914. This position was a personal victory for Keynes and reflected his preoccupation with economic efficiency, social welfare, and democratic accountability. A long-time critic of free-market orthodoxy, he had written in 1926, "It is *not* a correct deduction from the principles of economics that enlightened self-interest always operates in the public interest. Nor is it true that self-interest generally *is* enlightened; more often individuals acting separately to promote their own ends are too ignorant or too weak to attain even these. Experience does *not* show that individuals, when they make up a social unit, are always less clear-sighted than when they act separately."[13] The Great Depression had confirmed his view that markets did not always work optimally and might even malfunction if left alone. Fully free capital markets were in Keynes's estimate especially dangerous. Most fundamentally he worried that those controlling mobile capital could ride roughshod over any state's management of interest rates and currency values. Ultimately then basic decisions associated with sovereign state power would pass to unelected elites operating without any official or electoral restraint. Keynes also worried that currency markets would prove too volatile if left entirely alone and thus governments should stand ready to intervene to prevent potentially damaging swings. The grim economic state of most countries at war's end led the Roosevelt administration to lean to the side of caution even if supporting Keynes meant going against free-market doctrine and the preference of New York bankers.

The third element in the Bretton Woods cluster of initiatives was the commitment to free trade. It proved difficult to implement in the quick and sweeping terms that the Roosevelt administration wanted. The British government was loath to surrender its advantageous system of restricted trade within the empire. U.S. producers were fearful that steep tariff reductions would bring ruinous foreign competition and so mobilized supporters in Congress. Together they stymied repeated White House efforts to create an institution to function as a free-trade equivalent of the IMF or the World Bank. Only in 1947 did Congress agree to a modest measure, the General Agreement on Tariffs and Trade (GATT). It provided for a gradual and negotiated lowering of barriers to trade. Altogether lacking in institutional form, this mechanism made it possible to initiate international negotiations with any resulting agreements still subject to congressional approval. Only in the early 1960s did GATT begin to demonstrate its capacity to lower international barriers to trade with the launching of the negotiations known as the Kennedy round (after the president who sponsored them but would not live to see their results).

While Bretton Woods created a framework for globalization, significant economic integration was still some decades away. Into the 1970s capital remained in most places subject to state supervision. While foreign investment was rising, it stayed well below the comparative figures for the pre–World War I era. International trade, spurred at first by the United States' unilateral opening of its home market, was also increasing, but only in the 1970s did it begin to reach the relative level of the late nineteenth and early twentieth centuries. Even then, the socialist world of eastern Europe, the Soviet Union, and China, with a bit less than a fifth of world output, stood aside as a virtually separate system of exchange.[14] Labor mobility in the early post–World War II decades was nil compared to a half century earlier; potential immigrants, who once could have traveled without passport and with limited official inspection, now confronted stringent border controls.

RESCUE AND REFORM

Nowhere was the importance of recovery more important to the shape of the postwar world than in a stricken western Europe and Japan, and nowhere were American goods, capital, and leadership more essential. The United States alone had the means as the major surviving market for foreign exporters and as the sole source of capital to mount a rescue operation for those two strategic centers of the international economy. U.S. leaders also had a motive. They recalled how the troubled postwar settlement and the endless difficulties over war debts had poisoned the peace in Europe. Events had confirmed Wilson's insight: no prosperity, no peace. For the Truman administration, which had to work out a recovery program, the Cold War rivalry with the Soviet Union raised the stakes and added an element of urgency. A u.s.-assisted recovery was essential to closing the door to communist agitation and to creating positions of strength against Soviet aggression.

In this exercise in rescue and reform, u.s. leaders took the long view, moved with patience, and achieved extraordinary results. In addition to unilaterally opening the u.s. domestic market, they made money available for rebuilding and tolerated a revival of state economic power in defeated lands. Such measures helped restore capitalism in its birthplace (Europe) and reignite growth in a once dynamic capitalist offshoot (Japan). These successes in turn made possible not just the building of a powerful Cold War alliance but also the rise of an international economic system running along lines that reflected American preferences, albeit imperfectly.

The Grand Collaboration

The u.s. approach to western Europe was in one historian's intriguing formulation "empire by invitation." Americans and influential center-right European politicians entered a close partnership that served as the bedrock for the rescue effort. Robert Schuman of France, Konrad Adenauer of Germany, and Alcide de Gasperi of Italy—all conservative Roman Catholics—shared with the Truman administration an interest in speeding economic recovery, containing the appeal of their domestic rivals on the Left, and holding Soviet influence at bay. Britain, whether ruled by Labour or Conservative governments, joined the collaboration—but on its own terms as an established and trusted u.s. ally. This close transatlantic partnership enjoyed strong European public support. A survey in July 1945 asked French respondents whether they preferred to have the United States or the Soviet Union exercising a greater international influence; 47 percent favored the United States and only 23 percent were for the Soviets. In the American zone of occupied Germany an October 1947 poll found that 63 percent trusted the Americans to deal fairly with Germany, compared to 45 percent for the British and 4 percent for the French. No one trusted the Soviets. In Britain 63 percent of the public expressed approval of the government's pro-u.s. stance in an April 1948 poll.[15]

What turned out to be a grand North Atlantic collaboration was driven at first by simple privation. Cities across Europe had been repeatedly pounded, some reduced to rubble. Housing was in short supply; in hard-hit Germany, half the stock was gone. Industry, transport, and communications were all badly damaged. Food, hard to find at the end of the war, became scarcer because of weak agricultural production and distribution. Caloric intake in many places fell below the level to sustain life in the long run. The winter of 1946–47, the harshest in memory, intensified discontent among a cold, homeless, hungry population. Strikes and street demonstrations revealed that the public's patience was at the breaking point.

u.s. government assistance was critical to getting western European economies moving again. It began on a large scale in 1946 as Washington grasped the depth of the crisis. By the time assistance started trailing off in 1952, u.s. aid amounted to $21.7 billion, with the bulk of it going to France, West Germany, Italy, and Britain. The most famous increment (and also the largest) went with the Marshall Plan, announced in mid-1947 by Secretary of State

George C. Marshall. A senior State Department official had returned from a survey of Europe to report that Britain, France, and Italy were on the edge of economic, social, and political disintegration and by implication ripe for revolution that would play into communist hands. Reflecting alarm in the Truman administration, Marshall proposed a major aid program that would avert looming disaster and "permit the emergence of political and social conditions in which free institutions can exist."[16]

Although Marshall's initial proposal applied to all of Europe and the Soviet Union, Moscow declined to participate and made sure its clients in eastern European did the same. Over the next five years the Marshall Plan alone funneled into dollar-starved European treasuries some $13 billion—all in the form of outright grants to avoid the tangle and ill will created by American loans during World War I and the interwar years. Further stimulating the European economies was u.s. private investment. Already by 1950 it was nearly $2 billion, slightly higher than at the time of the 1929 crash, and by 1963 it had grown to over $10 billion.[17] Equally important as a contribution to recovery was Washington's decision to open the enormous, booming u.s. market to exports from Europe. Recovery would stall without strong foreign trade.

u.s. government assistance came with conditions. To win constituent support for foreign aid (never a popular measure), Congress stipulated that the Europeans spend roughly 70 percent of the Marshall Plan money on American-made goods. Cold War preoccupations led to another u.s. requirement—that governments accepting assistance oust any Communist Party members from governing coalitions. Washington was particularly worried by large Communist parties in France and Italy. Both parties had strong, well-organized labor support, a large electoral following, and high prestige derived from their leading role in the anti-German resistance. In France and Italy, the ruling Christian Democrats were happy to marginalize their Communist rivals, and so took the u.s. cue and split with them in the course of 1947. U.S. officials also sought with considerable success to drive a wedge between left-wing and centrist unions, thus in effect destroying the unity of the European labor movement.

Other conditions laid down by u.s. officials derived from a basic conviction that Europe needed to put more reliance on markets as the surest path to prosperity and stability. This emphasis on markets reflected the postwar hostility in some quarters to New Deal programs. It also reflected the tendency in Cold War rhetoric to identify the enemy with state planning and to equate freedom with economic choice and protection of property. In their eagerness to instruct the Old World, u.s. officials sought to reverse a long history of state ownership in strategic economic sectors and to discourage labor demands for welfare and higher wages. At the same time these officials encouraged European governments to coordinate their economic recovery programs and remove obstacles to trade among the fragmented national markets that made up Europe. A larger open market would work better to spur competition and specialization to the benefit of all.

The u.s. position on markets and the state was not doctrinaire. In fact many of the officials sent to Europe to work on recovery efforts came out of the New Deal bureaucracy and were comfortable with state activism, especially in an emergency. In the Cold War context, even rabid devotees of the free market understood the risk of forcing changes that might create a political opening for the Left. Thus, for example, u.s. administrators of Marshall funding in France had to accommodate local preferences. French planners had their eye on restoring their country's position as a modern economy and to that end favored investment in heavy industry, transport, and energy and gave low priority to consumer goods. When the French government nationalized electricity, coal, and airlines, u.s. officials reacted critically—and then acquiesced. At the same time they pressed for giving more attention to building housing, schools, and hospitals (all good advertisements for u.s. generosity) and for making the tax code more progressive.

The bold, relatively flexible, and sometimes intrusive u.s. role in postwar Europe was rewarded with a strikingly successful economic recovery. Much of that success was due to the Europeans themselves—their business skills and trained labor force that had survived the war's physical destruction, as well as a widespread resolve to put behind them state rivalry, military competition, and popular jingoism, which had inflicted monumental suffering. But opening the u.s. market at a critical moment and providing u.s. capital did much to facilitate the recovery. By 1952 industrial and agricultural production had substantially surpassed prewar levels. Though western Europeans still faced food and housing shortages, those lingering difficulties would dissolve in the extraordinarily prosperous years to come, as evidenced by high national growth rates, low unemployment, low inflation, expanding foreign trade, stable exchange rates, and liberal public expenditures on welfare, education, and health.

At the same time European leaders were taking the first practical steps toward regional integration, a cause that had European champions well before American officials had made it part of the Marshall Plan. French foreign minister Robert Schuman took a historical step in mid-1950 when he proposed a European Coal and Steel Community. Launched in 1952, it not only established cooperation between France and its old rival, Germany, but also provided the experience and political impetus for its members—France, West Germany, Italy, Belgium, the Netherlands, and Luxembourg—to create the still more ambitious European Economic Community in 1957. Rounding out the new regional framework was the North Atlantic Treaty of 1949. The alliance guaranteed the region's security from Soviet attack, with u.s. taxpayers bearing the lion's share of the costs.

Americans had had a significant impact but with notable limits imposed by the collaborative nature of their relationship with the governing European parties. There is truth in the witticism that the Europeans were ready to be dominated—but on their terms! Regardless of the leverage that Washington possessed, the postwar democratic ethos compelled European politicians to listen to popular demands for food, jobs, housing, and social security or risk losing votes, even falling from power. Moreover, a combination of political calculation and political integrity kept Christian Democrats from driving their Communist foes from the electoral process. For example, u.s. officials urging a quiet purge in Italy found the Christian Democrats there "not our natural allies in this campaign."[18] The leaders of the centrist party knew that they enjoyed some sway in Washington precisely because the Communist Party remained a lively, popular presence, and they genuinely supported postwar democratic norms that guaranteed the Communists a place in the political system even if the Americans in this case did not.

No less a constraint was the widespread skepticism—as strong on the Right as on the Left—of a free-market model in the stringent u.s. style. European leaders had seen the state playing a beneficial role in their countries' industrialization drive. They saw efficiency and competitive advantage not in free-for-all market activity but in industrial concentration and cooperation among firms that would have violated u.s. antitrust rules. But political ideology as much as practical economic experience guided politicians in Paris, Bonn, Rome, and the other western European capitals. They embraced social justice doctrines long promoted by the Catholic Church as a critical reaction against industrialization and the sweeping free-market principles favored by the Americans. Spiritual life could not develop, so the Vatican instructed believers, in a society governed by a soulless market, ridden with poverty and split sharply along class lines. Popular impatience, a belief in state power, and a strong commitment to social justice thus combined to give rise to a European welfare capitalism divergent from American preferences. Washington would have to accept rising state spending on popular programs and a continuing state role in the economy as the price for seeing capitalism survive in western Europe. U.S. control was partial and indirect; invitations to lead in this particular empire could be withdrawn as well as renewed.

Nowhere in the U.S. rescue of Europe was flexibility more in evidence than in the U.S. approach to Germany. The initial U.S. postwar plan, formulated by Henry Morgenthau, was starkly punitive. Its main preoccupation was to weaken Germany so that it could not plunge Europe into war for a third time in the twentieth century. Thus Germany was to be territorially dismembered, and the economy was to be "pastoralized"—reduced to an agricultural base. Industry was to be destroyed, with plants exported as reparations to injured neighbors. Not content with pushing for the execution of Nazi leaders at once (without trial), Morgenthau wanted ordinary Germans punished for their nation's crimes by forcing them to live on a subsistence diet. President Roosevelt approved Morgenthau's plan out of a shared sense of moral revulsion. "We have got to be tough with Germany and I mean the German people not just the Nazis. We either have to castrate the German people or you have got to treat them in such manner so they can't just go on reproducing people who want to continue the way they have in the past."[19]

Influential voices within the administration such as Hull and Stimson called for more accommodating terms rather than repeating the vindictive peace of 1919, which had ignited a smoldering German resentment. Public controversy over the Morgenthau plan together with dissent within the administration finally forced Roosevelt to begin a retreat from the hard-line approach. Truman continued it. The guidelines he announced in May 1945 called for a purge of Nazi Party members, demilitarization, a living standard no higher than the lowest elsewhere in Europe, and ultimately democratization as the best guarantee against the renewal of German aggression.

Increasing tensions with the Soviet Union prompted yet another shift— toward a revived if divided Germany. The former allies occupying Germany could not agree on a common policy, so in 1946 the Truman administration began looking to create a consolidated West Germany by joining the American, British, and French sectors of occupation together with the sections of Berlin that each held. In June 1948 these areas emerged as the new, de facto West German state. This step provoked Stalin late in the month to institute a Berlin blockade to force his former allies to negotiate for a unified but neutralized Germany and to make good on promised reparations. The tensions generated first by the blockade and then the outbreak of the Korean War pushed U.S. policy through its final stage. In September 1950 Washington publicly unveiled its plans for German military revival and integration into NATO (effected in 1955 over fierce French objections). Occupation and punishment of a defeated foe had given way to an emphasis on rehabilitation and collaboration. West Germany was on its way to full integration into the postwar western European system closely aligned with the United States.

If Germany was the enemy that became an ally, Britain might be best described as the already tested ally with delusions of grandeur. To be sure, those delusions were encouraged across several generations by American policymakers who had trumpeted Anglo-Saxon virtues, made Britain's wartime fate a matter of the greatest moment, and as a result twice intervened in European wars. The sense of community was captured dramatically during Sunday services held in the midst of the 1941 summit between Roosevelt and Churchill (whose mother was American). The two leaders, their staffs, and the ship's crew gathered on the afterdeck of the *Prince of Wales*; as they sang "Onward Christian Soldiers" in a ceremony meticulously arranged by the British leader, all had tears in their eyes. The war would generate differences over strategy, postwar trade, and decolonization, but these strains were more than balanced by shared values, which as in the past generated trust between the leaders. Moreover, British leaders realized that postwar influence depended in large measure on close U.S. ties. Collaboration with the rich, powerful relative would help preserve some fading imperial glory. With a heritage of world leadership to live up to, Britain was "not just another European country," so the British foreign secretary explained in mid-1947.[20]

The Anglo-American relationship did in fact remain close after the war. In 1946 Washington provided a $3.75 billion loan to keep the British economy afloat, and more support came with the Marshall Plan the next year. While Truman had summarily canceled joint work on nuclear weapons in 1946, he was later delighted to secure air and naval bases in Britain, which of course made the country a certain Soviet nuclear target in case of war. Elsewhere along the containment line, U.S. policymakers were incorporating into their global calculations overseas positions under British influence or direct control. Some embattled points such as Greece, Palestine, and Iran became primarily American concerns, while secure bases such as Gibraltar, Singapore, and Hong Kong were integrated into U.S. strategic planning. British armed forces as well as intelligence gathering activities substantially augmented those of the United States, and British troops served alongside Americans in Korea, at a cost not only of lives but of a confrontation with China that made London nervous and that prolonged a war Britain regarded as a distraction.

But U.S. leaders got British support in the Cold War largely on their terms.

As a distinctly junior partner, London had relatively little to say about critical u.s. decisions. In Britain, two world wars and a depression had left the treasury depleted, capital stocks sharply reduced, and the public more interested in improved living standards than imperial sacrifice. These straitened circumstances intensified London's dependence on Washington even as British leaders comforted themselves with the thought that they were playing the wise and wily Greeks to the upstart American Romans. Britain was not going to become "just another European country." Overstretched overseas, struggling to maintain the value of the pound as a leading currency, and reluctant to join the continent's experiment in integration, London lurched from one financial crisis to another, while living standards lagged behind those of western European neighbors. Repeated requests for u.s. bailouts came at a price—unquestioning support for u.s. policy. Prime Minister Harold Wilson, compelled to back an unpopular u.s. involvement in Vietnam, explained the simple logic of economic dependency. "We can't kick our creditors in the balls."[21]

A New Co-prosperity Sphere

Japan had sought in the 1930s to create what its leaders called "a greater East Asia co-prosperity sphere." This attempt to integrate regional economies and in the bargain establish regional dominance went badly awry. The attempted takeover of China provoked dogged resistance, while the collision with the United States resulted in a one-sided war that Japan was bound to lose. The American occupiers who sailed into Tokyo Bay in September 1945 thought they were about to turn a page in Japan's history, but they also set under way without knowing it a new stage in the old project of making Japan both secure and prosperous. As with Europe, this American attempt at a makeover was remarkably successful though far short of complete.

In contrast to the collaboration that marked the u.s. course in Europe, the u.s. approach to Japan was complicated by the bitterness of the Pacific conflict and the totality of the Japanese defeat. After the surprise attack at Pearl Harbor, many Americans viewed the Japanese with a hatred that had no counterpart in views of Germany or Italy. The fighting on the ground was no-holds-barred. In the final months of the war, with Japan severed from overseas sources of supply and certain of defeat, u.s. forces administered a brutal pounding. In August following firebombing of major cities, two atomic blasts, and the Soviet entry into the war, Emperor Hirohito announced surrender. The situation was by then grim. The destruction of housing stock was greater than in Europe while the level of subsistence was lower. Soldiers and refugees in the millions were flooding home from overseas with no work, housing, or other support. Inflation was quickly robbing savings of any value. Many Japanese anticipated a military occupation as unforgiving as their own wartime occupations and conducted by vengeful troops under the direction of an all-powerful proconsul, General Douglas MacArthur.

Reform and rehabilitation, not brutal revenge, proved the objective of the Americans who ruled Japan for nearly six and a half years—from August 1945 to April 1952. Given wide latitude by Washington, MacArthur set the course, with British and Soviet allies exercising only nominal control over occupation policy. From the start accommodation guided the u.s. plan. Occupation officials recognized that they could tap Japan's social discipline and its government bureaucracy in attending to the immediate task of feeding, housing, and policing a conquered population. As another step toward easing the transition from war to peace, MacArthur promptly made the controversial decision to leave the emperor—the very man who had sanctioned decisions as disastrous to Japan as to its neighbors—in place as what he called "a symbol which united all Japanese." The sovereign would not have to account for war crimes as his servitors did. Perhaps the most important step toward accommodation occurred in the heads of the Americans: they converted their former foe—once depicted as crazed and brutal—into respectable, well-behaved children eager to learn and become responsible adults. Fittingly MacArthur as the newly installed schoolmaster thought the Japanese "like a boy of twelve" at least compared to the Anglo-Saxons. The mass-circulation *Saturday Evening Post* put the task at hand more brashly: "The G.I. Is Civilizing the Jap."[22]

The remaking of Japan began as an exercise in New Deal reform even as the New Deal at home was coming under attack. From MacArthur's headquarters came instructions to remove imperial restrictions on political participation, reform the educational system, and permit labor organizing. The occupiers struck blows for economic democracy by ordering the more equitable distribution of farmland and the breakup of the massive family-owned business conglomerates (*zaibatsu*), regarded as accessories to Japan's aggressive policy. The Americans wrote a constitution for the new Japan renouncing war as an instrument of national policy. The Japanese military would thus focus only on self-defense, limit its operations to the homeland, and receive restricted funding. Finally, militarist elements associated with past aggression were purged from public life and the worst of them tried in international or military courts. From these measures MacArthur imagined emerging a peaceful, neutral nation, the "Switzerland of Asia." Some ordinary Japanese, traumatized by war and repelled by their callous leaders, hailed the occupation's early achievement: "I believe that the future of Japan will be brighter under American control."[23]

This New Deal approach succumbed in the course of 1947–48 as the Cold War increasingly intruded into the thinking of u.s. policymakers both in Tokyo and Washington. The new containment policy put a premium on stable allies and forward bases. The occupation accordingly underwent what has been called a "reverse course." Aided by conservative Prime Minister Yoshida Shigeru, MacArthur proceeded to convert Japan into an anticommunist bastion and a Cold War ally as important as any in western Europe. Encouragement of democracy gave way to political repression of the Left (including the Japanese Communist Party and radical labor unions) and an intensified censorship of perspectives critical of the u.s. presence or u.s. Cold War policy. On the economic front, MacArthur gave the green light to a new form of industrial concentration (*keiretsu*) because he thought it would hasten economic recovery and reduce pressure on an already stretched u.s. treasury to support the occupation. The new priority given to production in Japan resulted in calling a halt to reparations to neighbors who had suffered from Japanese aggression. Finally, the new policy quickly turned the Switzerland of Asia into an island redoubt. U.S. bases became permanent strong points for confronting Communist advances in China, Korea, the Philippines, and Vietnam. Backing u.s. forces was Japan's own 150,000-man "police force," a designation meant to get around the no-war clause in the American-imposed constitution.

A moderate, generous peace treaty, signed in April 1952, ended the occupation and moved the collaboration into a new phase. As a firm u.s. ally in the Cold War, Japan was on its way to realizing the security and prosperity that had previously eluded its leaders. A u.s. defense treaty and the continuing presence of u.s. forces on bases within Japan itself constituted a security umbrella. With Americans bearing the burden of Japan's defense, government planners could focus on promoting economic innovation and ever-higher levels of productivity. Already by 1952 the country had regained its prewar level of income thanks to hard work and sacrifice on the part of ordinary Japanese along with u.s. aid totaling some $2.2 billion and a surge of u.s. military spending (another $2.3 billion) in support of forces fighting in Korea. Fit securely within the u.s. system of free trade and given ample access to the u.s. market, Japanese producers would go from strength to strength in the decades ahead.[24]

By 1968 the Japanese had built the world's third largest economy. Their trade and investment activity as well as the example of their successful export strategy were stimulating a rising tide of economic activity in the very region that Japan had earlier tried to subdue. South Korea, Taiwan, Hong Kong, and Singapore were the first to get in step behind Japan, followed by China, Vietnam, and the rest of Southeast Asia. With Japan in the lead, eastern Asia was on its way to becoming the world's most economically dynamic zone.

But Japan was hardly a replica of its u.s. patron. As in western Europe, collaboration imposed limits on American reformers. Nominally a democracy, Japan functioned in fact as a one-party state. The Liberal Democratic Party, center-right like the Christian Democrats in Europe, dominated the political scene from the 1950s to the early 1990s, when it lost power for the first time—and then only briefly. No less significantly, the Japanese economy reflected little of the free-market orthodoxy championed by the Americans. The occupation had accepted industrial reconcentration, and once the occupation ended, Japan shifted to a kind of state-guided capitalism familiar from the wartime period, only now the war was for foreign markets, not territory. The state would play a major, wide-ranging role in creating and maintaining an advanced industrial sector geared to global competition. In that role it provided cheap credit to favored export-oriented industries, controlled access to foreign currency, stimulated savings so that Japan could generate its own investment capital, promoted consolidation of firms to improve their international competitiveness, protected the domestic market against imports, and even offered guidance on output and pricing. The parts of the economy that were not outward looking such as rice producers and small shopkeepers were treated to a soothing dose of protection viewed as appropriate in a society that valued domestic cooperation and social cohesion above competition and individualism. Some observers struck by the difference between American goals for Japan and the outcome have suggested that the occupation yielded a sort of "Japan, Inc." Stalwart Liberal Democratic politicians, powerful government bureaucrats, and favored corporate bosses worked together to create the Japanese economic miracle that was about to burst on the world.

THE CONSUMER MODEL GOES GLOBAL

U.S. postwar dominance, reflected in programs for international order and for Japan's and western Europe's recovery, was also expressed by a dramatic deepening of u.s. cultural influence. That influence can be summed up in the notion of consumer culture (introduced in chapter 3). Americans, who had already glimpsed the delights of widely spread abundance in the 1920s, were to find in the 1950s and 1960s that consumerism had become a pervasive domestic force and its overseas influence stronger than ever. Corporate executives, cold warriors, and proud nationalists each in their own way made the most of this u.s. role as a fount of goods and dreams reaching abroad. But whatever u.s. intentions, foreigners were not passively consuming the products or absorbing the values that Americans were sending out. The variety of responses from place to place and the outbreaks of resistance underlined the continuing diversity of peoples' lives and hopes around the world even as more and more lived in the sort of consumer society pioneered by the United States.

The Expanding Circle of Abundance

Postwar prosperity brought the u.s. consumer society to maturity. Wartime had prepared the way by raising incomes. More income meant not only higher living standards even while the fighting was going on but also savings in anticipation of a postwar purchasing binge. A 1945 survey revealed one out of every five dollars of disposable income was being socked away. "After total war can come total living." The words came from a corporate pamphlet but articulated a widely held public hope. After making a successful transition from war to peace in the late 1940s, the u.s. economy did indeed go on an unprecedented growth streak. Thanks to rapidly rising incomes, by the end of the 1950s slightly more than half of all families had become comfortably middle class, leaving roughly a quarter of the population still in poverty and thus outside the charmed circle of abundance.[25]

In this time of plenty, consumer goods flew off well-stocked shelves and into single-family homes rapidly spreading across suburban landscapes. By 1960 the penetration of the products associated with the good life was striking: 60 percent of all families owned their own homes, 75 percent a washing machine, and 87 percent a television. Spreading car ownership—three out of four families by 1960—began to endow the postwar landscape with some of its distinguishing features: the commute, the mall, the two-car garage, bedroom communities, the declining cities, roadside fast food, the motel, and interstate highways. More and more Americans could now afford to make a regular ritual of vacations to ever more distant and exotic destinations and to pack their children off to school and keep them there into their early twenties. Advertising and consumer debt kept the goods and the good times moving.

Europeans and Japanese embarked on their own consumer path thanks in part to the u.s. rescue effort. The former great powers pulled tightly into the u.s. orbit experienced in the postwar decades rapidly rising levels of material well-being. While the United States racked up an impressive annual per capita GDP growth rate of 2.4 percent on average between 1950 and 1973, the others did even better, with the result that their standards of living leaped into the blessed realm of previously unimagined abundance. France grew at 4 percent, West Germany and Italy at 5 percent, and Japan at an extraordinary 8 percent. Britain, diverted by imperial ambitions, was the chief laggard at 2.4 percent. The consequences of this impressive run of growth was to bring incomes generally in these countries within hailing distance of those of the United States. Between 1950 and 1973 West German and Italian per capita GDP tripled (reaching 79 and 63 percent respectively of the u.s. level), France more than doubled (rising to 78 percent of the u.s.), Britain fell short of doubling (reaching 72 percent), while the star Japanese performer climbed almost six times higher (to 66 percent).[26]

In Europe as in the United States, prosperity was accompanied by inexorable consumer inroads—what was by the early 1960s called the "auto-frigo" revolution. With more money in their pockets than in any time in history, western Europeans went on a spending spree not just for automobiles and refrigerators but also washers (especially prized by women as labor savers), televisions, public entertainment, travel, education, and perhaps most important of all better housing. Running water, an indoor toilet and bath, and central heating—a rare combination in 1945—had two decades later become commonplace. Mass-produced goods began to blur long-time European social distinctions whether rooted in region or class.

Japan was the third center of rising consumer activity in the early postwar period. The government's 1960 announcement that it planned to double incomes of ordinary Japanese marked the starting point. Astonishing results in economic performance soon allowed Japanese to join Americans and western Europeans in spending on nonessential goods and a more comfortable life. They bought new homes and adorned them with the items seen in the homes of the newly affluent in other parts of the world—a television, a refrigerator, a washing machine, and even for some a car. They too traveled and sent their children to high school and college in steadily rising proportions. But unlike others, Japanese avoided consumer debt, following instead a "save now, buy later" philosophy encouraged by government tax and welfare policies.

While the consumer model spread most quickly to the developed market economies of western Europe and Japan, those on the other side of an ostensibly "iron curtain" felt its seductive touch. By the early 1950s production in the Soviet bloc had recovered to prewar levels, opening an era of strong growth that continued well into the 1970s. Between 1950 and 1973 GDP in the Soviet Union and eastern Europe grew at an impressive 5 percent clip (as good as the best of the western Europeans during that period), and per capita GDP doubled even while remaining about half the actual level of western Europe. The successors to Stalin and their counterparts in capitals throughout social-ist eastern Europe understood that they faced rising popular expectations made possible by greater output but also fed by images of affluence picked up in foreign travel, movies, television, and magazines. U.S. propaganda under-scored the material advances associated with capitalism. In the mid-1950s the Eisenhower administration grasped the importance of playing up u.s. afflu-ence in regular radio broadcasts, magazines, and exhibits (such as the one in Moscow in 1959). The president pointed out to his advisers early in his first term the u.s. advantage in addressing "the common man's yearning for food, shelter, and a decent standard of living." Khrushchev had understood already in the 1940s that socialism's legitimacy depended on providing a better life for ordinary people. Once firmly in power in the mid-1950s, he pursued poli-cies to improve food and housing, to make television available for entertain-ment, and to funnel more state resources to light industry that could produce consumer products. Where Soviet leaders fell short, they faced grumbling (re-ported in secret police reports) and even on occasion consumer riots so out of hand that they had to be met with deadly force.[27]

As postwar economies recovered and life improved on both sides of the Cold War divide, foreigners became enthusiastic consumers of a wide range of mass-market American products from casual clothes and fast food to movies and music. Their rising appeal was strongest in areas where per capita income had passed a critical threshold so that consumers could afford discretionary spending on Coke's empty calories or an evening at the cinema indulging Hollywood illusions. As American consumer goods reached foreign hands in the early postwar decades in a way not seen since the 1920s, they bolstered the u.s. trade balance. At the same time advertising images and movie story lines stoked the appetite for even more consumption.

Coca-Cola is an apt symbol of this postwar u.s. consumer offensive. The soft drink manufacturer, which had its beginnings in Atlanta in the 1880s, first penetrated the Canadian market and then went overseas for the first time at the turn of the century to supply troops and other Americans in the newly acquired u.s. possessions and protectorates in the Pacific and the Caribbean. Only in the 1920s did a sustained and serious attack on foreign markets begin under the aegis of Robert Woodruff, Coke's long-time leader. Woodruff was born in into a well-to-do Atlanta family. His father seized control of the com-pany in 1919 and in 1923 put Robert, an accomplished marketer, in charge. The son dedicated himself to selling Coke (as he later put it) "to all segments of the social structure as one of the pleasantest things of life."[28] In 1926 he set up a foreign department in New York to promote franchises overseas—from Mexico to South Africa. The company provided advertising, quality control, and the secretly formulated concentrate to make the drink. By the 1930s Coke had franchise operations in twenty-eight countries, though the only major success in winning overseas consumers was in Germany. Most sales were still to Americans abroad.

The outbreak of war created an opening for expansion that Woodruff energetically exploited. Troops welcomed Coke as a pleasant reminder of home. Woodruff, who described his company's product as "morale food," had supposedly promised in the wake of Pearl Harbor to "see that every man in uniform gets a bottle of Coca-Cola for five cents wherever he is and whatever it costs."[29] He delivered—to the tune of 10 billion bottles—and in the bargain got preferential treatment from Washington on the wartime sugar ration essential to keeping his production lines moving. With military support, Coke set up plants behind the advancing frontlines, first in Casablanca in the wake of the North African invasion, then in Naples during the drive up the Italian boot, and finally across northern Europe as the Allies advanced on Germany. The same process repeated itself in the Pacific with plants going into operation in the Philippines and China. By war's end Coke had sixty-three bottling plants overseas.

These efforts not only helped consolidate the soft drink's standing as a national symbol but also laid the foundations for Woodruff's postwar overseas drive against a familiar set of challenges. Coke had to attract customers to a drink with no nutritional value. Domestic advertising had long associated drinking Coke with glamour, leisure, fun, youth, and family. These same messages were embodied in foreign media. Coke had also to sort through a welter of government regulations, legal provisions, and political sensitivities that varied from country to country. Coke's success on both counts is evident in rising foreign sales (more than a quarter of total revenue by the early 1950s) and in the expanding network of bottlers (418 in 92 countries and territories by the mid-1950s). Coke had established itself as a global force, an achievement that was even more remarkable for a corporation with roots in a largely poor and insular South.

Coke carefully cultivated and proudly embraced its dual role as a universally loved product that was also the embodiment of the American way. Billy Wilder's 1961 Hollywood comedy *One, Two, Three*, made with the company's cooperation, conveyed this message. Its central figure, a Coke executive in Berlin played by James Cagney, personified Coke's relentless drive that was so strong (so the film suggested) that even Communists were bound to succumb. Woodruff savored the iconic status his company had achieved and the profits that status ensured. He worked hard to protect Coke's position, cultivating influential leaders in Georgia and Washington, making a public fetish of Coke's secret formula, and working to defuse the potential embarrassments posed by the civil rights movement right in his own backyard. Woodward did not begin to relax his firm grip on the company until the late 1970s. His death in 1985 left the company in the hands of two protégés, both foreign-born (one Cuban and the other Egyptian), a testimony to the cosmopolitan transformation the company had undergone. By then Coke's operations extended into some 139 countries, and seven of every ten dollars of revenue came from foreign sales.[30]

Hollywood figured even larger both for the profits it earned overseas and for the fantasies that it communicated. Already in the interwar years millions of moviegoers, abroad no less than at home, had directed their rapt attention to the silver screen, filling the coffers of the major producers. After World War II u.s. producers retained all the advantages that had made the interwar export drive successful. Postwar movie attendance swelled along with the profits earned from exporting celluloid adventure, comedy, and romance. In Britain and Italy, for example, Hollywood films accounted for about two-thirds of all feature-length films shown in 1948–49 and by the early 1970s still made up two-fifths in Britain and a quarter in Italy. In Japan and in such major third-world markets as Mexico, Egypt, and India, Hollywood products made steady inroads over the same period, increasing from around a third or less to around half or better. The foreign earnings were substantial—for example, $293 million in 1963—and roughly equal to domestic earnings.[31]

Domestication and Resistance

It might be tempting to conclude that the United States was remaking the world culturally. The French philosopher Jean Baudrillard captured this sense that everyone was becoming a pale copy of the United States when he famously observed, "America is the original version of modernity. We are the dubbed or subtitled version."[32] U.S. government and business leaders might like to think that drinking Coke or watching *Gone with the Wind* fomented made-in-America dreams of individualism, democracy, and the free market.

But we have to be careful of any simple assumptions about cause and effect. In broad terms the United States was an embodiment of modernity but not one that others followed in any clear, predictable pattern (a point already made in chapter 3). London, Rome, Moscow, and Tokyo were already in the nineteenth century beginning to move toward modernity by routes arguably distinct from the track followed by New York, Chicago, and Atlanta. Moreover, each traveled not in isolation but in an interactive relationship with others. The spread of American goods and practices thus needs to be seen as part of a complex interplay of international and domestic influences. "Domestication" is a useful term to indicate the process by which imported products and practices have always been subject to transformation in order to become assimilated to daily life in a new cultural context with its own unique character. One careful student of Americanization has captured this complexity in his claim that u.s. culture circulating abroad—whether in the form of films, songs, jeans, or soft drinks—"does so mostly in disentangled bits and pieces, for others to recognize, pick up, and rearrange into a setting expressive of their own individual identities, or identities they share with peer groups."[33]

Consumer culture in the twentieth century was by definition mass culture—but its attraction was uneven. As income levels rose, ordinary people flocked to the films, tried the foods, listened to the music, and sported the clothes coming from the United States. The mobility and choice that went with abundance had an especially strong allure for young people, workers, and women—all interested in alternatives to social restrictions whether exercised by parents, bosses, or husbands and fathers. U.S. goods enjoyed a remarkable appeal not just because they were low in cost but also because they spoke of the possibility of another way of living, one in which material and social constraints gave way to material abundance and individual freedom. An Austrian who grew up in the u.s.-occupied sector of his country right after the war could still vividly recall years later the American products that defined that time of cultural transition: the chewing gum distributed by strikingly casual young American soldiers, the Levi jeans (an enormous prize to acquire), the Hollywood action movies, and perhaps above all rock 'n' roll.[34]

Elites by contrast remained the prime source of resistance. Cultural mandarins disliked the mass, materialistic society epitomized by the United States and worried about the threat that it posed to treasured local ways of life and hence to national identity. They attacked what they saw in the American mirror because it made them fear for the future of their country. The British intellectual Bertrand Russell—an aristocrat who had done distinguished work in philosophy—was enough of a freethinker to write appreciatively in 1951 of the postwar role he hoped that United States would play. Still he bemoaned the "the tyranny of the herd" that deformed u.s. politics and the cultural debasement that went with rising u.s. influence overseas. "Aesthetic standards, except in architecture, will probably be lowered. There will be less respect for art and learning, and more for the forceful 'executive.'"[35] Business leaders and trade groups facing competition from American goods allied with the cultural mandarins, invoking high-sounding arguments that had as their objective state subsidies or protection.

The classic novel skewering the empty consumer lifestyle associated with the United States appeared in 1965, appropriately enough in France. Georges Perec's *Things: A Story of the Sixties* offered a clinical picture of the psychology of avid consumers—their endless needs, their passing joys and diversions, their vague dissatisfactions. The novel's main characters were a Parisian couple in their early twenties uninterested in their work except that it yield an easy and substantial paycheck. "They possessed, alas, but a single passion, the passion for a higher standard of living, and it exhausted them. . . . They thirsted for a slightly bigger room, for running hot and cold water, for a shower, for meals more varied, or just more copious, than those they ate in student canteens, maybe for a car, for records, holidays, clothes." The only problem was that realizing their dreams, Perec told his readers, left the pair feeling sometimes "desperately empty" and "consumed" by the thought of money needed to perpetuate the cycle of acquisition and fresh desire. "The vastness of their desires paralyzed them." An instant success, *Things* was admired throughout Europe for its acutely observed picture of a major feature of the postwar period. The banality of the lives Perec created in *Things* contrasts sharply with his own family's poignant story. His parents, both Polish Jews who had immigrated to France in the 1920s, died in the course of World War II—one in the French army and the other in a German concentration camp. The gap between the Europe of the war and of the postwar was huge no matter how one assessed the outcome of the transformation.[36]

The U.S. products that rode the rising tide of consumerism abroad had to surmount a variety of obstacles. Coca-Cola's difficulty in France in the late 1940s offers a good illustration of this resistance. With only one bottler there before the war, Coke planned a major postwar expansion. An alliance of interests rallied against this case of Coca-colonization. Producers of wine, mineral water, and other local products pronounced the American drink "a poison." The French Communist Party launched a polemic against Coke as the leading edge of a U.S. invasion. The French finance ministry joined the critics, opposing Coke operations because profits sent home would drain a hard-pressed French economy and slow recovery. Coke executives fought back with the help of the State Department and the U.S. media. All raised the issue of gratitude. "Coca-Cola was not injurious to the health of Americans who liberated France from the Nazis," fumed the Coke official in charge of the export drive. Coke won the battle in the early 1950s. France's center-right governments, dependent on U.S. Marshall Plan support, access to U.S. markets for its own products, and NATO protection, tamped the controversy down. In any case the French indicated to pollsters that they didn't much like Coke anyway.[37]

Hollywood exports faced their own set of problems, which were resolved in a variety of ways particular to the place. For example, in France the film industry joined with the government to continue the resistance to U.S. products dating back to the interwar years. As the dispensers of reconstruction assistance and gatekeepers to the rich U.S. market, U.S. officials were able to force the door for U.S. films in a 1946 agreement, but the French fell back on a combination of quotas on imports and subsidies for producers, distributors, and exhibitors. This arrangement allowed home-grown products to control half the market into the 1970s. But their slipping competitive position thereafter would force an adaptation in French national film style. Survival meant borrowing U.S. methods—more capital invested in larger-scale individual projects, stars and stories appealing to an international audience, and filming in English. Coproductions with U.S. and other foreign producers would begin to blur the national origins of the final product just as was happening in other industries. Increasingly, these changes would transform French films into something neither French nor American but transnational in financing, production, and appeal. French filmmaking remained a vital industry, the largest of any in Europe.

Sub-Saharan Africa reveals another set of problems that traveled with Hollywood products. Cowboys and Indian films, the most popular genre for a growing and enthusiastic film audience, began to circulate first in towns during the 1930s and increasingly in rural areas in the 1940s and 1950s. Colonial administrators and sometimes educated Africans worried that flickering images of sex and violence and references to struggles against oppressors would plant immoral, criminal, or subversive ideas in "primitive" minds. Censors went to work excising objectionable scenes. But quite contrary to those fears, audiences—at their core young working-class men—professed shock at the sex and violence that slipped past the censors. What they carried away from the mutilated story line conveyed in difficult-to-follow dialogue were fragments of the "modern" sophistication that they could integrate piecemeal into their clothing, language, gestures, bearing, and dance. Whatever cultural coherence the film had had when it left the studio had been thoroughly undone by the time a noisy audience of a hundred to several thousand in Zambia, Ghana, or South Africa had socialized in the open-air screening areas, responded to the on-screen excitement, and headed home on bicycle or on foot. One woman in 1988 recalled her images of the films, which had once been her supreme pleasure: "Horses, cowboys, big hats, America." Films had neither remade nor corrupted her.[38]

The hold of American music over urban youth in the Soviet Union offers yet a third example of the mix of repulsion and attraction that u.s. cultural products generated. Young people had access to u.s. musical styles through films captured during World War II, Voice of America broadcasts across the Iron Curtain, and records smuggled into the country and then crudely reproduced on discarded X-ray plates. Jazz enjoyed an underground revival in the early 1950s. Small clubs became hotbeds of jazz as well as boogie and swing. The enthusiasts that they attracted were men with adopted names like Peter and Bob wearing fashionably narrow ties and tight-fitting suits and women with tight slit dresses and bright lipstick. In the mid- and late 1950s rock 'n' roll led by Bill Haley and His Comets and then the folk music genre championed by Joan Baez and Bob Dylan filtered across the Iron Curtain, followed by a Beatles mania in the mid-1960s. As earlier, bands sprang up to imitate the songs and dress of the currently popular foreign model. Alexander Gradsky, the head of one of the first rock 'n' roll bands, recalled his reaction to first hearing the Beatles in early 1963: "I went into a state of shock, total hysteria. They put everything into focus. All the music I'd heard until that time was just a prelude."[39] By the late 1960s Moscow alone had hundreds of rock groups with names like Purple Catastrophe, Bald Spot, and Nasty Dogs.

Soviet officials repeatedly went on the offensive against this cultural infiltration—and repeatedly failed to break the Anglo-American musical hold. During the late Stalin years officials banned jazz, which they denounced for its "epileptic, loud-mouthed compositions." Khrushchev had no better an opinion of these capitalist imports. (Listening to jazz, he complained, made him feel like he had "gas on the stomach.") Officialdom cracked down on the illegal record trade, patrolled dance halls and restaurants, published denunciations of decadent music, and tried to lure young people to alternative entertainment. They failed to turn the musical tide and occasionally faced violent confrontations. For example, on May Day 1967 during a youth rally in Red Square, right at the foot of the Kremlin wall, twisting (the latest dance craze that had couples ecstatically gyrating) broke out spontaneously. The police scattered the crowd only to see dancing start up elsewhere on the square or on nearby streets. Anglo-American popular culture was out of control in some segments of the population and even influencing such quasi-official cultural products as movies, television, and youth festivals.[40]

In eastern Europe the situation was if anything worse. For example, in Prague the political reform fever of Spring 1968 was accompanied by cultural subversion. The American beat poet Alan Ginsburg paid a visit that inspired a beatnik vogue—long hair, loose disheveled clothes, sandals, drugs, impromptu social gatherings ("happenings"), and a new kind of music. Immediately following the Soviet military intervention in August to curb political reforms, the most famous of the underground rock bands, the Plastic People of the Universe, took the stage for the first time. Influenced by the psychedelic New York group the Velvet Underground, the band was apolitical but dangerous in its challenge to official culture. Singing lyrics in English that the band members at first barely understood, they saw themselves creating an "authentic" alternative to a society they found bland, repressive, and boring. Officials denounced them as morbid, vulgar, and antisocial, but the band maintained a furtive existence, performing its experimental music before enthusiastic fans. (One of those fans was the famous political dissident and future Czech president Vaclav Havel, who made his country home available for a recording session.)[41]

The complex ways that foreigners interacted with the American consumer model is well illustrated by a final example—the postwar evolution of Italian fashion.[42] Milan's textile industry, famed for its high-quality fabric, restarted production in 1945 with the help of U.S. reconstruction assistance. To succeed the industry needed foreign sales, especially given the weak domestic market in the immediate aftermath of war. An ambitious new generation of designers and promoters in Florence and Rome set about securing that market in the United States and in the bargain keeping textiles strong. They included Italians of modest background such as the Fontana sisters (Zoe, Giovanna, and Micol), who were adept at intricate quality work, but also cosmopolitan aristocrats such as Giovanni Battista Giorgini and Emilio Pucci, who had good political and economic connections. Together they wooed American tastemakers—the editors for leading fashion magazines and the buyers for leading department stores—hoping to win them away from the long-dominant Paris fashion houses. Already in 1947 one of those tastemakers was convinced that Italy had "everything necessary to a vital and original fashion industry: talent, fabric, and beautiful women."[43] A presentation of the new "Italian Look," elegantly staged by Giorgini in Florence in February 1951, signaled success. Buyers found much to like: well constructed clothing made from quality fabric with a strong sense of color, design, and interesting detail—and less costly than goods from Paris. The Italians for their part catered to the requirements of the U.S. buyers, especially that clothes be casual and comfortable. Good publicity added to the glamour of the exported Italian goods as Hollywood stars such as Grace Kelly, Ava Gardner, and Linda Christian and socialites such as Jacqueline Bouvier (later Kennedy) turned during the late 1940s and early 1950s to Italian designers such as the Fontana sisters for their high-fashion gowns. By the early and mid-fifties export sales were soaring with an estimated three-quarters of those sales going to the United States. By 1958 Italy had taken the lead in Europe's export of clothing and accessories to the United States.

The opportunities that U.S. consumers created for Italian fashion houses also led to production challenges for which Americans had an answer. The rapidly climbing demand for both lower-priced "ready-to-wear" goods and more expensive boutique items required an overhaul in production—a shift from the established handicraft system of production (small-scale and high quality) to the U.S. mass-production, assembly-line model. The fashion houses invested in cutting and other machines that could save time and labor, so that a jacket that took fifteen hours to make in 1952 could be done in two hours by 1965. But the Italian industry was careful not to go completely American. It preserved the technical and aesthetic qualities that had given their goods an edge in the first place, and some fashion houses preserved a remnant of the small-scale, craft-based production that stood alongside mass production and gave prestige to the mass-produced goods. Flair and workmanship could coexist alongside the assembly line.

This story of Americanization had already run from Milan to Rome and Florence and thence to U.S. department stores and back to Italian work rooms. The story took one last twist as casual U.S. clothing styles began to win a following among fashion-conscious Italians, themselves moving into a period of consumer abundance. In the 1950s they began to take an interest in the kind of items bound for the U.S. market and demanded the same. They were learning from Americans that fashion like other consumer activities could be fun and help the buyer transcend social status. No one learned this lesson better than young Italians. By the 1960s they had inaugurated the age of blue jeans and T-shirts. What began as Italian producers conquering the U.S. consumer market ended with American styles altering Italian consumer tastes.

Americans at midcentury had managed to marry well-established economic and cultural influence to their newly won military and political dominion. Dominion could be exercised more effectively, cheaply, and durably if based on positive appeal. As a demonstrable success, the U.S. model elicited both admiration and emulation and gave legitimacy to U.S. attempts to create international consensus over the rules governing the globe. Americans would be conquerors of a different kind. This proposition had gotten its primary test in Europe and Japan, the focus of u.s. initiatives from the late 1940s through the 1960s.

But this far-reaching economic and social effort together with the no less expansive Cold War campaign led inexorably to far-flung commitments in places from which the Europeans were in retreat and from which the Japanese had been expelled. Creating a better world involved Americans ever more deeply with problems on the global periphery. In most cases these problems were legacies of that era of colonialism and national rivalry that the postwar u.s. order was meant to transcend. Expanding commitments at a host of points along that periphery would soon introduce Americans to the difficulties that went with their now ascendant position.

6

THE THIRD-WORLD CHALLENGE

1941★1968

Fidel Castro was a cartoonist's dream. "The bearded one" (as his followers called him) had swept an unpopular dictator from power in January 1959 and in a rush administered summary justice to leaders of the old regime, implemented populist programs, and curbed u.s. influence on the island. U.S. observers quickly assimilated Castro to the familiar image of the Latin leader—the brat whose tantrums required adult disciplining. Exactly a year after he had come to power, a cartoon captured this sense of him as a pistol-packing, trouble-making kid (fig. 6). The cartoon made the case for bringing him into line by replacing gentle diplomatic strokes with a punishing economic paddle. But Castro and his revolution would survive.

The Cuban Revolution was more than a standing affront to u.s. pretensions to hemispheric dominance. It was one part of a broad, steadily intensifying third-world challenge to u.s. global dominance every bit as important to the u.s. global order as the Soviet rivalry and the international market economy. Though formally committed to self-determination, Washington beat a quiet retreat from that principle at the end of World War II. In the course of the 1950s and 1960s mounting attacks on u.s. positions on the periphery and an eruption of embarrassing criticism of racial practices at home left policy-makers deeply worried. They responded with a counteroffensive at a host of points abroad and with domestic civil rights legislation. They were determined to master the third world and at the same time to vindicate their claim to stand for freedom whether in the United States or in other lands.

"Third world" like other influential formulations such as "totalitarianism" has to be used with care. Contemporary Americans would have known it as a term coined in the late 1940s to signify the countries that were left on a map

Figure 6. "Spare the Rod and Spoil the Child," News and Courier
(Charleston, South Carolina), 29 January 1960, 6A.
Cartoonist not identified.

after subtracting the first (free) world and the second (socialist) world. Looking back, the term can be used in a second sense to suggest another, more historically grounded geography—a wide range of lands under some form of foreign control swept at midcentury by powerful forces of liberation. Castro's smoldering resentment of the United States, his association of foreign control with social injustices, and his determination to create a new Cuba was part of a worldwide pattern. From Asia to the Middle East, Africa, and on to Latin America, nationalist elites were intent on redefining their relationship with the long-dominant North Atlantic states. Once established as the leading power in that region, the United States figured as one of the main obstacles to realizing their goals. The ferment attending this process would affect— sooner or later, in one way or another—most of the earth's surface and most of its inhabitants. The two largest countries involved, China and India, alone accounted for more than a third of the world's 2.5 billion people in 1950.[1]

Under the best of circumstances the third-world revolt against all forms of imperial control was bound to pose a stiff challenge to u.s. dominance. That this revolt hit with such force on such a broad front following a war that had destroyed or undermined the leading colonial powers added to the challenge. Making it even more problematic, the upheaval on the periphery worked against a long-standing u.s. policy of advancing corporate interests and of assuring access to resources critical to an industrial economy. Finally, the competition with the Soviet Union made u.s. policymakers hypersensitive to radicals whose success might create gaps in the containment line and inspire a bandwagon flight to the Soviet side.

Underlying these concerns was a cultural animosity rooted in the American experience as a settler society and reflected in earlier phases of u.s. involvement in Latin American and East Asia (treated in chapters 2 and 3). U.S. policymakers and observers carried strong assumptions about third-world immaturity that inspired doubts that colonial peoples could wisely manage their independence and resources. American leaders reacted to the rise of the Cuban leader and others like him with a mix of impatience, contempt, and hostility. In this postwar perceptual framework, the leaders and people of the third world assumed familiar guises. They were children for the knowing American to tutor. They were miscreants for the u.s. policeman to curb and if necessary call to account. They were a force of nature—a flood, a hurricane, an avalanche—driven by racial fury, civilizational animosity, or communist fervor. In this case the appropriate u.s. response was to patiently withstand, wear down, and outwait.[2]

The pervasive sense of superiority and paternalism toward newly independent peoples was doubly problematic. It accentuated u.s. resistance to change and thus fed the very challenge that American leaders sought to blunt or channel. Moreover, it led u.s. leaders to misconstrue the situation in the distant lands they sought to manage. They possessed a sketchy to nonexistent knowledge of the particular circumstances—the histories and the cultures—out of which the third-world challenge had emerged, and thus ignorance and illusion hobbled u.s. policy and raised the price Americans would have to pay. But u.s. leaders possessed considerable power to compensate for any lack of insight. As the cartoon suggests, they could persuade (the feather) or coerce (the nailed paddle). The rise of the imperial presidency was especially important for putting in their hands a wide array of potent instruments that usually produced the desired effect. That the costs paid by peoples in the third world, especially those most determined in their resistance, were high was of little matter to u.s. policymakers confident in their right to inflict destruction, massively if need be.

FACING THE END OF EMPIRE

Early in the century discontent was already building among nationalist elites who were educated abroad and had a sense of the wider world. Having failed in their suit at the peace conference ending World War I, they stood more determined as World War II reached its end. European colonial powers were badly weakened, so opponents of the colonial status quo could demand, not plead. The rush to independence turned into a postwar stampede. Liberation movements in Asia—in India, Indonesia, the Philippines, Vietnam, and China—led the way. But sub-Saharan Africa, Latin America, and the Middle East were close behind. Formal wartime support for self-determination had seemed at first to closely align Americans with this gathering movement toward decolonization. That principle was inscribed in popular u.s. discourse and enshrined in seminal policy statements, but it stood alongside doubts about third-world peoples charting their own course and belief in the efficacy of enlightened outside guidance.

The Looming Colonial Collapse

World War II did much to kick the legs out from under empire. Japanese conquests in 1941 and 1942 dislodged the French, British, Dutch, and Americans, stripping these colonial masters of their mystique. U.S. leaders went out of their way to make self-determination a fundamental Allied principle. The Atlantic Charter in August 1941 made a sweeping commitment to "respect the right of all peoples to choose the form of government under which they will live," while the U.S. declaration on national liberation of March 1943 flatly affirmed that this right applied to all people.[3] The wartime alignment of the United States with the Soviet Union created what many thought would be a potent anticolonial front in the postwar period. A defeated Japan would surely forfeit its overseas possessions. While the British, French, Belgian, Dutch, and Portuguese might want to keep their imperial holdings, they would face disapproval from Moscow and Washington.

These developments sharpened expectations among third-world elites of a postwar international environment favorable to their cause. Many were thinking about independence but not simply as a formal condition easily met once the offending foreigners decamped. Independence was rather only the first step toward genuine liberation from foreign economic and cultural control and the ultimate goal of rapid, autonomous economic development. These ambitions entailed still others—transforming a national psychology of dependency, healing social divisions created by long-term foreign influence, fashioning programs with popular appeal, and constituting a supportive international community of like-minded states. However varied their countries' circumstances, whether formally colonized or nominally independent, third-world leaders were conscious of shared concerns. They were all sensitive to the damage done their societies by foreign domination and to the costs and perils entailed by the struggle to end that domination. They all took a keen interest in postindependence policies that would bring their people prosperity and genuine self-determination, not colonialism in some new form. Four cases—India, Ghana, China, and Guatemala—underline the intense commitment to national liberation and domestic renovation that had taken shape by the time of Japan's collapse in August 1945.

India, the heart of the British Empire, slipped out of control in the course of World War II. The Indian National Congress led the drive for liberation. Formed in 1885, the Congress Party was a loose association of nationalist elites that lacked mass support until a charismatic, British-trained lawyer, Mohandas Gandhi, launched a nonviolent campaign for self-rule in 1919. Repeated rounds of arrests and imprisonment for Gandhi and other Congress leaders failed to stem the rising nationalist pressure. In 1942 Congress demanded immediate independence, proclaiming that it could no longer accept "an imperialist and authoritarian" rule.[4] British rulers cracked down on this "Quit India" campaign, but they also understood that nationalism had sapped imperial legitimacy and that the material and moral costs of repression were too high to salvage the colonial status quo. In 1947 Britain decamped, leaving India independent and facing the trauma of communal violence that accompanied partition of the colonial domain into a predominantly Hindu state of India and the new Muslim state of Pakistan.

An India governed by the Congress Party followed a relatively conservative course in third-world terms. Its leaders were English speakers, most university-trained (some in Britain) and most from the upper reaches of society. Neither they nor their allies at the local level, within the business community, and in the British-trained civil service entertained dreams of revolution. India's first prime minister and heir to Gandhi's leadership of Congress, Jawaharlal Nehru, deplored the sharp inequalities between city and countryside and the severe discrimination suffered by untouchables and women, but he did little to remedy these problems. The government failed to invest in education, health care, and social welfare, and per capita GDP grew a paltry 1.4 percent annually between 1950 and 1973.[5] Rural poverty, illiteracy, and illness persisted while the population of the poor exploded.

What Washington noticed was not the instinctive caution of the Congress Party but its rejection of sweeping free-market policies in favor of a mixed economy influenced by the British Labour Party principles and Soviet-style planning. India thus gave a prominent role to public enterprise and bureaucratic regulation alongside the free market, and heavy industry enjoyed priority as the symbol of India's modernity. Worse still from the U.S. perspective, New Delhi promoted a neutralist stance in the Cold War. Asians had had enough of being "petitioners in Western courts and chancellories," Nehru announced in 1947. "We do not intend to be the plaything of others."[6] He emerged as one of the most vocal exponents of nonalignment—and demonstrated its benefits by securing economic aid from both the Cold War rivals.

The ferment that would for the first time break colonial control in sub-Saharan Africa is evident in the second case—Ghana and its founding father, Kwame Nkrumah. An adventuresome spirit, Nkrumah had left the British Gold Coast (Ghana's colonial name) in 1935 for Philadelphia to continue his studies at Lincoln University, an all-black school favored by other young African nationalists. During the war years he moved to the political Left and expressed a marked impatience with the imperialist system gripping not just his own country but also much of the African continent and the black diaspora beyond. His views reflected the influence of W. E. B. Du Bois, the African American activist, writer, and proponent of pan-African unity. Marxism too attracted Nkrumah with its claims that a new, nonoppressive order was a historical inevitability and indeed within the reach of those willing to organize and press forward. At the same time he was electrified by Africa's sudden wartime prominence and by the Allied promise of postwar self-determination. He knew that already the peoples of India and Vietnam were demanding independence on the basis of that principle. He anticipated that the colonial powers might want to hang on to their possessions, but a resolute resistance could, he explained in a 1943 talk, defeat them. "We cannot get what we want by asking, pleading and arguing. . . . We are in a world of action, not talk."[7] In May 1945 the thirty-six-year-old Nkrumah, now the subject of FBI inquiries, moved to London. There he would hone his political skills and continue his political education among the active West African community, itself in the grip of independence fever.

When he finally returned home in 1947, Nkrumah carried a bold vision of the changes that were necessary and a confidence that he and other black leaders could put them into effect. He imagined freeing Ghana from imperial control, cooperating closely with neighboring African states in creating a fresh destiny for the continent, and launching Ghana itself on a rapid, state-directed program of modernization. In 1957 Nkrumah realized his dream of independence, and then he pressed forward with plans that Washington regarded as unsound. As the foremost voice for a liberated Africa, Nkrumah championed state-guided development within a united and anti-imperial Africa siding with neither Cold War camp.

China was a third instance in which World War II brought nationalist sentiment to a boil, though with consequences far more dramatic than in either India or Ghana. A broad spectrum of China's politicians and intellectuals had come to see their country's condition as semicolonial, and virtually all agreed on ending the iniquitous international system of great-power domination that had done such harm to their land. None entertained brighter or more consequential thoughts of a new day coming than the leader of the Communist Party, Mao Zedong. As a young man, Mao had been agitated by the international battering that his country was taking and angered by the social injustices he saw all around him. Plunging into the dizzying currents of reformist and revolutionary ideas sweeping China in the early twentieth century, Mao had ended up in the Communist Party. A founding member, he had watched it flounder under Soviet guidance and then in the latter half of the 1930s had assumed control. He exploited nationalist anger over Japanese aggression to rally support and build Communist base areas. While the invaders kept the forces of Mao's long-time Nationalist rival distracted, Communists organized, armed, and honed their popular appeal.

Already by 1941, Mao expressed marked optimism about China's postwar liberation. He was heartened by the Atlantic Charter commitment to a new world order and Anglo-American expressions of interest in cooperating with the embattled Soviet Union. Mao declared that these developments represented nothing less than "the opening of a new stage in the history of the world."[8] American entry into the war several months later struck him as a guarantee not only of an antifascist victory but also of a lasting international alignment favorable to peace and far-reaching reform within China.

By early 1945 Mao was in even higher spirits and confidently predicting that the U.S.-Soviet alliance would endure well into the postwar period. Popular forces everywhere seemed to be gathering strength; the reactionaries were in retreat; and the successful Soviet political and economic system was setting the pattern that other peoples would take as their model. Even American capitalism seemed in a conciliatory, progressive phase. China could look forward to an era of peace and progress. In this benign national and international environment, Mao calculated that he could force the Nationalists to accept a power-sharing arrangement as the first step toward winning political power. The longer-term prospects were even brighter. While the United States seemed for the moment economically vital, Mao held to the orthodox Marxist view that ultimately, within a decade perhaps, that country would find itself in the grip of a shattering crisis. The Soviet Union would then come into unchallenged preeminence, and fundamental change within nations and within the global system would be assured. Mao held to this markedly optimistic view well into 1946. He was set on a course that would carry China well beyond the American orbit and far away from the American model. Mao famously declared in 1949 in the wake of his civil war victory that "the Chinese people, compromising one quarter of humanity, have now stood up."[9] He was equally confident that revolutionary forces around the world were in the ascendance. The achievement of the Chinese Communists would almost at once quicken unrest in the region, while aid from the new Beijing government would begin to strengthen the Vietnamese struggle against the French.

In Latin America as in South Asia, East Asia, and Africa, the close of the war coincided with a rising demand for change. Reformist regimes and populist movements sprouted throughout Latin America, drawing sustenance from Allied propaganda that victory over fascism was but the prelude to building more prosperous and open societies. Reformers wanted to encourage popular political participation, and so they took such steps as expanding the franchise beyond the ranks of propertied males and legalizing labor unions. Reformers also concerned themselves with pressing questions of social justice and redistribution of wealth in societies marked by glaring inequalities. The urban middle class and the working class as well as students and intellectuals were the chief advocates of these changes. As dictators fell and repression lifted, parties on the Left (including Communist parties) began to play a prominent political role, and unions became more assertive and increased their membership. Though still under the sway of the good neighbor policy, Washington followed these developments with an anxious eye.

Guatemala offers an excellent case in point of how the war years fed optimism and progressive political action that would in turn sharpen those u.s. anxieties. A long-repressed and ethnically divided society had embarked in 1944 on an era of moderate reform. Popularly elected presidents, first Juan José Arévalo and then Jacobo Arbenz, promoted policies geared to national integration and political mobilization but also the assertion of greater independence vis-à-vis the United States. No step in their program was more important than land reform—what its sponsor, Arbenz, called the "heavy debt the ruling class and governors contracted with the humble people, with the people of the field with cheap cotton shirts and palm-leaf sombreros who do not have shoes, or medicine, or money, or education, or land."[10] The controversial initiative sought to close old and deep ethnic and socioeconomic divisions that had left Guatemala a fragmented nation. At the top was a small, rich, and ethnically European minority. At the bottom was a large, impoverished, rural population of Mayan descent. Arbenz expropriated and redistributed large landholdings under the control of his country's planter class as well as of the u.s.-based United Fruit Company. He also shifted toward greater neutrality in the Cold War and placed Communists prominently among his advisers. Anxiety in Washington was turning to alarm.

These four cases were driven by a profound hunger for change. Inspired by elites, demands for a new order assumed a popular character and took aim at colonial domination, foreign control exercised through informal means, and settlement patterns that privileged Europeans and their descendants. These elites were impatient to implement their agenda and eclectic in their strategies. Whatever the variations in their goals and policies, everywhere they were putting u.s. policymakers on the defensive.

Self-Determination Qualified

The ferment breaking out all along the global periphery left leading Americans in the 1940s troubled if not outright hostile. Part of the response was rooted in American doubts about the very people creating the ferment. The gathering Cold War suspicions soon significantly underlined those doubts. But the American response was also a function of strong attachments to the Europeans facing the calls for liberation. These embattled colonialists had been wartime allies and figured as potential partners in any confrontation with the Soviet Union. This set of concerns—a mix of antipathy, sympathy, and calculation—started to eat away at any meaningful U.S. commitment to freedom in the third world.

Even as World War II was in progress, U.S. officials began privately to back-pedal on formal self-determination pledges. Their response to the rising liberation chorus was shaped in part by sturdy notions of cultural superiority already seen earlier in the continental drive against Native Americans, the assertion of dominance within the Caribbean region, and the colonial drive across the Pacific. President Franklin D. Roosevelt and his aides were heirs to the view that the distinction between civilized and savage was fundamental, pervasive, and persistent. Coming to political maturity at the turn of the century, they had watched with approval as their country had launched its forays overseas even as racial segregation at home became the law of the land and the social norm. They continued to believe in the duty of more advanced peoples to uplift lesser ones and if necessary drag them into modernity.

This racially conscious view of a world divided between virile, civilized peoples and their "little brown brothers" was significantly reinforced by ignorance of the third world. Americans were familiar with the Old World. They spoke its languages. They felt culturally connected to it. They had fought two world wars on its soil. Policymakers who came from privileged families such as Franklin Roosevelt knew Europe from leisurely visits, friendships, study, and even professional activities. Roosevelt and John Foster Dulles had no trouble finding Germany on a map; they had walked its major cities; and they knew the country's leading personalities. The third world by contrast was a profoundly foreign, dimly imagined realm of nonwhite people, mostly peasants whose struggle to extract a subsistence from the land was alien to midcentury Americans save perhaps rural southerners. Policymakers and the public knew next to nothing about its leaders, its societies, and its histories. They thus could easily project hardy American assumptions about the child-like nature of these foreigners, the essential goodness of ordinary people instinctively sympathetic to the United States, and the wayward tendencies of their leaders.

Roosevelt himself offers ample evidence of how a conviction of third-world inferiority helped to gut a meaningful commitment to decolonization. He referred to Asians as a "yellow peril" to be guarded against and as "children" to be directed.[11] Thus he imagined the Vietnamese as small, peaceful, and dependent. They as well as the Koreans required in his estimate twenty to thirty years of foreign tutelage so that they could learn to stand on their own. Continued tutelage was also his prescription for the British colonies. In keeping with his sense of Anglo-American kinship, Roosevelt ultimately conceded that Britain as a superior country and a great power had a special claim to play the tutelary role in colonial areas. Before the war was out, he had given those claims precedence over competing calls for independence issuing from brash, unprepared peoples about whom he knew next to nothing. The president concluded that even the French, to whom he felt less close culturally and whom he condemned for their colonial mismanagement, might yet overcome their deficiencies and attend to long-neglected obligations as tutors in the colonial world. But American observers had no expectation that the French any more than the Belgians, Dutch, or Portuguese could rise to the British standard in colonial affairs.

Roosevelt's retreat from self-determination began even while proclaiming it in the Atlantic Charter in 1941. The u.s. president privately assured British prime minister Winston Churchill that his interest was limited to "the development of backward countries" and to the elimination of "a backward colonial policy."[12] Indian demands for independence predictably met a tepid response from the Roosevelt administration, which avoided openly challenging Churchill. At Roosevelt's boldest in March 1942, he pressed Churchill to make concessions to the Indian National Congress, but even then he stood on the practical rather than the principled grounds of keeping India a stable base for wartime operations. Roosevelt's accommodation of wartime partners became if anything more pronounced as the war drew to a close. At Yalta he explicitly exempted Britain, the leading colonial power, from any formal trusteeship arrangements. The British would be allowed to guide their colonies to independence at a pace and along lines of London's choosing. With Churchill pressing for similar concessions for the French and no fresh face to serve as trustee in Indochina, the u.s. president acquiesced early in 1945 to the demand of Charles de Gaulle to restore French control there. Roosevelt had rendered the principle of national self-determination meaningless for all practical purposes.

The new Truman administration had no problem with that outcome. Consistent with Roosevelt's ultimate stance, u.s. officials made sure that the United Nations charter in May 1945 did not endorse immediate independence but instead stipulated that colonial powers had an obligation to help dependent peoples take "progressive" steps toward self-government "according to the particular circumstances of each territory and its peoples and their varying stages of advancement." A State Department paper prepared the next month for the Potsdam conference candidly conceded that the best course for colonies was their continued subordination so that Europeans could guide them into freedom and create permanent bonds between them and the West. The United States could not, the paper added, afford alienating prime European allies.[13]

Truman was receptive to these concerns not least because he harbored a crude and generally condescending view of other peoples. In his early years he referred to Mexico as "Greaserdom" and Slavic peoples as "bohunks." His military service during World War I introduced him to "kike town" (New York), evoked the stereotype of the avaricious Jew, widened his range of reference to include "frogeater" for the French and "Dago" for the Italians and stimulated a hatred for Germans. "They have no hearts or no souls," he wrote home in 1918. The next world war introduced "Jap" into his vocabulary. Once in the White House, Truman continued to think along well-worn racial lines. The Japanese were, he wrote in Potsdam in 1945, "savages, ruthless, merciless and fanatics." Accustomed to the southern pattern of race relations that had prevailed in his hometown of Independence, Missouri, Truman continued to refer to blacks as "nigs" and "niggers" at least as late as 1946. Such was Truman's reluctance on civil rights that he did not at first respond to postwar African American demands. Black servicemen had returned from fighting for freedom overseas to demand some of the same for themselves. The president had nothing to say about the violence visited on veterans in the name of defending segregation. Only in 1948, facing a tight race to remain in the White House, did he begin to shift. His most important measure, desegregation of the military, remained a hollow gesture until manpower shortages during the Korean War forced the army to take equal-opportunity rhetoric seriously. When the president directed his gaze abroad to newly independent countries, he still thought in crude stereotypes. For example, he confessed in 1951 that he imagined India "pretty jammed with poor people and cows wandering around the streets, witch doctors and people sitting on hot coals and bathing in the Ganges." He lavished on the British, whom he saw as the source of American law and as close allies, the most fulsome praise he could manage for any foreigners, noting that "fundamentally . . . our basic ideas are not far apart."[14]

The kinds of concerns that Truman gave voice to became increasingly urgent as the Europeans began their destabilizing colonial retreat while the u.s.-Soviet rivalry grew sharper. With their morale tattered, their economies in shambles, and their troops decimated and weary, the Europeans were left with vainglory their chief remaining asset—and it quickly wore thin in the face of the rising anticolonial pressure. Hardly had the war ended than the British abandoned India, the start of a general exit from South and Southeast

Asia. London was soon in retreat from the Middle East. It abruptly gave up control of an unruly Palestine in 1947, leaving Jews and Arabs to settle their differences by force of arms. Next door in Syria, France had already granted independence without a struggle in 1944. The Dutch surrendered the East Indies in 1949, lacking the stomach and troops to restore control of this colonial prize. Washington was inclined to see these and other possessions in the Middle East, Africa, and Southeast Asia as bulwarks of containment rather than outdated exercises in colonialism. Although Washington did not want its NATO allies to be humiliated in their colonies, it preferred that they focus their military resources on the defense of Europe; yet U.S. leaders feared instability if the Europeans abandoned their colonial posts too quickly.

By 1950, in the midst of the deepening Cold War crisis, the Truman administration was increasingly turning its attention to third-world problems. It disliked and discouraged the Cold War neutralism championed most visibly by the newly independent Indian government. It made the new revolutionary government in China the poster child for what happened if communism went unchecked. It pronounced France's struggle in Vietnam part of the worldwide containment effort and began sending substantial aid. After formally surrendering the Philippines in 1946, the Truman administration stepped back in to help the Manila government fend off a Communist-backed rural insurgency. In Korea a temporary occupation, launched with a view to guiding the locals and containing the Soviets, turned into a permanent U.S. commitment and then into a limited war. The periphery had become difficult in a way no American observers had imagined in 1941 or even in 1945—and worse was yet to come.

SHARPENING CONTRADICTIONS

Through the 1950s and 1960s, even as the Cold War was stabilizing and U.S. economic and cultural power was riding high, U.S. policymakers confronted serious challenges all along the periphery. The initial postwar stirrings had yielded nationalist, socialist, neutralist, and revolutionary advances in Latin America, Asia, the Middle East, and sub-Saharan Africa. The agents of change in those regions saw themselves not in isolation but as part of a broad international transformation. This sense of international solidarity included a wariness of Cold War pressures that might obstruct their nationalist ambitions, a prickly indictment of imperialism, a suspicion of capitalism as an outmoded and exploitative system, and a fascination with socialism as the fast track to development and social justice. Both Moscow and Beijing saw a rich opportunity unfolding before them and began expressing strong support for liberation movements. Further accentuating u.s. fears was the weakened European position. The reverses of the 1940s turned into a rout in the course of the 1950s. The British lost their grip on an oil-rich Iran in the early 1950s. The loss of the last shreds of imperial influence in Egypt was attended by the Suez fiasco in 1956, an attempt to take control of the canal coordinated with France and Israel but undermined by the Eisenhower administration. Britain lost definitive control of its client state Iraq in 1958 along with bases and oil concessions there. France retreated from Indochina in 1954 and Algeria in 1962, each after eight years of bitter fighting. Ghana's independence in 1957 marked the beginning of a colonial collapse across sub-Saharan Africa. The British, French, and Belgians had liquidated their holdings by the end of the 1960s. The Portuguese finally abandoned the field in the mid-1970s. Only white settler regimes in Rhodesia and South Africa still held out against demands for majority rule.

The official u.s. response to this dangerous set of developments was strikingly conflicted. Eisenhower, Kennedy, and Johnson—even more than Truman before them—worried about major breaks in the containment line. They faced "a wave of revolution sweeping around the world" (as Ike phrased it at the end of his time in the White House).[15] With the third world figuring as a long string of vulnerable points susceptible to the lure of communist ideology or assistance, u.s. presidents were constantly examining the tools at their disposal—whether conventional pressure, covert operations, or social science insights on development—that would help them head off or limit convulsions on the periphery. But at the same time they were gripped by self-doubt as they learned that racial failings at home were costing the United States support abroad and further depressing its credibility among the world's "people of color." Commentators overseas, most embarrassingly in third-world countries, were decrying the contradiction between the u.s. claim to stand for freedom and the on-the-ground domestic practices.

The Radical Vogue

Buoyed by postwar successes against the faltering colonial powers, third-world leaders intensified and broadened their drive in the 1950s and 1960s. In the process they began to coalesce around shared aspirations and common policies. The conversation was well under way by the late 1940s, with the focus on strategies of economic development. Latin American states, sensitive to their long-time domination by the United States, took the lead. In 1947 Cuba hosted a meeting of developing countries anxious for more equitable trade rules, including the opening of developed world markets for their agricultural products. Some within the hemisphere called for an alternative import-substitution policy to overcome deep global inequalities. Championed by the Economic Commission for Latin America headed by Raul Prebisch, this policy gave priority to building domestic industry and protecting it from ruinous foreign competition by effectively stepping outside the u.s.-devised and dominated free trade system. Unless governments intervened in the economy in this way, so the champions of this alternative development model contended, poor countries would continue to pay for high-value finished goods from abroad with low-value agricultural exports. As a result, their countries would fail to industrialize and they would remain locked in a subordinate position, the backwater of the international economy with their people languishing.

The emerging third-world agenda took a major step forward in 1955 at Bandung, Indonesia. Delegates from twenty-nine African and Asian states gathered to form a neutral bloc working outside the Cold War framework. Led by India's Nehru, Egypt's Gamal Abdul Nasser, and Yugoslavia's Marshal Tito, the emerging nonaligned movement called for a halt in the wasteful and dangerous arms race, funding of economic development programs, and a definitive end to colonialism. These positions outraged staunch u.s. cold warriors such as Secretary of State John Foster Dulles. The prominent role of a Chinese delegation headed by Premier Zhou Enlai underlined the challenge this neutralist current posed to u.s. hopes for containing communist influence.

The growing assertiveness in the third world was reinforced by the emergence of Moscow as an active sponsor of third-world causes. Soviet leaders were as Eurocentric as their counterparts in Washington. Overwhelmingly preoccupied with the fate of Europe, they saw the third world as a realm of developmental backwardness that was hard to manage and that tended to produce perplexing, often difficult leaders. But Moscow also realized that it had an asset in the worldwide network of Communist and Workers' parties and in the high prestige of the Soviet model of industrialization. Already during the 1920s the Moscow-based Communist International had demonstrated the advantages to be won in the colonial world, cultivating politically engaged elites, encouraging political organization, and providing support in the form of money, advisers, and schooling.

Stalin had put the international movement on a leash by the 1930s and kept it there down to his death in 1953. With resources scarce after the war, Stalin gave priority to consolidating control of eastern Europe. He was in any case doubtful about the revolutionary potential of the colonial world. A conventional Marxist outlook told him that Communist parties in such feudal lands could not be reliably proletariat. His doubts were reinforced by his own personal instinct to avoid commitments in places that he could not control. U.S. military superiority added to his reluctance to become entangled at distant points of marginal importance. He had his hands full devising a defense closer to home. For example, he dealt warily with the Chinese Communists until their victory in 1949. Only then did he provide substantial and open backing in the form of a defense treaty and development aid. In Korea in 1950 Stalin engaged in one uncharacteristic bit of adventurism. He authorized Kim Il Sung's invasion of the South, but then when the enterprise went wrong, he reverted to form. He refused to come to Kim's rescue and instead left the task to Mao. Similarly, when Ho Chi Minh called for support against the French, Stalin passed the responsibility—and the risk—to the Chinese leader.

Stalin's successors—first Nikita Khrushchev and then Leonid Brezhnev—were more aggressive in exploiting opportunities in an increasingly restive third world. As Khrushchev consolidated his control in the mid-1950s, he began to court neutralists such as Afghanistan, India, Burma, and Indonesia with offers of substantial development aid while also endorsing third-world calls for rapid decolonization. His 1956 speech on peaceful coexistence, which sought to soften the Cold War conflict, called attention to "the present disintegration of the imperialist colonial system" and praised those throughout Asia, the Middle East, Africa, and Latin America "resolutely fighting for a life of freedom and independence." In January 1961, against the backdrop of an intensifying dispute with China over socialist bloc leadership, Khrushchev burnished his credentials as a champion of the third world. He reaffirmed the importance of wars of national liberation such as the one that Castro had led against the u.s.-supported Batista regime in Cuba. The Soviet leader pronounced these third-world struggles "not only admissible but inevitable, since the colonialists do not grant independence voluntarily." Brezhnev, who helped to topple Khrushchev in 1964, continued the cultivation of third-world clients, hesitantly at first and then with greater assertiveness during the 1970s.[16]

From the early 1960s into the 1970s voices from every point in the third world heralded the prospects for a radical shift in world politics that struck directly, perhaps even fatally at the dominant u.s. international position. The last colonial regimes in Africa were on the defensive, Mao's Red Guards were restoring revolutionary vitality to China, Cuba's Castro breathed defiance of the United States, and Vietnamese Communists brought to a victorious conclusion their long independence struggle. Exponents of the third world celebrated the popular enthusiasm for liberation so evident in China and Cuba, championed violence as an antidote to social injustice and foreign domination, and praised Vietnam's struggle against France and then the United States as an inspiration for others. The United States figured as the main obstacle to decolonization and development and to the creation of a just international order. But like the imperialist system, so champions of the third world argued, the United States was on the defensive and ultimately doomed. The tide of history seemed to favor their cause.

In 1961 Martinique-born Frantz Fanon published one of the classic statements of this radical perspective. *The Wretched of the Earth* was an extended reflection on the traumatic emotional effects of colonial domination based on his experience as a doctor in Algeria during the anti-French struggle. Revolutionary violence, he argued, was critical to transforming once dominated "natives" psychologically as well as politically. "The mobilization of the masses, when it arises out of the war of liberation, introduces into each man's consciousness the ideas of a common cause, of a national destiny, and of a collective history." Fanon thus highlighted the critical role of anticolonial struggle in producing the "cement which has been mixed with blood and anger" that would make possible the next phase of nation building.[17]

Four years later China's Lin Biao, Mao's mouthpiece and heir apparent, commanded worldwide attention when he also wrote in praise of armed struggle. He saw in the Vietnamese confrontation with the United States evidence for a "revolutionary upsurge" in the developing world. Lin characterized Latin America, Africa, and Asia as the world's populous countryside, while North America and western Europe constituted the privileged, exploitative city. As powerful revolutionary movements triumphed in rural regions, they were putting the imperialist core under siege and throwing the United States as the leading imperialist power on the defensive. Developments since World War II in China, Korea, Cuba, and Algeria as well as Vietnam made clear to Lin that history was on the side of revolutionary change: "The whole capitalist-imperialist system has become drastically weaker and is in the process of increasing convulsion and disintegration." The prospects for the global triumph of the socialist cause were excellent.[18]

The theme of anti-imperialist struggle similarly dominated Ernesto "Che" Guevara's famed call for "many Vietnams." The Argentine-born Guevara was a doctor by training and a revolutionary by political instinct. He saw in Castro's revolution the promise of social justice long denied ordinary people all across Latin American. In 1967 on the eve of an expedition to incite insurrection in Bolivia that would make him a revolutionary martyr, he wrote of the arduous conflict ahead in which "the repressive forces shall go seeking easy victims." But like Lin, he pointed to Vietnam as evidence that third-world countries could overcome even the most powerful oppressor. Confronted by "two, three or many Vietnams," imperialism would have to scatter its forces and ultimately suffer defeat.[19]

Ghana's Nkrumah spoke from exile in 1968 to hail the opening of yet another front in the third world's struggle—a violent black resistance in the United States. He had long promoted pan-African unity as a means to end colonialism and advance development. The emergence of a "Black Power" movement inspired him to dream of solidarity on an ever grander scale. The descendants of slaves scattered across the Atlantic world—in North and South America and the Caribbean—would unite with peoples of Africa in what would become "part of the world rebellion of the oppressed against the oppressor, of the exploited against the exploiter."[20]

The high tide of decolonization and radicalism in the third world gave the impetus to the most sustained call to date for rewriting the rules of the international economic game so that the poor would fare better. Those calls echoed in a General Assembly increasingly dominated by new nations. In 1964 poor countries organized into the Group of 77. Member states (ultimately well over a hundred) demanded what they called a New International Economic Order involving above all a revival of the import substitution strategy pioneered in Latin America. They also advocated for a strong state role in economic development. An unchecked free market would, they contended, perpetuate foreign domination, slow and distort development, and spawn social injustice.[21] Those same poor countries launched a parallel effort, the New World Information and Communication Order (a term coined in 1969) to get third-world peoples out from under the media control of the developed world. Promoting and protecting local media and restricting the power of multinationals to control information and entertainment seemed the only way to escape foreign political and cultural perspectives at odds with local experiences and needs. Third-world voices, dismissed out of hand a half century earlier, were dominating their own national stages, making themselves heard in international forums, and advancing demands that had the North Atlantic states on the defensive. A more dramatic global transformation is hard to imagine.

Caught in Crosscurrents

The thinking behind u.s. policy toward the third world became more complex during the 1950s and 1960s. Deeply rooted anxieties about the maturity of third-world peoples and doubts about the stability of their countries persisted in U.S. policy, indeed intensified as radical programs gained in appeal. Behind those anxieties and doubts were assumptions about cultural superiority and paternalism that social scientists repackaged into a pragmatic program for managing the third world. But in an unpleasant turn Washington found itself the target of blistering foreign criticism of U.S. racial attitudes and practices. This unprecedented scrutiny caused considerable embarrassment to cold warriors engaged in the struggle for hearts and minds along the periphery. This propaganda setback prompted mainstream U.S. media and leading officials to engage in some serious soul searching about whether the United States was living up to its obligations as the standard-bearer for the free world.

Eisenhower and his advisers offer evidence for the grip of familiar, timeworn images of other cultures even as the third world loomed larger as a Cold War front. The president regarded the Indians as "funny people," politically emotional, and not fully trustworthy; the Vietnamese as "backward"; and the Chinese as "completely reckless, arrogant, . . . and completely indifferent to human losses." Secretary of State Dulles had a formula for the proper treatment of Latin Americans: "You have to pat them on the head and make them think that you are fond of them." C. D. Jackson, a White House adviser, lamented in 1954 the lack of practical experience among "the swirling mess of emotionally super-charged Africans and Asiatics and Arabs that outnumber us." Ike thought that third-world leaders who displayed "ambitious pretensions," such as Nasser of Egypt, would have to be put in their place, a point seconded by the U.S. ambassador to Egypt Jefferson Caffrey in 1954 when he advised that the best way to deal with the Egyptian leader was to assume the role of "an intelligent parent faced with a 'problem child.'" Above all these strange, troublesome children stood the true adults—"the English-speaking peoples of the world," in the words of the president. He had a strong sense of solidarity with "those British" even in the midst of the Suez crisis in 1956 when London sought to deceive Washington—"they're still my right arm."[22]

But by the late 1950s the Eisenhower administration was feeling the sting of intense criticism from allies and neutrals no less than enemies that prejudice permeated the vaunted American system. Shocking images of mobs attacking schoolchildren in Little Rock in 1957 and Bull Connors's police dogs lunging at protesters in Birmingham in 1963 circulated widely overseas. The charges of racism lodged abroad echoed at home and highlighted the divergence in values between the United States and the growing number of newly independent states, many in sub-Saharan Africa. Under pressure, officials responded at first with "information campaigns" and tours by black performers such as Louis Armstrong to rescue the national reputation. Even though Eisenhower and others in his administration understood the ruinous international effects of a stubborn segregationist order, he was not ready to champion change. Formative years had schooled them in the ways of social segregation and the attendant notions of fundamental human difference. His defense of southern advocates of segregation as "not bad people" was telling. "All they are concerned about is to see that their sweet little girls are not required to sit alongside some big overgrown Negroes."[23]

John Kennedy seemed equally conflicted. In the rethinking of race in relation to foreign policy, Kennedy was a revealing figure. For reasons that were personal, generational, and electoral, he was less tightly wedded to Jim Crow. At the same time he was more ready to acknowledge the legitimate claims of nationalists to self-determination. He expressed sympathy in public for the aspirations of third-world peoples and especially the new states of sub-Saharan Africa. In the late 1950s, in response to outbursts of anti-American sentiment, he began criticizing the Eisenhower administration's support for the colonial policy of NATO allies. As senator, he reserved his most pointed criticism for the French effort to pacify Algeria. Once in the White House, Kennedy continued to stress the importance of third-world nationalism and the inevitability of decolonization. In July 1962 he insisted, "The United States has no intention of abdicating its leadership in [the] movement for independence to any nation committed to systemic human oppression."[24]

But Kennedy was surprisingly inert. When African diplomats complained of being refused service along the highway between New York and Washington, his cavalier response was "Let them fly!"[25] Not until mid-1963 did he offer civil rights legislation, having become embarrassed by continued southern defiance and pushed by burgeoning demonstrations. Even then nothing would happen until Kennedy's assassination put presidential powers in Lyndon Johnson's hands. It would take a southerner to break the moral paralysis. Taking up Kennedy's languishing legislation, he rammed it through Congress in 1964 and followed the next year with a voting rights bill. Johnson's bold vindication of equal rights finally provided an effective responses to overseas criticism even if it came at a heavy political cost, the loss of the solid Democratic South.

The politics of race paled for Kennedy in the face of intensifying Soviet and Chinese efforts to capture the loyalty of nationalists in new states. As early as January 1961, during his first weeks in office, he had found Khrushchev's endorsement of wars of national liberation a disturbing "clue" to Soviet intentions. The following April he described such wars as "a monolithic and ruthless conspiracy" aimed at the third world. When Kennedy turned to policy specifics, he worried as much as his predecessors about whether newly independent peoples could responsibly exercise their freedom. The third world seemed (as he put it somewhat vaguely in regard to the Congo) "where everything falls apart." On policy toward Vietnam, Cuba, the Congo, and Angola, a persistent fear of communist inroads muddied his verbal support for nationalism and led him to his famous formulation that it was better in the final analysis to embrace authoritarians than to allow misguided moderates to create an opening for a communist seizure of power. Seen from the heights now occupied by u.s. cold warriors, the third world was still a collection of trouble spots where freedom was a mixed good and sometimes even downright dangerous.[26]

The Kennedy administration clutched at "modernization theory" as an enlightened way of managing these troubled spots. Interest in "modernization" had had its inception within the academy in the late 1940s as a way of accounting for the nationalist unrest that was driving decolonization and inviting communist inroads. The notions generated by academics spread within the foreign policy establishment in the late 1950s and early 1960s just as visitors and observers from newly independent states were generating unfavorable international publicity about a racially burdened America and just as foreign aid priorities were shifting from Europe to third-world crisis points. Social science techniques promised to restore to Americans the luster of good intentions, to offer an effective program for using the redirected economic support, and ultimately to provide an antidote to radical trends in unsettled lands.

While couched in social science terminology, the notion of modernization incorporated old views about the backwardness of people on the periphery and the special u.s. obligation to serve as a tutor. Who better to help a third world struggling to catch up with the West politically and economically than the United States, the country with the most advanced economy, a model constitutional system, and an altruistic approach untainted by colonialism? Advocates of modernization advised developing countries that with the help of funding and guidance from the United States they could overcome the "traditional" attitudes and practices that held them back and achieve results in decades that had taken the more advanced centuries. While the proponents of modernization imagined themselves elaborating rigorous and practical theory, they were in fact affirming sturdy notions of the United States as a benevolent agent of historical progress, a transformative force in a troubled world in which some

countries were mired in the past. The simple but disturbing fact was, a ranking State Department official observed in 1953, "the hands of the clock of history are set at different hours in different parts of the world."[27] Action intellectuals—prominently Harvard and MIT professors—thought they knew how to
make those hands move faster for the laggards. They promoted their ideas on
how to get economies to take off, how to pursue counterinsurgency strategies
to maintain order, and how to transfer techniques and values through such
programs as the Peace Corps, mobilizing enlightened and dedicated young
Americans to win friends abroad.

In a Kennedy administration filled with action intellectuals, W. W. (short
for Walt Whitman) Rostow was most closely associated with the modernization faith. A professor at MIT, he had emerged during the 1950s as one of its
high priests. He had the chance to practice what he preached when called to
work in the Kennedy White House on third-world policy. After a time in the
State Department, he returned to the White House, now as Lyndon Johnson's
national security adviser. Throughout his government career he was consistently a leading advocate of tackling insurgencies breaking out in the third
world. Communists, whom he deemed the "scavengers of the modernization
process," could be stopped. Social and political reforms together with foreign
aid could, he promised, get developing nations through periods of internal
tensions and vulnerability to subversion. At the same time he was not shy
in stressing that special forces and military advisers might be necessary to
hold insurgents at bay and give development programs a chance to work. The
longer Rostow stayed in Washington the more the high-sounding language
of modernization gave way to blunt calls to exercise brute military power. By
the time of the Johnson presidency the latter had eclipsed the former—and
began to reawaken the charges of vicious American racism that enlightened
Democrats in the White House thought they had managed to silence. Johnson's support for civil rights at home did not prevent him from conceiving of
third-world peoples in demeaning stereotypes that made strongmen attractive and thinking in paternalistic terms that facilitated the resort to gunboat
diplomacy and covert operations.

The sustained scrutiny U.S. leaders had given the third world and themselves had resulted in, if nothing else, a capacity for vigilant self-censorship.
They wanted no condescending public remark to slip out that might impair
their working relationship with new states or provide grist for communist propaganda mills. But even with their consciousness steadily rising and the domestic discourse on race in flux, policymakers remained captives of a domes-

tically derived, color-conscious view of other peoples and states. The officials most favorably disposed to civil rights could still be heard making sweeping references to "dark-skinned nations," "yellow-skinned peoples," and "non-whites." Dividing the world by shades of skin pigmentation suggested not cultural sophistication but rather a strong racial consciousness, the amazingly persistent product of a long and troubled settler history on the North American continent.

PATTERNS OF REGIONAL INTERVENTION AND CONTROL

Increasingly anxious about an increasingly assertive third world, the u.s. government created a multiplying set of commitments that extended well beyond the old haunts in the Caribbean and the Pacific and came by the 1950s to encompass the entire globe. As Washington began to see virtually every point on the periphery as a potential vulnerability, it scrambled to shore up its position in country after country. These commitments proliferated even though Washington regarded Europe as the main Cold War battleground. Dean Rusk, secretary of state during both the Kennedy and Johnson administrations, explained how sideshows could become the main event in this global conflict when he declared in May 1961, "If you don't pay attention to the periphery, the periphery changes. And the first thing you know the periphery is the center."[28] The most obvious manifestation of this expanded u.s. role in the third world took the form of "pactomania." Washington concluded a steadily rising number of alliances with countries adjoining the Soviet Union and China.

At each point u.s. policymakers could apply an arsenal bulging with tools to win and sustain clients, punish foes, and define the limits of change. Some of these tools were tried and true, including notably support for strongmen, diplomatic isolation, economic pressure, and dispatch of the marines. The stronger post-1945 u.s. position helped make policymakers even more persuasive. For example, the u.s. control of the IMF and World Bank as well as Washington's new power to make direct loans and grants bolstered the economic options available to secure compliance. U.S. officials could dangle offers of advanced technology and weaponry. They could also resort to covert operations and psychological warfare. Thanks to this wealth of options, Washington could tailor its approach from region to region and make defiance a costly proposition. While u.s. forward positions in western Europe and Japan proved stable and strong (as seen in chapter 5), those within the emerging third world would turn out to be more problematic and require far more effort to sustain them, including costly limited wars in Korea and Vietnam.

Good-bye Good Neighbor

The 1940s opened with U.S. officials celebrating their good neighbor relationship to Latin America. By the 1950s the approach had shifted dramatically. Postwar nationalism in Latin America had set off alarm bells in Washington. Nationalists threatened investment and trade, opened the door to communist influence, and encouraged the potentially dangerous mobilization of popular forces. The stronger the nationalist demands for carving out a truly independent course in foreign and domestic policy, the more intense the U.S. resistance. By the 1950s and 1960s U.S. officials had assumed the tough-guy approach. They combined support for repressive military regimes, manipulation of intra-elite cleavages, covert operations, and in extremity the dispatch of U.S. forces with a frequency not seen since the early twentieth century.

The Truman administration had continued in the Cold War the wartime policy of shoring up hemispheric solidarity but with a growing sense of urgency and impatience. An inter-American alliance system put together in 1947 was one safeguard against Soviet penetration. U.S. training and funding of Latin American militaries provided another way to promote anticommunism and political stability within the region. Washington bowed to military coups in Peru and Venezuela against duly elected governments in 1948 and signaled support for the dictatorship run by Anastasio Somoza in Nicaragua and Rafael Trujillo in the Dominican Republic. Immature Latin Americans needed a firm hand if they were not to succumb to communist blandishments. Once they succumbed, so the foreign policy establishment was beginning to reason, they would never escape from the totalitarian grip of the communists. By contrast, despots might deny democracy in the short term but they would keep the door open to eventual democratic development. Latin Americans living in what George Kennan called after a tour of the region "confused and unhappy societies" still needed time to mature.[29]

Truman recognized that development programs might stimulate economic growth and thus head off communist appeals to the poor, but his budget, constrained by Republicans and a public tired of sacrifice, had no room for an ambitious new aid program for Latin America. The best that he could do was announce his Point Four program that put private investment in place of U.S. government assistance. So, for example, when Latin Americans asked for U.S. economic help comparable to that given Europe, Truman responded unsympathetically, "There has been a Marshall Plan for the Western Hemisphere for a century and a half."[30] He was referring to the Monroe Doctrine. If states in the region wanted to attract investment from abroad and hold accumulated wealth at home, they had only to follow a free-market formula and make foreign bankers and businessmen feel welcome. That in turn meant maintaining stability against leftist or populist agitation, limiting state intervention in the economy, and in general respecting private property.

Truman's successors learned to like covert operations, a capability always on call after the creation of the CIA. A coup in Iran carried out in Ike's first year in office had suggested covert operations were a silver bullet. Not only did they seem effective against communists worming their way into power; they cost little and proceeded quietly, thus preserving the public U.S. claim to stand for freedom and self-determination. Convinced that Guatemala was going communist, Eisenhower authorized a CIA operation against the democratically elected, reform-minded Arbenz government. A small army of exiles joined with the Catholic Church, powerful landowning families, and a panicked military to oust Arbenz in 1954. Eisenhower exulted publicly, "The people of Guatemala, in a magnificent effort, have liberated themselves from the shackles of international communist direction."[31] The coup had indeed "stopped communism" to Washington's satisfaction, but the price was the perpetuation of wide economic and ethnic division in Guatemala and ultimately a long and bloody civil war.

In March 1960 Eisenhower decided to try covert action again, this time to remove Castro. The Cuban leader's rise to power evinced the usual concerns about flawed Latin leadership. A State Department analysis sized him up on the eve of victory as "immature and irresponsible," while the head of the CIA, Allen Dulles, took the position that Castro and his associates "had to be treated more or less as children."[32] Their increasingly populist program and trade ties with the Soviet Union deepened the animosity. When public warnings and economic pressure failed to bring Castro to heel, Eisenhower gave the job to the CIA. By the time Kennedy had settled into the White House, the CIA plans to solve the Cuban problem were ready. Kennedy gave the green light, only to discover at the Bay of Pigs that the covert stick could be ineffective. Guevara had witnessed the U.S. machinations that had brought Arbenz down and conveyed to Castro the lesson of Guatemala: brace for a covert U.S. assault. Castro took the warning seriously, readied his military for the attack, and survived.

Kennedy had alternatives to covert operations. One was his Alliance for Progress, the first concerted attempt to make a U.S.-funded development program a weapon against the communist advance in the third world. In March 1961 he announced the initiative with its commitment to spending $20 billion over ten years and to sending U.S. advisers to ensure effective use of the money.

As an application of the modernization strategy, the Alliance for Progress did less to promote growth and reform and more to strengthen indigenous elites intent on countering any threat to class privilege and the political status quo. The other alternative to covert operations was the tried-and-true method of relying on strongmen. Despite Kennedy's soaring rhetoric about promoting democracy and popular reforms, in 1962 he came down in favor of recognizing a military coup in Argentina that had divided his advisers. Conversely, the assassination of the long-time Dominican dictator, Trujillo, in 1961 left Washington worried about instability that worked to communist advantage and that evoked the specter of a potentially embarrassing new "Cuba."

Lyndon Johnson had no reservations about working with right-wing governments and few of Kennedy's hopes for the Alliance for Progress. His chief adviser on Latin America, Thomas Mann, nicely captured the new hard-nosed, macho approach: "I know my Latinos. They understand only two things—a buck in the pocket and a kick in the ass." Johnson's backing of a military coup against Brazil's left-leaning government headed by João Goulart set the tone. Kennedy had begun helping the Brazilian military and keeping aid programs out of Goulart's hands. Johnson increased the pressure, encouraging the generals to act and dispatching a u.s. carrier task force to signal his concern. When the coup plotters succeeded in early 1964, he rewarded them with immediate diplomatic recognition and an increased level of aid. (Brazil became the third-largest recipient, behind South Vietnam and India.) The next year he reverted to methods familiar from earlier in the century and dispatched some 23,000 u.s. troops to the Dominican Republic to prevent what he called "a band of Communist conspirators" from taking control. The political infighting and outbreaks of violence that marked the post-Trujillo years finally had exhausted Johnson's patience and convinced him it was better to act and avoid another Cuba (just as he was struggling to keep South Vietnam from becoming another China).[33]

Countering Revolution

While a hard-edged policy kept Latin America under overall u.s. control, the same resolution failed to produce the desired effects against determined East Asian revolutionaries who pressed ahead with Soviet, Chinese, and popular support in combinations that varied from China to Korea to Vietnam. Where military and economic aid and support for strongmen failed to stop the communist advance, Washington resorted to direct military intervention. But turning the region into a battleground led to trouble in the field and unrest at home.

The Chinese revolution was the trauma that set the stage for a bloody quarter century along the Asian periphery. The Truman administration tried to block the Communist Party's rise using military and economic aid (at least $3 billion in current dollars) to bolster a conservative strongman, Chiang Kai-shek. But the Communists emerged victorious in 1949, after three years of civil war, and drove Chiang's Nationalists to Taiwan. Washington was left facing a well-organized, determined revolutionary regime hostile to the u.s. presence in East Asia. Truman rejected diplomatic relations with the Communists, whom he described as "those people who believe in government from the top—the totalitarian state."[34] He pursued instead diplomatic and economic isolation backed by containment enforced from u.s. bases in Japan and the Philippines. Neither he nor the public was spoiling for a fight.

The North Korean invasion of South Korea turned the China-u.s. stand off into the Cold War's first limited war. The temporary division of Korea at the end of World War II had by 1948 hardened into a permanent division along the thirty-eighth parallel. In the South, Washington opted for a conservative strongmen, Syngman Rhee, to counterbalance the Soviet-backed regime in the North. The North's invasion in June 1950 breached the containment line and thus posed a new, dangerous threat. "Communism has passed beyond the use of subversion to conquer independent nations," the president told Americans.[35] Truman quickly ordered u.s. forces to the peninsula and secured the backing of the un Security Council. He also signaled fresh determination to defend the defeated Chinese Nationalists (interposing the Seventh Fleet in the Taiwan Strait) and stepped up support of both the French in Indochina and the government in Manila battling Communist-led forces.

The Korean War went sour on the battlefield and then at home following the Chinese intervention in October–November 1950. In April Truman sacked his insubordinate commander, General Douglas MacArthur, who wanted to expand the conflict into China and give the containment front in Asia higher priority than Europe. Truman's contretemps with MacArthur and his inability either to win or to end the conflict eroded public support. Already in early 1951, less than a year after the war had begun, half of Americans polled thought the military commitment in Korea a mistake and three out of four were averse to "an all-out war with Communist China."[36] The damage to Truman's presidency and to the Democratic Party grew greater as the war dragged on. The Republican Dwight Eisenhower's promise in 1952 that he would end Truman's war helped win him the presidency. He delivered in July 1953 in a cease-fire that restored the division of Korea along the 38th parallel and left the peninsula two armed camps, each hair-trigger ready for the next round of fighting.

Three years of fighting had devastated the peninsula. U.S. bombing techniques honed during World War II took an especially heavy toll on North Korea, leveling cities, obliterating villages, and showering civilians with incendiaries. It could have been worse; the Truman administration repeatedly discussed using nuclear weapons and the Eisenhower administration threatened an atomic strike. They both finally resisted the temptation. The war could have been shorter by some two years had Truman himself not insisted on handling prisoner repatriation on the basis of free choice (a procedure that vindicated u.s. values and was intended to embarrass the North Korean and Chinese Communist enemy). He refused to follow international conventions stipulating return to the country of nationality. With cease-fire talks deadlocked, the death and destruction continued. In all some 3 to 4 million Koreans (most civilians) died during the war, together with at least 152,000 Chinese who had joined the fray. The land that emerged from the war was not only politically divided and constantly shadowed by the prospect of renewed fighting. Its population was numerically diminished, materially deprived, and psychologically demoralized amid physical ruin running all the way from north to south.

The Korean War ended with a firm u.s. hold on East Asia. The war itself was not the trauma for Americans it had been for Koreans. The American dead were relatively few (54,000) while in a time of peace and plenty those at home easily put the distant, unpleasant war out of their minds, even as u.s. aid programs, treaty commitments, and military deployments secured South Korea as a key Cold War outpost. On Taiwan u.s. assistance helped build an economy that could sustain the military ambitions of Chiang's ruling Nationalist Party. While the Nationalists dreamed of a return to the mainland, u.s. policymakers were more interested in a secure island base even if it meant accommodating to a state-directed development policy similar to Japan's, accepting strict limits on u.s. companies seeking to enter the market, and putting up with military confrontations Mao initiated in 1954 and 1958 as reminders of China's claim to Taiwan. The Philippines was another key East Asian outpost successful defended. Formally declared independent in 1946, the country remained under Washington's watchful eye. A home-grown Leftist insurgency (the Huks) set off alarms in early 1950, but it soon sputtered out, the victim of its own misguided strategy and timely u.s. assistance. U.S. forces retained access to major bases (ultimately critical to waging war in Vietnam). But little changed for Filipinos. Their economy remained burdened by crony capitalism and lagged behind their neighbors' increasingly successful development programs. Their government remained the plaything of provincial elites. And rural discontents that had fueled the insurgency continued to simmer.

The seeming U.S. successes in Taiwan and the Philippines contrasted with the missteps in China and Korea, the main focus of U.S. concern in the immediate aftermath of World War II. Crude information had badly skewed policy decisions. Washington concluded that Mao was a creature of the Soviet Union, relying heavily on intelligence appraisals coming from the opposition Nationalist Party. Once the Korean War began, the Truman administration refused to take seriously Chinese warnings about possible military intervention. As the commander in the field, MacArthur plunged ahead confident that "Orientals" only respected force. The result was a painful military reversal followed by a prolonged, deadlocked war. The same pattern was to repeat itself in Vietnam. Its Communists figured as part of a monolithic movement threatening to the region and far beyond. Its leaders lacked genuine nationalist credentials. Its popular support was shallow and dependent on terror. A demonstration of U.S. determination in South Vietnam would be enough to intimidate the North. These miscalculations meant once again that as the conventional tools of U.S. policy failed, military force became the ultimate but inconclusive resort.

Truman took up on Indochina where Roosevelt had left off, taking a vague French pledge of ultimate independence as a fig leaf to cover a stark denial of self-determination. The Communist-led Viet Minh (short for Vietnam Independence League) had declared French control at an end in August 1945, ostentatiously invoking the American Declaration of Independence and appealing to Truman to endorse this exercise of national self-determination. Truman made no response. As the Cold War took shape, his administration's backing for the embattled French became ever less grudging. Secretary of State George Marshall contended that the Viet Minh leader, Ho Chi Minh, had "direct Communist connections," while France deserved support because it was in the best position to supply Vietnamese "enlightened political guidance" and encourage economic development. Finally, in early 1950 the Truman administration made a formal commitment of aid to the French forces and accorded diplomatic recognition to their Vietnamese puppet government. Relying on the colonial power seemed the best hope for restoring regional stability, blocking Communist China's expansion, and preserving a market for a recovering Japanese economy. Sticking to the Roosevelt-Truman path, the Eisenhower administration backed the French. They might yet master a situation in Vietnam marked (as John Foster Dulles put it) by a "lack of political maturity on the part of the people themselves." By 1954 the United States was bearing three-fourths of the cost of the war—but to no avail. Dienbienphu, imagined by French strategists as a decisive conventional battle, turned into a slow strangulation of French forces, a defeat that snuffed out any lingering colonial ambitions.[37]

The French retreat left Eisenhower scrambling to save the southern half of Vietnam from the victorious Communists. He banked on Ngo Dinh Diem, a strong-willed, one-time collaborator with the French. Diem proved at first a shrewd nation builder, but he also stirred political discontent with his autocratic ways. By the early 1960s Diem was on the defensive in his urban strongholds and losing control of the countryside. Intensified Kennedy administration support, including a growing team of u.s. advisers (up to 16,000 by 1963), failed to check the gathering insurgency. With Diem on the ropes and perhaps even exploring a secret deal with Hanoi, the Kennedy White House decided to encourage a coup. The generals who seized power in late 1963 proved no more effective. The colonial option had failed. So had the strongman strategy. A decade's worth of aid and advice had also proven unavailing. Washington now had only one tool left in its arsenal—a major commitment of u.s. air and ground power—if it did not want to risk losing all.

The decision on a direct and costly u.s. troop commitment fell to Kennedy's successor. Johnson tiptoed toward the commitment. He bombed North Vietnam for the first time in August 1964 following what he took to be two attacks on u.s. Navy destroyers. In the bargain Johnson got Congress to pass the Tonkin Gulf resolution, a blank check authorizing use of force in the region. With the presidential election behind him, Johnson resumed the bombing in early 1965, only now on a larger scale and a continuing basis. The first u.s. combat unit arrived in March, and by July the president had decided on a major troop commitment (to climb to half a million). He had unleashed a war that would ravage the peoples and land of Indochina and shake the American political system.

Taking Over from the British

The Middle East was the stage on which an increasingly prominent United States eclipsed a fading Britain. The transition occurred late and piecemeal. Until World War II missionaries and oil companies were the leading u.s. players. The war expanded the official u.s. stake in Iran (a supply line to the Soviet ally) and interest in oil under the control of the Saudi ruling family. The beginning of the Cold War further raised the region's profile without disturbing its long-standing image of a backward place peopled by thieves and fanatics and ruled by despots. Its defining qualities were, in Eisenhower's crisp characterization, "violence, emotion and ignorance."[38] Policymakers were interested in military bases and communications routes right at Europe's back door, oil to keep the developed world's economy humming, and the welfare of the Israeli state that arose from British-controlled Palestine in 1948.

The parts of this emerging regional commitment did not fit well together. Immediate U.S. diplomatic support for Israel followed by growing military assistance alienated opinion throughout the region and sent some regimes looking to the Soviets as a counterweight to the Americans. In an effective regional division of labor, the U.S. policymakers at first took the northern tier—Turkey and Iran as well as Greece—fronting the Soviet Union as their prime concern, while leaving Britain to maintain order behind that line, especially in Egypt, Iraq, and Jordan. Nationalists, socialists, pan-Arabists, and advocates of other secular ideologies suspected that U.S. ambitions were neocolonial, a point confirmed by Washington's close cooperation with the arch-colonial power. Rising radical sentiment and an inexorable weakening of British influence forced U.S. policymakers to cover the region single-handedly and to rely ever more heavily on conservative regimes for assured access to oil. Thus Washington became even more identified with the status quo.

This mix of objectives—keeping the Soviets out, the Israelis territorially secure, radicals neutralized, and the oil flowing to European and Asian allies—called for resorting to the full range of policy tools. Covert operations and support for strongmen figured prominently in the creation of a pro-U.S. government in Iran in 1953. In 1951 a nationalist government headed by Mohammed Mossadeq had taken over a major British oil concession. London countered by attempting to topple Mossadeq. When that effort collapsed, Eisenhower's CIA stepped in and finished the job with help from the Iranian military. Now that the "wily oriental" (Dulles's label) was out of the way, the young monarch, Mohammed Reza Shah Pahlavi, rushed home to reclaim his throne, and Washington invested heavily in his survival (to the tune of over $1 billion in economic and military assistance between 1953 and 1960).[39] For a quarter century, first as a dependent but increasingly as a regional military surrogate, the shah assured the United States a steady flow of reasonably priced oil, kept the lid on domestic discontents, and furtively cooperated with Israel.

Economic carrots and sticks were the tools of choice at the other end of the region where Egypt dominated. Britain had clung to military bases there and the Suez Canal while demanding deference from Egyptian political leaders. Blessed with resources the British lacked, Eisenhower tried to buy Nasser's good behavior with the promise of help with a massive Aswan dam project.

Dulles abruptly withdrew the offer in 1956 after discovering that Nasser, a "Hitlerite" personality and "an extremely dangerous fanatic," was also dealing with Moscow. Nasser responded by nationalizing the Suez Canal, which in turn prompted the Anglo-French-Israeli attack on Egypt. Faced with a situation rapidly spinning out of control and livid over the plotting by his allies, Eisenhower brought the military assault to a halt by refusing to rescue the collapsing British pound. London had finally realized it was playing second fiddle in a region it had once dominated. Dulles drew what seemed the obvious conclusion: "We must fill the vacuum of power which the British filled for a century—not merely the ability to act in an emergency but day in day out presence there."[40]

Eisenhower acted on this conclusion in early 1957 when he asked Congress to endorse a major aid program backed by authority for the president to use military force if necessary. Britain was in full imperial retreat and plans for a regional alliance against the Soviets was floundering. Syria was beginning to develop Soviet trade ties, and a military coup in Baghdad undercut the last British influence in Iraq. With stability in peril and the Soviets making headway, the president needed some dramatic show of resolve, especially to reassure Iran and Turkey, the states on the containment frontline. In March 1958 Congress acceded to Eisenhower's request by a margin of 72 to 19 in the Senate and 350 to 60 in the House, granting him the power to wield a big stick in the region and eventually appropriating $200 million to build up u.s. influence. This combination of initiatives signaled a new level of u.s. commitment in the Middle East, which became known as the Eisenhower Doctrine.

In July 1958 the president used his new authority in Lebanon—but at a price. When a Muslim uprising against the country's pro-Western Christian president threatened to create more trouble in an already volatile region, he ordered a military intervention. U.S. Marines waded onto Beirut beaches crowded with bikini-clad beauties and frolicking children. This show of force helped calm the situation, but it also did nothing to shake the appeal of Nasser's Arab nationalism. Nasser himself had come to stand for driving Britain from the region, avoiding entanglement in the Cold War, and securing support for economic development from Moscow if not Washington. As a weary Eisenhower himself had to concede, "The people are on Nasser's side."[41]

The tightening u.s. ties to Israel deepened the problems for u.s. policy in the region. To the end of his term Eisenhower continued to try to square the circle—supporting and restraining Israel while trying to maintain some influence in Egypt. His Democratic successors gave up on the balancing act, swayed by party ties to an American Jewish community fiercely supportive of Israel. Kennedy began to step up the provision of advanced military hard-ware and blinked away evidence that Israel was developing nuclear weapons. Johnson had even fewer hesitations about support for Israel. The outbreak of fighting between Israel and its neighbors in 1967 (the Six-Day War) revealed that the United States and Israel had arrived at a level of cooperation that amounted to a virtual alliance.

The Neocolonial Solution

Like the Middle East, Africa came late to the u.s. policy agenda. One minor exception was Liberia, which had emerged in the nineteenth century as a u.s. protectorate dominated by American blacks who had fled the land of slavery to this new homeland. In a second exception leading African Americans had sought to rally opposition in the 1930s to the Italian invasion of Ethiopia. They had remained outspoken during World War II, calling for a policy of genuine liberation throughout Africa consistent with the Atlantic Charter. After the war their demands collided with the Cold War concerns that put anticommu-nism ahead of anticolonialism. Prominent blacks who stubbornly backed the African freedom struggle were swept aside by McCarthyite currents at home. The singer and civil rights campaigner Paul Robeson encountered repression that ended his professional career and undermined his political influence. W. E. B. Du Bois, an influential voice for black internationalism within the National Association for the Advancement of Colored People, left the orga-nization and went into exile in Ghana. The head of the NAACP, Walter White, grasped the new limits imposed by the Cold War. So rather than fight a losing cause, he dropped talk of black liberation in broad international terms and instead focused on using the Cold War rhetoric of freedom to advance the civil rights cause at home.

Africa began finally to command serious official attention in the late 1950s with independence demands echoing across the continent and colonial powers in retreat. Policymakers responded to these developments guided by a deep and strikingly persistent conviction of African incapacity. Their views accentuated the sense that the continent was vulnerable to disorder and thus to communist penetration. A National Security Council report in 1957 reveals how views on race found their way into serious policymaking. The secret re-port characterized Africans as "still immature and unsophisticated" on the foremost question of the day, the conflict between nationalism and commu-nism. Nineteenth-century colonialism was bad, the report intoned, but pre-mature independence was no better. Washington had to seek a middle way in which colonial powers were to guide their charges into the modern world—away from the "extremely primitive" outlooks associated with tribal and family loyalties, away from the lure of radical doctrines and toward responsible self-government.[42] Vice President Richard Nixon couched these racist doubts in cruder terms when he observed to his colleagues on the National Security Council in January 1960, "Some of the peoples of Africa have been out of the trees for only about fifty years."[43] Worried about instability, Washington preferred military strongmen over the impatient leaders who had championed independence. Typically President John Kennedy complained that Kwame Nkrumah, the president of Ghana and the herald of decolonization, was "unnecessarily difficult," while the u.s. ambassador in Ghana offered Kennedy a thumbnail sketch of "a badly confused and immature person."[44]

Even though Africa was a Cold War backwater, worry over independence movements led policymakers during the late Eisenhower and the Kennedy years to initiate aid programs as well as covert operations. But to a degree not seen in other regions, Washington looked to the colonial powers to work out arrangements that would constrain emerging African states in a neocolonial web of economic and political ties. Keeping Africans on a leash held by London and Paris seemed the best way in the short run to frustrate the communists (whether home grown or sent by Moscow) while also guaranteeing western Europe's access to natural resources so important to recovery. Already anxious about the destabilizing effects of decolonization, Americans were also determined to preserve solidarity with European colonial powers, who also happened to be NATO allies and controlled access to valuable bases. In the American estimate, the British offered the best model for implementing a responsible neocolonial transition. By the late 1950s French colonial practice was also getting the American seal of approval. Even Portugal, that most recalcitrant of the colonial powers, secured Kennedy's acquiescence to its policy of military repression in Angola. In return the u.s. military got to keep its valuable Azores bases.

The Algerian conflict, one of the most brutal and long-lasting of the liberation struggles, illustrates the attractiveness of the neocolonial solution. The Eisenhower administration accepted that the Algerians would in time get their independence and had no intention of involving the United States directly in resolving this colonial flare-up. Rather Washington hoped for what it called "independence within interdependence."[45] The large French settler community, French business, and the government in Paris should accept formal independence and then work together to give their former subjects the guidance they would need. Informal tutelage wielded through commerce, culture, and a military presence would secure a stable, moderate Algeria, in what would amount to a protectorate, right at Europe's back door.

Strongmen figured prominently in the emerging Euro-American formula for stability. American policymakers looked for leaders who could maintain order and cooperate with businessmen and diplomats from the former colonial powers. The Belgian Congo, which won independence in 1960 as the Republic of the Congo, offers a case in point. The Belgian-trained Mobutu Sese Seko became a favorite of the local CIA station chief as well as the Belgians. Mobutu played a leading role in getting rid of Patrice Lumumba, a nationalist with views close to those of Nkrumah. Eisenhower said he wanted Lumumba stopped; an assassination followed in January 1961. Two years later Kennedy welcomed Mobutu to the White House and praised the commander of the Congo's army for his contribution to order in the postindependence period. "General, if it hadn't been for you, the whole thing would have collapsed and the Communists would have taken over."[46] After seizing power in 1965, Mobutu sustained U.S. backing by exercising a firm hand at home and opposing leftist states in the region. That his rule down to 1997 also badly mismanaged the economy of Zaire (the new name he gave his country) and saw the brutal repression of dissent counted for less in the American grade book.

South Africa was a welcome island of industrial activity and political calm in what one State Department official described as "a restless stirring continent." Its mines fed gold and strategic minerals such as uranium, manganese, and chrome onto the international market. Its government neutralized Soviet subversion and irresponsible black radicals, while assuring the security of vital sea lanes passing its southern tip and welcoming U.S. missile tracking facilities. Guaranteeing these Cold War benefits was the ultimate neocolonial arrangement. South Africa's European population—mainly Dutch but also British—were sufficiently large, rooted, and armed to control the majority African population. The formal means for exercising that control was the apartheid system, immediately recognizable to Americans as a variant on Jim Crow. But neocolonialism here as in other parts of Africa had a fundamental flaw: it provoked increasingly well-organized domestic resistance. Apartheid also evoked by the late 1950s increasingly strong criticism from the U.S. civil rights movement. U.S. officials had long recognized the practical risk of apartheid "driving the natives to communism." Under pressure Eisenhower conceded that apartheid was "a touchy thing," but neither he nor his Democratic successors would go beyond pro forma public condemnation. Even as South Africa turned into an increasingly repressive white police state, overt

Cold War concerns with stability and subterranean racist fears continued to govern u.s. policy. The leading opponent of apartheid, Nelson Mandela, had good grounds as he began his quarter century in confinement in 1962 for wondering about the u.s. commitment to freedom.[47]

Americans had intervened on a broad third-world front and more often than not beaten back nationalist challenges to u.s. dominance. This achievement stands on a par with the parallel efforts to stymie the Soviet Union and shape the international order. The hyperrealist observation that Thucydides put in the mouth of the Athenian ambassador to Melos—"the strong do what they can, and the weak suffer what they must"[48]—seemed borne out by events. Twenty-five hundred years had apparently changed little. Third-world dreams of effecting fundamental change at home and internationally would have been hard to realize in the best of circumstances. Once Americans joined what they saw as a global ideological battle against communism, the obstacles in the way of the likes of Castro, Nkrumah, Mao, and Arbenz became formidable and in some cases even impassable. Defiance of the United States carried major and lasting consequences. Washington squelched some radical regimes and insurgent movements and made others pay a high price. U.S. pressure pushed Castro toward a garrison state and the allocation of a large proportion of national resources to security. China paid heavily in life and treasure to protect its Korean and Vietnamese frontiers, while the peoples of those regions suffered human losses in the millions and had their lands laid waste. The u.s. success in aborting nationalist reform in Guatemala set the stage for a prolonged internal conflict in which some two hundred thousand would lose their lives, almost all at the hands of a repressive right-wing military.

But as another devotee of realism pointed out at the very outset of the Cold War, the United States too might pay a price in the effort to impose its will. Walter Lippmann, Washington's leading journalist and a widely respected wise man, warned in 1947 that pressing containment on a global scale would put u.s. policymakers at the head of "a coalition of disorganized, disunited, feeble or disorderly nations, tribes and factions around the perimeter of the Soviet Union."[49] With great prescience he predicted that Americans would inexorably be drawn into local contests about which they knew little and which were of scant relevance to u.s. interests. But commitments once made were not easily repudiated, and thus Americans stored up trouble for another day.

Lippmann's prediction of a price to pay came dramatically to pass in Vietnam. The commitment there plunged u.s. leaders into perplexity. It brought dramatically to the fore the contradiction that made some Americans wince:

a nation formally and emphatically identified with freedom engaged in a brutal, bloody effort to control the future of another people in a distant land. The resulting domestic resentments and in time resistance would put policy-makers on the defensive, ignite bitter public controversy, and seriously strain the u.s. political system. The decades to come would reveal ever more clearly that ascendancy even for the strongest could have its price: mounting costs associated with global crusading, debilitating cracks in the foreign policy consensus, and presidents weakened and driven from office.

7

DISORIENTED GIANT

1968★1991

On 31 July 1968 President Lyndon Baines Johnson sat down at a table in the White House Cabinet Room to listen to a tape his son-in-law, Captain Charles Robb, had sent from Vietnam (fig. 7). Standing inconspicuously in the background was a bust of John Kennedy, who had bequeathed the Vietnam commitment to Johnson. His head bowed, the president absorbed the harrowing details of where this third-world intervention had taken him. Ambitious, proud, and politically skilled, Johnson had come into office confident in his direction at home and abroad. His foreign policy was guided by the orthodoxies of the early Cold War absorbed during long service in Washington. He took containment along with the specter of totalitarianism and the lessons of Munich as gospel and combined them with a can-do confidence in the United States as a global force great enough to pursue its goals abroad as well as at home—to have both guns and butter. Proven badly wrong, he had announced the previous March that he would not seek another term in office. Politics had been Johnson's life; the man listening to the tape knew that his political life was about to end, his reputation in tatters.

The bloody, stalemated conflict in Vietnam had brought Johnson down. A major enemy offensive earlier in the year had caught u.s. and South Vietnamese forces off guard and shocked the u.s. public. The war had isolated Washington from allied governments, sparked anti-Americanism across western Europe and in Japan, intensified strains in the u.s. economy, and seriously weakened the dollar as the solid center of international finance. Robert McNamara's doubts about the war forced Johnson to ease him out only to find his successor in the Pentagon, Clark Clifford, expressing skepticism. Public and congressional opinion was in disarray. Some called for liquidating the war. Others wanted to stay the course or even follow a more aggressive strategy

Figure 7. Lyndon B. Johnson, by White House photographer Jack E. Kightlinger, July 1968. (Courtesy of Lyndon Baines Johnson Library and Museum, Austin, Texas. B-1274-16.)

even if it meant cutting Johnson's prized Great Society programs. When the Democratic convention meeting in Chicago rejected an antiwar platform and moved to nominate Johnson's choice, Hubert Humphrey, angry protesters clashed with out-of-control police. Television captured the violent scenes for a shocked national audience. The domestic Cold War consensus was shattering.

Johnson's successors faced the challenge of constructing a new foreign policy in the context of continued hard times. The period of adjustment running through the 1970s and 1980s was marked by twists and turns as successive presidents and their key advisers rethought the u.s. role in the world. The efforts of Richard Nixon and Jimmy Carter between 1969 and 1980 met with distinctly mixed results. Ronald Reagan and George H. W. Bush reverted in the 1980s to the familiar Cold War framework. The collapse of the old Soviet foe along with its eastern European clients seemed to restore faith in the country's mastery of global forces.

The resolution may have been illusory. By fixing dominance at midcentury on multiple fronts, the u.s. state became subject to crosscutting pressures—both at home and internationally—that made a sound, widely accepted course of action unusually difficult to devise. The lurching from one policy to another from the 1970s onward was an expression not of some personal failing of men in the White House. The presidents from McKinley to Truman who had guided the country to ascendancy were no more skilled or insightful than their successors. The prime difference was that the latter operated within a more difficult position created by a wide range of global commitments (from alliances to client states to international institutions and norms) that in turn made heavy, almost daily demands on national resources, presidential judgment, and domestic politics. Ascendancy so recently won was already under stress. It would prove not just complicated but packed with cares.

GLOBAL FORCES STRIKE BACK

Forces operating on a global scale did much to create the time of troubles that engulfed u.s. policy. At the forefront was the nuclear arms race entering its third decade; a still perplexing and increasingly diverse third world, the outbreak of intergenerational discord on a worldwide scale, and an international economy whose dynamism had spun beyond u.s. control. Cumulatively these developments sowed disaffection and disarray at home and limited the exercise of u.s. global power. They also forced policymakers into thinking outside well-worn Cold War grooves.

U.S. entanglements and initiatives overseas had a paradoxical effect: it created a more cosmopolitan public that grew restive under Cold War constraints and dangers. Millions of soldiers had gained an informal international education. The numbers serving in France during World War I were dwarfed by some 11 million sent to points all around the world in the course of World War II. From the latter group of veterans exposed to the broader world would emerge the leaders in the rapidly expanding fields of international and area studies in the 1950s and 1960s. The soldiers and diplomats manning Cold War outposts and the employees of multinational corporations continued the schooling of an entire people. A boom in tourism added to the popular sense of a broader world. Visitors to France alone climbed from .26 million in 1950 to 1.35 million in 1970. By then Americans were making 2.9 million trips across the Atlantic to Europe and the Mediterranean. Universities became hotbeds of international interest spurred by the Fulbright Program, the Peace Corps, and other overseas opportunities. According to a 1965 survey, one in ten college students had visited Europe before graduation.[1]

This increasing awareness of and engagement in the world translated for some into activism aimed at such transnational problems as nuclear testing and the arms race, human rights, and the environment. Grassroots campaigners in the United States linked up with counterparts in Europe and Japan. Similarly professionals from scientists to historians met with colleagues overseas to share perspectives and devise common programs. Nongovernmental organizations with an international portfolio mushroomed in the United States but also in western Europe and Japan. There were ten times more of them worldwide in 1984 (12,686) than there had been in 1960.[2] Ascendancy functioned within a more and more dense web of global connections that undercut narrow nationalist perspectives and challenged the Cold War state's monopoly of information.

Wrestling with the Nuclear Genie

American ascendancy arrived at the dawn of the nuclear age. The conjuncture created nightmares that grew steadily worse, and indeed have yet to go away. By the 1960s they had prompted the first limits on strategic nuclear weapons, an effort at the heart of improving u.s.-Soviet relations (described in chapter 4). Leaders on both sides talked of the nuclear peril. Technical means of verification such as satellites, ground sensors, and upper-atmosphere air sampling helped them clear the hurdle of mutual suspicion and negotiate agreements with greater confidence. But the anxiety that fueled the arms race persisted. Moscow increased its nuclear force to preclude a successful u.s.

first strike or attempts at nuclear blackmail. The Soviets' move toward parity in the 1970s soon inspired calls in Washington for countermeasures.

Arms controllers had a hard time getting the nuclear genie back in the bottle. The fundamental problem was the allure that ever more sophisticated and reliable weapons of mass destruction exercised over Soviet and U.S. policy-makers. A striking case in point are MIRVs (short for "multiple, independently targeted re-entry vehicle"), which placed several warheads atop one rocket. Each warhead could be programmed to seek its own distinct target. As rockets got larger, they could carry more of these MIRVs, thus multiplying the destructive power on each side while threatening the sense of stability and predictability that nuclear strategists were coming to prize. Technological inventiveness was also evident in antiballistic missile defenses, placed around Moscow in the 1960s to ensure against a U.S. first strike. These defenses added another element of uncertainty to nuclear calculations and created pressure on the U.S. side to create comparable defenses or build more missiles to overcome the Soviet defenses.

The nuclear genie proved elusive for a second reason—the know-how had insidiously spread, giving rise far and wide to national ambitions to join a select, prestigious club. Washington and Moscow had sought to limit membership. A nonproliferation treaty concluded in July 1968 restricted the spread of fuel and technology and invited others to renounce nuclear ambitions. (It gained enough signatures to come into force two years later.) Proliferation was by then already well advanced. Britain had tested its first nuclear device in 1953; France and China broke into the charmed circle in 1964. Israel followed stealthily just behind, breaking unannounced into the club with help from France in the late 1960s. (By 1990 Britain, France, and China each had arsenals in the range of 300–500 warheads, and Israel about 100 warheads.) Third-world states such as Brazil, India, and Pakistan indicated support for nonproliferation but only if the superpowers made a commitment themselves to pursue nuclear disarmament and to promote security and development in the third world. India conducted its first test in 1974, spurring neighbor and rival Pakistan to keep pace. (Pakistan finally joined the club in 1998; current estimates are that each of the South Asian powers has around 40 nuclear weapons.) South Africa was the only state to go nuclear and then reverse itself. Isolated internationally and fearful of its neighbors, the apartheid regime produced weapons in the 1980s, likely with Israeli assistance, but dismantled its stockpile of six crude weapons in the early 1990s.[3]

The U.S. public awoke in the late 1950s to the nuclear danger, stirred by fallout from atmospheric testing by both the United States and the Soviet Union.

One of the first public statements by SANE (National Committee for a Sane Nuclear Policy), established in 1957, highlighted the rising sense of international solidarity before a common danger: "The sovereignty of the human community comes before all others—before the sovereignty of groups, tribes, or nations. In that community, man has natural rights. He has the right to live and grow, to breathe unpoisoned air, to work on uncontaminated soil." Women's groups were especially effective in speaking for the welfare of children around the world threatened by radioactive fallout. A new round of Soviet and u.s. testing in late 1961 and early 1962, followed in October 1962 by the Cuban missile crisis further accentuated popular fear and sparked fresh public protests. Kennedy's June 1963 American University speech and nascent Soviet-American cooperation on arms control had a calming effect. Most Americans did not want to think about the prospect of cataclysmic destruction. So they were content to leave the mysteries of nuclear strategy to experts who had mastered its arcane details, understood its language filled with acronyms such as ICBM and SIOP, and could contemplate the awful implications behind such reassuring terms as "nuclear exchange" (which brought to mind some kind of gift-giving). But the slightest hint coming out of Washington that nuclear war was thinkable would snap the public awake and ignite protests.[4]

Troubles in the Third World

As with the nuclear issue, the third world had by the 1960s begun to pose an acute problem for policymakers (as seen in chapter 6). That problem did not abate. American policymakers confronted a pair of difficulties. One was conceptual. Even though the Cold War consensus was eroding, containment remained the one obvious, widely understood paradigm to apply to an unruly periphery. Containment in its heyday during the early Cold War had arguably been too simple a framework for formulating policy toward the third world, and it became steadily less appropriate as the third world itself became more diverse and as its leaders began to explore nonsocialist development paths. The other was the scale of the discontent. Could Washington curb the challenges when they kept appearing on so many fronts?

The Vietnam War had confirmed what the Korean conflict earlier had suggested—that East Asia was dangerous terrain for u.s. policymakers. But extricating u.s. forces was difficult because Hanoi was implacable in its demand that u.s. troops had to leave, clearing the way for a final drive toward long-sought national unity. This looked from the perspective of Johnson and then Nixon too much of a defeat, so diplomatic negotiations, launched in mid-1968, languished while U.S. forces remained bogged down, the fighting spread into Cambodia, and public disaffection mounted.

The Chinese Communists demonstrated equal staying power—here too to Washington's great frustration. Beijing's assistance to North Vietnam helped stalemate the United States there as it had earlier in Korea. Mao remained militant in pressing China's claim to Taiwan, and despite the domestic tumult brought on by the Cultural Revolution (1966–69), he continued to support genuinely radical third-world forces. The turn to the market following Mao's death in 1976 seemed to American observers finally to promise a "normal" China. They would soon discover otherwise. The Communists retained a firm grip on the government, cultivated regional influence, and still pressed their Taiwan claims.

Latin America remained a restive sphere of influence. Castro's Cuba was a thorn in the U.S. side that became more painful as Havana championed revolutionary movements in Central America. In Guatemala an insurgency backed by disgruntled army officers inspired by the Cuban Revolution sputtered in the 1960s and then died out, only to be followed by renewed unrest in the late 1970s as the country's indigenous people became politically active. In El Salvador too a persistent insurgency wore away at government control. Bloody and indiscriminate official and right-wing terror failed in both Guatemala and El Salvador to end the resistance. In Nicaragua the end of Somoza family rule in 1979 placed power in the hands of a left-wing movement whose name memorialized that early antagonist of U.S. intervention, Augusto Sandino. The only bright spots for U.S. policymakers were Chile and Argentina, where the military, following the Brazilian example, seized power and hounded the left.

The Middle East joined the list of policy worries in the 1970s, the third decade of deepening U.S. involvement. The central event was a revolution in Iran in 1978 against the U.S.-backed regime of Mohammad Reza Shah Pahlavi. The opposition had been broad based, but the clerics, who had taken a leading role, emerged as the dominant force. Not satisfied with toppling a key U.S. client, the most prominent of the clerics, Ruhollah Khomeini, proceeded to denounce America as "this Great Satan" and "the number-one enemy of the deprived and oppressed people of the world."[5] The creation of an Islamic republic demonstrated the potential for a new kind of politics that consciously repudiated secular ideologies imported from the West. The conflict in Afghanistan drove home the point following the Soviet invasion in 1979. The call to holy war mobilized Afghans and drew volunteers and funding from across the Arab world. The sharpening sense of Palestinian nationalism and desperation inaugurated a second new regional trend that was challenging to u.s. policy: the Palestinian Liberation Organization's turn to violence against the Israeli occupation. Finally, dependence on Middle Eastern oil boomeranged in the 1970s. An Egypt-led attack on Israel in 1973 became the occasion for a boycott by oil producers. Though aimed at the United States, the boycott pitched the economy of the entire developed world into turmoil. Six years later the Iranian Revolution again interrupted oil supplies and provided a second reminder that a resource critical to the world economy lay outside u.s. control.

In sub-Saharan Africa Washington watched the shadow of Marx fall across more and more of the continent. His influence was evident in insurgencies in Angola and Mozambique, radicalized by stubborn Portuguese defense of their colonial holdings. His influence was also evident in Ethiopia, where pro-Soviet policies put at risk a strategic u.s. communications line. Finally, the African National Congress's assault on South Africa's official policy of apartheid left u.s. officials anxious. The ANC had a dubious partner in the South African Communist Party and an ambiguous position on the ultimate disposition of South Africa's mineral wealth. As earlier, Washington worried that liberation and majority rule might carry the region with its natural resources farther away from the "free world." Better for freedom to come slowly than risk disorder.

Social Ferment

Beleaguered by nuclear nightmares and third-world crises, u.s. policymakers felt the ground at home give beneath their feet. The 1960s witnessed the opening of a striking generational divide that was not limited to the United States or even to developed countries. Young people, the products of unprecedented postwar affluence, poured into city streets from Chicago to Paris to Tokyo to Mexico City. Local discontents, often issues of campus governance, sparked these protests, which then took aim at larger targets such as destructive, dehumanizing Cold War values and national elites seemingly compromised by those values. The range of the youth assault on the status quo was by itself shocking to u.s. leaders. That so many of their fellow citizens would come to sympathize with parts of the youth critique added to the shock. The cumulative effect was to mark a social and ideological turning point in the postwar era and to set in question the legitimacy of the dominant role the United States now claimed.

The first signs of social discontent in the United States, the epicenter of international unrest, appeared in the 1950s and early 1960s. Young people led protests over civil rights, university affairs, and the Vietnam War, which gave rise in turn to black power, feminism, environmentalism, gay activism— all reflections of a broader sea change in u.s. society. The generation of the sixties grew up amid prosperity, a striking contrast to the hard times their parents had experienced. Singled out by advertisers, young people were thoroughly versed in the workings of a flourishing consumer society. Their other companion as they came of age was the Cold War with its atomic dread and its multiplying overseas commitments. Demographic and educational trends equaled in no other developed country gave this new generation special social prominence. The postwar baby boom dramatically increased the youth cohort, while the rapid expansion of public universities meant that those going to college leapt both absolutely (from 3 million total in 1960 to 10 million in 1973) and as a proportion of all young people (from 27 percent in 1955 to 40 percent in 1965). There were, in other words, more young people generally, and to a greater degree than earlier they were congregated on college campuses, where sustained contact could generate a distinct generational outlook.

The first hint of building social ferment and intergenerational tensions appeared in the African American community. Cold War claims to stand for freedom around the world came home to roost in demands for full civil rights for black Americans. In 1960 African American college students formed the Student Nonviolent Coordinating Committee. They were impatient with the caution and paternalism of their elders such as Martin Luther King. Activism soon spread to white college students. The organization of Students for a Democratic Society (in the same year that SNCC was founded) and the protest at the University of California at Berkeley spanning the 1964–65 academic year put students in the vanguard of protests that would in time become nationwide. The Port Huron Statement (the influential SDS manifesto) saw them "breaking the crust of apathy," while a leader of the Berkeley movement famously urged them to stop an "odious" university administrative machine by putting "your bodies upon the gears, upon the wheels, upon the levers, upon all the apparatus."[6] Paralleling college unrest were riots by African Americans in the major cities beginning in 1964 and the rise of the Black Panthers and Black Muslims, again with young people to the fore, driven by anger over continuing racial prejudice and economic inequality.

Early 1965 marked the beginning of opposition to the Vietnam War, with college campuses the focal point. The protests, which intensified year by year, directly challenged the wisdom of Cold War leaders in making the commitment in Vietnam, and increasingly attacked the intellectual foundations of the Cold War. Protesters indicted u.s. policymakers for betraying the long-standing national commitment to self-determination and for failing to see that communists could have strongly nationalist motives. Some critics attributed this betrayal of core national values to the influence that a military-industrial complex wielded over Washington and more broadly to the rise of an essentially undemocratic atmosphere at home, which allowed a self-appointed elite to exercise control. They characterized as doubly racist the war in Vietnam, where whites were engaged in profligate destruction of an Asian country and used black Americans to do the dirty work. With this attack on racism went a more sympathetic view of "the social revolution that is sweeping through the impoverished downtrodden areas of the world."[7] For the first time since the beginning of the Cold War, some Americans watched with open interest, even admiration, the unfolding of revolutionary experiments in such third-world countries as China, Vietnam, and Cuba.

Multifaceted social ferment not only created deep divisions within American society but also eroded the Cold War consensus. A bit more than two decades after it began, the Cold War no longer evoked unthinking assent among the broader population. What began as rising criticism in the course of the 1960s turned by the early 1970s into political alienation spurred by the persistent Vietnam-generated controversy and the Watergate scandal and reflected in the increasingly cynical conviction that the u.s. commitment to freedom was not serious and political leaders were not trustworthy. As the Munich analogy gave way to the slogan "no more Vietnams," Washington found it hard to mobilize the electorate for overseas struggle, especially in the third world. Looking over their shoulder at the domestic scene, policymakers could not feel the old confidence or express the familiar moral fervor. At the same time Congress, chagrined by its record of passivity, tried to reclaim its prerogatives from an "imperial president," a term tellingly coined in 1973. Foreign affairs staff on committees as well as in individual offices increased while Congress passed measures to force the president to involve the legislature in matters of war and to curb his power to initiate military and covert activity in the third world.

The Downsides of Economic Growth

Even under the best of circumstances finding the resources to manage ascendancy was a tall order. An international economy turned unruly and a domestic economy gone sour made that task nearly impossible. These developments came as a surprise after the auspicious postwar beginning (treated in chapter 5). In restarting and restructuring the international economy, the United States had laid the basis for an era of global prosperity welcome all the more for the contrast with the suffering and deprivation that proceeded it. But what amounted to a golden age at home and abroad in the 1950s and 1960s ended in the 1970s and 1980s. Sluggish growth, rising prices, and growing international competition fueled popular discontent that put u.s. cold warriors under yet another set of constraints.

The foremost development was the rise of Japan and the European Community as new centers of economic power, each roughly on a par with the United States. By 1973 total western Europe output exceeded that of the United States, while Japan alone was a bit better than a third as large, with more dramatic growth to come in the decades to follow. U.S. products no longer dominated international trade as they had in the aftermath of World War II. While the revival of competition was natural, u.s. trade policy hastened the process. Cold War presidents time and again used access to the u.s. market to draw and hold allies without insisting on genuine reciprocity. Exposed to competition at home from subsidized foreign producers enjoying protected home markets, u.s. industry and agriculture operated at a distinct disadvantage. In 1964 Harvard economist John Kenneth Galbraith warned Johnson that getting "screwed on tariffs" would result in serious, long-term harm to the country. Low-skilled Americans would bear a disproportionate share of that harm. Workers' weekly wages began to fall in the 1970s and by 1991 were 20 percent below the level of twenty years earlier. Alone the textile, apparel, steel, and auto industries lost over a million jobs over that period. Wide swaths of the heartland reduced to "rust belts" graphically told the story of hard times come to industrialized America.[8]

Prosperous and productive, both western Europe and Japan were not only strong competitors but also independent-minded advocates for positions that sometimes diverged from those of their u.s. ally. They were as eager to promote trade with the Soviet bloc as they were averse to confrontation. Nuclear war evoked high levels of popular anxiety, intensified whenever Washington engaged in loose talk about nuclear wars or backed away from arms control. The u.s. war in Vietnam evoked equally strong opposition and gave color to charges that an emergent American imperialism, not the Soviet Union, was the real enemy. Finally, western Europe and Japan posed an even more profound and lasting challenge to the United States by simply showing that other economic developmental models could work as well as the stringent market capitalism championed by Washington (as seen in chapter 5). Japan had embraced a guided capitalism and an "illiberal" democracy that was notably suspicious of unbridled individualism and aggressive pluralism, while western Europeans developed a comparable devotion to a strong, activist state (attentive to social welfare as well as economic growth). These divergences from u.s. preferences often expressed themselves in disputes over protecting agriculture and mom-and-pop stores, promoting national film industries, and safeguarding culinary traditions.

The rise of new competitors intensified stresses already developing within the u.s. economy. Eisenhower glimpsed the dangers at the very outset of his presidency: a strong economy, he warned, was critical to support high levels of military and foreign aid spending. The burden of heavy federal spending might on the other hand weaken the country's capacity for long-term defense. He proceeded to rein in the military budget, ended the war in Korea, and sidestepped the French appeals for help in Indochina in 1954.

The signs of trouble nonetheless appeared in the late 1950s and 1960s. The u.s. trade balance steadily shrank until finally going into the red in 1971 for the first time since 1883. Here was one sure sign of slipping competitiveness. A regular imbalance of payments—more funds going out of the country than coming in—was another. Even when the trade balance was positive, this adverse flow of capital put more and more dollars in foreign hands, so that by 1958 those holdings exceeded the gold reserves that were supposed to back the dollar. Yet a third deficit opened up as government spending outstripped revenues, sending federal deficits rapidly upward and piling the national debt higher year after year. Behind these trends was runaway consumer spending, stimulated by a taste for foreign products and vacations and a concomitant rise in personal debt and fall in the savings rate. Improvidence at home coupled with heavy u.s. investment overseas and spending on military forces abroad began to undercut the value of the dollar. As foreigners began to wonder if the greenback was as good as gold (the promise of the Bretton Woods agreement), some began to unload their dollar holdings and thus put downward pressure on its value. The bullion in storage at Fort Knox could sustain this demand for only so long.

The late 1960s marked the onset of economic turbulence. Johnson grudgingly began to concede that spending on the Vietnam War was not only squeezing his Great Society program (itself consuming rising portions of the federal budget) but also required a tax increase. Inflation was taking hold even as growth slowed, and the dollar was under attack as the premier international currency. By the 1970s the country was in the grips of general economic malaise. The trade deficit worsened, while imports from competitors "deindustrialized" traditionally strong manufacturing states. An already struggling economy was hit by soaring oil prices, first in 1973 and again in 1979. The mix of slow growth and rising inflation known as stagflation intensified. The purchasing power of ordinary families no longer rose as it had since the late 1940s. Strains in the economy were beginning to threaten the Cold War compact with the public of having both guns and butter. Was the American dream of delivering a better life to each new generation in peril? Should the United States squander resources abroad while pressing needs at home cried for attention? Popular discontent with the economic situation was finding expression at the ballot box, while polls revealed the public was losing interest in the Cold War. By late 1971 the economy loomed as the prime national problem for four of ten Americans surveyed. Only one in seven mentioned Vietnam.[9]

The oil price hikes, engineered by the Organization of Petroleum Exporting Countries, highlighted the vulnerability of the u.s.-sponsored and dominated international economy. Oil had made the twentieth century a time of incredible growth. Oil had displaced coal as the prime transport fuel by 1930, and it had become the main power source for industry by the late 1950s. It had also become critical to making commercial fertilizer and keeping residences and offices comfortable. Producing countries, mainly in the Middle East, made a quiet bid to make the most of their good luck and bring the major multinational corporations such as Standard Oil of New Jersey, Royal Dutch Shell, and British Petroleum under control. With Iran and Saudi Arabia in the lead, opec took shape in 1960 to assert control over production levels and manage prices. The developed world, which enjoyed a postwar boom in part thanks to ever-increasing use of imported oil, was now vulnerable to any large upward jump in price. Many developing economies were if anything more vulnerable. Costly energy imports drained their limited foreign exchange holdings and slowed growth at the very time the markets in the developed countries for third-world exports was going into an oil-induced recession. The resulting hardship stirred popular discontent around the globe, and officials everywhere worried over the possible consequences of the oil crisis. A cascade of international loan defaults or a rising chorus demanding trade protection were but two of the possible developments that could shake the entire international economic system. Officials in Washington recognized yet one more weakness on a lengthening list.

Economic troubles persisted into the early 1990s, with federal budget deficits soaring as a result of an impressive military build-up coupled not with tax increases but with tax cuts. The total federal debt ballooned from $1 trillion at the beginning of the Reagan administration to $4 trillion by the end of the first Bush administration. The steady diet of grim economic news—weak exports, low saving rates, and neglect of investment in infrastructure—continued even as the Soviet Union collapsed. As one pundit put it in 1991, "The dollar is devalued, the Treasury awash in red ink; virtually every social problem existing in the country has worsened. Detroit is a ruin; Hollywood a colony of Japan; American banks, 20 years ago the most brilliant objects in the financial skies, now flicker dully in the background."[10] A country in thrall to its consumerist instincts could not check its spending, raise its taxes, or boost its savings level. This was a worrisome set of developments for an American state bent on wielding global dominance.

By the late 1980s three decades of economic troubles had raised the specter of u.s. decline. The most pointed case for slipping u.s. dominance came in 1987 from the British historian Paul Kennedy. In *The Rise and Fall of the Great Powers*, he argued that the United States had, like other great powers operating out of the North Atlantic, built its international predominance on a vital, growing economic base. But Kennedy saw signs that the United States had reached a painful, potentially terminal state of "imperial overstretch" as the costs of Cold War commitments undermined economic strength and inevitably eroded international standing. The question of whether the United States was about to follow the earlier dominant powers into decline sparked sharp debate within the foreign policy establishment. Had u.s. goals come to exceed national resources? Did u.s. security policy need a thorough rethinking.[11]

CAUGHT IN THE POLICY THICKET

A globally oriented u.s. policy that had crystallized during World War II and the early Cold War turned dysfunctional in the late 1960s. Johnson's difficulties in Vietnam signaled a new Cold War phase. He and his immediate successors confronted limits that even an ascendant United States ignored at its own peril. Their search for a new basis for policy led during the decade from 1969 to 1979 to a distinct if temporary lowering of Cold War tension but not a new policy equilibrium. While the old consensus came apart, no new consensus was emerging to take its place.

During these difficult times the northeastern establishment began to lose the grip it had exercised over policy for some seven decades, through Republican and Democratic administrations alike. Johnson was not part of that establishment even if he did rely on advisers originally recruited by Kennedy. Nixon nursed a grudge expressed in regular private outbursts against privileged figures and powerful institutions from the Northeast. Carter had no personal or professional ties to the region before coming to Washington. Those two presidents' leading advisers, Henry Kissinger and Zbigniew Brzezinski, had a shadowy claim to a place in that establishment by virtue of their education and connections that they had cultivated in advancing their careers (including notably membership in the Council on Foreign Relations). But neither had the requisite Waspy, upper-crust social background. Both had opted for academic careers rather than the law, and both were émigrés whose realpolitik world-view derived from their central European homelands (Germany and Poland). Carter's first secretary of state, Cyrus Vance, was the sole reminder of the glory days of the northeastern lawyers turned policymakers—and he would ultimately resign after losing influence at the White House. The changing of the policy guard was a sign that policy was coming unhinged.

Nixon and Realpolitik

As clearly as any leader of the time, Nixon grasped the new challenges to u.s. dominance. His tattered reputation—the drinking bouts, the introverted personality, the ethical and legal lapses that destroyed his presidency, and the unduly prolonged war in Vietnam—should not blind us to his insights and studied attempt to construct a more modest and thus sustainable Cold War policy.

An accumulation of problems confronted Nixon from his first days in the White House. At home the Cold War consensus was in collapse, public discontent over Vietnam was mounting, and relative u.s. economic decline was well under way. International challenges were if anything more serious. Key allies were getting restive. Anti-American feeling in Japan, rooted in opposition to close military and political ties early in the 1960s and sharpened by the Vietnam War, had erupted in violent demonstrations. Everywhere across western Europe public fear of nuclear war and support for the complete elimination of nuclear weapons was sky high. France's Charles de Gaulle and West Germany's Willy Brandt began to assert distinctly European interests. During his years of presidential power between 1959 and 1969, de Gaulle had rebuffed u.s. demands for further opening of the French market, criticized u.s. intervention in Vietnam, helped talk the dollar into crisis, and minimized France's role in NATO. He saw himself countering Americans' "taking over all of the economic, financial, military and political networks in the world. In it is an invasion that spreads like the flow of a river."[12] Brandt took up in 1969 where de Gaulle had left off. He worked out trade deals and diplomatic understandings with both Moscow and its eastern European client states with an eye to building ties between the two Germanys and encouraging long-term change in socialist eastern Europe. This policy known as Ostpolitik sought to bring détente to central Europe.

Nixon's ability to deal with these problems depended on foreign policy insights accumulated over a long political career. Raised in California, he made his reputation as a staunchly anticommunist congressman from that state. His style reminded some of Joe McCarthy. His apprenticeship in international affairs began in earnest during the eight years that he served as Eisenhower's vice president. It continued during his own presidential campaign against Kennedy in 1960, during which foreign policy issues figured prominently. The years in the political wilderness following his defeat gave Nixon a chance to read, reflect, and cultivate international contacts. In 1968 he made a second bid for the White House and in a three-way race garnered enough support (43 percent of the vote) to win. The main story was not that he had edged out the Democrat Hubert Humphrey by a mere 1 percent but that Nixon's share of the vote together with third-party candidate George Wallace totaled 56 percent and reflected considerable popular resentment against the antiwar, youth, and black power movements.

Nixon's was a presidency strongly focused abroad. (He observed a year before his election, "I've always thought this country could run itself domestically without a President. All you need is a competent Cabinet to run the country at home. You need a President for foreign policy.")[13] Once in office he immediately embarked on a bold experiment in realpolitik that aimed to bring U.S. policy in line with the constraints that it operated under. In January 1969, his first month in the White House, he instructed his National Security Council staff headed by Henry Kissinger to explore ways of getting out of Vietnam and ending a fruitless policy of no contact with China. The heart of his program was a relaxation of tensions with the Soviet Union (détente for short) and by extension a critical adjustment of U.S. military strategy. Détente would allow him to significantly reduce the military budget and repudiate the lure of nuclear superiority over the Soviets in favor of the less costly doctrine of sufficiency. That latter stance meant he would not expand the nuclear arsenal beyond what was needed to inflict serious damage on the Soviet Union in case of an attack. By settling for deterrence Nixon ruled out building a strike force big enough to wipe out Soviet bombers and missiles before they could get off the ground and thus possibly to make a nuclear war winnable. At the same time he scaled down the Pentagon's plan to prepare to fight simultaneously two-and-a-half wars (the standard first put in place by the Kennedy administration); one and a half wars became the new, more modest and less costly goal.

These initiatives together represented a major, fundamental shift, taking U.S. policy back to the notion of a great-power condominium first envisioned by Franklin Roosevelt during World War II. Nixon was not abdicating U.S. dominance but recognizing that its prudent exercise required accommodation of other major powers, which would in turn reduce u.s. costs and help sustain domestic support. In his balance-of-power approach, China and the Soviet Union figured not as ideological threats or moral mutants against which the United States had to crusade. Rather they were genuine world powers with their own set of legitimate interests. Nixon favored diplomatic dialogue as the means to identify areas of compromise and avoid a clash of core interests and possibly war. As he told his staff in July 1971, "The world will not be worth living in if we can't get the great potential explosive forces under control." No less important, he noted publicly that same month, was the relative decline of u.s. economic power. A world dominated by "just two superpowers" had given way to one under the sway of "five great power centers"—the Soviet Union, China, western Europe, and Japan as well as the United States. In keeping with this shift away from a stark Cold War division toward a multipolar order in which economic strength weighed heavily, Nixon wanted to shift spending from the military to areas in which government activism might improve citizens' lives and the competitiveness of the economy such as education for better paying jobs, more available health care, a cleaner environment, and incentives for emerging industries.[14]

A program that broke so sharply with Cold War orthodoxy would, Nixon fully realized, provoke serious opposition. The president and Kissinger were especially mistrustful of the vast foreign affairs bureaucracy; it could not keep secrets, nor could it move quickly; nor did it want policies that threatened its budget or turf. Nixon more broadly distrusted the leadership class, which "no longer has any character" and was thus unreliable.[15] The new administration's foreign policy thus put a premium on the concentration of power in the hands of the president and his immediate staff to a degree never before seen. Secrecy, maneuver, and surprise would be critical to moving forward with his policy adjustments without getting bogged down in public controversy. In this policymaking by stealth, key foreign policy initiatives would have to come out of the White House. Once the policy was in place, the White House could then make a surprise announcement, catching its domestic critics off guard, depriving the bureaucracy of time to leak and obstruct, and exploiting the power of the presidency to persuade the public.

Nixon pursued his priority concern, détente with the Soviets, through summit meetings with Leonid Brezhnev, Nikita Khrushchev's successor. Out of these meetings came cultural and economic agreements, but control of strategic nuclear weapons threatening to both sides dominated the Nixon-Brezhnev relationship. In May 1972 the two leaders laid out the implications of the fearsome strategic standoff between the United States and the Soviet

Union. "In the nuclear age there is no alternative to conducting their mutual relations on the basis of peaceful coexistence. Differences in ideology and in the social systems of the USA and the USSR are not obstacles to the bilateral development of normal relations based on the principles of sovereignty, equality, non-interference in internal affairs and mutual advantage."[16] Nixon's partnership with Brezhnev produced the most ambitious attempt to date to diminish the nuclear danger. The first Strategic Arms Limitations Treaty (SALT I), signed in May 1972, froze at existing levels the number of land- and submarine-launched intercontinental missiles (2,558 for the USSR and 1,710 for the United States) as well as the number of long-range bombers (140 for the Soviets and 455 for the United States). In an effort to preserve a stabilizing retaliatory capacity on both sides, each agreed to accept a limit of two fixed, land-based antiballistic missile systems, one to protect the capital and the other a missile complex.

Nixon pursued rapprochement with Beijing in parallel with détente with Moscow. He had helped create the gulf with China in the 1950s by invoking the "red peril," by championing the defense of Taiwan, and by identifying China as the chief threat to U.S. interests in Southeast Asia. In the early 1960s, in the wake of the Sino-Soviet split, he had continued to oppose U.S. diplomatic contact with Beijing. Once in the White House Nixon moved quickly to dislodge the very China policy that he had helped to lock in place. He signaled to Beijing that he was interested in contact. Clashes on the Sino-Soviet border made the Chinese responsive. Finally, in July 1971 Kissinger took a secret trip to talk with Zhou Enlai and Mao Zedong that in turn paved the way for a dramatic meeting between Nixon and Mao in February 1972. The Shanghai communiqué issued at the end of Nixon's China visit defined a new relationship in which the U.S. side recognized China's important international standing and in which the Chinese side downplayed sharp and long-standing differences with Washington over the future of Taiwan. Nixon's three years of patient diplomacy conducted in great secrecy and guided consistently by a search for a balance of power and by a disdain for ideology had created a new basis for Sino-American relations. Over the coming decades the new relationship would withstand recurrent tests posed by crises in the Taiwan Strait and clashes over human rights, Tibet, and trade.

The accommodation with China, important in its own right, was part of a retrenching of U.S. commitments in East Asia so sweeping that they effectively marked the end of the Cold War in the region even while the U.S.-Soviet Cold War rivalry continued. The new sense of limits was articulated in the Guam (or Nixon) Doctrine of July 1969. Nixon put regional allies in the western

Pacific but also in the Persian Gulf on notice that they would henceforth have to defend themselves primarily through their own efforts, with u.s. assistance and nuclear protection playing a secondary role.

The u.s. combat role in Vietnam, which had given rise to a sense of limits in the region, was itself not so easily ended. Like Johnson, Nixon had arrived in office determined to defend South Vietnam. He agreed that its survival was essential to American international credibility and to avoidance of a domestically divisive "who lost Vietnam" debate. But also like Johnson, he found that Hanoi could outlast American patience, so his pursuit of disengagement from Vietnam proved both awkward and frustrating. At the outset of his presidency, Nixon sought to quiet the domestic uproar. He turned the war over to the South Vietnamese military (an approach begun in Johnson's last year and dubbed "Vietnamization"), steadily withdrew u.s. troops, ended the unpopular draft, and held out hopes for a negotiated settlement. At the same time he applied pressure on Hanoi by bombing enemy supply lines and rest areas throughout Vietnam as well as in Cambodia. He ratcheted up the pressure in 1970 by sending u.s. forces across the border into Cambodia. On another front he pressed Moscow and Beijing to use their influence to moderate Hanoi's peace terms. No closer to a settlement in May 1971 than two years earlier when he had come to office, a frustrated Nixon made a major concession. He signaled to Hanoi that he would accept an agreement that left North Vietnamese troops in the South while requiring the withdrawal of all u.s. forces. Nixon well understood that the u.s.-backed Saigon government was not likely to long survive that arrangement. Finally in January 1973, after another year and a half of diplomatic talk and battlefield deaths, Hanoi and Washington struck a deal over the continuing objections of the South Vietnamese government.

Nixon did not have experience in economic issues, nor did Kissinger; great-power politics was their consuming passion. Nixon nonetheless recognized the rise of a multipolar international economy in which the United States was hobbled by a loss of competitiveness on global markets, falling confidence in the dollar, and multiple deficits. Rather than trying to protect the u.s. dollar and maintain control of the international economic system, Nixon pursued a defensive policy of revising the Bretton Woods arrangements that the United States could no longer sustain single-handedly. In 1971 he ended the dollar's assigned role under the Bretton Woods accords—to serve as a steadying point of reference for the currency market. He did this by breaking the fixed link between the dollar and gold. Even so, the u.s. dollar remained the preferred currency for other nations to hold in reserve; they valued it even in its new free-floating form for its relative safety and stability. Washington began to share the burden of managing the international economy with the western Europeans and the Japanese. These changes left the critical Bretton Woods institutions, the IMF and the World Bank, still in place and the Bretton Woods commitment to an open international economic system still the animating idea among the leading free-market economies collaborating together in what became known as the Group of Seven (or the G-7).

Nixon's effort at revamping U.S. foreign policy proved vulnerable. Part of the problem was that Nixon himself was still in some ways mired in the past. The Cold War rhetoric that continued to fill his head left him fixated by the maintenance of American prestige and credibility. He worried that his country would become "a pitiful, helpless giant."[17] He feared unrest in the third world that might favor communism, an anxiety often expressed in crudely racist terms. With little knowledge of local conditions and little concern for the ultimate fate of peoples along the periphery, Nixon made stability the touchstone of policy. In Chile he colluded in the overthrow of the elected socialist government of Salvador Allende in 1973. In the Middle East he looked to strongmen best represented by the shah of Iran. In Africa he backed colonial regimes (notably the embattled Portuguese in Angola and Mozambique), the white minority government in Rhodesia, and the repressive apartheid regime in South Africa. Finally, as much as any of his predecessors he fell victim to the technological temptation and kept MIRVs outside the arms-control framework because the United States for the moment enjoyed an advantage in this area. However, the Soviets mastered this innovation as they had all the others, thus offsetting the achievements of SALT and accelerating the costs and dangers of the arms race.

But Nixon's personal flaws—suspicion, meanness, and ultimately isolation and paranoia—did even more to undercut his policy innovations. These flaws contributed to the Watergate break-in and the resulting constitutional crisis that seriously distracted the president from March 1973 onward and finally forced his resignation nearly a year and a half later. His go-it-alone style also got in the way of building support. Impatient with interference, protest, debate, and criticism, Nixon stayed behind closed doors and kept the public, the bureaucracy, and Congress all at arms length. He would decide, they would follow. Privately he spelled out his notion of democratic politics: "The American people are like helpless children yearning for leadership."[18] This telling comment reveals Nixon's lack of a soft political touch that left him isolated and helped make his new, tough-minded approach to foreign policy vulnerable to attack. Following Nixon's resignation over the Watergate scandal, the attacks by hard-line cold warriors picked up even though Nixon's successor, Gerald Ford, and Henry Kissinger, still secretary of state, tried to maintain continuity. An increasingly assertive Congress, the humiliating defeat in Vietnam in 1975, and emboldened critics combined to cast a shadow over détente, a term that was soon in such bad odor that Ford avoided it during his 1976 campaign to win election in his own right.

Carter Takes the High Road

Like Nixon, Carter entered the White House determined to set a new agenda for a country buffeted by economic problems and gripped by general malaise. Carter had won the 1976 election with the promise of following "a foreign policy that reflects the decency and generosity and common sense of our own people." With a political career limited to the Georgia governorship, Carter knew little about international problems, the national security establishment, or foreign leaders. But he was confident that his ability to master detail and his enlightened outlook would enable him to manage effectively. Carter's born-again Christian faith was especially important in inspiring a moral fervor and humanitarian earnestness that had made him a critic of Nixon-Kissinger secretiveness, imperial pretensions, and pursuit of an amoral realpolitik. The antidote to Nixon's demonstrable moral failure at home and internationally, so Carter believed, was a morally inspired leadership. Carter secured the experience that he himself lacked by his appointment of Vance as secretary of state and Brzezinski as the White House national security adviser. The president and his two chief aides brought to the table divergent but potentially complementary perspectives, what one historian of the administration has described as "morality, reason, and power."[19] Vance, the lawyerly voice of reason, came out of the venerable northeastern establishment. He shared Carter's desire to move beyond the Cold War. But he was not an idea man. That role fell to Brzezinski, an academic and advocate of power politics, whose personal experience as a Polish émigré ill disposed him to Nixon's sellout to Moscow.

Promoting human rights quickly emerged as the core idea around which Carter hoped to organize his foreign policy. Influencing this development was a growing international community of activists determined to make good on the early postwar commitments to human rights. Amnesty International, which had set up shop in London in 1961, was the leading organization. Its sections operating around the world, including eastern Europe and the Soviet Union, sought to expose abuses of political and civil rights. The u.s. section flourished in the 1970s thanks to innovative fund-raising techniques and a dedicated staff trained in earlier civil rights and antiwar activities. The Helsinki accords signed by the superpowers and the Europeans in 1975 revealed the growing appeal of the human rights agenda. The accords advanced Willy Brandt's goals of legalizing and stabilizing the European borders settled at the end of World War II, promoting trade across the Iron Curtain, and facilitating the free movement of peoples and ideas. But the signatories also promised to respect human rights. Brezhnev and other leaders in the Soviet bloc accepted the agreement as a harmless piece of paper, but soon found themselves bedeviled by determined local rights groups and by activists such as the Soviet Union's Andrei Sakharov operating in the full glare of the international media. The potent appeal of rights was also evident in a campaign to improve the position of women. Already in 1963 Soviet bloc and third-world representatives in the UN General Assembly had joined to pass a resolution condemning discrimination against women. In 1975 the same coalition took up the issue again, this time pressing for UN-sponsored conferences to address the special burdens carried by women as a result of state violence and patriarchal practices and beliefs. The first was held in Mexico City that year, followed by another in Copenhagen in 1980, and a third one in Nairobi in 1985. These gatherings focused international attention on government policies unfriendly to women.

Against this backdrop of burgeoning human rights talk, Carter announced his own concerns in a Notre Dame commencement address in May 1977, and he translated those concerns into policy in a February 1978 presidential directive. Both reflected his strong convictions about the sanctity of human life and the U.S. obligation to defend individual rights around the globe. He told the Notre Dame audience, "We can no longer separate the traditional issues of war and peace from the new global questions of justice, equity, and human rights." The obligation to press human rights seemed clear but the implementation would prove difficult. Were allies and enemies to be held to the same standard? What was to be done about violators? How did human rights bear on such key issues as arms control and third-world unrest? Carter's own uncertainties on these points were reflected in meandering speeches that aggregated issues, piling one disjointed point on another. With no organizing vision at the outset to pull the pieces of his policy together or supply priorities, Carter was vulnerable to confusion and drift, became lost in details, and could sound no clarion call to win public support in economically troubled times. His reliance on senior advisers with distinctly different points of view compounded his own conceptual confusion.[20]

Carter clung to Nixon's approach to the Soviet Union and China even as his inexperience and formal commitment to human rights rendered that approach less coherent. He sought improved relations with China, building on the earlier Nixon-Mao understanding. In December 1978 during a u.s. visit by Mao's successor, Deng Xiaoping, the two sides agreed to exchange ambassadors for the first time in the thirty years since the creation of the People's Republic of China. This step came at the expense of Taiwan, a controversial move that put in question Carter's commitment to human rights and prompted Congress to pass the Taiwan Relations Act committing the United States to the defense of the island. Beijing complained bitterly but did nothing more. In his dealings with the Soviets, Carter put arms control center stage (here too following Nixon), but his approach alternately provoked and perplexed Moscow. The new president had thrown the SALT talks into confusion in 1977. Under Brzezinski's influence, he made the precipitous decision to try to break out of the established negotiating framework and press instead for the elimination of heavy missiles, an area of relative Soviet strength. After Moscow dismissed the idea out of hand, Vance took the talks back to the original lines and successfully negotiated a SALT II treaty, signed in June 1979 by Carter and a decrepit Brezhnev. The new agreement tightened the terms of the arms control regime by requiring each side to reduce its antiballistic missile systems from two to one and by containing the threat of proliferating MIRV'ed missiles. It imposed a ceiling of 2,400 missile launchers, of which 1,320 could carry MIRVS.

By then u.s.-Soviet relations were laboring under accumulated strain that arms control successes alone could not dissipate. Watching Carter cozying up to China, Moscow concluded correctly that Brzezinski was pressing for a strategic relationship to weaken the Soviets. Carter's championing of human rights for Soviet dissidents angered the Kremlin, which saw a contradiction between détente and this u.s. ideological campaign aimed at eastern Europe and the Soviet Union itself. The two sides also clashed over their respective arms spending, with each convinced that the other was engaged in a military buildup that gave the lie to their talk of accommodation. One source of the problem was exaggerated CIA estimates of Soviet arms spending supplied to Carter; they erred by ignoring weaknesses in the Soviet economy. Finally, the strategic balance in Europe became a sore point following the appearance of the Soviet ss-20s rockets threatening western Europe. Carter responded by deploying a new generation of u.s. weapons (Pershing II and ground-based cruise missiles). Capped at the strategic level, the nuclear arms race was erupting at the regional level. By mid-1978 Ambassador Anatoly Dobrynin was telling Moscow that the Carter administration had "a selective, half-hearted conception of détente."[21]

The third front on which Carter acted was the third world, and there he assumed the role of the Good Samaritan indifferent to Cold War conventions. He promoted peace in the Middle East by sponsoring talks between Egypt's Anwar Sadat and Israel's Menachem Begin. The Camp David accords in September 1978 seemed to set the two countries on a new path toward cooperation. Carter pushed to conclusion a treaty returning the Panama Canal and surrounding zone to Panama in September 1977. Here was a chance to right old wrongs and address what Carter saw as legitimate nationalist grievances. But both initiatives confirmed the old political adage: "No good deed goes unpunished." Carter's considerable effort to extract the Camp David accords won him few friends. Getting the Senate to approve the Panama treaty required the expenditure of even more political capital early in his administration. Critics howled that Carter was giving away u.s. territory not to mention a strategically valuable transit point.

Finally, Carter explored forward-looking policies geared to protecting the environment and promoting energy independence. He was influenced by the rising level of environmental consciousness in the United States. Rachel Carson's 1962 account of DDT poisoning, *Silent Spring*, was not only a best-seller but also the catalyst for a movement first in the United States and then internationally. By 1970 Americans were celebrating Earth Day and telling pollsters about the high value they put on the environment, while Green parties emerged to advocate for strong environmental policies in New Zealand, Germany, and other parts of the developed world. International meetings sponsored by the UN started to grapple with the future of the planet. Consistent with this nascent environmental outlook, Carter made energy conservation his signature environmental program. When the second oil shortage of the decade slammed the u.s. economy in 1979, he called for greater energy efficiency on the part of industry and ordinary citizens. He sold the initiative poorly at first, but even after he formulated a rallying cry less burdened with technical details, he found that consumers insisted on cheap fuel as a right. Their devotion to large cars, long drives, and big houses made his energy policy politically toxic and put in question the u.s. commitment to meaningful environmental measures.

Carter policy underwent a dramatic transformation in 1979–80 that shattered détente and spelled failure for another presidency. The sudden loss of a seemingly secure u.s. position in Iran began the process. Khomeini's revolution succeeded in driving the shah into exile in January 1979. This setback turned into a problem and then a major crisis in November after Carter admitted the ailing shah to the United States for medical treatment. In Tehran outraged students promptly seized the u.s. embassy and held its staff hostage. After diplomacy failed to secure their release, Carter authorized a rescue mission in April 1980. It too failed, driving Vance to resign and publicly underlining Carter's continued impotence. Still unresolved on election day, the Iran imbroglio dealt Carter's hopes for a second term a damaging, perhaps fatal blow. Not content with Carter's defeat, Khomeini refused to release the hostages until inauguration day, just after Reagan had taken the oath of office.

The Soviet invasion of Afghanistan in December 1979 further weakened Carter while spelling finis to both his human rights concerns and his lingering hopes for détente. Moscow had been desperately trying to shore up a failing client government under assault from Islamist forces and head off unrest spreading among the Muslim population of Soviet Central Asia. But Politburo members as well as Soviet advisers in-country were reluctant to intervene with their own troops, fearing that Afghanistan would become a quagmire and poison relations with the United States. Faced with a choice between defeat or forceful action, they set aside their reservations.

When Brzezinski, now dominant in policymaking, learned of the December invasion, he saw not a Soviet Vietnam in the making but a renewal of "the age-long dream of Moscow to have direct access to the Indian Ocean." He explained to the president that this apparent Soviet push into South Asia and the Middle East constituted "an extremely grave challenge." Devising a response was simple, he recalled in his memoir: Carter had only to grasp that the Russians "tended to respect the strong and had contempt for the weak." Standing before Congress in January 1980, Carter announced that the country faced possibly "the most serious threat to peace since the Second World War." His answer was the Carter Doctrine: the United States would defend by force if necessary its interests in the Persian Gulf. At the same time Carter shelved the salt II treaty awaiting ratification by the Senate (though he as well as the Soviets would informally observe its limits). He also raised military spending, imposed a grain embargo on the Soviet Union, and canceled u.s. participation in the upcoming Moscow Olympics. The rivalry between the United States and Soviet Union was spawning tensions not seen since the 1960s.[22]

Finally in July 1980 Carter authorized a formal shift to a nuclear doctrine that was both costly and dangerous. It focused u.s. strategic forces not just on Soviet cities but also on command posts, missiles, and bombers. No longer were nuclear weapons simply about deterrence, with a failure involving loss of human life too terrible to think about. This new policy, favored by Brzezinski, made it possible to entertain the idea of a controlled nuclear war in which each side might strike only the leadership centers and strategic weapons of the other. This strategy generated anxiety and instability while also favoring increases in each side's strategic weapons to ensure survival in case of an attack against its main nuclear force. As one side added weapons, the other had to respond not just in kind but in greater numbers, so that policymakers could be sure of absorbing an attack and still having the capacity to hit back.

Rising Cold War emotions also spilled over into third-world policy. Carter had already in mid-1979 ordered the CIA to provide covert support for the anti-Soviet resistance in Afghanistan. Continued under his successor, that program would eventually cost $3 billion and contribute to the devastation of an already poor country. When the Soviets' Vietnamese ally invaded and occupied Cambodia in January 1979, Washington ignored the repeated Cambodian military provocations against Vietnam. Preoccupied with what seemed a worldwide Soviet offensive, Carter imposed sanctions on Hanoi, joined in an anti-Vietnam coalition that included Pol Pot's genocidal Khmer Rouge and China, and gave the green light for China to launch a military expedition against its former Vietnamese allies. In Central America Carter watched leftist inroads with growing concern. After the overthrow of the Somoza government in Nicaragua in 1979, the Carter administration tried to block the Sandinistas from taking power even though they had led the revolution. When that measure failed, Washington made it clear that aid depended on the new regime's moderating its Marxist impulses. In neighboring El Salvador Carter backed a government listing heavily to the right even as he tried to restrain its violent repression. He could not politically afford to see another victory by the Left. In the horn of Africa, a now aroused Washington charged the Soviets with exploiting a dispute between Somalia and Ethiopia to make local inroads.

Carter had come to Washington promising a foreign policy based on fresh ideas and humanitarian considerations; by the time of his decisive electoral defeat at the hands of Ronald Reagan in November 1980 his policy was in shambles and his public standing had crumbled. A recession on the eve of the election had wounded the incumbent. No less important was his bungled attempt to escape the Cold War framework. The 1977 Panama Canal treaty had been a costly victory. The failure to protect a strategically critical ally in Iran made the United States look weak and Carter inept; the subsequent hostage crisis there humiliated him. Finally, his human rights policy had introduced an irritant into détente while a misreading of the Soviet invasion of Afghanistan made it seem that the Kremlin was embarked on a new course of aggression. A chagrined Carter had to confess that he misjudged the Cold War foe even as he took steps to intensify the Cold War that he had sought to ameliorate.

BACK TO THE COLD WAR—AND BEYOND

Even as Nixon, Ford, and Carter sought to shape a Cold War policy that took account of international and domestic constraints, outspoken members of the foreign policy establishment championed a freshly assertive stance in the world. Ronald Reagan's election in 1980 seemed to restore national morale and ambitions lost to policy over the previous twelve years. But Reagan ended up highlighting the continuing constraints that the American state labored under. Like his predecessors, Reagan suffered from setbacks dealt by Congress, the public, and his prime allies. The collapse of yet another foreign policy approach was averted by the appearance of a new Soviet leader. Mikhail Gorbachev offered Reagan and his successor, George H. W. Bush, a way out of the u.s.-Soviet Cold War deadlock, but even the collapse of the Soviet Union that quickly followed did not remove the sturdy constraints on u.s. powers.

Militant Backlash

A group of unreconstructed cold warriors had led the backlash against détente and human rights. Though dubbed neoconservatives, they were more like militant Wilsonians. The United States was in their view the repository of universal values and carried a historical national obligation to battle for those values around the globe. Their crusading vision entailed a commitment to building an unrivaled military force and wielding it as the prime instrument advancing u.s. goals. It did not entail (as real conservatives were to discover) respecting fiscal discipline, limiting presidential or federal power, or dealing candidly with the public.

These militants first pressed their cause through the Committee on the Present Danger, which had taken shape in 1975 in reaction to Nixon's "sell out" to the Soviet Union and China. It remained active in the face of what its members saw as Carter's fuzzy-minded, ineffectual policy that had invited the Soviet invasion of Afghanistan and the hostage humiliation in Iran. They disliked the SALT limits on the u.s. nuclear arsenal, wanted sharply higher military spending, and had no tolerance for third-world insurgencies with a Marxist tinge. Only the United States as the strongest of the free countries could turn back this threat, but to do so Americans had to abandon the illusions behind détente, reject claims of a weakened u.s. position in the world, and resume the bold leadership role seen early in the Cold War. This policy transformation was about more than tough diplomacy and military rearmament. It required moral revitalization that would infuse a spirit of patriotism and sacrifice in u.s. politics. A confident president unimpaired by congressional restrictions or the doubts of an ill-informed public, could at last act again on the old Cold War axioms: the dangers of appeasement and the implacably aggressive nature of totalitarian states. In the view of these militants, global constraints were to be overcome, not accommodated.

The militants were a bright, articulate, assertive, and ultimately influential group, all members in good standing of the foreign affairs establishment. Paul Nitze, the drafter of the nsc-68 call to arms in 1950 and an experienced arms-control negotiator, issued regular reminders of Moscow's goal of world domination and the risk entailed by arms control. Eugene Rostow, a Yale law professor and brother of W. W. Rostow, was especially prominent as chair of the cpd's executive committee. He articulated the group's strong attachment to Israel as an ally deserving strong u.s. backing against Arab aggression and Palestinian terror. Norman Podhoretz edited *Commentary*, a widely read outlet for militant views, and in 1980 published *The Present Danger*, a manifesto crisply articulating the committee's antagonism to an alarming, immobilizing "culture of appeasement." Jeanne Kirkpatrick, a feisty Georgetown political scientist, provided the militants an appealing rationale for downplaying human rights in the developing world. Her reasoning was familiar: strongmen were the best guarantee against communist takeovers; once totalitarians took control they would never release their grip.

A traumatic encounter with German aggression and genocide had shaped the outlook of most militants. They carried the memory of the disastrous appeasement by the democracies. Having tacitly encouraged Hitler's aggression, they were forced to open the war on disadvantageous terms while a horrific holocaust unfolded and ultimately the Red Army advanced into the heart of Europe. Through World War II and the early Cold War the future militants had backed New Deal policies and supported the Democratic program of intervention in World War II followed by containment of the Soviet Union. But official and public questioning of the moral foundations of that Cold War policy in the 1960s and 1970s conjured up in their imagination the dark days of the 1930s returning. Students burned draft cards, defied authority, and mouthed nihilist slogans. Militants blamed these brash dissenters together with a defeatist media for undermining the war effort in Vietnam. Nixon's misguided policies made a bad situation worse. He pursued arms control with the Soviets rather than an arms buildup that would have guaranteed u.s. superiority. He sought an accommodation with Moscow and Beijing that betrayed the fundamental American faith in freedom. And he set the stage for a poorly disguised defeat in Vietnam that revealed a loss of national will. In western Europe the trends toward appeasement were even more pronounced as the political Left rose to prominence in France and Italy and as antinuclear pacifism increasingly marked public opinion in West Germany. U.S. allies seemed to be rejecting a firm resistance to communism in favor of peace and prosperity at any price.

The spirit of appeasement persisting into the Carter years blinded Americans (so at least the militants argued) to the threat from a robust, confident foe. The Soviets were, Podhoretz emphasized, "dedicated to the destruction of the free institutions which are our heritage and the political culture which is our glory."[23] While Washington clung to a hollow policy of détente, a Soviet arms buildup opened a "window of vulnerability." Confident in its strategic superiority, the Kremlin would seek to expand its heavy-handed control from eastern to western Europe and advance into the oil-rich Persian Gulf using Afghanistan, Iraq, and Syria as stepping stones. U.S. weakness would also encourage the Soviets to probe for openings in Latin America and sub-Saharan Africa. Militants were consumed by a sense of worldwide strategic threat.

The militant cold warriors abandoned their long-time allegiance to the Democratic Party. They found a new home in the Republican Party and a champion of the new, resolute Cold War ethic in Ronald Reagan. This former Hollywood actor and New Deal Democrat turned anticommunist Hollywood labor leader, turned spokesperson for General Electric, turned conservative California politician was as innocent of foreign policy experience as any Cold War president, perhaps the most innocent. His views were simple and sketchy, but in broad terms they coincided with the militant position. His United States was a unique country with a special mission as "an empire of ideals": "For two hundred years we have been set apart by our faith in the ideals of Democracy, of free men and free markets, and of the extraordinary possibilities that lie within seemingly ordinary men and women." The Communism that challenged u.s. policy was, he told a radio audience in May 1975, not a political or economic system but rather "a form of insanity—a temporary aberration which will one day disappear from the earth because it is contrary to human nature."[24]

Reagan made a warm-up run for the Republican nomination in 1976, attacking Ford for his support of détente and decrying talk of the Panama Canal giveaway. In 1980 Reagan won the nomination and moved to the general campaign against a wounded Carter. His call for a return to Cold War crusading and revived national pride made him a winner. Just short of seventy years old when inaugurated, the new president made appointments suggesting that he was ready to translate election-year rhetoric into policy. Militants won high-level policy positions: Richard Allen as the president's national security adviser, William Casey as CIA director, Robert Gates as Casey's deputy, Paul Nitze and Eugene Rostow heading up arms control, Jeanne Kirkpatrick at the United Nations, Richard Perle in the Defense Department, and Richard Pipes (a Harvard historian) as the White House Soviet specialist. They were joined by other hard-liners, notably Secretary of Defense Caspar Weinberger.

During his first term in office Reagan advanced a program that corresponded closely to the calls of the militants. He focused on the Soviet peril, sought a stronger military, and struck a distinctly Wilsonian tone. Yet Reagan proved a cautious cold warrior whose hard-line stance was qualified from the outset and then further compromised by his awareness of the mounting costs and discontents spawned by his program. The old constraints had not gone away—as his dramatic shift in 1985 back to the path of détente would demonstrate. A March 1983 speech to a convention of Christian evangelicals illustrates the two faces of Reagan. He labeled the Soviet Union the "evil empire." It was bent on world revolution, a goal it pursued heedless of morality. There was no room in u.s. policy for compromise with such a force, and those in the West who thought otherwise were deluded. But alongside this resounding affirmation of the moral foundation of the Cold War, he indicated a readiness to negotiate. "I intend to do everything that I can to persuade them of our peaceful intent." Moscow had only to understand that "we will never compromise our principles and standards. We will never give away our freedom. We will never abandon our belief in God." (Can we assume that Reagan knew that Moscow had neither u.s. freedom nor religiosity in its crosshairs?) And then he declared again: "We will never stop searching for a genuine peace."[25]

In his first years in office, Reagan gave substance to his hard-line policy but in a way that suggested less a moral crusade and more a righting of a strategic balance gone wrong. After having consistently condemned the Beijing regime during the election, the new president accepted the practical value of China as a makeweight against the Soviet Union and the danger of driving the two old allies back together. Moral condemnation went out the door. He continued the arms buildup set in motion by Carter in 1979. By 1985 the military budget was $129 billion higher than it had been in 1979. Thanks to the fresh infusion of funds, the Defense Department moved from the one-and-a-half-war doctrine embraced by Nixon, Ford, and Carter to a two-and-a-half or even three-war doctrine (the capacity to fight in Europe, the Middle East, and the western Pacific all at the same time). The Pentagon spent lavishly on conventional forces as well as nuclear weapons to close the alleged window of vulnerability created by the Soviet program. In March 1983 Reagan made a surprise announcement, deeply personal in nature, that added a fresh wrinkle to his nuclear policy. He was going to pursue a technologically ambitious Strategic Defense Initiative (SDI or Star Wars) that held the promise of defense against missile attack. He asked his audience, "Wouldn't it be better to save lives than to avenge them?" Like earlier Cold War presidents, Reagan lived with the black box as a constant reminder of Armageddon possibly just moments away. He recoiled from the terrible logic of mutual destruction that had come to define the arms race. By exploiting the U.S. technological edge, Reagan hoped to make the country safe. Congress and the public found much to like in this multibillion dollar project that promised (as Reagan had put it) to render "nuclear weapons impotent and obsolete."[26]

Reagan's strategic offensive against the Soviet Union provoked considerable controversy and eventually alarm and resistance. The increased spending came at a time of economic difficulty. Neither Congress nor the public wanted to sacrifice to intensify the Cold War struggle. Unwilling to increase taxes and unable to make cuts in domestic programs, Reagan resorted to deficit spending. The resulting massive federal deficits evoked dire warnings that fiscal irresponsibility would hurt the U.S. economy and ultimately undermine U.S. global power. Critics of SDI charged that it would destabilize the nuclear balance of terror, fail to work, cost too much, and run afoul of cheap and effective Soviet countermeasures. Public opinion surveys in western Europe as well as in the United States registered rising anxiety over nuclear war not seen since the late 1950s and strong support for bringing a halt to the arms race through hard-nosed negotiations. Some 50,000 warheads were already in the hands of the Soviets and the Americans when 500 were enough for either to destroy the other. By the end of 1983 nearly half of all Americans surveyed thought Reagan's policies were pushing the country toward war. Jonathan Schell's *Fate of the Earth*, a best-seller in 1982, captured this pervasive anxiety: "Now we are alive, but in a moment we may be dead. Now there is human life on earth, but in a moment it may be gone." The sense of human vulnerability and civilization's fragility was heightened by talk of "nuclear winter" that would finish off those who survived a nuclear war. Leaders in western Europe kept their distance from Reagan's hard-line policy and instead pursued trade deals with the Soviet bloc. The Reagan administration tried to stop one of the biggest of these deals, a gas pipeline from the Soviet Union, out of fear it would leave the western Europeans in thrall to Moscow economically and hence impotent politically. The European response was defiance, and the deal went through.[27]

Reagan confronted what he took to be Soviet inroads in the third world with the same combination of verbal toughness, practical caution, and political constraints evident in his Soviet policy. In December 1981 Reagan authorized covert operations against Nicaragua. The CIA would arm and direct exile forces ("freedom fighters") in a dirty war meant to wear down that country's "totalitarian" Sandinista regime. In February 1982, acting on the maxim that it was better to have authoritarians than pro-Soviet insurgents in power, he announced his strong support for an embattled government in El Salvador. He continued in Afghanistan the anti-Soviet covert activities begun by Carter. In Angola he revitalized a policy of intervention initiated by Kissinger and Ford in 1975 after Portugal dropped the ball and granted its colony independence. Reagan wanted to keep the new government, aligned with the Soviets and the Cubans, on the defensive by supporting the guerrilla opposition that was also backed by China and South Africa. In Ethiopia and Cambodia, as well, the administration sought allies, however unsavory, to contain Soviet influence.

Behind Reagan's bold words was a reluctance to put the U.S. military in harm's way. His defense secretary laid down a list of preconditions for the use of force (known as the Weinberger Doctrine) designed to avoid another half-hearted commitment epitomized by the Vietnam defeat. But so exacting were the preconditions—including a clearly defined objective, broad and lasting public support, employment of overwhelming force, and a clear endgame—that all the might Reagan's arms budget was building seemed tightly tethered. The U.S. invasion of Grenada in October 1983 proved that decisive military action was possible—as long as the enemy was a hopelessly outmatched ministate. A violent struggle within the island's revolutionary regime, its alignment with Cuba, and concern for the safety of Americans there provided the rationale for the invasion. U.S. forces quickly prevailed. On the other hand, Reagan's decision to send marines to help stabilize a strife-torn Lebanon in 1982 went wrong. After more than two hundred marines were killed the next year in a bombing of their barracks, an embarrassed president faced a public outcry and by early 1984 had pulled all the troops out of harm's way. The Lebanon setback had by then prompted Weinberger to make public his restrictive criteria for the future use of military power. Though some within the administration called for a direct U.S. combat role in fighting communism in Central America, even covert support for the U.S.-backed Contras in Nicaragua proved controversial. Reagan's policy proved unpopular with the public (with seven out of ten Americans polled in mid-1984 worried about another Vietnam in the making). That policy faced sharp opposition in Congress and from a determined peace movement.[28]

A Surprise Turn and a Sudden End

The Cold War tensions that erupted during the late Carter years and continued into the first term of the Reagan administration proved a blip—with good reason. U.S. policy continued to labor under the familiar set of constraints: a restive public, a strained economy, wayward allies, and the nuclear peril. Within four years of entering the White House Reagan had redirected his concerns from confrontation to accommodation. A series of summits with Mikhail Gorbachev marked the abrupt turnaround. By 1989 Reagan's successor, George H. W. Bush, and Gorbachev would be proclaiming the end of the Cold War, and two years later the collapse of the Soviet Union left no doubt about the outcome. No one was more surprised by this turn of events than dyed-in-the-wool cold warriors with their adamant belief in a formidable, enduring Soviet threat.

Gorbachev's role was critical both to Reagan's policy shift and to the ultimate Soviet collapse. When he came to power in 1985, he was unusually young and well educated for a Soviet leader. Travels in western Europe in the 1970s left him wide eyed and wondering, "Why do we live worse than other developed countries?" He brought to the Kremlin not only vigor but also an expanding sense of what was needed to revitalize a socialist society that was (in the words of one of his supporters) "lagging behind the world economically, technologically, and scientifically" and suffering from "an underlying mass alienation of working people from significant social goals and values." The first priority was thus not just to accelerate growth rates but also, Gorbachev concluded, to cultivate greater political openness and public support. The Cold War figured mainly as a burden and distraction that could retard, perhaps even undermine, reform by devouring resources and elite attention. Gorbachev pressed reform on the socialist leaders of eastern Europe so that their survival would cease to depend on Soviet subsidies and tanks. He wooed western Europeans with talk of the Soviet Union taking a place in the European family of nations. He proposed cuts in military spending and ambitious steps to control the arms race while refusing after 1987 to let SDI stand in the way of an agreement with Reagan. Finally, he readied Soviet forces for withdrawal from the draining war in Afghanistan. Gorbachev became something of an international celebrity whose popularity extended across Europe to the United States.[29]

Gorbachev gave Reagan his first plausible diplomatic partner since coming to office. Brezhnev had been ill when Reagan entered the White House and died in 1982. The first successor, Yuri Andropov, was in poor health and died in 1984. The second, Constantin Chernenko, followed him to the grave the next year. The newly installed Gorbachev was not only energetic; he also quickly put Reagan on the defensive. His rapid-fire initiatives at home and internationally were scoring propaganda points and discrediting the "evil empire" charges coming out of Washington. Reagan responded by making a policy reversal as striking as Carter's. He moved toward a policy of accommodation that amounted in everything but name to détente.

The president's personality and outlook does much to explain this sudden shift. Reagan was a genial rather than a theological anticommunist. The secret to his political success was not to be found in his work ethic and analytic skills. Unlike Nixon and Carter, he had no taste for delving deeply into the details of policy. (One of Reagan's standard jokes was about hard working never killing anyone, but then—he asked—why take a chance?) His long suit was rather "his charm, good looks, and memory" (as Richard Darman, a White House adviser, noted). Conservative columnist George Will added his "talent for happiness."[30] His 1984 reelection campaign slogan—"morning again in America"—captured that rhetorical optimism that many Americans found appealing. Lending substance to that optimism was a strong, simple nationalist vision that he communicated with conviction. He told German leader Helmut Kohl that "we were the most moral and generous people on earth." He called the parents of a marine killed in Beirut and told them, "America is a country whose people have always believed we had a special responsibility to try to bring peace and democracy to others in the world." Looking back in his memoir, he observed, "Americans have always accepted a special responsibility to help others achieve and preserve the democratic freedoms we enjoy."[31]

The president was not invested in a particular position or strategy, only in knowing that the United States was a force for good. This kind of trademark Reagan talk contained as much room for working with Gorbachev as for crusading against the evil empire. Indeed, he began his reelection year with a declaration on U.S.-Soviet relations that could have come from Richard Nixon: "The fact that neither of us likes the other system is no reason to refuse to talk. Living in this nuclear age makes it imperative that we do talk." One student of Reagan policy has put the matter in blunt but helpful terms: "Reagan was a fairly ignorant optimist surrounded by knowledgeable and ideologically sophisticated pessimists. These pessimists had constructed a Manichean worldview of great detail, inner consistency and plausibility. But Reagan, the sentimentalist, had a better grasp of reality."[32]

Reagan's weak grasp of critical policy issues was another important part of his flexibility. His lapses on nuclear weapons are famous and revealing. For a time he thought that a nuclear missile once fired from a submarine could be recalled.[33] He did not realize until the fall of 1983 that 70 percent of Soviet missiles were land based versus only 20 percent of the u.s. missile arsenal, a basic difference in force structure that was critical to any arms control agreement. Only then did he grasp why the Soviets had rejected his proposal for their making cuts in land-based missiles without similar American concessions. Similarly, sdi appealed to Reagan so powerfully at least in part because he knew and cared so little about the details. Unconstrained by a rigid or elaborate conceptual framework of the sort carried around by the militants in his administration, Reagan could proceed by instinct.

If Reagan's style and views left him free to adjust, his own political difficulties gave him a reason to do so. He went into his second term suffering from falling approval ratings. The "Teflon" president seemed to be losing some of his coating. His reputation suffered a major blow when scandal broke in late 1986. He had publicly condemned terrorists and vowed never to deal with them. But his concern for the fate of American hostages in Lebanon led him to authorize a secret deal in 1985 to sell Iran arms in exchange for using its influence to secure their release. The proceeds from that sale went, thanks to the ingenuity of White House staffers, into a secret fund to support the Contras after Congress had refused them appropriations. When the press learned of these developments in defiance of the president's own public position, congressional will, and the Constitution, the administration plunged into crisis. The independent investigation that followed showed the president in violation of the law and not in control of his own policy, but no one had the stomach for another impeachment so close to the Nixon ordeal. In his usual genial way, Reagan confessed to the public that what was now called the Iran-Contra scheme was wrong but that he could not say whether or when he might have approved it.

For a presidency on the decline George Shultz, Nancy Reagan, and British prime minister Margaret Thatcher had just the prescription. They teamed up to lobby for working with Gorbachev to create a new era of peace and security. Such an achievement would not only revive Reagan's popularity but also burnish his historical reputation. Thatcher had been the first to encounter Gorbachev—and pressed her positive appraisal on Reagan. Shultz, an old Reagan associate who had replaced Alexander Haig as secretary of state in mid-1982, understood that Reagan was ready to apply his powers of persuasion on the Soviet Union and "turn it into a good empire."[34] Shultz also had the breadth of vision—academic training as an economist and leadership of a major construction firm (Bechtel) with sizable overseas operations—to understand that the 1980s were not the 1940s whatever the militants might think. He found himself at first checked by the mixed bag of advisers surrounding the president in a highly competitive and maddeningly disorganized White House decision-making process. But increasingly in the second term, working in tandem with Nancy Reagan, Shultz was able to secure the president's ear.

A series of summits carried Reagan and Gorbachev toward the new détente. Their first meeting came at Geneva in November 1985. Reagan liked Gorbachev, Shultz glimpsed an opening for improved relations, and the two leaders put on the agenda the goal of cutting their nuclear arsenals in half. Following this impressive start, a meeting in Reykjavik, Iceland, in October 1986 went astray as Reagan and Gorbachev got away from their handlers and began exploring ways to totally eliminate nuclear weapons. Belatedly brought into the picture, Reagan's staff went into shock and then pulled the president back to more modest, established administration positions. The two leaders resumed their arms talks at the third summit in Washington in December 1987. There they signed an intermediate-range nuclear force agreement (INF), destroying nearly 2,700 Soviet and U.S. missiles with a range of 300–3,400 miles. The fourth summit in Moscow in late May–early June 1988 produced no breakthrough on negotiations over strategic weapons (rechristened Strategic Arms Reduction Talks or START to distinguish them from the much criticized SALT). But Reagan by his warm public demeanor and upbeat comments revealed that the evil empire no longer held any terror.

Having paid his dues as vice president, Bush finally got to take charge of the Oval Office in 1989. He arrived just in time to preside over the quiet end of the Cold War, though he did little to either hasten that outcome or shape the aftermath. Bush had grown up quintessentially northeastern establishment. Born in 1924 in Milton, Massachusetts, he was from a wealthy family prominent in Connecticut politics. World War II interrupted his path from an elite prep school to an Ivy League college. After serving as a navy pilot during World War II, he resumed his studies at Yale and then moved to Texas to work in the oil-drilling business. Bush began his political career as a Sunbelt conservative in 1966. He had two terms in the House of Representatives before Nixon appointed him ambassador to the United Nations in 1971; then in 1973 he was made chair of the Republican National Committee just as the Nixon administration went into its Watergate death throes. In 1974 Bush became the head of the liaison office in China and the next year director of the CIA. A bid in 1980 for the Republican presidential nomination failed. When Reagan offered him the vice-presidential slot, Bush accepted and waited for another shot at the top prize.

Bush's victory in the 1988 presidential election put someone at the policy helm with a fairly conventional mind and a solid record of achievement. He had served competently in the national security bureaucracy and kept a low profile during the Reagan years of sharp internal disagreement and ultimately dramatic reversal. Attached to the familiar Cold War framework, he watched warily as the world that he knew so well disappeared. Bush may also have suspected, as did many Cold War hardliners, that Gorbachev only pretended to be a reformer to lull Americans and western Europeans into passivity while in fact maneuvering to revive Soviet power. Whatever the reason, Bush spent his first months in the White House in 1989 dithering over a policy toward the Soviet Union while holding Gorbachev at arm's length. The Soviet leader was by then in trouble. His reputation at home had declined as his reforms failed to deliver economically. Elections held in March 1989 gave vent to political forces that began to tear the Soviet Union apart.

The collapse of socialism in eastern Europe beginning in the spring of 1989 and Gorbachev's mounting domestic difficulties finally roused Bush, but even then he did not move quickly to provide economic aid either to the new eastern European governments or to Gorbachev. Bush's own caution along with a yawning federal budget deficit and a lack of popular support for foreign aid stood in the way. The European Community and Germany stepped into the gap beginning at the G-7 summit in July, while the IMF was left to impose terms for what it assumed would be a smooth, rapid shift from central planning to a market economy in former socialist states. When Bush finally met with Gorbachev for their first summit in December 1989, held on shipboard in a stormy Maltese harbor, the Soviet leader flatly declared the Cold War over: "The world leaves one epoch of Cold War and enters another epoch."[35] Bush was after a year of scrutiny finally if vaguely ready to agree.

The following two years saw more of the same. Bush stood on the sidelines (perhaps prudently) while the two Germanys moved toward reunification, a major development at the very heart of Europe. West German chancellor Helmut Kohl worked out a deal that Gorbachev could accept, imposed terms on the East Germans, and arranged for the West German taxpayers to bear the costs of integration. Similarly, with Slobodan Milosevic embarked on building a greater Serbia from the ruins of the collapsed Yugoslav federation, Bush was passive. He watched ineffectually as the Soviet Union dissolved in 1991 with nuclear weapons, once under Soviet control, now shared out among Russia, Ukraine, Belarus, and Kazakhstan and with the Soviet economy in a downward spiral.

The only notable Bush achievement came on the arms-control front. There he pressed ahead with START. As the Soviet Union teetered on the brink of collapse, Bush signed the START agreement in July 1991 with a distracted Gorbachev. It provided for the reduction of u.s. strategic warheads from 11,602 to 8,592 by the mid- to late 1990s, while Soviet warheads were to fall from 10,877 to 6,994. Following the Soviet collapse, Bush conducted talks with the leader of the new Russia, Boris Yeltsin, and in January 1993 they signed START II reducing the arsenals by an additional two-thirds (down on each side to 3,500 bombs and warheads).

Bush's caution may have served him better after China erupted in violence in June 1989 following a spring of protests aimed at corrupt, one-party rule. American observers tended to assume China would follow the Soviets along the path of far-reaching economic and political reform. Student demonstrators in April and May 1989, soon joined by broad sectors of the urban population, confirmed those expectations of a China about to undergo change. Deng Xiaoping, however, had his own ideas about where to take China. On the evening of 4 June he had the Chinese army crush this challenge to Communist party control. Republicans and Democrats alike howled for punishment of the "butchers of Beijing." But Bush resisted, and just weeks after the chilling massacre of protesters dispatched his NSC adviser Brent Scowcroft on a secret mission to talk to the Chinese leadership. The president preferred stable relations to renewed confrontation. The Mao-Nixon rapprochement had once again survived.

While the Chinese Communists stayed in power and presided over continued rapid economic growth, the Soviet Union unraveled, its economy in free fall. By December 1991 Bush had lost his interlocutor in Moscow. Gorbachev's resignation marked the end of an era for the Soviet Union, now splitting into its constituent republics with Boris Yeltsin in control of the massive Russian core. It was also the definitive end of the Cold War and the beginning of a running debate over what had occasioned the Soviet collapse. The answer was controversial because it amounted to a verdict on the conduct of the Cold War and even the u.s. response to Bolshevism since its appearance as a political force in 1917. For some the answer was ultimately about the moral foundations of u.s. ascendancy, inspiring a powerful temptation to reach a triumphal conclusion.

The popular argument that Reagan's arms spending had driven the Soviet economy to the brink and thus left Gorbachev no option but to seek security through peace is too simple. This interpretation not only indulges in caricature by juxtaposing a cunning American to a reactive Russian; it also conveniently omits critical developments on the Soviet side. The Afghanistan quagmire (1979–89) was demoralizing. Lagging economic growth and technological innovation limited the regime's choices while deepening popular alienation over unmet consumer expectations. The Soviet bloc was a fragile alliance that suffered its first defection (Yugoslavia) in the late 1940s and then saw in the 1950s the defection of Euro-communists, restiveness in the eastern European satellites, and the defection of China. The allies that the Soviet Union did keep, such as Cuba and Vietnam, required a heavy and continuing transfer of economic resources.

But underlying most of these problems and bearing most fundamentally on the Cold War outcome was the fact that the two superpowers were not roughly equal but rather a striking mismatch. Once begun, the course of the Cold War was regulated by relative economic power more than anything else. So far ahead was the u.s. economy in both size and sophistication that the Cold War might be summarized as begun by the United States, dominated from the outset by the United States, and won by the United States. Soviet leaders' general caution in handling their rival and their recurrent interest in economic reform in the post-Stalin era were the logical outcome of this uneven contest.

The Soviet economic disadvantage had a variety of serious consequences. It imposed limits on military spending and foreign aid. Throughout the Cold War, Washington could afford to throw money at Cold War problems — whether in producing new weapons or in providing military and economic assistance to third-world allies — in a way that the Soviets could not. Even after the Carter-Reagan buildup, u.s. military outlays accounted for around 6 to 7 percent of GDP. Soviet leaders on the other hand were still straining to make their smaller, less dynamic economy produce the weapons, support the troops, and generate new military technologies needed to keep up with the United States. Rough estimates indicate that Soviet military spending in the mid-1980s made claims on the overall economy several times greater than in the u.s. case. The very difficulty the Soviet Union experienced in supplying both guns and butter helped over time to undercut the appeal of its development model among allies and in the third world. Even in the Soviet Union during the Khrushchev and Brezhnev years, influential members of the Soviet elite felt that the system created by Lenin and Stalin was mired in the past and needed renovation, a point strongly seconded by the general population longing for the kind of consumer abundance available in the leading market economies.

But to say that the United States had from the start overwhelming economic superiority is not to say that the Soviet Union had to capitulate. Despite their relatively weak position, Soviet leaders from Stalin to Gorbachev repeatedly sought to make Washington take the Soviet Union seriously as a world power and fumed whenever u.s. leaders denounced the Soviet system as illegitimate and immoral. Moscow's long-term response to the u.s. advantage was not surrender but a search for ways to become stronger and secure respect. What made Gorbachev unusual was the boldness of his reforms and ultimately the risks that he was prepared to run in implementing them. His gamble intended to invigorate socialism and the Soviet state failed with deadly consequences for both. An aide looking back called Gorbachev "a genetic error of the system."[36] Cold warriors had assumed that a totalitarian regime was so repressive that it would never be brought down from within. Gorbachev proved that assumption wrong and leaves historians wondering whether another more cautious leader might have kept the Soviet Union on track and how the u.s.-Soviet relationship and the global order might then have evolved.

Great global commitments carried a wide array of potential consequences. The United States had by its ascendancy become hostage to fortune to a degree that few foresaw in the 1940s. The country had accumulated commitments at a hundred points around the world. Repeated interventions had spawned resentment, disaffection, even bitter enemies along with gratitude and friends. These interventions cost money the public begrudged, and they were more likely to divide than unite Americans. Even where those interventions were spectacularly successful, the United States paid a price—in domestic markets opened on favorable terms to bolster allies, in the rise of economic competitors, in foreign leaders questioning u.s. policies, and in societies and economies organizing around values at odds in critical ways with those of the United States.

Gradually the position of global dominance so carefully built up over half a century was coming under increasing pressure, and u.s. leaders struggled to master the chaos abroad and contain the tensions at home. The end of the

Cold War and the disappearance of the Soviet Union seemed a triumphant resolution of these troubles and opened an era full of promise for the spread of u.s. values on a truly global scale. Perhaps the moment of Wilsonian transformation had come. But the underlying structural problems would not go away. Even though Americans could close the book on the Cold War, familiar perplexities would persist into the 1990s and beyond.

8

THE NEOLIBERAL TRIUMPH

1991★

David Horsey's cartoon "What a Difference a Day Makes . . ." (fig. 8) captured the sharp, painful sense of rupture that many Americans felt in the wake of September 11. Before that fateful morning, they imagined themselves cavorting carefree amid peace and prosperity. That morning took them into a less friendly world. Perplexities piled high in this new time of adversity and testing. The American state bolstered its instruments of domestic surveillance, detention, and punishment—encroaching on freedom in the name of defending it. Military campaigns launched in Afghanistan and Iraq proved open-ended commitments and problematic contributions to national security. The war on terrorism promised, like predecessor crusades against poverty and drugs, to be long and dispiriting and inconclusive. From this perspective u.s. leaders, unsteady on their feet ever since the late 1960s, looked like they were still struggling to get their bearings.

What the emphasis on the drama of this single day may obscure is the triumph of values dubbed "neoliberal" that had brought a remarkable clarity and consistency to u.s. foreign relations around the turn of the new century. The term can be confusing because "liberal" in common American usage suggests support for government welfare programs such as Roosevelt's New Deal and Johnson's Great Society and government intervention in the economy along the lines advocated by John Maynard Keynes. Neoliberalism in fact stood against these positions so influential at midcentury. Its advocates looked back to the nineteenth-century doctrine of laissez-faire for inspiration and guidance. This classical liberal doctrine, most deeply rooted in Britain and the United States, called for freeing markets from social, political, or moralistic constraints. Thus liberated, the "invisible hand" of supply and demand could

Figure 8. "What a Difference a Day Makes . . . ," by David Horsey, Seattle Post-Intelligencer, 8 September 2002. (Republished in David Horsey, From Hanging Chad to Baghdad: Editorial Cartoons [Seattle, Wash.: Seattle Post-Intelligencer, 2003], 18. Reproduced by permission.)

do its work to the benefit of all—rich and poor alike. For advocates of this marketplace society, the state was the enemy, social welfare programs a bane, and notions of public good a snare. The good life was about giving individual buyers and sellers the space to act on their interests.

Powerful domestic political currents carried the neoliberal public philosophy toward its dominant place within the post–Cold War foreign policy establishment. In the 1960s and 1970s a new breed of Republicans took up the neoliberal cause. In the lead were political pundits and operators such as William F. Buckley, Richard Viguerie, and Paul Weyrich. They had warmly embraced the arguments of the economists critical of the Keynesian hold on public policy as well as the academy. Friedrich Hayek's influential polemic *The Road to Serfdom*, published in 1944, reinforced their fear of the welfare state as a stop on the road to a totalitarian takeover. Milton Friedman, best known for his 1962 essay *Capitalism and Freedom*, provided a clear, compelling argument for free markets as models of economic efficiency but also guarantors of political freedom. When the stagflation of the 1970s failed to yield to a Keynesian solution, neoliberals called for a fundamental change of course—toward cutting government regulations, taxes, and programs that disrupted markets and strangled individual choice. Within their own party, these free-market Republicans took a jaundiced view of leading moderates such as Richard Nixon who had made their peace with big government. They looked for allies in corporations anxious over intensifying foreign competition and thus eager to shed government restrictions and weaken labor unions. They set up think tanks—notably the American Enterprise Institute and the Heritage Foundation—to propagate their policy proposals, while their political action committees made sure that probusiness candidates got elected to Congress. To improve Republican chances on the national stage, they allied with conservatives such as Pat Robertson and Jerry Falwell more focused on the cultural issues that constituted the other half of the resurgent party's appeal. The politicized evangelicals imagined creating a good society was less about encouraging money making and free individual choice and more about outlawing abortion, promoting public prayer, and driving out pornography. Ronald Reagan kept the coalition together and carried it to victory. His forceful articulation of themes of free-market prosperity, individual autonomy, and restored morality and national pride began to transform the debate in Washington, with Democrats by the end of the 1980s echoing the Republicans' neoliberal line.

Amplifying these domestic trends were developments playing out on a global scale. The socialist collapse between 1989 and 1991 signaled the failure of the centralized, planned economic model as an alternative to the market model. East Asia was becoming a poster child for the potency of the latter. Japan had secured its place among the ranks of the leading economic powers and preserved it despite a prolonged stall in the growth rate, while neighbors who had embraced guided capitalism along Japanese lines went from strength to strength, none more impressively than China. International agreements freeing trade and capital movements together with new technologies such as computers and cell phones began to knit connections among peoples and regions to a degree not seen since the first age of globalization in the decades around 1900. In this era in which goods, capital, people, and cultural practices traveled further and mixed more than at any time in recent memory, multiculturalism became a buzz word along with globalization to express this sense of barriers coming down and fixed identities dissolving. Americans were to various degrees agents of these transformative developments and recipients of their influences.

Under the neoliberal sway, u.s. policymakers gave high priority to the integration of the international market economy. They pushed for the removal of obstacles to trade and capital movement, the privatization of state-run enterprise, and an end to market-distorting government subsidies. The resulting intensification of global commerce and the loosening of restrictions on international markets put states on the defensive and inculcated consumer values and individualism congruent with the neoliberal agenda. The new order, already taking form in the 1980s and increasingly clear in the 1990s, was to survive September 11. Continuity, not rupture, was the order of the day. U.S. policy kept as its ultimate goal and bedrock faith free markets, restrained government, and unrestrained individualism.

The neoliberal triumph did not adjourn controversy or end difficulties. Champions of freedom found themselves in disagreement as a result of their different understandings of what freedom meant and of how they sized up the global order they hoped to advance freedom in. The differences came into sharp relief as u.s. policymakers attended to their self-assigned role as policeman and manager of the emerging neoliberal world order. With greater u.s. claims to global influence following the Soviet collapse went greater u.s. global obligations—the maintenance of minimal security, the formulation of international rules, and their enforcement. Attending to those obligations in turn created their own set of problems for u.s. leaders both at home and internationally. Finally, neoliberal policy encountered unexpected resistance in a surprisingly wide variety of contexts—at home, in the developed world, in the rapidly growing states of East Asia, and above all within the Muslim world.

By the early twenty-first century, u.s.-sponsored neoliberalism was no longer unchallenged and unchecked on the world stage.

VISIONS OF FREEDOM

The neoliberal faith that came to dominate u.s. social thought and political discourse underwent some striking shifts in emphasis. Three related visions of freedom had their day in the sun. Leaders and commentators concerned with advancing freedom at the outset of the 1990s regarded success a foregone conclusion. The collapse of communism lent credence to the view that neoliberal victory was a done deal. No sooner had the celebration of Cold War and Gulf War victories died down than pundits awakened to the fast-moving currents of globalization, which seemed to give freedom a strongly economic spin. Yet a third perspective on freedom emerged in the wake of the 9/11 attacks on New York and Washington. The world suddenly seemed a dangerous place with the American project facing a long, hard slog. Military interventions in Afghanistan and Iraq as well as the prosecution of a worldwide "war on terror" were the first steps toward what all neoliberals took as the ultimate goal of political and economic freedom.

Post–Cold War Euphoria

Before the Cold War was even over, the celebration of victory began. In a fine piece of anticipation, Francis Fukuyama published in 1989 an essay titled "The End of History?" which would set the tone for early post–Cold War pronouncements. Fukuyama was hardly a household name. His service in the RAND Corporation, a Cold War think tank affiliated with the air force, and in the State Department as a Soviet specialist had attracted little notoriety. Nor did the essay at first blush seem likely to have much punch. He contended that a social model that favored the free movement of ideas and free economic activity was on the verge of final, global victory—but he made his point in a way that asked a lot of his readers. His often abstruse philosophical meditation required patience, and accepting his argument required a leap of faith. The outcome of events in eastern Europe were by no means clear, while Communist parties were still in control in Moscow and Beijing as well as Havana, Hanoi, and Pyongyang. But suddenly even as the essay went into print, China was gripped by a "democracy spring" that seemed to foreshadow the end of Communist control, while eastern Europe came alive with antisocialist ferment. By the end of the year regimes from Poland to Bulgaria had shaken off Soviet-era constraints. The prospects for a neoliberal future were further enhanced by the collapse of the Soviet empire itself. Russia and the other constituent elements of the USSR had broken free of the socialist straitjacket.

At the heart of Fukuyama's argument was that history had reached "the end point of mankind's ideological evolution." The idea of "Western liberal democracy" now held universal sway as "the final form of human government." One by one in the course of the nineteenth and twentieth centuries opposing ideologies—militarism, autocracy, monarchism, fascism, and Nazism—had lost out to freedom. Communism would soon be gone, Fukuyama predicted, thanks in part to Reagan's strong international stand, and then the victory of freedom would be virtually complete. Freedom already prevailed in all the countries that mattered, and where liberalism had not already taken hold along the global periphery, it would surely triumph because it now had no competitors with any broad appeal.[1]

Reagan's successor, George H. W. Bush, was by his own admission not adept at "the vision thing." But in the latter years of his presidency he converted Fukuyama's lofty philosophical reflections into his own stirring nationalist terms suitable to the celebratory mood following the end of the Cold War and the Soviet collapse. Bush's State of the Union addresses dwelt with growing enthusiasm on the themes of democracy and free markets. In January 1990 he announced the end of the postwar era dominated by the Cold War and "the beginning of new era in the world's affairs." He continued: "America," not as a nation but as an idea, is "alive in the minds of people everywhere. As this new world takes shape, America stands at the center of a widening circle of freedom—today, tomorrow and into the next century." A year later, standing before Congress just as he prepared to drive Iraqi forces from Kuwait, the president forcefully rejected the view that "America's best days are behind her." He looked ahead instead to an American-sponsored "new world order, where diverse nations are drawn together in common cause to achieve the universal aspirations of mankind—peace and security, freedom, and the rule of law." He returned to these grand themes in January 1992 with the Gulf War victory and the Soviet collapse just behind him and a reelection campaign looming. Bush told the nation, "By the grace of God, America won the Cold War." The United States was now, he asserted in his most celebratory language, unchallenged as the "freest," "strongest," "kindest" nation on earth. It was the "one sole and preeminent power" that the world trusts to be on the side of decency, fairness, and righteousness.[2]

This euphoric neoliberalism acquired a more distinctly economic dynamic in the middle of the 1990s as the concept of globalization gained ground as the substitute for the now defunct Cold War framework that had guided the country's elite for almost half a century. By the end of the decade globalization had become a buzzword in wide circulation. Promiscuously invoked, globalization served as shorthand for the spread of a free-market capitalism. The market had triumphed in the former Soviet Union and eastern Europe. It had brought rapid growth to much of East Asia, including notably China. The press was filled with news of globalizing trends on all fronts—trade, investment, technology transfers, migration, tourism, and culture. The sense that globalization was not only a force to reckon with but also benign was strengthened by the sustained growth of the u.s. economy. Good times brought unemployment down, closed the worrisome federal deficit, and restored the dollar to a position of strength on world markets. At the same time a vigorous Japanese economy was stuck in the doldrums, and Germany struggled to integrate the once socialist and woefully run-down eastern part of the country. The United States had regained first position whether measured by size of market, attractiveness to investors, or trust in the dollar as the reserve currency of choice.

William Jefferson Clinton, whose presidency coincided with these good years, warmly embraced globalization as a force creating societies of abundance and choice. In the White House as during his presidential campaign, he invoked a faith virtually indistinguishable from that of his predecessor. "Because previous generations of Americans stood up for freedom and because we continue to do so, . . . all around the world more people than ever before live in freedom. More people than ever before are treated with dignity. More people than ever before can hope to build a better life."[3] This declaration by a product of the iconoclastic 1960s testifies to the power of the new bipartisan dispensation. But Clinton's political heart was in the transformative power of free markets. He drew from his experience as an Arkansas governor dedicated to creating desperately needed jobs. Despite his inexperience in foreign affairs, Clinton as presidential candidate underlined the importance of economic globalization, offered a strategy to ensure competitiveness for u.s. industry, and called for assisting the socialist economies to make the transition to the market.

Clinton's response to the North American Free Trade Agreement (NAFTA) provided an early signal that these priorities had carried over into his presidency. Signed by his predecessor, the agreement was pending in Congress with a majority of Democrats opposed. After hesitating, Clinton threw his weight behind ratification. His language amounted to something of a confession of faith in the benefits of globalization: "No one has shown how a wealthy country can grow wealthier and create more jobs unless there is global economic growth through trade."[4] His success in pushing the treaty through with the help of Republicans alienated elements within his own party, while it bemused former cold warriors habituated to think of economic issues as secondary to geopolitical strategy in the affairs of state.

During his eight years in office Clinton remained preoccupied with free markets. At home he built on the Reagan revolution, removing government economic regulations, cutting welfare programs, and privatizing government services. "The era of big government is over," the president proclaimed in 1996.[5] Outdoing Reagan as a fiscal conservative, he brought the federal budget into balance. At the same time he focused on advancing and protecting the free-market international economy with an enthusiasm that exceeded Reagan's and Bush's. Resolving trade disputes and containing international financial crises would prove the single consistent foreign policy thread running through the Clinton years. Not surprisingly, the Treasury Department would have as much clout as the State Department, and the star of the Wall Street investment banker Robert Rubin would rise highest. Starting as an economic adviser to the president before moving over to head Treasury, he eventually outshone Secretary of State Warren Christopher (whose careful lawyer-like style mirrored the manner of his patron, Cyrus Vance) and his successor, Madeleine Albright (a Zbigniew Brzezinski protégée). Rubin's New York roots, his Ivy League education, his corporate success, and his devotion to public service carried faint echoes of the northeastern establishment tradition.

Increasingly Clinton defined national security in terms of threats to globalization. A financial panic was one of those threats. No less worrisome were terrorists, cyber attacks, and rogue states or groups armed with biological, chemical, or nuclear material who could exploit technological vulnerabilities and create havoc in an integrated world. Though Clinton did not say it, his vision of freedom benefited corporations above all. Freed from government regulations, they were to cruise the global market and seize on whatever opportunities for profit presented themselves. As prime engines of growth, they had a kind of sovereign right to ignore the preferences of local populations, run roughshod over weak governments, shed labor and shift production as they pleased, provide extravagant pay to executives, and circumvent environmental restrictions. Unfortunate though it might be in the short term, corporate-driven globalization would have to come at a cost to those with less power, and in the long run, so defenders of the new international system of production and supply argued, all would benefit—not just managers and stockholders but also workers and consumers. Democrats such as Clinton had traveled a long way from the New Deal.

What Clinton stated episodically and unsystematically Thomas Friedman, a *New York Times* journalist turned pundit, converted into a snappy manifesto. *The Lexus and the Olive Tree*, published in 1999, encapsulated the newfound enthusiasm taking hold among educated, influential Americans. Friedman contended that free-market capitalism had created a new, powerful, dynamic, all-encompassing system. His breezy and upbeat treatment made clear that the United States was tightly tied to an irresistible force. "Globalization is not just a trend, . . . not just an economic fad. It is the international system that has replaced the cold-war system. And like the cold-war system, globalization has its own rules, logic, structures and characteristics." Globalization, he explained in language that revealed his enthusiasm, was also largely benign. It "involves the integration of free markets, nation-states and information technologies to a degree never before witnessed, in a way that is enabling individuals, corporations and countries to reach around the world farther, faster, deeper and cheaper than ever."[6]

If Friedman's stress on the power of markets was not enough to cheer neoliberals, they could swoon over his claim that globalization had diminished the importance of states as fundamental units of international affairs even as it elevated the importance of u.s. leadership. In his rendering of the brave new world taking shape at the end of the twentieth century, state borders were now more porous while global market pressures forced governments everywhere to downsize and shift once core functions to the private sector. Whether developed or developing, states had no choice, he argued, but to accommodate to a more limited role. They had to stop constraining and exploiting markets for their own dubious ends and at the expense of economic efficiency as well as individual advancement. The new task of states was to help their citizens adjust to the competitive dynamism of the international economy.

The major exception to the general pattern of state decline was, as Friedman saw it, the United States. Americans occupied a special place in his vision of globalization. They were, in the first place, "the prophets of the free market and the high priests of high tech."[7] They were also the caretakers of the emerging global regime. As the only surviving superpower, the United States had to serve as the leader and stabilizer of the new system. The u.s. destiny was now to champion not just the political ideals that had dominated previous decades but an entire way of life that was inexorably taking over the world. Friedman's perspective bore more than a passing resemblance to the extroverted, confident outlook seen at earlier stages of the American ascendancy: John O'Sullivan's manifest destiny, Albert Beveridge's call to imperial uplift, Woodrow Wilson's Fourteen Points, and Henry Luce's announcement of the American century.

By the end of the 1990s, the neoliberal case for globalization had begun to create a backlash in the United States. The rising chorus of complaints echoed criticism already circulating in the developing world and in Europe. Potentially catastrophic environmental degradation, the inevitable result of mounting levels of production and trade, threatened human health and welfare. Lax labor standards allowed multinational corporations to exploit the working poor. As businesses transferred jobs to low-wage areas overseas, American workers lost their livelihood. Surging capital flows could capsize national economies. Widening inequalities spawned political discontent and violence. Big corporations with transnational interests and the resources to bend local politics and politicians to their will were destroying democracy and endangering fragile ecosystems and cultures. The technocrats who interpreted the rules that governed the international economy were not subject to review or recall by any electorate even though their decisions might have a greater impact than any piece of national legislation. As one critic put it, globalization had imposed on American democracy "a supergovernment of unelected trade bureaucrats." Finally, the critics charged that a world defined by market forces and a society shaped by market metaphors might be materially rich but would lose spiritual and collective meaning.[8]

Opposition to globalization reached a critical mass in the United States in November 1999 when protesters disrupted the World Trade Organization's Seattle meeting and closed the city down. This resistance was feeding into a broader, global stream of discontent dating back to the Group of 77's complaints over the harm the global market did the third world. Signs of disquiet had been evident in Europe by the mid-1990s in demands for constraining the dangerously massive amounts of capital flowing from country to country and for addressing global poverty in ways other than simply through the market. Following the events in Seattle, international gatherings with a globalization agenda drew crowds of protesters and gave the meeting sites the look of a siege as police and demonstrators squared off. But the critics failed to shake the neoliberal consensus that made globalization seem such a good idea. A loose coalition from across the political spectrum, they had no common political program. The diversity of their challenge was reflected in the two anti-globalizers who jumped into the 2000 presidential race—Pat Buchanan from the Republican Party's right wing and Ralph Nader, best known as a left-leaning consumer-rights activist. The electorate was not impressed. Despite considerable popular disquiet over globalization, Buchanan and Nader combined accounted for a mere 4 percent of the vote.[9]

The Return of the Militants

As Horsey's cartoon suggests, the 9/11 attacks dramatically darkened the national mood. They also created an opening for a distinctly militant neoliberalism sidelined over the previous decade. The first post–Cold War hints of militancy had emerged within the administration of the senior Bush. While the president talked of "a new world order" as a virtual reality, his secretary of defense, Dick Cheney, laid the intellectual groundwork for a neoliberalism muscular enough to overcome any resistance to u.s. dominance. In 1990 he set the staff of Paul Wolfowitz, a leading militant, to work on global strategy. The resulting Pentagon paper made the prime u.s. goal stopping any country from reaching a position that would allow it to challenge the United States either in broad global terms or in a narrower regional context. The declassified version of the report, toned down for public consumption, called for using the post–Cold War u.s. dominance to "secure and extend the remarkable democratic 'zone of peace' that we and our allies now enjoy."[10]

While Bush left the Cheney recommendations on the shelf, the militant view got a fresh injection of energy from a 1993 essay by Samuel Huntington, an influential Harvard professor of government. He proposed a "clash of civilizations" as the central feature of the post–Cold War world in place of the other, softer articulations of the neoliberal faith. His basic premise was that international conflict was an invariable feature of the world scene. Proliferating civil wars and ethnic quarrels in Bosnia, Kosovo, Haiti, Rwanda, and Somalia as well as struggling democratic initiatives in Russia and China seemed to support Huntington's pessimistic reading of global trends. The "new world order" had not arrived, and the international economy was more likely in his view to generate cultural friction and political conflict than draw countries together. In a world of competing regionally based civilizations, the sharp resurgence of the Islamic and Confucian zones and the threat they posed to the West most worried Huntington. In the face of this new threat, he called for the United States and its long-term European allies to join in defense of those Western values of "individualism, liberalism, constitutionalism, human rights, equality, liberty, rule of law, democracy, free markets, [and] the separation of church and state." The language Huntington used suggested that the troops he sought to rally were Anglo-American, but he reserved the dominant place for the United States. It had "to promote the strength, coherence, and vitality of its civilization in a world of civilizations." Otherwise, neoliberal values would soon be isolated globally and thrown on the cultural defensive.[11]

By the end of the decade the old Cold War militants were stirring. They were troubled by Clinton policy and gripped by a nostalgia for the early Reagan years as a heroic moment of conceptual clarity and domestic unity in foreign affairs. That clarity and unity was again needed in a dangerous world, but it was not to be found in either Fukuyama's view that neoliberalism had definitively triumphed or Friedman's conviction that the forces of globalization were relentlessly moving forward. In 1996 an influential essay calling for "a neo-Reaganite foreign policy" proposed that the goal of U.S. policy should be "benevolent global hegemony." "Military supremacy and moral confidence" provided the basis for dominance; preempting potential challengers would guarantee the United States its favored position over the long haul. A year later militants gathered under the umbrella of the Project for the New American Century to prepare a call to geopolitical arms and to state their faith in military strength. The list of those "resolved to shape a new century favorable to American principles and interests" (including explicitly political and economic freedom in the world) would prove a who's who in the diplomatic and military establishment of Clinton's successor, George W. Bush.[12]

Cheney's doctrine, Huntington's thesis, and the Project for a New American Century's manifesto provided the bearings for an administration caught off guard and thrown off balance by the shocking attack on home ground. George W. Bush had arrived in the White House eight months earlier with less exposure to the broader world and experience with foreign affairs than any president in living memory. What he lacked in knowledge and curiosity he made up for in the certitude of a born-again Christian, a public swagger meant to convey confidence, and a trusted circle of skilled political operatives drawn from the stable of loyal Bush family retainers. Faith in the market, never in doubt in the Clinton years, was even more fundamental to the new president and those surrounding him. But his election-year stress on a foreign policy that reflected "the humility of real greatness" and that steered between the extremes of isolationism and empire left in doubt how vigorously he would press the neoliberal cause abroad.[13] The attacks on September 11 dealt a shattering blow to any lingering confidence that the new world order was firmly in the saddle and that a neoliberal world was inevitable or even benign. The president emerged an unabashed militant. Hard-liners had his ear. Operating from a Cold War frame of reference, they imagined a world starkly divided along clear ideological lines. In the grand struggle to decide its future, they knew appeasement would be disastrous and military strength and moral certitude essential. Cheney, a powerful vice president, was one of those influential hard-liners. The assertive Donald Rumsfeld, in charge of the Department of Defense, was another. Each had on their staff former Cold War militants: Deputy Defense Secretary Paul Wolfowitz; Undersecretary of Defense Douglas Feith; Defense Policy Board member Richard Perle; National Security Council member Elliott Abrams; and Cheney's chief of staff, Lewis "Scooter" Libby.

Bush echoed his hard-line advisers in the way he defined the issue at hand. While publicly denying the "clash of civilizations" thesis, the president nonetheless linked u.s. policy to civilizational struggle and claimed pride of place for the United States as the crusader in chief. The president was confident in the righteousness of his cause and in the necessity for the United States to act alone if necessary. In the immediate aftermath of the 9/11 attack, he delivered a televised speech before Congress that invoked the keywords from a century and more of public foreign policy discourse: national mission, world leadership, and providential support in the face of a dark threat. But the fate of human freedom was the overriding theme. He announced, "Freedom and fear are at war. The advance of human freedom . . . now depends on us." The country had arrived at a time of testing. If it acquitted itself well, "this will not be an age of terror; this will be an age of liberty, here and across the world." Speaking again to the country four months later, the president put the spotlight on the "axis of evil." In keeping with Huntington's emphasis, the axis ran through the Middle East (Iraq and Iran) to East Asia (North Korea). He once again accentuated the moral imperative behind a u.s. policy dedicated to defending universally applicable values: "the rule of law; limits on the power of the state; respect for women; private property; free speech; equal justice; and religious tolerance."[14]

In short order, the Cheney Doctrine came off the shelf to become the administration's governing strategic concept. In June 2002 a president with a tendency to use speeches to make policy gave West Point's graduating class a preview of what would emerge the following September as the Bush Doctrine. He declared the passive strategies of containment and deterrence out of date. "We must take the battle to the enemy, disrupt his plans, and confront the worst threats before they emerge. In the world we have entered, the only path to safety is the path of action." That goal in turn meant keeping the u.s. military so strong that it was "beyond challenge." At the same time he repeated his commitment to defend neoliberal values under assault from ruthless tyrants and fanatical terrorists. In February 2003 he singled out the entire Middle

East as the testing ground for his democratization drive. A president with virtually no prior knowledge of international affairs had taken up, verbally at least, the most ambitious crusade in the history of u.s. foreign relations. His goal was not the defeat of a particular country or ideology but a global transformation on u.s. terms and the simultaneous elimination of powers who might obstruct this sweeping u.s. project. The White House seemed bent on repeating a story line from nearly a century earlier, confident that this time great ambitions would not go wrong. As Bush explained just as war with Iraq began, "I don't expect Thomas Jefferson to come out of this, but I believe people will be free."[15]

A variety of personal considerations may have energized Bush's neoliberal faith and directed it toward Iraq. A tin-horn dictator had defied his father and then outlasted Clinton. Saddam Hussein's survival was an irritating reminder of a family as well as a national failure in the Middle East. Popular outrage over the attacks in New York and Washington created a political environment favorable to forceful action. A macho streak that was part of Bush's Texas ethos and compensated for a lifetime of underachievement may have at this point come into play. By removing Saddam Hussein, he could not only vindicate family and national honor but also demonstrate his personal mettle and bring distinction to what had begun as a lackluster presidency. The notion of a war against Iraq appears to have seized the president's imagination even before the fires had died out in the Manhattan rubble, and thereafter the martial impulse grew stronger.

The new militant neoliberal program, with its focus on expunging evil, eliminating security threats, and promoting democracy in the Middle East, gave rise to enormous controversy. Some such as the Columbia University cultural critic Edward Said considered Huntington's views, recycled by the Bush administration, dangerous in their conceptual simplicity. He warned against making "'civilizations' and 'identities' into what they are not: shutdown, sealed-off entities that have been purged of the myriad currents and countercurrents that animate human history, and that over centuries have made it possible for that history not only to contain wars of religion and imperial conquest but also to be one of exchange, cross-fertilization and sharing." Others within the policy establishment expressed practical doubts. Philip Zelikow, who had worked on Bush senior's nsc staff, found the doctrine associated with the younger Bush "aggressively opaque." It did not offer a guide to dealing with specific policy questions. Others inclined to see the world in balance-of-power terms worried that the stark insistence on preserving u.s. dominance against emerging challengers would have a perverse effect. Friends and foes alike would safeguard their security by finding ways to offset u.s. advantages, whether by withholding cooperation, improving their weaponry, or constructing new alliances.[16]

Prominent neoliberals responded to the new militant tone in strikingly diverse ways. Some former celebrants of the "new world order" such as Bush senior kept their counsel, while his former associates Brent Scowcroft and James Baker expressed their doubts about the wisdom of the militant-inspired Iraq invasion. Friedman the globalizer signed on to the Iraq war precisely because it promised to promote democracy, free-market prosperity, and enlightened individualism in the Middle East. (He would later express chagrin at the botched outcome.) Clinton by contrast affirmed his essentially optimistic view of a globalizing world that stood in dramatic contrast to the emerging militant approach. In a speech given at Harvard two months after September 11, he focused on "the most breathtaking increase in global interdependence in all of history" as still the central fact of international life. Sticking with a strategy of enlightened globalization—making the most of international markets while confronting the problems they generated—was, in his view, the best response to terrorism. Huntington, who confessed himself "dead-set against us going into Iraq," sheared off from the militants. But neither he nor the other neoliberal critics of Bush's Middle East policy would let it shake their faith. The issue for them was not whether but how to defend and promote that faith under changing circumstances. Neoliberalism remained the governing guide to the u.s. role in the world.[17]

DIMENSIONS OF DOMINANCE

This increasingly influential neoliberal faith raised the salience of two long-standing u.s. policy concerns—but for the first time on a genuinely global scale. First, freedom could not flourish in a disordered world. To that end, the u.s. military turned increasingly to the task of bringing defiant strongmen, bloody-minded dictators, and shadowy terrorists to account. Moreover, freedom depended on giving full rein to global market forces. That meant shrinking the state sector in both developed and developing countries, minimizing labor and environmental provisions that created market inefficiencies, and providing corporations with ample latitude for entrepreneurial activity.

Military and corporate leaders figured prominently as advocates and enforcers of the neoliberal agenda. Military leaders began to gain greater policy influence in the early Cold War (George Marshall under Truman, Eisenhower in his own right, and Maxwell Taylor under Kennedy and Johnson come immediately to mind). Recent decades have seen that influence dramatically enhanced. Reagan made his first secretary of state General Alexander Haig, a Henry Kissinger protégé who had served as the White House chief of staff during the final, Watergate-dominated phase of the Nixon presidency. Four of Reagan's six national security advisers (Richard Allen, Robert McFarlane, John Poindexter, and Colin Powell) were military men. George Shultz, the most influential figure at least during the latter part of the Reagan presidency, had a corporate background as well as ties to the University of Chicago's strong tradition of neoliberal economics. Under the elder Bush a mix of military and corporate figures continued to dominate. Brent Scowcroft, the president's right-hand man in the White House, was a retired Air Force general who had worked with Kissinger in the Nixon and Ford administrations, while Secretary of State James Baker came out of the same Texas oil business milieu as the president. Within the Clinton circle of advisers, Robert Rubin, a Wall Street insider, was arguably the most influential. The military, in retreat under Clinton, made a limited comeback under the younger Bush with Colin Powell taking over the State Department. But even so, he was overshadowed by Dick Cheney, who shared an oil business background with the president. Though a presence in Washington politics going back to the 1950s, Rumsfeld had also spent a good part of his time from 1977 onward in private business, most notably at the head of a major international pharmaceutical company.

Global Policeman

Neoliberalism's preoccupation with global order translated directly into the frequent exercise of overwhelming u.s. military might. The Vietnam defeat had inspired talk of using u.s. forces cautiously. But by century's end any sign of a so-called Vietnam syndrome seemed to be fading. Indeed, the United States had become *the* policeman of the global system, embarking on eight major overseas operations between 1989 and 2003. The exercise of u.s. military power was most frequent in the third world, consistent with a pattern evident during the Cold War and even earlier. The colonial era was long gone, but the gross violation of the sovereignty of the weak by the strong remained a familiar feature of international life. While "regime change" might sound new, it reflected an interventionist impulse directed at the periphery that was quite old—and that could still lead to grim consequences.

To support its global mission, the military enjoyed post–Cold War budgetary largesse that dwarfed outlays in any other country. In 2002 the United States accounted for 40 percent of total world military spending, which meant in actual dollars more than the next nine combined. By the dawn of the new century, a quarter of a million troops were scattered across some seven hundred bases around the world and backed by thirteen formidable carrier battle groups and an array of technologically sophisticated weapons.[18]

A long-standing devotion to technowar led Pentagon planners to seek swift, decisive engagements that would yield quick victories at low cost in American lives. Innovations in communications, computerized battlefield control, smart munitions, and drones gathering information and delivering explosives were just some of the ways that advanced technology gave the United States the ability to fight "virtual war."[19] But this kind of comparative advantage was of dubious help—perhaps was even a handicap—in a range of politically sensitive operations. American leaders had the impressive capacity to inflict heavy damage on a country but not necessarily to police, occupy, or pacify with finesse.

True to a century-old pattern, military power played a prominent role in keeping a restive Caribbean region firmly under u.s. control even as the Soviet threat receded and then vanished. Panama's strongman, Manuel Antonio Noriega, was the first target. The Reagan administration had at first tolerated his involvement in the drug trade in exchange for support of u.s. policy in Nicaragua and El Salvador. The relationship began wearing thin during Reagan's second term as the drug issue became public. The Department of Justice indicted Noriega in early 1988, but Reagan resisted a military action as costly in lives and u.s. reputation in Latin America. Under pressure to leave the country quietly, an angry Noriega mobilized anti-u.s. sentiment, overturned presidential election results, and harassed u.s. soldiers and civilians living in the Canal Zone. The newly installed Bush administration first tried military threats and then backed a coup to dislodge Noriega. When both failed, Bush ordered an invasion in December 1989. The sheriff got his man and promptly packed him off to stand trial in a u.s. court for drug trafficking. (Noriega was subsequently convicted and imprisoned.) The Bush administration could now boast about democracy restored, and the u.s. military could draw confidence from an operation that went smoothly with only twenty-three soldiers killed. On the other hand, Panama came out of the invasion with some three thousand civilian dead and a badly damaged economy. One bitter Central American drew a comparison designed to make North Americans cringe: "You laugh at the Russians—what a mess they've made of Eastern Europe. But what a mess you've made of Central America."[20]

Haiti became the next target of u.s. intervention. Fixed firmly in the u.s. orbit, Haiti stood as the perfect example of a "failed state." Its per capita GDP, already low at the outset of the postwar period, had by century's end fallen by a fifth. Its strife-torn politics continued to destabilize the country. In 1991 the country's military had overthrown Jean-Bertrand Aristide only eight months after his election as president. Economic sanctions and UN mediation had failed to restore civilian control. When an armed mob turned back a token U.S.-Canadian force attempting to land in Port-au-Prince in October 1993, Clinton was embarrassed. He was also worried by the flight of Haitian refugees to Florida. After securing UN Security Council backing, he announced in September that he was prepared to use the U.S. military to vindicate democratic principles and restore order critical to the operation of the free market. Clinton saw himself a reluctant policeman with no choice but to respond to a problem in his own neighborhood. With a showdown looming, a delegation headed by Jimmy Carter (seconded by Colin Powell and Senator Sam Nunn) got the coup leaders to agree to stand down. But the U.S. president had no obvious strategy beyond brute gunboat diplomacy. He turned the policing over to an international force while a restored Aristide struggled with mounting disorder until the populist president was once more ousted, this time under U.S. duress. Haiti remained a failed state.

The Middle East had already in the 1970s and 1980s begun looming large as a zone of conflict for the United States. The Persian Gulf alone contained 40 percent of the world's oil. The fuel shortages of the early and late 1970s had demonstrated the vulnerability of an energy-hungry world economy—and the consumer lifestyles most Americans prized. The leaders of the region's major oil exporters understood their stake in keeping the global economy afloat. But the Iranian Revolution at the end of the decade gave notice of a trend troubling to neoliberals: rising Islamist sentiment challenging—sometimes violently—the U.S. grip on the region and the legitimacy of the secular elites that collaborated with the United States. Not only had the revolution alarmed the Soviets, with fateful consequences in Afghanistan, but it had also led to war with Iraq after Tehran had offered its support to Iraq's Shia majority against the government of Saddam Hussein. Shaken by events in Iran and Afghanistan, Carter had asserted his doctrine in January 1980 to signal a formal commitment to use military force in the Gulf. Reagan had kept the pressure on Iran's new Islamic republic, aligning with Saddam Hussein in his eight-year war with his neighbor. Reagan had also provided generous support for Islamic forces resisting the Soviets in Afghanistan. Elsewhere in the Middle East, which was rapidly emerging as a major theater of U.S. operations, Reagan sent the marines into Lebanon (1982–84) and ordered air strikes against Muammar al-Qaddafi's Libya in April 1986 after rising tensions over terrorism.

The Iraqi invasion of Kuwait in early August 1990 thrust the Persian Gulf into still greater prominence. Preoccupied by the dramatic demise of socialist regimes in eastern Europe and the Soviet Union, the Bush administration may have seemed to Saddam Hussein indifferent to rising Iraq-Kuwait tensions over petroleum production, a disputed boundary, and war debt. Indeed, the clear priority Washington had given to containing and punishing Iran and the bland reassurances provided by the u.s. ambassador on the smoldering Kuwait problem gave Saddam Hussein good reason to expect no difficulties from his superpower patron. Caught by surprise by the invasion, the u.s. president quickly rallied, swearing in an apparently impromptu declaration before television cameras that this act of aggression "will not stand."[21] Whatever the motive—Kuwait's oil, Iraqi aggression, or some other concern—he ordered 200,000 u.s. troops to Saudi Arabia to block any further Iraqi advance, and then committed another 200,000 to free Kuwait. Bush also quickly forged a broad, thirty-nation coalition, including Gorbachev's Soviet Union as well as two Arab states, Syria and Egypt. In November the Security Council gave its blessings to this u.s.-led effort by authorizing the use of force. Following his Cold War predecessors, Bush bypassed constitutional provisions for going to war and even avoided serious congressional consultation. Once his military plans became public, he told the Congress in effect to either endorse them or humiliate the commander in chief and undercut American world leadership. Not until the eve of the fighting did he extract an endorsement for this presidential fait accompli from a deeply divided Congress. The vote on 12 January 1991 was 250 to 183 in the House and 52 to 47 in the Senate (with Democrats preponderantly in the nay column in both houses).

Saddam Hussein refused to surrender his trophy even in the face of a half-million-man multinational force superior in numbers and equipment to his own. On 16 January the Bush administration began a six-week campaign of heavy bombing, followed six weeks later by a u.s.-led ground attack. A hundred hours of combat ended with Iraqi troops in flight from Kuwait and a cease-fire. In this lopsided victory u.s. forces suffered nearly three hundred dead compared to what can only be roughly estimated to have been ten to twenty thousand Iraqis killed during the war (mainly soldiers but also civilians). Amid national celebration, Bush exulted, "By God, we've kicked the Vietnam Syndrome once and for all." But in fact Bush operated under limits familiar to his predecessors and suggested by prudence. Any attempt to overthrow Saddam Hussein by force of arms might, he and his advisers feared, result in heavy u.s. casualties, destroy the international coalition that gave u.s. policy legitimacy, and leave a shattered Iraq in u.s. hands. Bush settled instead for a UN-backed program of military pressure, arms inspections, and economic restrictions that seriously weakened the Iraqi regime while causing severe and widespread popular hardship. Kurd and Shia resistance at the end of the war along with deteriorated public health conditions in the immediate aftermath of the fighting probably cost in the range of 200,000 Iraqi lives. Under UN sanctions infant mortality between August 1991 and March 1998 rose sharply, according to one careful study. It estimated a minimum of 100,000 and more likely 227,000 excess deaths during that period.[22]

Though the region seemed under control through the balance of the 1990s, anti-U.S. sentiment was on the rise. U.S. support for Israel was a long-time irritant, to which was now added anger over the continued basing of U.S. forces in Saudi Arabia. In Somalia sentiment turned violent. With the end of the Cold War that country no longer served as a counterweight against Soviet-backed Ethiopia and thus had lost its generous U.S. assistance. The resulting internal political strains led to civil war, which combined with drought to create by 1991 widespread hunger and death. Much of the civilian population was by then vulnerable to starvation. The Bush administration found itself faced with growing public controversy over the Somali crisis and simultaneously calls to respond to mounting warfare in Bosnia. The president decided to focus on the seemingly less risky and less costly Somali problem. He ordered a U.S. airlift to help with food relief in August and then in November sent in some 28,000 troops as part of an international force protecting the UN relief operation. The essentially humanitarian mission turned into a police action when it expanded to include disarmament and political accord. The leading Somali warlord, Mohammed Farrah Aidid, got in the way. The U.S. forces launched an attack in July 1993 that killed elders of Aidid's clan. Payback came the following October when U.S. forces got mauled in a running gun battle in the capital, Mogadishu. A dismayed Clinton, worried about public reaction to eighteen U.S. dead and many more wounded, quickly wound up direct U.S. involvement and began working out complicated ground rules to guide future involvement with UN peacekeeping operations. The Somalia syndrome now reinforced the Vietnam syndrome.

Americans in the Middle East remained in harms way thanks to Osama bin Laden and his loose, decentralized organization known as al Qaeda (or "the base"), which was created to wage the anti-Soviet struggle in Afghanistan. Having proven that determined holy warriors could defeat one major power, bin Laden set about proving it was possible to wound a second. He forged ahead, recruiting throughout the region and attacking U.S. troop barracks, naval vessels, and (most spectacularly of all) U.S. embassies in Nairobi and Mombassa. Clinton's response to the embassy attacks were also spectacular but ineffectual—cruise missile strikes against Afghanistan and Sudan. Technowar simply missed the point.

The permissive political atmosphere following the 9/11 attacks gave George W. Bush the chance to pick up the pace of military operations. Though professing to fight only one war (against terrorism), the Bush administration prosecuted two. One was against bin Laden and al Qaeda's operational base in Afghanistan. A December 2001 invasion of that country removed the Taliban government that had hosted bin Laden. U.S. bombers and four thousand American troops on the ground working with anti-Taliban warlords did the trick. A new government, installed with U.S. blessings and NATO backing, faced the formidable task of bringing the warlords to heel, extending central government control over a culturally diverse population, and in the bargain introducing democracy. A U.S. president who as a candidate had foresworn nation building had embarked on precisely that course under some of the most challenging circumstances imaginable.

The second war was against Iraq. What the senior Bush cautiously began, his son boldly sought to complete. Immediately after the 9/11 attacks, Bush demanded "any shred" of evidence implicating Iraq and reacted testily to doubts expressed by knowledgeable staff. By July 2002 the White House was set on war, the visiting head of British intelligence concluded, with "intelligence and facts . . . being fixed around policy" and with scant concern for managing the postwar situation. The president and his allies went on to cook the intelligence on Saddam Hussein's weapons of mass destruction and publicly link the Iraqi ruler to the 9/11 attacks, convincing the great majority of Americans. Despite the official propaganda offensive, the prospect of an invasion stirred great controversy among the foreign policy elite and a substantial slice of the broader public. Once launched in late March 2003, the invasion proved a cakewalk for U.S. forces. Baghdad fell after three weeks of fighting. One of the commanders arriving on the scene observed ruefully, "We've conquered a country today and for the first time we started it."[23]

The Iraq adventure, however, badly miscarried as U.S. forces shifted from technowar, at which they were superb, to occupation duties, for which they were unprepared by virtue of their cultural blinkers, their training, and their doctrine. Rumsfeld had not minimally prepared for running the country despite repeated reminders from military officers and government experts of the complexity of that task. The militants in the Pentagon and in the vice president's office envisioned U.S. troops mobbed by joyous crowds hailing the liberators. Democracy and free markets in this fantasy would swiftly and naturally take root.

The u.s. government of occupation thus followed directives based on the easy if flawed assumptions of the militants. It dismantled Saddam Hussein's bureaucracy, police force, and army and quickly found itself without the means to maintain order. To make matters worse, u.s. forces faced an increasingly determined, popular, and well-organized insurgency. The superior firepower available to American troops turned into a liability as they gave priority to protecting themselves. They shot or bombed first and asked questions later—with serious consequences to civilians. Within months the occupiers had worn out whatever welcome they had had. By the late fall the Bush administration was embattled in Iraq, under sharp criticism at home, and isolated internationally. This facet of the war on terrorism had proven a windfall for the terrorists and a shattering blow to Iraq's political structure and popular welfare. With u.s. troops caught in a new quagmire, the military resumed the debate over the use of military power dating back to the Vietnam War. The troubled outcome of the Iraq war called to mind the old warning: "Woe to the statesman whose reasons for entering a war do not appear so plausible at the end as at its beginning."[24]

Surprisingly, Europe was the third neighborhood into which the u.s. policeman ventured. In the final days of the Cold War, the Yugoslav federation began unraveling, the victim of economic crisis and political division exacerbated by Serbian and other nationalist firebrands. In 1991 Slovenia and Croatia opted for independence. Determined to carve out a "Greater Serbia" from the remaining territory, Slobodan Milosevic responded by directing his forces into Croatia. In 1992 they moved to secure the Serb position in a multicultural Bosnia while also cracking down on the majority Albanian population in the Serbian province of Kosovo. The televised agony of a Serb-besieged Sarajevo and media reports of ethnic cleansing began to prompt calls for decisive outside intervention. Mounting numbers of deaths (ultimately several hundred thousand) and millions made homeless, climaxing in the mass murder of Muslim men in Srebrenica in July 1995, raised the specter of Europe's ugly past revived. With the leading European powers unwilling to go beyond economic sanctions against Serbia, the spotlight shifted first to the Bush administration in its final months and then to the new Clinton administration.

As a presidential candidate, Clinton had pummeled George H. W. Bush for his inaction in a human crisis that he compared to the Holocaust, but once in office he dodged calls for action on the "problem from hell" (a phrase widely credited to Secretary of State Warren Christopher). The president wanted to focus on domestic policy, and any thought of intervening overseas soured after the public relations disaster in Mogadishu. The deep divisions within the foreign policy establishment were reflected within the administration. The military balked at getting into another morass. On the other hand, Clinton's national security adviser Anthony Lake saw a serious moral challenge, and Madeleine Albright, the u.s. representative at the un, pointedly asked why the country should have a "superb military . . . if we can't use it?"[25] Finally, in August and September 1995, with Croat and Bosnian forces beginning to turn back the Serbian army and its paramilitary allies, Clinton authorized u.s. bombers to strike under a nato umbrella. An intimidated Milosevic agreed to a cease-fire and to the dispatch of nato peacekeepers to stabilize the Bosnian state now divided into two ethnic parts (one Serb and one Muslim-Croat). In early 1999, with Kosovo the new focus of Serb ethnic cleansing, air power was again Washington's weapon of choice. Between March and June u.s.-led nato bombing of Serbia backed by the threat of ground operations forced Milosevic to withdraw the Serbian military from that strife-torn province and again accept nato peacekeepers. A fragile peace at last prevailed in both Bosnia and Kosovo.

The u.s. policeman who patrolled the Caribbean region, the Middle East, and southern Europe refused to answer two desperate calls from Africa. The first came from Rwanda. Ethnic antagonism had erupted in an organized Hutu campaign of killing Tutsis. Ignoring detailed reports from un observers on the scene from April to mid-July 1994, the Clinton administration verbally danced around the word "genocide" in a blatant exercise of willed ignorance. Neither the administration nor the public had any appetite for risking u.s. forces in what might turn into another Somalia. Tutsi forces fighting their way into the country finally brought the massacres to a halt. By then at least 800,000 had died, most Tutsi. All that the president and Secretary of State Albright could do was make journeys of penance to Rwanda for the thousands upon thousands of deaths that they might have prevented. Humanitarian action was hard to muster when racism diminished the humanity of the massacred, when their land had minimal strategic value, and when their economy was marginal to the rest of the world. Not surprisingly, the sheriff decided to sit this one out. Darfur issued the second call. Ethnic violence in Sudan's western region displaced several million and resulted in the death of several hundred thousand by early 2006. The George W. Bush administration responded with some talk but no meaningful action. The pattern of passivity seemed bipartisan.

Regime Manager

The broad exercise of U.S. military power was matched by an aggressive campaign to bring the international regime that Washington had done so much to construct after World War II into line with the increasingly neoliberal U.S. agenda. Individualism figured as an unalloyed good. Political rights took precedence over economic rights. Democracy American-style represented the ideal political system with a claim to moral superiority over authoritarian regimes that stifled their people. Above all the free-market purists who led this campaign sought to roll back state involvement in the economy not only at home but internationally. This broad free-market push with its origins under Reagan and Prime Minister Margaret Thatcher in Britain had by the 1990s acquired a name, the Washington consensus.

The name was appropriate given the U.S. role in shaping, defending, and managing the international economy. The United States commanded its largest chunk, possessed the international currency of choice, and controlled the major international economic institutions. In keeping with strong neoliberal currents, Washington gave increasing emphasis to removing obstacles to the free movement of trade and capital. Repeated rounds of negotiations under GATT had steadily and substantially reduced trade barriers so that by the mid-1990s world tariffs were on average an eighth of what they had been half a century earlier. Global commerce had nearly tripled from the 1970s to the mid-1990s. As a tribute to GATT's success, its member states in 1995 converted the loose mechanism into a formal organization, the World Trade Organization (WTO), with its own bureaucracy and the power to press for further cuts and to adjudicate disputes over complicated trade agreements. The other half of the neoliberal drive, creating greater space for capital movement, entailed revision of one of the basic parts of the Bretton Woods structure. The designers of the postwar international economy had accepted state restrictions on the movement of capital as insurance against a disabling system-wide panic of the sort that they had witnessed following the 1929 crash. However, as western Europe and Japan recovered economically after World War II, Washington began calling for an end to those restrictions. In the 1970s and 1980s that pressure began to see results. As governments ended currency, investment, and other controls, capital moved more and more freely around the globe. Direct investments in overseas production alone were seven times higher in the late 1990s ($400 billion) than in the 1970s.

According to the Washington consensus, what was good for the international system generally was also good for individual countries. U.S. leaders used their leverage to nudge other states toward "restructuring"—abandoning an active government role in the economy in favor of free market principles and guaranteed access to foreign investors and corporations. Repeated financial crises in the developing world created a golden opportunity for promoting these market reforms. States there had taken on heavy debt to industrialize at a time when u.s., European, and Japanese banks were flush with excess capital, including earnings deposited by major oil producers. The oil shocks of 1973–74 and 1979 sent the banks' favored borrowers in sub-Saharan Africa and Latin America hurtling toward default as a result of having to pay high imported oil prices and losing markets in the developed world also hurt by expensive fuel. With Argentina, Chile, Mexico, and Brazil struggling between 1981 and 1983, the u.s. government took action. The u.s. Treasury and the u.s. Federal Reserve joined with the International Monetary Fund and the banks in putting together rescue packages conditioned on the debtors' implementing "structural adjustment programs" (or saps). Recipients of emergency help were to open markets and cut state spending, which in turn meant slimming state bureaucracies but also eliminating food and other popular subsidies and cutting spending on education and health care. The poor suffered, social tensions intensified, and economies continued to struggle. This same combination of forcing open markets and imposing social austerity guided the Washington-imf response to cries for help from the former socialist regimes in the early 1990s and a string of countries engulfed by panic during 1997–98.

The corollary to the faith in private initiative to fuel sustained economic development was a steady retreat from u.s. government-funded development programs, so prominent during the early postwar decades. Neoliberals doubted the efficacy of these programs, never in any case popular with the electorate. Better to rely on saps as the prime instrument of any development policy, so the new orthodoxy argued. Already in the final decades of the Cold War, official u.s. development assistance fell from .31 percent of GNP in 1970 to .24 percent in 1980 to .15 percent in 1989. The end of the Cold War removed one long-standing, practical argument for helping the poor as pawns in the superpower struggle. Accordingly, assistance remained low—at around .1 percent (a rate that allowed the United States to set the standard for stinginess among the rich countries of the world). A substantial part of u.s. assistance was in any case focused on Israel and Egypt, the two largest aid recipients. Counting what Americans gave privately did not significantly alter the picture. That figure was about .03 percent of GDP, roughly what citizens in other advanced industrial democracies were on average giving.[26]

Economic bloc building provided yet another u.s. mechanism for bringing others into the neoliberal system of trade and investment. The North American Free Trade Agreement was Washington's response to the vitality of a European bloc oriented toward welfare capitalism and the influence of a Japanese model in East Asia that allowed for a prominent state role. Bush senior laid the basis for NAFTA in 1989 with the conclusion of a U.S.-Canada free-trade agreement. He then drew in Mexico and left the resulting agreement for his successor to get through Congress. Bill Clinton's decision to back NAFTA established his neoliberal credentials and emboldened enthusiasts of the bloc-building strategy to think in hemispheric terms. The Bush administration concluded a deal in 2005 that drew five Central American states and the Dominican Republic into the neoliberal embrace even while it dreamed of pulling in the entirety of South America. But the major economies of the region, above all Brazil and Argentina with their strong traditions of state-directed industrial development and social welfare, reacted coolly.

Along with promoting the neoliberal agenda, Washington assumed a critical role as guarantor of last resort against financial panics. As checks on international capital mobility had eroded in the 1970s and 1980s, massive amounts of money began to move ($1.5 trillion *daily* by the late 1990s). A panic could quickly empty an economy of foreign investment, send it into a tailspin, undoing decades of hard-earned growth and setting off tremors threatening other economies and even the entire global system. Third-world countries that had attracted large foreign investment were the most immediately vulnerable because a stampede could have an outsized impact on their small economies. Moreover, their central banks had limited resources to contain a crisis. Arranging bailouts became a U.S. obligation—and a chance to demand market reforms. In 1995 Clinton responded to a looming financial meltdown in Mexico with Treasury guarantees to reassure investors and stem capital flight that was devastating that country's economy and spreading fear through international financial markets. He got in return commitments that locked Mexico more tightly within a set of free market rules. In 1997 Thailand slipped into a crisis with serious consequences for Malaysia, Indonesia, and South Korea. This time the IMF came to the rescue with U.S. support—and predictably imposed free market reforms as the price for its help. In 1998 the cycle repeated itself when Russia defaulted on its international loans in August. By December the panic had reached Brazil. Salvage operations for both countries carried the usual price—implementation of measures favored by Washington. They also evoked the usual response—widespread resentment against the U.S. imposition.

The Russian crisis dramatically demonstrated the danger of contagion and the importance of a quick response. At special risk was a major American investment firm, Long-Term Capital Management, operating outside U.S. government oversight or regulation. It had piled up astonishing profits by relying on computerized trading. Its investments had risen to $125 billion but were covered by only $4 billion in actual capital. When the financial markets took an unanticipated dive in August following the Russian default, the firm suffered huge losses and teetered on the brink of bankruptcy. Wall Street was near panic by September over the prospect of a failure in the U.S. financial system. Deciding that this free-wheeling firm was too big to let fail, the Federal Reserve engineered a takeover by a consortium of major banks and investment companies. The bankers sighed in relief but knew the next crisis was only a matter of time in such a large, complex, dynamic, and integrated international economy.

The master of the international economy was also the scapegrace of the international community. While the IMF, the WTO, and NAFTA were responsive to U.S. preferences, other international organizations and agreements, even those that the United States had helped create, provoked American resentment, criticism, and even resistance when they failed to take their cue from Washington. Its notions of international leadership was heavily freighted with nationalist presumptions. The tacit but powerful conviction that the country was exceptional gave rise to a strong sense of entitlement in international gatherings and to an emotional rejection of any suggestion that the United States was merely one participant of many in a global democracy.

Of all the major international organizations, the UN inspired the most conflicted attitudes among Americans, both leaders and the public. It embodied two goals that U.S. leaders had championed early in the twentieth century: collective security and a democratic forum for the countries of the world. The UN as a vehicle for these goals generally enjoyed warm U.S. public approval. The failure to live up to expectations, particularly in the late 1940s when Cold War rivalry immobilized the Security Council and again in the late 1970s when new third-world states bucked U.S. control of the General Assembly, diminished that support—but only for a time and in the main no more than in other founding countries. By the 1990s public support had recovered (70 percent expressed approval in 1999). At the same time a solid minority (27 percent) clung to an unfavorable view, the highest in a sample of thirteen countries.[27]

The more outspoken of the critics saw the UN as troublesome and unreliable. The General Assembly served as a soapbox for the world's anti-American rabble. The UN specialty organizations seemed bureaucratically bloated, suspiciously partial to "global governance," and generally out of sympathy with neoliberal goals. The Security Council, a frequent thorn in the u.s. side, gave those old Cold War nemeses, China and Russia, a chance to wield a veto along with that putative ally, France. A long-standing go-it-alone strain, especially potent in the Republican Party, led to calls to reduce or even sever ties to the United Nations. A Heritage Foundation study, for example, argued that "a world without the u.n. would be a better world," while a Heritage vice president pronounced the un "out of control." It had become "exceedingly anti-u.s., anti-West and anti-free enterprise." In the 1980s Reagan's un representative, Jeanne Kirkpatrick, scored public points by denouncing the organization's "excesses." Jesse Helms took up the anti-un chorus from his position as head of the Senate Foreign Relations Committee. The feisty North Carolina Republican blocked payment of u.s. dues and told a un assembly to its face that any attempt to encroach on u.s. sovereignty or limit the exercise of u.s. power around the world would drive the United States from the body.[28]

This powerful current of disaffection was increasingly reflected in u.s. policy decisions. For example, Washington regularly refused to fund un population programs that involved abortion or un AIDS programs that seemed to sanction casual sex. When un general secretary Boutros Boutros-Ghali proved insufficiently responsive to u.s. wishes, the Clinton administration effectively blocked his reappointment. But the un remained too useful to ignore. Bush senior and Clinton secured valuable Security Council blessings for the first Gulf War as well as for the Bosnia and Kosovo interventions. Washington also valued the un for taking on more and more policing outside u.s. areas of interest. As of 1994 the un had seventeen peacekeeping missions under way, involving 73,000 troops and costing $3.6 billion (better than three times the cost of the regular un operating budget). The largest of the post–Cold War operations were in Cambodia, Somalia, and Bosnia. The election of the younger Bush brought the vociferous critics of the un into the heart of the policy process—with predictable results. The new president did what neither of his predecessors was prepared to do—go to war without some kind of international sanction.

The gathering u.s. go-it-alone sentiment was even more marked in the case of international accords that might constrain u.s. military power. The rising appeal of supranationalism, which Washington had once helped to promote, left u.s. leaders feeling squeezed. They sprang to the defense of national sovereignty. Pentagon objections blocked u.s. adhesion to the convention against antipersonnel land mines (most dangerous to civilians). The Clinton administration in its closing days signed the treaty creating the first permanent International Criminal Court to try those charged with war crimes, crimes against humanity, and genocide, the very offensives that U.S. officials had helped to enshrine in international law in the aftermath of World War II. However, the younger Bush scuttled U.S. membership by refusing to submit the treaty for Senate ratification, and his administration pressured other governments not to ratify it. When the court, based in The Hague, came into existence in 2002, the Bush administration pressed for explicit exemptions from the its jurisdiction and threatened aid cuts to any who signed the agreement without granting a special U.S. exemption. In June 2002 the Bush administration also unilaterally set aside the SALT limits on antiballistic missile development on the grounds that the agreement was out of date, a needless obstacle to the defense scheme first envisioned by Reagan. A comprehensive test ban treaty, signed by President Clinton in 1999 as a check on nuclear proliferation, ran into sharp opposition in the Republican-controlled Senate. One of the first acts by the new Bush administration was to set the agreement aside. That administration also whittled away long-standing international conventions defining the treatment of prisoners of war. The struggle against terrorism called for new rules — unilaterally imposed — regarding the treatment of combatants, so the Bush team argued in the face of widespread condemnation at home and internationally. The deeper argument may have been (as the Bush administration delegate to the UN put it) that "those who think that international law really means anything are those who want to constrict the United States."[29]

Instances of genocide created for the United States the most difficult bind. The Holocaust had become in widely retailed versions of the twentieth century a defining event that regularly evoked emphatic statements by U.S. leaders about "never again." But in fact the Senate delayed ratifying the 1948 UN genocide convention until 1986. The United States was the last of the major powers to do so and even then with reservations. By then the Cambodian genocide of 1975–79 had come and gone — 2 million lives in all. When the Carter administration finally reacted, it lined up behind the perpetrators, the Khmer Rouge, against the Vietnamese forces that had brought the horrors to a stop. The administration of Bush senior did no better. It sat by silently while Saddam Hussein killed 100,000 Kurds in 1987–88. In Bosnia between 1992 and 1995 some 200,000 Muslims died while the Bush and Clinton administrations hid. The massacre of 800,000 Tutsis and Hutu-moderates in Rwanda in 1994 prompted a repeat performance. Only in the late 1990s did hints of a shift become apparent thanks to stubborn State Department bureaucrats who understood the stakes, intrepid journalists supplying shocking eyewitness accounts, and outspoken members of Congress. Under political pressure over Bosnia, Clinton gingerly tried bombing his way to higher moral ground in 1995, and he did the same when Serbia attempted to sweep Kosovo clean in 1999. U.S. officials now gave support for special courts to try those accused of genocide in former Yugoslavia, Rwanda, Cambodia, and Iraq. These courts were a means of vindicating an important principle, but they were also an afterthought. The lives were gone; the passivity of presidents from Carter to Clinton in the face of human horror was all too clear. "Never again" really meant—as one observer put it mordantly—"Never again would Germans kill Jews in Europe in the 1940s."[30]

The official u.s. response to the international environmental movement was also guarded. Americans in ever greater numbers expressed support for action, but policymakers doubted (perhaps correctly) the citizenry's willingness to make significant sacrifices. Any serious global response would put heavy burdens on the United States as the world's third most populous country, its largest economy, its hungriest and least efficient consumer of energy, and its most avid devotee of consumer abundance. Reinforcing these doubts were free-market fears that both principle and corporate profits would suffer from elaborate international environmental restrictions. Advocates of the market had not cut back state regulations in order to let them come back to life in new form. Market forces would solve environmental problems. Washington accordingly played a detached and sometimes obstructive role in the international efforts to negotiate solutions, starting with the Stockholm conference in 1972 and culminating at the Rio Earth Summit in 1992 where the elder Bush found himself at odds with a broad international consensus on the need for a quick and concerted program. The most recent environmental measure to suffer a u.s. rebuff was the Kyoto accords, negotiated in December 1997 to effect a reduction in the greenhouse gases causing global warming. U.S. critics questioned the science behind the agreement, and when evidence of rising temperatures and sea levels became indisputable, they clung to their faith that the free market would provide an effective, low-cost solution. If others refused to accept this self-evidently sound approach, the United States would go its own way.

PITFALLS

The intensity of the neoliberal vision and the scale on which u.s. leaders sought to advance it understandably generated a variety of problems. Some became evident in American life as efforts directed overseas produced strains and incongruities at home that either contradicted neoliberal values or made it difficult to sustain the neoliberal campaign internationally. Others were inherent in the magnitude of the u.s. project. It was not easy to make peoples around the world conform. To inventory these various problems is to ask about the durability of the neoliberal moment. Does it have staying power or is it a flash in the pan?

Domestic Dysfunction

Democratic theory with its stress on the power of the people to decide has shortcomings increasingly evident in a u.s. foreign policy dedicated to neoliberal values. Most Americans have known little about the broader world and thus have had difficulty in coming to an informed opinion on pressing issues. They were also (to judge from the polls) inclined to put domestic priorities first. Thus protection of jobs at home came ahead of free trade principles, and an aversion to taxes and military service left them suspicious of sustained overseas military engagements. Whether guided by considered self-interest or unthinking passivity, the public had a bias toward hanging back even as the range of u.s. commitments overseas and by extension the number and variety of consequential decisions multiplied dramatically over the course of the twentieth century.

In a neoliberal age the tensions intensified between public preferences and the international policies pursued in the public's name by its elected chief executive. Presidents were strongly committed to an activist course overseas, determined in defense of free markets, and ever more able to act autonomously. Despite much talk about downsizing government, the White House staff—the indispensable agent of the imperial-style presidency—continued its steady growth. Over five hundred under Nixon, it had increased to eight hundred by the mid-1990s under Clinton. By then the entire White House work force, not just those directly serving the president or vice president, numbered around six thousand.[31] The White House was more than ever the nerve center for policymaking, where a skilled staff secretly set the course, "educated" the public, cut the Constitution to the incumbent's liking, and built his celebrity with the collaboration of the national media. Amplifying the White House call for playing an active international role was the increasingly large and loud foreign policy establishment made up of ex-officials, professional commentators, and academics.

As the president grew more powerful, a society organized along neoliberal lines suffered from an ever-more clouded vision of commonweal. Putting the individual first not only drained meaning from citizenship and blunted any impulse to political participation; it also removed any incentives for ordinary Americans to know about the world or take a responsible hand in the management of global dominance. The last three decades of the twentieth century saw only half of eligible voters show up for presidential elections. (Off-year elections were even lower, attracting fewer than four in ten.) A rising level of alienation from government accentuated this trend away from confidence in the public sphere. Asked if they can "trust Washington to do what is right all or most of the time," 78 percent of Americans in 1964 said "yes" but only 19 percent agreed thirty years later. By 1994 75 percent endorsed the proposition that "government is pretty much run by a few big interests looking out for themselves."[32] The public policy that usually mattered the most at the ballot box was the performance of the domestic economy. Notions that the citizen owed something to the state gave way to popular expectations that the state's prime role was to maintain national economic growth, take care of struggling sectors of the economy (such as airlines and agriculture), help those subject to disaster, and more broadly guarantee opportunities for individual self-realization and psychic gratification. Political leaders came to recognize the bargain and accommodate consumer preferences. It thus made good social and political sense to talk in the language of consumer choice and abundance, setting aside expectations of sacrifice, indeed arranging the elements of u.s. foreign policy so as to avoid demands on the public.

The power of individualism and the retreat from public concerns into private spaces spawned yet another worrisome neoliberal trend: rising social inequalities. Many Americans, chronically poor and un- or underemployed, lacked the formal education and skills not only valued in the marketplace but also critical to meaningful political participation. Literacy and numeracy suffered a marked decline, suggesting a widespread educational failure. By the early 1990s, nearly half of all American adults (some 88 million) were in functional terms barely literate and hence could not handle such seemingly basic tasks as writing a letter about a billing error, making sense of a newspaper article, or filling out a form. These social disparities reflected in turn income inequalities that have widened under the neoliberal dispensation. In 1970 the ratio of the income received by the top fifth and the bottom fifth of the population was 4 to 1. By 1993 it had climbed to 13 to 1. This concentration of wealth at the top was evident in 2003 data indicating that the upper 5 percent of families claimed half of the nation's income while one in five families with children under six years of age were in poverty, and one in six Americans had no health insurance. With jobs moving abroad, welfare programs weakened, and labor unions losing both numbers and political clout, lower-income Americans were in serious trouble.[33]

A consumer-driven, neoliberal society marked by political alienation and rising inequality had also to confront social violence. The u.s. homicide rate, a good proxy for assaults of all types, ran better than three times the per capita figure for other developed market economies. The U.S. incarceration rate, a good proxy for social breakdown, led the world in 2004 with 726 inmates per 100,000 of population and set a record high for the United States. African American neighborhoods were hit especially hard. One of every eight black males between the ages of twenty-five and twenty-nine was in jail on any given day, and the total number of blacks in prison fell just short of a million (910,000). Determined to exercise military dominance internationally, the U.S. state fell far short of securing a monopoly on violence domestically.[34]

An electorate preoccupied by the sovereign self espoused at least nominally a strongly nationalist view of the U.S. role in the world, perhaps because an increasingly atomistic society clung to this reassuring vestige of shared identity and purpose. While a substantial majority of Americans took satisfaction in membership in a special club — select, powerful, righteous — they shied away from paying the dues and lost patience with heroic commitments abroad requiring sustained sacrifice of American money or lives. Personal and family satisfaction and not propagation of neoliberal values and institutions seemed to top the public's agenda. The prevailing self-centered vision of the good life and reluctance to sacrifice has left bold policymakers in the lurch and rendered policy itself schizoid and thus incoherent. The imperial presidency had the most to gain and the most to lose from public ambivalence about foreign commitments. Many Americans esteemed the occupant of the White House as the embodiment of national identity and mission and trusted the incumbent to know enough to use wisely the considerable powers at hand. But the public could turn on a president whose policies required genuine sacrifice or seemed to imperil the prospects for steadily improving living standards. In effect, the public had assumed the role of providing a check on presidential powers that Congress had virtually abdicated — but the check was crude in its judgment and delivered well after the fact with the damage done. This arrangement was, to put it mildly, awkward for a global power in a way it had not been before 1945 for a country with a more modest international role.

Post–World War II examples abound of the public restraining presidents or repudiating those whose decisions resulted in higher taxes, constraints on consumption, or significant loss of American lives. The Cold War lost its luster when the public realized in the late 1950s and again in the early 1980s the risk of nuclear destruction. Strong backing for limited wars in Korea and Vietnam gave way to politically crippling discontent that mortally wounded the incumbent president. By early 1951 a majority of those with an opinion thought Truman's war a mistake. In 1964 most Americans could not even place Vietnam on a map even as Kennedy and Johnson steadily ratcheted up the u.s. commitment there, and by late 1967 Americans who judged the Vietnam War a mistake outnumbered those who endorsed it. Carter's appeal for energy conservation in the name of national security in the late 1970s provoked consumers, who wanted more and cheaper power, not less and higher priced. The Iraq invasion and occupation offer the most recent demonstration of this pattern. The public bought into a notion that was (to put it politely) glaringly contrary to fact—that Saddam Hussein was personally involved in the 9/11 attack (the view of 69 percent in August 2003). Having given the president virtual carte blanche to go to war, a disengaged and barely attentive mass public increasingly pronounced the war a mistake in the face of mounting casualties and costs. Disillusionment with the Iraq debacle helped raise sentiment in 2005 in favor of international retrenchment if not retreat to its highest level in forty years of surveying.[35]

The counterexamples of presidents attentive to public limits are instructive. Eisenhower liquidated the Korean War and spared the country further military engagements, thus burnishing the reputation of the 1950s as a golden age of peace and plenty. Reagan's notion of national greatness without the need for sacrifice perfectly fit the preferences of a consumer society in a neoliberal age. The elder Bush's Gulf War was similarly successful because it accommodated popular preferences for quick, cheap victory achieved with a minimum of disruption. Not only were u.s. casualties extremely low, but oil-rich Arabs and oil-dependent Europeans and Japanese footed the bulk of the $60 billion bill, leaving the u.s. Treasury to fork out only $7 billion.

The ambivalence toward the exercise of presidential power also shows up in the public's relationship to its armed forces. Most Americans have since the end of the Vietnam War professed a high regard for the military, esteeming it above virtually all other national institutions, including the presidency, Congress, the media, and even in recent decades organized religion.[36] The reasons for the high regard are easy to guess: its competence served as a yardstick of national power, its operations put on display national valor and skill, and its successes vindicated national claims to special standing. But the reluctance to sacrifice, so marked a feature of the neoliberal society in general, removed military service as an obligation of citizenship. Ever smaller proportions of the citizenry and elected officials in Washington had experienced military service.

With the hugely unpopular draft gone since 1973, the armed services were left to fill their ranks, as any business would, with offers of good pay and benefits most likely to appeal to those on the lower end of the income ladder. To minimize the size of that force and to achieve market efficiencies, the Department of Defense privatized a wide range of military functions. Between 1994 and 2002 the Pentagon signed contracts worth $300 billion to "outsource" not only food services, base upkeep, and supply but also intelligence, translation, the management of advanced weapons systems, covert operations, training of foreign forces, and even running ROTC programs. These military firms were (with the exception of Halliburton) not household names. But they have found favor among Democrats as well as Republicans eager to control costs even at the price of diminished public involvement and oversight.[37]

These trends have helped set the officer corps apart from and in critical ways at odds with the consumer republic. Career officers have increasingly identified with the Republican Party over the last three decades (Republicans now outnumber Democrats in their ranks by an eight to one margin, a marked contrast to the ratio in 1976, when over half of military elites rejected any party identification). They saw themselves at odds with interfering politicians, a liberal media, and a society in long-term moral decline. They were like other conservatives reacting against the perceived betrayal of the military during the Vietnam War and the 1960s assault on "traditional" values and institutions. A far cry from the ideal of citizen-soldiers who mirrored the society they defended, officers looked like a distinct and discontented warrior caste devoted to discipline, hierarchy, obedience, loyalty, and sacrifice. Predictably, some officers had fantasies of saving a society in decay by force of their example and of standing up to their misguided, interfering "civilian masters." It was time, so the editor of an army journal declared in 1996, for the military to "tell them how it must be done."[38]

The tensions between the consumer-oriented public and an assertive neoliberal foreign policy has one final, material dimension—the emergence of serious economic vulnerabilities with the potential to undermine the U.S. capacity to act forcefully and autonomously in the world. American consumers made profligate use of oil that left the U.S. economy and lifestyle hostage to the decisions of foreign producers, war and political turmoil in producer countries, and rising worldwide demand. Americans were also responsible for a low rate of savings. By 1990 it was down to about a third the rate of the 1950s, 1960s, and 1970s and far behind that of the main U.S. economic competitors. In 2005 the rate fell into the negative range, the lowest since the Great Depression. Whether due to stagnating income growth or material aspirations outrunning means, low savings rates meant a diminished domestically generated pool of capital available for investment in infrastructure, research and development, plants, and machinery. Finally, Americans became massively dependent on foreign capital to cover large, recurrent trade and federal budget deficits. For a quarter century u.s. imports had regularly and substantially exceeded exports. Similarly alarming, the gap between what Americans were ready to pay their government and what they expected from it in services and subsidies produced persistent deficits in Washington beginning in 1969. The annual deficit increased from $74 billion in 1980 under Carter to a high of $221 billion in 1986 under Reagan to an even higher $290 billion in 1992 under Bush Senior. Closed during the Clinton years of strong growth and greater fiscal discipline, that deficit began to balloon again under the younger Bush (reaching $318 billion in 2005 and pushing the total federal debt to $4.6 trillion). As long as foreign investors saw the United States as an attractive risk, capital for investment and debt service remained reasonably priced. Shake that confidence and the retreat of European, Chinese, and Japanese capital could have damaging effects—higher interest rates, slower growth, and falling real estate, stock, and bond markets. Ordinary Americans might suddenly find their jobs in peril, their personal debts hard to carry, and the values of their homes (the main asset of most families) falling. Such a meltdown would strike at the livelihoods of many, almost certainly destabilize the international economy, and leave the United States in a considerably less secure world.[39]

Losing Friends, Making Enemies

By the twentieth century's end the United States offered the oldest and most widely broadcast model of modernity. The world was awash in American economic and cultural influences. U.S. medical and biotechnological research defined the cutting edge, supplying u.s. pharmaceutical firms with a steady flow of new drugs and techniques. Computer systems around the world relied on software and circuits created and supplied by u.s. firms such as IBM, Intel, and Microsoft. Three-quarters of all Internet messages passed through the United States. Entertainment Hollywood-style dominated the movie screen and television in virtually every country. The three top-grossing films in 1994 in twenty-one different countries were, with only a handful of exceptions, made in the u.s.a. Foreigners embraced McDonald's and Disney theme parks the way they had earlier taken on jazz and jeans.[40]

However powerful as a neoliberal force, the United States faced limits. In July 2002 a secret British cabinet paper gave voice to a common notion: "In practice, much of the international community would find it difficult to stand in the way of the determined course of the us hegemon."[41] To be sure, Washington could have its way when it wished, but defying or ignoring the views of other governments and peoples came at a price, not least to u.s. reputation.

Surveys around the world revealed continuing admiration for u.s. society, notably its ethnic and religious openness, economic and educational opportunity, technological achievement, and economic freedom. Some half million of the world's most talented youth voted with their feet in 2000–2001 by enrolling at u.s. universities. (Half came from a newly dynamic Asia.) But those same surveys also expressed suspicion of official u.s. intentions and hostility toward the uncompromising "fundamentalist" u.s. positions on political and market freedoms. Doubt and dislike were especially marked on four regional fronts, each with the potential for creating problems for the United States.

The most dramatic disaffection took hold in Europe. The transatlantic partnership began drifting apart even before the Cold War had ended. Carter had been a puzzle. Reagan had shifted abruptly from too tough with the Soviets to too soft. Nuclear strategy had been perennially divisive. The drift apart continued through the 1990s and accelerated under the Bush militants. An increasingly integrated Europe on the whole clung to its mixed economy and social welfare policies. Tinkering proceeded in such strongholds of welfare capitalism as France, mainly in the form of trimming benefits, and the new eu members from eastern Europe followed strong free-market policies even though polls showed popular sentiment in line with the western European welfare philosophy and elections revealed a still strong current of socialist politics. Cutting welfare was politically palatable in the parts of Europe emerging from socialism, but elsewhere the likely results were electoral grumbling and even public demonstrations that could shake government resolve. Thus European states on the whole continued to play a far stronger role than u.s. neoliberals thought proper, and greater public resources went to public goods than they deemed wise. Differences in economic culture erupted into repeated transatlantic collisions over protection of food supplies, subsidies for farmers, and cultural protection against u.s. imports.

To this set of divisive issues Europeans added long-standing doubts about u.s. international leadership. European integration was at its outset in the early postwar years driven at least in part by the dream of restoring European influence in a world dominated by the Cold War superpowers. As the French minister of foreign affairs, Maurice Faure, put it in July 1957 when he appealed to the French parliament to approve the Rome treaties advancing Europe integration: "Well, there are not four Great Powers, there are two; America and Russia. There will be a third by the end of the century: China. It depends on you whether there will be a fourth: Europe."[42] Charles de Gaulle and Willy Brandt had given voice to a vision of Europe's political future that diverged from Washington's. Those differences, especially over the virtues of détente, continued into the 1980s. The gathering impetus behind European integration intensified talk of an Old World less dependent on the New World. A u.s.-dominated NATO alliance, a relic from the era of Cold War cooperation, began to lose its common reason for being and survived largely because Washington was eager to preserve the alliance as a tool in support of u.s. initiatives outside Europe and as a means of heading off the rise of a Europe-only defense force.

While Washington fixated on nationalist goals and resisted restraints on the exercise of national military power, Europeans proved themselves strong proponents of supranationalism. The European Union, itself an expression of that faith, early in its history embraced the cause of human rights, creating along the way special courts, commissions, and guarantees of those rights for its citizens. The EU states applied that same commitment to rights internationally, playing a leading role in the process of elaborating and defending them. Similarly the EU states got behind the very international initiatives such as banning landmines, controlling climate change, and establishing an international court of justice from which in the 1990s irritated u.s. nationalists began turning ostentatiously and sometimes petulantly.

Within a Europe that already harbored suspicions about Americans as violent, bigoted, heartless, and wasteful, the younger Bush's leadership style and militant policies provided confirmation and stimulated disaffection. In a 2004 poll 58 percent pronounced themselves averse to u.s. global leadership, and 76 percent disapproved of Bush's international policies. Seven in ten surveyed looked to the European Union as a substitute power center to protect the region's vital interests and counterbalance the United States. To European commentators critical of the Iraq invasion, the Bush administration seemed to fall prey to a discredited imperial pattern. For example, Régis Debray remarked, "With its proconsuls and its aircraft carriers, the rapacious and generous America revisits the time of colonizers drunk on their superiority, convinced of their liberating mission, and counting on reimbursing themselves directly." This erosion in confidence in u.s. leadership threatened NATO and more broadly jeopardized transatlantic cooperation in a wide range of areas from culture and economics to tourism and immigration. Whatever this trend may mean for the global system, it foreshadows formidable constraints on the exercise of u.s. power and the advance of neoliberal values.[43]

Russia posed a different sort of obstacle to the neoliberal charge. The collapse of the Soviet Union did not eliminate suspicions of the United States. The decision by a u.s.-dominated NATO to push right to Russia's doorstep and Washington's post-9/11 drive to establish bases in Central Asia both seemed to strike at Russia's tattered great-power status. The popular reaction against the United States, so pronounced in EU countries, was somewhat more muted in Russia. While indicating slightly more favorable than unfavorable views of the United States, Russians responding to surveys in early 2004 had an unfavorable view of Bush as a leader (60 percent) and had less trust in the United States as a result of the Iraq war (63 percent).[44]

East Asia was already before the 1990s the region most outspokenly critical of U.S. neoliberalism, and resistance persisted beyond the Cold War. Leaders and politically active intellectuals in the region have time and again turned to the strong state to ensure prosperity and security. Free markets have not commanded theological loyalty; their practical advantages have had to be weighed against other, often broader societal considerations. Similarly, democratic development has tended to follow a distinctly unorthodox, even "illiberal" path. Japan has functioned through virtually the entire postwar period as a one-party state, while China's Communist Party has clung to power even as it has opened markets and given greater scope to elections. Not surprisingly, elites throughout East Asia have recoiled against U.S. calls for market and democratic reforms. These calls seem to them paternalistic at best and at worst a strategy for destabilization of an increasingly successful and self-confident region. They have also resisted Western interpretations of human rights as essentially political and applicable to individuals. Beginning in 1993, Asian delegations to international conferences made the forceful case that rights varied by region and culture. Thus, individual rights might have to give way in some cases to the collective interests of the family, clan, village, or state. Social solidarity, economic development, or political stability might take precedence over personal freedoms.

American hectoring has combined with economic and strategic irritants to inspire a popular literary genre urging East Asians to "say no" and follow their own course. The Japanese were the first to speak out during the trade wars of the 1980s when their state-guided, export-driven growth was leaving the United States in the dust. Japanese commentators rejected U.S. demands for breaking up the clubby internal market, responding that naked market forces and rampant individualism would stir conflict and harm social cohesion, perhaps even undermine the gains achieved by the country's fragile, resource-poor economy. By the early 1990s three-fourths of Japanese polled thought reform-minded Americans were looking for a scapegoat for their own economic and social problems and about half saw their country locked in a competition to become the number-one economic power in the new century. Resentments and anxieties so pronounced in Japan had by the 1990s spread to China. U.S. pressure on its economy, attacks on Communist Party control, complaints about human rights violations, and support for Taiwan generated a sharp backlash. Suddenly China had its own "say no" literature. Its denunciation of u.s. leaders for alternately preaching to and threatening China as though it were a third-rate power attracted an avid nationalist readership. Singapore's outspoken leader, Lee Kuan Yew, joined the critical chorus, deploring the socially disruptive effects of the aggressive individualism Americans practiced and held up as a model for others.[45]

In the Middle East, attitudes toward the United States were already by the 1990s wary. The Iranian Revolution had not only shaken u.s. control but also set off ideological reverberations throughout the region. It demonstrated the power of religious ideas and leaders to mobilize the public and effect change. Washington's long-standing support for Israel and its dispatch of forces into Saudi Arabia in the lead-up to the first Gulf War added to the popularity of the Islamist political ideology not only in the Middle East but in a sweep of territory running from northern Africa to Southeast Asia and containing well over a billion Muslims. Hardly a monolith, public, political Islam assumed as many guises as there were countries, each with its own language, ethnic, and historical profile—the venerable and influential Muslim Brotherhood in Egypt; the clergy who controlled Iran; the parliamentary pragmatists in Turkey; a militant Hamas with grassroots support in Israeli-occupied Gaza; a mass-based and nationalist Hezbollah in Lebanon; and Saudi Arabia's missionizing Wahhabi establishment. Al Qaeda, which would leap to prominence as the author of the 9/11 attacks on the United States, was an expression of the ideological ferment roiling virtually every Muslim country and dispersing beyond national borders in a complex pattern of mutual influence.

What advocates of political Islam had in common was a dislike of u.s. policy and an impatience with their own rulers, who had both collaborated with u.s. policymakers and failed to deliver on their pledges to build a "modern" society on the basis of socialism, nationalism, or industrialization along Western lines. The appealing alternative to these secular ideologies was a vision of social and political development derived from indigenous, Qur'anic principles. The u.s. declaration of the war on terrorism followed by the invasions of Afghanistan and Iraq deepened the conviction, most forcefully articulated by Islamists, that the United States was embarked on a crusade in which oil figured prominently. The Bush administration's talk of promoting a neoliberal order in the Middle East had the ring of hypocrisy at best and neocolonialism at worst.

Public opinion seemed to move with the Islamist critics. Among opinion leaders around the world surveyed at the end of 2001, those in Egypt, Turkey, Pakistan, and Uzbekistan were most inclined to see a conflict looming between the West and Islam (41 percent). They thought that the United States was too supportive of Israel (95 percent) and was overreacting in its war on terror (62 percent). They believed that ordinary people in their country had a negative view of the United States (49 percent) and attributed the 9/11 attacks to a loathing of long-standing u.s. policy (81 percent). A survey conducted in early 2004 revealed that popular hostility remained intense. For example, respondents in Morocco, Pakistan, and Jordan gave bin Laden vastly higher favorable scores than the u.s. president. So intense was the hostility generated by the Bush Middle East policy that it was breaking down the distinction between u.s. policy and u.s. society. A twenty-five-year-old graduate student at Cairo's American University, Ali Ahmed, articulated that distinction, "I like America so much. I like the American people. I want to go to America to study computer science, but I hate American policy in the Middle East and against Afghanistan. I hate it so much." A man in McDonald's in Cairo expressed similar mixed feelings: "We like the American people; we just don't like America." But polling done in early 2004 showed that even appreciation for the United States as a society and culture was in sharp decline. For example, respondents in Jordan with a favorable view of the United States fell from 53 percent in 2002 to 21 percent in 2004. The moral if not the economic resources on which u.s. ascendancy depended were dwindling.[46]

History did not end with the fall of the Soviet Union, as Francis Fukuyama famously suggested. The most recent chapter of American history marked by a strong, outward-looking neoliberalism was far from stable or static. Intervention was relatively easy given u.s. military might; nation building along democratic and free-market lines proved much harder and much more controversial. Keeping restive allies and former rivals in line was a constant challenge, yet the functioning of the international system depended on comity and cooperation. A Republican Party dependent on cultural conservatives alienated by an anomic, amoral, multicultural consumer society and with a Manichaean international outlook added to the tensions within u.s. policymaking. Demands that godliness, manliness, and morality guide u.s. choices in the world not only polarized u.s. politics but also fed disaffection abroad — and in both these ways made a policy grounded in neoliberal principles harder to sustain.

The neoliberal moment has been attended by perplexities and challenges that leave uncertain the fate of the American attempt to remake the world in its own image. Is the American-dominated order vulnerable and transient or sturdy and enduring? Will Americans and other peoples around the world flourish under its auspices or falter under the weight of accumulating national suspicions, regional resentments, and global problems? The citizens of the mightiest republic in history might well ask themselves these questions — before alarming world trends confront them with answers they don't like.

conclusion

HEGEMONY IN QUESTION

This volume opened with a simple question: how did the United States gain its current ascendancy? The answer, developed in the previous chapters, can be found in the accumulation of economic might, the development of a keen sense of national purpose, and the rise of a formidable state with a knack for pursuing international goals with deliberation and patience. To these material, ideological, and institutional features must be added a fair degree of luck in location and timing. Americans made the climb as a settler society at a favorable moment in a region—the North Atlantic—that was outstripping the rest of the world in output, power, and pride. By the middle of the twentieth century the United States stood as a colossus astride the world. Through the balance of the century and into the next, Americans wielded unmatched military power with a genuinely global reach. They shaped and sustained an international economy embodying widely appealing socioeconomic values. When their political and corporate leaders spoke, people everywhere listened even when the message was disagreeable.

ON THE IMPORTANCE OF NAMES

There is no shortage of labels available to apply to what the United States has become. A sampling with varying degrees of merit would include reluctant imperialist, imperial republic, democratic crusader, world policeman, or the first nation of modernity. To these choices, French foreign minister Herbert Védrine added "hyperpower" (*hyperpuissance*). Leading Republican Tom Delay, perhaps irritated by this bit of fancy French name-calling, countered with the down-to-earth "super-duper power." Madeleine Albright liked the reassuring sound of the "essential nation."

Determining the label that both fits and illuminates does matter. As the French writer Albert Camus is supposed to have observed, "Naming things badly adds to the misfortunes of the world."[1] An exercise in naming can force us to grapple with defining features—to sort through those elements in a situation that are central to understanding and those that are peripheral or distracting. Working with the right label may not end "the misfortunes of the world" but may minimize mishaps. Finding a prudent way ahead surely depends on a clear understanding of the current u.s. ascendancy and its likely durability in the years to come.

Against "Empire"

"Empire" is the term currently in vogue in the controversies set off by Bush administration policies. The invasion and occupation of Iraq, the creation of a client state in Afghanistan, and the u.s.-dominated international coalitions that encompassed these feats are recent examples of what might properly be deemed the exercise of imperial power. An abundance of earlier examples of u.s. regional projects can be found in Latin America, East Asia, and Europe. In each area representatives of the American state established explicitly colonial administrations as well as exercised informal control through proconsuls, economic and military aid programs, covert operations, and diplomatic carrots and sticks. Though boasting no colonial service, u.s. officials have practiced the art of pacification and administration and struck bargains with local collaborators—all with an eye to that most imperial of aims, making particular people and regions directly responsive to the wishes of a distant power. All these activities have gone forward under the cover of a set of rationales that neatly echo justifications for earlier imperial enterprises. We know empire by its claims to uplift others, respond to duty, advance progress, and secure advantage—and by its travails, not least the local resistance that it generates, the brutality that gives the lie to benevolence, and the rising costs that it imposes on the folks at home.

Champions of the militant neoliberal position (described in chapter 8) have embraced empire as a sign of national greatness and badge of national pride. They ask Americans to shoulder the imperial role and with it accept the unembarrassed exercise of u.s. power. Conquest and pacification, they contend, played a central role in establishing the u.s. position in the world; the imperial patterns that have emerged in sharp relief over the last several decades are an extension of the nation's past experience and arise from the same democratic, reformist wellsprings. They insist that empire in its "Anglophone" variant has made the world a safer, more prosperous, and enlightened place.[2] What Britain began to do to improve the lot of humankind, Americans are obliged to continue.

Those making this unabashed case for empire stand sharply, even self-consciously at odds with a prominent anti-imperial strain of thought. It has defined the overarching u.s. mission in the world in terms of a genuine, consistent commitment to freedom and self-determination. Proponents of this position have held that "imperial" behavior, which blurs the distinction between the United States and traditional expansionist, self-aggrandizing powers, is simply un-American. This opposition to empire first appeared in the contest for independence with Britain. It reappeared as sharp criticism of u.s. leaders who embarked on a war with Mexico in the late 1840s and who seized the Philippines at the turn of the century. In this last case the McKinley administration found itself on the defensive as a colonial war, denounced by critics as overtly and violently imperial, divided Republicans and rallied Democrats. The solution was to bring the fighting to a quick end by making concessions to leading Filipinos in the resistance. The opposition to empire persisted, turning postwar Americans against involvement in World War I on the grounds that u.s. soldiers had fought and died not for a better, freer world but to save the British Empire and make money for bankers and arms manufacturers. Those same fears of democracy's betrayal in a world of imperial rivalry evoked a burst of opposition to deepening u.s. involvement in the European conflict in 1940 and 1941. In the eyes of critics in the late 1960s the struggle in Vietnam seemed yet another instance of the country losing sight of its liberating mission. So central was the anti-imperial theme that even advocates of greater international involvement had to assimilate it into their case for action. German *imperial* expansion twice justified sending u.s. forces into European wars. Once more during the Cold War policymakers and pundits took a stand against a Soviet system built on the old-style territorial empire of the czars and aspiring to an ideological empire that was global in scope.

This tension between imperial aspirations and anti-imperial traditions has carried into current policy controversies. A range of critics today invoke empire in their attack on the troubled occupation of Iraq and the hubris of the Bush administration. They give voice to long-standing fears about the United States falling prey to empire and in the bargain betraying its historical role as a proponent of freedom and foe of militarism. What's wrong with empire? Patrick Buchanan asked rhetorically in 2002 amid the debate over "regime change" in Iraq. "Only this. It is a century too late. Jefferson's idea, that 'all just powers come from the consent of the governed,' and Wilson's idea of the self-determination of peoples have taken root in the souls of men."[3] Anti-imperial arguments issue from a second set of critics operating within the time-tested realist framework. Though preoccupied primarily with the practical difficulties raised by imperial projects (especially the gap between sweeping aspirations and limited means), these commentators factor into their calculations the power of ideological traditions to curb u.s. global ambitions. Empire may, they recognize, confront the country with a political taboo fatal to long-term support.

The real problem with empire as a label is not that it clashes with a central strand in the dominant American self-conception or even that it implies an overreaching policy. Rather, empire does not suffice. It evokes a picture of colonies and spheres of influence that falls well short of describing the u.s. position. Empire is appropriate for ancient Rome, imperial China at its height, the Ottomans, or Victorian Britain but fails to fully capture the impressive reach of the United States in its post-1945 ascendancy. Of these comparisons, Britain may come closest. But even London's exercise of international influence was constrained by its relatively limited economic resources. The British economy accounted for only 9 percent of global GDP in 1870 (far short of the astounding u.s. figure of 27 percent in 1950 and 22 percent as late as 1998).[4] In contrast to the u.s. case, British strategists faced a growing crowd of competing powers, thus making alliance building indispensable to security. And British leaders had to work within the constraints that the technology of the time (communications, transport, production, and warfare) imposed on its direct and indirect influence. U.S. policymakers have enjoyed considerably greater leeway thanks to a century of unmatched technological innovation and a half century of sustained spending on a technologically advanced military force.

Three features of the u.s. case stand out and together suggest that empire fails to capture the historically unprecedented geographical scope and depth of u.s. influence. Most obviously the u.s. dominance is reflected in its potent political and military power with a long record of using it to bend major powers and even entire regions to its will. In the realm of great-power politics, the American state mobilized to help the Soviets crush Germany and to overwhelm Japan, and it applied pressure until the Soviet Union retreated from its forward position in Europe and then imploded. No longer was the United States checked by rivals of even roughly comparable destructive power. In recent years the major developed countries a rung below the United States have figured for the most part as allies, with Britain linked especially closely. Russia, which has struggled to remain in the second tier of states, and China, which has gained membership in that second tier, have an ambiguous relationship with the Washington—neither allies nor open antagonists. Beyond this now unmatched military might, policymakers have had at hand an arsenal jam-packed with tools that provided alternatives to brute force.

The u.s. impact on the developing world was no less dramatic: Washington demonstrated time and again the capacity to blunt and in places break radical movements and governments. Repeated interventions had a kind of "demonstration effect" that by the 1970s and 1980s served strong notice on those considering defiance of u.s. preferences. "Bad actors" that survived u.s. pressure—such as North Korea, Vietnam, and Cuba—paid a high price. The more predictable fate was not to survive at all. No surprise that many leaders in the developing world thought twice about challenging Washington and gave instead serious consideration to prudent accommodation. As the century drew to a close, accommodation meant accepting the international free-trade regime designed and backed by the United States and the resulting constraints on development choices.

Reinforcing conventional American power was the u.s. model of modernity that has spawned dreams of abundance and opportunity around the globe. This modernity first became evident at the turn of the century. The fluidity and inventiveness of the u.s. economic system provided the material basis for the first modern, mass consumer society. Consumer patterns that gathered force in the United States during the first global age began to spread to Europe and even the major metropolises of the developing world. By the 1920s the export of u.s. goods and the ideals were igniting alarm as well as envy and enthusiasm abroad. The advance of u.s.-inspired consumer culture picked up speed after World War II. Mickey Mouse, Levis, pop music, Hollywood films, and TV programming exercised enormous appeal. By the beginning of the twenty-first century so widely had elements of the u.s. consumer model spread that it was difficult to tell where the original ended and the translation began. Children traveling in the United States for the first time remarked in wonder on discovering that even Americans had McDonald's outlets!

The Case for "Hegemony"

Combined military-political and economic-cultural power (what some have called hard and soft power) have widely if not universally established u.s. legitimacy as a global leader. That legitimacy is tacit and ad hoc yet far reaching as well. At its heart are values shared with other peoples and a confidence in the dominant power's fairness. Not only have Americans insistently claimed that their values were universal and their leadership in defending and advancing them indispensable, but also and more to the point those claims have often been embraced internationally as appropriate or at least acquiesced in as the most attractive of the available options. Western European center-right leaders assumed the role of junior partners in order to hasten recovery after World War II, contain their domestic challengers on the Left, and safeguard themselves from Soviet pressure. To take another case, China's Communist leaders have over the last several decades set aside their party's long-standing resistance to u.s. interference in the region in return for access to u.s. capital and consumer markets, technology, and university classrooms—all critical to advancing their ambitious development strategy. Thanks to the range of benefits it can dispense, the United States has held sway to a notable degree through persuasion rather than brute force—or (as Machiavelli memorably put it) through love rather than fear, attraction rather than conquest. In securing that love much depends on a power's ability to frame its goals and realize them in ways that minimize resentment and offset the perceived costs of cooperation.[5]

American legitimacy is reflected in the international regime (norms and institutions) that u.s. leaders have built and maintained not only by force but through international discussion and even example. Wedding conventional great power to a strong nationalist creed and a widely admired and demonstrably successful developmental model gave the United States the basis for setting international rules and creating international organizations. Hints of a u.s. commitment to regime building began to appear at the start of the twentieth century and blossomed amid Wilson's planning for the Paris peace conference. It revived with new intensity after World War II. Over the last half century, u.s. vision, generosity, and leadership have done much to shape the global order. The fingerprints of the United States are everywhere. Washington promoted European integration at its fragile start as well as Japan's recovery from crushing defeat. Major international institutions such as the United Nations, the World Bank, and the International Monetary Fund exist as a result of u.s. initiative and support. The same can be said for the worldwide free trade system, the elevation of human rights to international prominence, and the precedent of holding leaders responsible for what have become widely endorsed notions of genocide and crimes against humanity.

The fitting term for a state-wielding power and influence on such a broad scale is not "empire" but "hegemon." Derived from the ancient Greek designation for a leader of a federation of states, the term has come into wide if loose usage over the last several decades to characterize the role great powers can play beyond merely exercising force or promoting narrowly self-interested goals. In one sense the hegemon supplies public goods, for example, by creating conditions conducive to security and prosperity for all within its system. In a second sense associated with the Italian political theorist Antonio Gramsci, the hegemon associates itself with or even inculcates values or norms with broad appeal, such as protecting human welfare or advancing social justice. Taken together, these two notions suggest that hegemony involves both rich material and institutional resources as the prerequisite for exercising international influence and a legitimizing ideology to elicit cooperation from others. The reward for the hegemon comes in securing international consent or at least acquiescence to what might otherwise require coercion with its immediate costs and long-term possibilities for creating a unified opposition. Hegemonic states also secure a side benefit at home: international dominance successfully exercised can create a presumption of the role being right or inevitable, with the result that popular support is easier to secure, domestic claims on resources are deferred, and social values are reshaped to the benefit of elites invested in hegemony politically or economically.

The hegemonic position that Americans carved out for themselves—overwhelming preponderance stretching around the globe—was rooted in the steady accretion of U.S. power. As we have seen, Americans laid the foundations for their hegemony in the course of the nineteenth century. By putting in place the material, ideological, and institutional prerequisites, they readied themselves for making a claim as the paramount global power. In a mere three generations they made good on that claim. By 1945 and the purging of the ranks of the great powers, Americans were on the brink of hegemony. The Cold War spurred an already preeminent United States to greater activity. The collapse of European and Russian socialism in 1989–91 left the U.S. state the unchallenged head of a coherent global system. Americans could claim the world's largest economy, far-reaching political influence over others, an unmatched military prowess, the most widely admired model for social mobility and technological innovation, and the knack for generating worldwide cultural trends. If ever the term "hegemony" was appropriately applied, it is to what the United States became in the latter half of the twentieth century and now remains. To equate "hegemony" with "empire" or use them interchangeably is to obscure the significance of this recent unprecedented, pervasive U.S. role all around the world.

CONFRONTING THE FUTURE

How durable is the astonishing hegemony that Americans now enjoy? How long can we expect to see persist the combination of strengths that made the U.S. ascendancy possible? We might wish a future of boundless opportunities in which the wondrous national achievements of the past endlessly repeat themselves. But equally possible is an erosion of the U.S. position in the world playing out in a downward spiral of deteriorating national morale and diminishing material power. History suggests taking the pessimistic scenario seriously. As this account has shown, U.S. ascendancy arose from a long and often fortuitous historical process. What past processes created future forces can destroy.

The Problem of Decline

While prudence might suggest at least contemplating the possibility of decline, such an exercise is not likely to become a national pastime. One obstacle is the very nature of hegemony. The influence of the hegemon is pervasive and thus difficult to pin down. U.S. hegemony is hard to understand and discuss, not to mention manage, because it is everywhere. The task is rendered all the more formidable by a u.s. public and large segments of the political elite that know little of the broader world and are largely oblivious to the historical and cultural forces that have shaped it. How much more difficult to grasp the limits of hegemony if the critical context is missing. The result is a hardy national complacence. Embedded in a world that they have helped form, Americans find it is easy to take as predestined what is in fact created and to assume eternal what is in fact perishable.

The long reach and overwhelming strength of the hegemon at the moment may hide from observers the essential fragility of that position. Authority exercised at many points and in multiple ways gives the United States deep influence (with one area reinforcing another), but it also creates a wide range of vulnerabilities. What comes together in a virtuous cycle can also fly apart as weakening in one element spreads to the others. Imagine economic adversity combining with popular disaffection over costly overseas entanglements to set off a crisis in nationalist faith. Could a country divided over its identity and thus fundamental common goals mobilize the necessary domestic support to sustain a coherent, consistent foreign policy that is indispensable for a hegemon? A rising chorus of criticism abroad no less than at home might only deepen the u.s. crisis of confidence and further hobble u.s. policymakers.

Americans bent on considering decline confront an enduring if unpleasant paradox inherent in the exercise of power. A hegemon can intervene to shape developments around the world, but the train of events thus set in motion is bound to yield unpredictable outcomes. The broader the reach, the wider the array of unwelcome results. Instances from the realm of "soft" economic and cultural power tend to be less threatening. Consider the free-market model, which Washington promoted in both western Europe and East Asia. To the surprise and irritation of some American observers, the outcome in those two regions—welfare capitalism and state-directed capitalism—bears a strong but hardly full resemblance to the economic practices promoted by the United States and gives rise to sometimes distinctly divergent preferences and interregional friction. Examples from the realm of "hard" conventional power highlight considerably more dire consequences flowing from the exercise of hegemony. Blowback, an apt term for the unanticipated but damaging consequences of blatant intervention in the affairs of other peoples, has been a pronounced feature of u.s. foreign relations over the past half century. Examples of adverse effects flowing from u.s. intervention abound from South Korea to Cuba to South Vietnam to Iran and, of course, most recently Afghanistan and Iraq.

Perhaps most challenging of all, thinking about decline involves accepting the importance of that insubstantial thing called legitimacy. The exercise of hegemony ultimately depends on securing an international seal of acceptance. A persistent, blatant failure to attend to collective welfare can cause peoples all around the world to withdraw the approval they have accorded u.s. leadership or at least to end their acquiescence. The resulting disaffection would leave the United States more isolated and raise the direct costs of playing a hegemonic role. If those costs rise, so too will the domestic tensions over how to absorb them and win back international support. As disagreements at home sharpen and u.s. policymakers scramble to devise fallback positions, resources and popular support can dribble away decade by decade.

The Neoliberal Straitjacket

Nowhere is the neglect of legitimacy more evident than in the determination by u.s. policymakers over the last decade and a half to follow a marketplace vision so narrow that they could deal only fleetingly, hesitantly, and intermittently with a broad, gradually building set of global problems. From human inequality to environmental degradation, these problems have the potential to cause serious, far-reaching mischief. An awareness of these problems had become widespread in the course of the 1990s and fed rising hostility to the prevailing global economic arrangements so evident in the streets of Seattle in November 1999. A fixation on free trade and investment, so the critics claimed, put in question the air Americans breathed, the climate they lived with, the microbes they absorbed, the networks of commerce and confidence they depended on for a livelihood, even the moral responsibility they bore for needless suffering within the human family. The neoliberal response was a mix of defensiveness, avoidance, and hesitant efforts on the margin. In the main neoliberals buried their heads in the sand, hoping that either markets would eventually correct the world's woes or that those woes were not salient to u.s. security and welfare.

The most blatant assault on the neoliberal promise of prosperity was the persistence at the beginning of the new millennium of that old human enemy, hunger and disease. Hunger alone ravaged the lives of some 800 million people (more than a tenth of humanity) and harvested 6 million children a year. Another 6 million died annually from preventable diseases, with malnutrition as a major contributory cause. Extreme poverty, which meant trying to survive on a dollar a day, defined the lives of over a billion people according to the World Bank. This incidence of poverty—one in six people around the world—persisted despite the spectacular rise in living standards in many regions. An army of diseases, some easily preventable or treatable, continued to stalk and fell large parts of the human population. In sub-Saharan Africa AIDS ate away at the sinew of societies and dramatically reduced life spans. The spread of the epidemic to Asia threatened human misery and social instability on a mind-numbing scale. The neoliberal response to these problems was necessarily hesitant. Having the state provide minimum subsistence and basic health care clashed with an insistence on keeping government safely small and constrained. But relying on markets rather than the state seemed a dubious strategy. Markets have no intrinsic incentives to save the lives of people without resources.

A demographic explosion has created intense population pressures threatening neoliberal hopes on a second front. Between 1800 and 1900 world population increased by 50 percent—from 1 to 1.5 billion. Then between 1900 and 1960 it doubled, reaching 3 billion. By 1999 the number had doubled again to 6 billion, with three-quarters of the increase occurring in the developing world. In country after country, population growth created a vicious cycle. An ever-larger number of people negated the gains of economic growth. Moreover, more people added to the pressure on limited land in densely settled countrysides. As a consequence, environmental conditions deteriorated and the discontent of the poor fed civil unrest, itself harmful to production and investment and the provision of government services such as health care and education on which future stability and prosperity depended. There are hopeful signs of a demographic turnaround. It began in the 1960s in the developed world as well as parts of the developing world and recently started to slow population increases in such high-growth regions as sub-Saharan Africa, Central America, and South Asia. But the momentum of a growing population is great and, without intensified birth control, is likely to carry the world to a peak currently estimated at 9.2 billion people by 2075, a total half again as high as today's.[6] Until that point and probably beyond, the challenge to care adequately for so many people will almost certainly remain daunting. To judge from past performances, market mechanisms are not panaceas; they may indeed encourage larger, not smaller families, may aggravate income inequalities and social strains, and thus may make the transition to lower birthrates more difficult to reach.

Of all the threats to a neoliberal world, the most serious and systemic may be environmental degradation. It is the product of rising levels of consumption made possible by fossil fuels and pushed higher still by a world population that was four times larger at the end of the twentieth century than at the start. Poor people devouring marginal land and locally available fuel supplies carried some responsibility, but the rich with their gargantuan appetite for goods bore greater blame. The waste that was the natural byproduct of more goods and more people put growing pressures on the earth. Much of the impact was localized, yet the cumulative and generalized pressure on land, air, and water made the twentieth century a watershed in human history. The stress showed up in many ways—from global warming and rising sea levels, to climate swings, to species and tropical forest losses, to depletion of freshwater sources, to the deterioration of oceans and seas. Humans (in the words of one respected environmental historian) had "begun to play dice with the planet, without knowing all the rules of the game."[7] Even though attitudes toward the environment have undergone a revolution, especially in the developed world, environmental problems have mounted in severity and breadth.

The relentlessly increasing environmental stress on the earth has posed a threat that is not easily measured by the market model. The favorite yardstick is GDP, which counts the output of goods and services that enter the market but not their environmental effects. To get beyond the simple arithmetic of market transactions, an alternative "social" GDP has gained converts. It includes environmental damage (for example, the loss of scarce resources and the damage to air quality) associated with production, the adverse societal impact of economic activity (for example, the local costs in unemployment and neighborhood breakdown of a factory leaving a city for a lower-wage region), and even the contributions of unpaid workers such as child-care providers and hospital volunteers to overall societal well-being. One rough estimate of U.S. economic performance that incorporated these ecological and social costs of growth concluded that GDP between 1969 and 1995 registered a steady decline, a jarring contrast to the overall rise recorded by conventional GDP calculations.[8]

The market model cannot easily come to terms with the environmental crisis for a second reason: the long time frame in which any remediation will have to work. A concerted effort at cleaning up industrial pollutants might require several decades. Dealing with desertification and ozone-layer depletion could well extend over a century. Soil erosion and tropical deforestation might require twice as long to reverse. And efforts to turn back global warming might reach over a thousand years before achieving significant results. Effective solutions involve concerted action over generations on multiple fronts. Market mechanisms can play a role but within a grand strategy that subordinates the transactions between buyers and sellers to some broad, long-term politically determined project. "States plus markets" seems the most promising and perhaps the only effective formula.

The widening gap in wealth and welfare among the world's peoples, a striking feature of the neoliberal order, has posed yet another challenge. While virtually everyone has benefited to some degree from the rising tide of international economic activity, the benefits overwhelmingly have gone to those already well off. The resulting inequalities have appeared along three different dimensions. First, the developing world fell behind the developed. Overall by 1993, the richest fifth of the planet's population received sixty times the income of the poorest fifth. That figure was up from thirty times in 1960, and the gap continued to widen during the 1990s. Second, women have lagged behind men, a trend that is particularly serious in the developing world where the spread of free markets has opened up opportunities to men that women often cannot exploit for want of literacy, legal rights, access to capital, and socially sanctioned access to public space. The third dimension of inequality appears within countries in both the developed and the developing worlds. The widening income gap between the top fifth and the bottom fifth of the population afflicts the United States (as noted above) and even more dramatically poorer countries such as Brazil, Guatemala, and China. Everywhere groups without capital and skills favored by the marketplace and with strong local attachments that rule out relocation to more prosperous places have fallen behind. Notable among these are peasants who still constitute over half the population of Africa and Asia, industrial workers in the proliferating rust belts of the developed world, and the urban poor everywhere.

Finally, the nuclear cloud, which had faded from view with the end of the Cold War and the collapse of the Soviet Union, has returned in a new round of proliferation and rising fear of nuclear weapons and other weapons of mass destruction. The genie uncorked in 1945 has traveled widely, abetted by the global trade in nuclear technology, fuel, and expertise. The demand has been especially strong in recent decades in the Middle East, South Asia, and East Asia. A determination to keep up with regional rivals and to deter the United

States has driven weapons projects, most notably in Iran, Iraq, Pakistan, India, and North Korea. Some forty states in all have developed peaceful nuclear facilities that offer a basis for creating nuclear arsenals.[9] With a flourishing international black market facilitating proliferation, no one expects free-market solutions to resolve the underlying pressures that have made nuclear weapons such a critical asset. Nor are market solutions likely equal to the challenging and costly task of cleaning up the residue of U.S. and Soviet nuclear programs, closing down production facilities, and addressing contamination resulting from lax standards. The total costs may run at least as high as the initial production costs.

States claiming hegemony have a special obligation of stewardship. The greater their claim, the greater their obligation to promote global prosperity and safety in ways that are in fact effective and are perceived as such. By neglecting its responsibilities with regard to these most critical of human problems, the United States runs the risk of losing legitimacy as architect and keeper of global order. Poll after poll over the last several years reveals world-wide suspicion and opposition to U.S. policy, even among long-time allies. This aversion has in turn prompted greater critical scrutiny of U.S. culture and society and ultimately basic questions about the worthiness of the United States to lead.

Choices

While U.S. hegemony entails perplexities and burdens, an abandonment of hegemony may carry risks. Diminished U.S. leadership could prove dangerously disruptive of the international system and imperil the well-being of peoples everywhere, Americans included. A U.S. retreat could undermine an international economy that has generated impressive global abundance and peace beneficial to many. Simply consider the resources now available today (an annual worldwide output of $30 trillion at the end of the twentieth century) compared to fifty years earlier when it was a tenth that figure. Imagine what this amazing, unprecedented leap in global productivity has meant to health and welfare in all lands. Without U.S. leadership, so the defenders of hegemony claim, these gains might well have been limited, even nonexistent. A future of diminished abundance might prove distinctly unpleasant: greater discord among states and peoples leading to rising cultural intolerance, flaring nationalist fervor and rivalry, deepening international divisions, and fraying economic ties that would slow growth and press down longevity and health in wide swaths of the human population. This would be a world of narrower horizons, fewer choices, and less interaction among peoples and cultures. It would also be a world with diminished capacity for addressing mounting global problems.

Advocates for maintaining U.S. dominance along current neoliberal lines hold the ideological high ground. The predominant version of American nationalism took a distinctly activist turn in the course of the twentieth century. From the 1890s to the 1920s the notion of the United States as a dynamic republic with the vision and energy to manage the world's affairs began to come into its own. Republicans dedicated to an assertive policy along a broad front contributed to this shift in thinking. So too did Woodrow Wilson with his fervent support for the ideal of a progressive international society. In 1941 Henry Luce blended this set of nationalist ideas in his vision of an American century marked by the advance of political freedom, unhampered commerce, and general economic abundance. The most activist U.S. leaders after World War II drew from this creed, as appealing to visionary Wilsonians such as Harry Truman as to corporate-minded Republicans such as Ronald Reagan and the younger Bush. Over the past half century it has become an orthodoxy so potent in its appeal that challengers risk exile from membership in the foreign policy establishment and exclusion from government posts. Such is the allegiance commanded by the one true faith. Or as John Adams observed pungently, "Power always thinks it has a great Soul, and vast Views."[10]

Even so, a good case can be made for a U.S. retreat from hegemony and toward a more modest and sustainable role in the world. A searching critique has no reason to linger on matters of style, particularly such easy targets as a policy governed by restless unilateralism or simplistic assumptions. Such a critique should instead turn to the hegemonic project itself.

The place to begin a critical evaluation is with the tendency of the champions of hegemony to oversell the product. They point to its historical achievements to the neglect of the costs it has imposed on others. The leaders of the United States have managed hegemony with a lamentably heavy hand—with scant respect for human life and scant respect for human diversity. Millions died and many societies suffered profound disruption as a result of the U.S. interventions that dot the pages of this account. To those costs would have to be added an intolerance of views on markets and the state that diverge from U.S. preferences. As a result, U.S. pressure has in some cases blocked or disrupted socioeconomic and political experiments favored by others, especially in Latin America, Africa, and the Middle East. In other cases, an insistence on an American way has generated tensions with major states such as China or regions such as western Europe with divergent interests and values; that insistence has also strained ties with genuinely international organizations such as the UN. On virtually every front U.S. leaders have left themselves open to charges of hypocrisy — of ignoring if not violating the ideals of democracy and self-determination that they publicly profess.

A look into the future reveals more grounds for doubts about the hegemonic project. Put simply, the time for U.S. hegemony may have passed. As the relative U.S. advantage in economic might and cultural appeal slips, attempts to exercise hegemony may prove increasingly counterproductive, doing more to further undermine than to confirm U.S. dominance. The U.S. economy labors under limits. Persistent structural problems include oil dependency, low domestic savings, and deep trade and federal budget deficits. The core U.S. cultural model — a faith in unending corporate-driven growth and the unending delights of consumerism — may be fading at least in the developed world. Western Europe and Japan have both drawn alongside the United States in their technological capacity, their income levels, their capital resources, and the depth and integration of their home markets. They need no longer look to the United States as a model in any of these areas. The consumer revolution led by Americans may have at least in these two regions run its course. Rising per capita income beyond a point (in the range of $15,000 in a fair sampling of countries recently surveyed) seems to produce no greater individual satisfaction while imposing costs captured not by conventional GDP data but by social GDP estimates.[11]

In military affairs, the United States has retained, even increased, its dominance. But to what end? Its massive nuclear stockpile can be used only at the risk of profound and widespread moral revulsion and in some circumstances of devastating counterstrikes. Its high-tech forces may be the wonder of the world. But they are effective only against the most peripheral and isolated of states (in what one observer has dismissed as "theatrical micromilitarism"), and they have limited capacity to rebuild what they have destroyed.[12] The exercise of military might has proven a poor substitute for the intricacies of diplomatic negotiation, the trade-offs indispensable to international comity, and the long-term commitment of resources to economic development and human welfare.

Finally, hegemony may hurt the hegemon. Evidence can be found in the privileging of corporate interests harmful to popular welfare, a fixation with military power that amounts to a national obsession, an increasingly infantilized and inert public, and the rise of an imperial presidency antithetical to genuine democracy. These trends validate a sharply critical view of foreign adventures that prevailed during the country's first century. Proponents of republicanism claimed that crusades, even crusades conducted in the name of freedom, threatened freedom at home. The history of republican experiments across history showed that foreign entanglements and adventures created dangerous concentrations of political power within and undermined the very civic virtues on which the survival of any republic depended. Vindicating this republican fear is the rise of the imperial president and the concomitant atrophy of the democratic process.

While most Americans today may not see hegemony through this anxious republican lens, many have voiced their discontent with the outward thrust of u.s. policy. Some express it in frustration and chagrin directed not against u.s. leaders but against a seemingly ungrateful, unyielding, dangerous world and call for scaling back international commitments. The most restive have contended that a more isolated, less burdened America would be better off—less vulnerable to attack, less dependent on fickle friends, less likely to get entangled in distant quarrels, and more secure in its homeland and its domestic liberties. Others refuse to go this far and instead put the blame squarely on u.s. leaders—political and corporate—whose free-market, environmental, and human rights policies have betrayed values as important at home as in the international community. Taken together, these critical reactions suggest a broad-based skepticism about hegemony. But the critics may be so fundamentally divided philosophically, politically, regionally, and socially that they cannot cobble together a common program to serve as an alternative to hegemony.

A retreat from hegemony need not lead to isolationism. This myth about the nature of u.s. foreign relations in the past, which was constructed in the first place for the very purpose of justifying u.s. dominance, is likely to figure prominently in any defense of the status quo. But the notion of isolation is flawed as history and as a source of lessons. Today as earlier, the United States has a major stake in a productive, peaceful, and just global society. By extension, the United States has an obligation rooted in self-interest if not calculations of altruism and long-term human welfare to help mobilize a collective international response to the problems generated by that society. A retreat implies that the United States would act in world affairs not as *the* leader but as *a* leader, perhaps in some circumstances the first among equals. Engaging in a genuinely collaborative relationship with other states and taking international institutions and norms seriously may hold out the best hope of extending the considerable achievements of the previous fifty years and in the bargain maintaining u.s. influence and advancing u.s. well-being.

The historical case for the efficacy of collaboration is compelling. The u.s. role after World War I calmed, for a time at least, the arms race, gave the Europeans a chance to sort out their monetary tangle, and sustained the turn-of-the-century drive to create humane standards of international conduct. The post–World War II record is even more striking. The achievements in setting norms (such as outlawing genocide), rehabilitating defeated Germany and Japan, and creating a framework for global prosperity were the result of collaboration richly repaid in international support and respect, not to mention enhanced u.s. security. This collaborative element helped not only to distinguish the u.s. from the Soviet side during the Cold War, but also to determine the outcome of a competition that was as much about systems and values as military might. International cooperation is not an illusion; it yields results far better than a course defined by narrow self-interest and pursued by brute force.

Whatever the attractions of a more modest, collaborative internationalism, winning broad acceptance of such an approach faces serious difficulties. It requires that Americans think about their role in the world in a fresh, genuinely global way quite distinct from the cautious opportunism familiar from the first u.s. century and the rising assertiveness that has marked recent decades. It also requires a sensitivity to the intricacies of the global system and the cultural diversity of its parts. That sensitivity will not come easily to today's body politic, which features a disengaged, ill-schooled public and a political class beholden to interest groups and trapped by shallow rhetoric and narrow, short-term calculations. Above all, the middle way offers nothing heroic to a country of individualists that may be dependent on civic nationalism as one of the few sources of collective identity. Indeed, calls for serious, long-term support for economic development programs, genuine respect for international norms, and tolerance for regional diversity collide with prevailing nationalist and neoliberal notions, which continue to inspire bold dreams of global transformation under the American aegis and in the American image. A retreat from hegemony would require a lot: a more cosmopolitan understanding of other cultures, a more sophisticated grasp of u.s. limits, a genuinely democratic electoral system responsive to popular preferences, and a better informed electorate able to think through those preferences. The fate of the current ascendancy with its hegemonic dimensions may well hang on how Americans measure up to these high standards and how rapidly structural problems eat away at the foundations of our hegemony. What the next page of the national story has to say may depend on how well we take into account the possibilities and constraints created by a history of burgeoning state power, strong nationalism, and intrusive global forces.

NOTES

INTRODUCTION

1. National Security Council Study 68, in U.S. Department of State, *Foreign Relations of the United States, 1950*, vol. 1 (Washington, D.C.: U.S. Government Printing Office, 1977), 238. American ascendancy, a notion long integral to this project and a term featured in my title, also appears in the subtitle of Charles S. Maier, *Among Empires: American Ascendancy and Its Predecessors* (Cambridge, Mass.: Harvard University Press, 2006), announced and published just as this work was going to press. The basic concerns of the two volumes are sufficiently distinct that readers should not confuse them. Maier examines the U.S. case within a comparative imperial framework to determine if the United States is an empire, whereas my interest is in tracing how the United States won and sustained its dominance.

2. Data from Angus Maddison, *The World Economy: A Millennial Perspective* (Paris: Development Centre of the Organisation for Economic Co-operation and Development, 2001), 135.

CHAPTER 1

1. See J. Valerie Fifer, *American Progress: The Growth of the Transport, Tourist, and Information Industries in the Nineteenth-Century West* (Chester, Conn.: Globe/Pequot Press, 1988), 200–204, for a discussion of the Crofutt-Gast collaboration.

2. Quoted in Brian W. Dippie, "The Moving Finger Writes: Western Art and the Dynamics of Change," in *Discovered Lands, Invented Pasts: Transforming Visions of the American West*, ed. Jules David Prown et al. (New Haven, Conn.: Yale University Press, 1992), 97.

3. Population figures from Angus Maddison, *The World Economy: A Millennial Perspective* (Paris: Development Centre of the Organisation for Economic Co-operation and Development, 2001), 250.

4. Data from Alan Taylor, *American Colonies* (New York: Viking, 2001), 44, 120, 306–7, 368.

5. This section builds on the treatment in my *Ideology and U.S. Foreign Policy* (New Haven, Conn.: Yale University Press, 1987), 52–58.

6. Quotes from Taylor, *American Colonies*, 195 (Pequot in 1637); and Albert K. Weinberg, *Manifest Destiny: A Study of Nationalist Expansionism in American History* (Baltimore: Johns Hopkins Press, 1935), 83 (Georgia in 1830).

7. Jefferson, January 1809, quoted in Reginald Horsman, "American Indian Policy in the Old Northwest, 1783–1812," *William and Mary Quarterly*, 3rd ser., 18 (January 1961): 52.

8. Jackson quotes from his annual message to Congress, 6 December 1830, in *A Compilation of the Messages and Papers of the Presidents, 1789–1897*, comp. James D. Richardson, 10 vols. (Washington, D.C.: U.S. Government Printing Office, 1896–99), 2:521, 522.

9. Quote from Chief Joseph's account, "An Indian's View of Indian Affairs," *North American Review* 128 (April 1879): 432–33.

10. For a recent careful reconstruction, see Jeffrey Ostler, *The Plains Sioux and U.S. Colonialism from Louis and Clark to Wounded Knee* (Cambridge, U.K.: Cambridge University Press, 2004), chaps. 14–15. Orders by General Nelson Miles quoted on p. 334.

11. Data from Taylor, *American Colonies*, 45 (1800); and John D. Daniels, "The Indian Population of North America in 1492," *William and Mary Quarterly*, 3rd ser., 49 (April 1992): 298–320.

12. Quote from Ruth Miller Elson, *Guardians of Tradition: American Schoolbooks of the Nineteenth Century* (Lincoln: University of Nebraska Press, 1964), 81.

13. This now venerable theme is associated with Samuel Flagg Bemis, *A Diplomatic History of the United States*, 4th ed. (New York: Holt, 1955).

14. Palmerston comment in December 1857, quoted in Kenneth Bourne, *Britain and the Balance of Power in North America, 1815–1908* (Berkeley: University of California Press, 1967), 203.

15. Quote from Robert V. Remini, *Andrew Jackson and the Course of American Empire, 1767–1821* (New York: Harper and Row, 1977), 383–84.

16. George Washington, "Farewell Address," 17 September 1796, in *Writings of George Washington*, 39 vols. (Washington, D.C.: U.S. Government Printing Office, 1931–44), 35:234.

17. Olney to U.S. ambassador in London, Thomas F. Bayard, 20 July 1895, in U.S. Department of State, *Papers Relating to the Foreign Relations of the United States, 1895*, part 1 (Washington, D.C.: Government Printing Office, 1896), 558.

18. Maddison, *World Economy*, 241.

19. Data from Maddison, *World Economy*, 185; and Paul Bairoch, "International Industrialization Levels from 1750 to 1980," *Journal of European Economic History*, 11 (Fall 1982): 275, 284.

20. Maddison, *World Economy*, 126, 186, 262. Growth at a 1 percent annual pace yields over twenty years an overall economic expansion of 22 percent. Growth at 3 percent, seemingly a small difference, yields a substantially higher jump of 81 percent.

21. Harold Brydges (pseud. for James Howard Bridge), *Uncle Sam at Home* (New York: Henry Holt, 1888), 49 ("vast hive") and 52 ("advanced position"); H. G. Wells, *The Future of America* (1906; repr., New York: Arno Press, 1974), 51–52; Charles Wagner, *My Impressions of America*, trans. Mary Louise Hendee (French original, 1906; translation, 1906; repr., New York: Arno Press, 1974), 144.

22. Observations probably by Inoue Ryokichi, 1872, in *The Japanese Discovery of America: A Brief History with Documents*, ed. Peter Duus (Boston: Bedford Books, 1997), 195; quote from Yasuo Wakatsuki, "Japanese Emigration to the United States, 1866–1914: A Monograph," *Perspectives in American History* 12 (1979): 433; and comments by Liang and Tan excerpted in *Land without Ghosts: Chinese Impressions of America from the Mid-Nineteenth Century to the Present*, trans. and ed. R. David Arkush and Leo O. Lee (Berkeley: University of California Press, 1989), 88–89, 120.

23. Angus Maddison, *Monitoring the World Economy, 1820–1992* (Paris: Development Centre of the Organisation for Economic Co-operation and Development, 1995), 233.

24. William F. Channing quoted in David Hochfelder, "The Communications Revolution and Popular Culture," in *A Companion to 19th-Century America*, ed. William L. Barney (Malden, Mass.: Blackwell, 2001), 309.

25. Quoted in Thomas P. Hughes, *American Genesis: A Century of Invention and Technological Enthusiasm* (New York: Viking, 1989), 14.

26. Maddison, *World Economy*, 361–63.

27. Trade data in Robert E. Lipsey, "U.S. Foreign Trade and the Balance of Payments, 1800–1913," in *The Cambridge Economic History of the United States*, vol. 2: *The Long Nineteenth Century*, ed. Stanley Engerman and Robert E. Gallman (Cambridge, U.K.: Cambridge University Press, 2000), 691. GNP, like GDP, provides the value of all goods and services produced in a given year. GNP goes beyond GDP by including income earned abroad while conversely excluding income earned by foreigners from domestic production. The practical difference between the two terms is usually minimal.

28. Lipsey, "U.S. Foreign Trade and the Balance of Payments," 700–701, 704; and Robert E. Gallman, "Growth and Change in the Long Nineteenth Century," in *Cambridge Economic History of the United States*, 2:50 (on sectoral change within the U.S. economy).

29. Quote from Robert B. Davies, "'Peacefully Working to Conquer the World': The Singer Manufacturing Company in Foreign Markets, 1854–1889," *Business History Review* 43 (Autumn 1969): 319.

30. Maddison, *World Economy*, 35, 250.

31. U.S. Department of Commerce, *Statistical Abstracts of the United States, 1998*

(Washington, D.C.: U.S. Census Bureau, 1999), 11, for numbers of immigrants; U.S. Census Bureau website at <http://www.census.gov/population/www/documen tation/twps0029/tab01.html> (accessed 8 July 2004) for data on foreign-born population; and Maddison, *World Economy*, 128 (for 1870–1913 total), 345 (for total work force).

32. Quote from Philip Taylor, *The Distant Magnet: European Emigration to the U.S.A.* (New York: Harper and Row, 1971), 74.

33. Quotes from Taylor, *Distant Magnet*, 171; Walter D. Kamphoefner, Wolfgang Helbich, and Ulrike Sommer, eds., *News from the Land of Freedom: German Immigrants Write Home*, trans. Susan Carter Vogel (Ithaca, N.Y.: Cornell University Press, 1991), 436 (Dorgathen), 476, 477, and 478 (Kirst), 500 (Dilger).

34. This and the following paragraph draw heavily on the essays in *Cambridge Economic History of the United States*, vol. 2, particularly Gallman, "Growth and Change in the Long Nineteenth Century," 39; Lipsey, "U.S. Foreign Trade and the Balance of Payments, 1800–1913," 698; and Lance E. Davis and Robert J. Cull, "Capital Movements, Markets, and Growth, 1820–1914," 736–37, 740–41, 747, 771, 784–88, 809. See also Maddison, *World Economy*, 99, which puts total U.S. capital invested abroad in 1914 at $3.5 billion (a mere 8 percent of all investments overseas at that time).

35. The treatment through the balance of this section draws, directly at points, from my *Ideology and U.S. Foreign Policy*, chaps. 2–4.

36. John L. O'Sullivan, "The Great Nation of Futurity," *Democratic Review* 6 (November 1839): 426.

37. Quotes from Reginald Horsman, *Race and Manifest Destiny: The Origins of American Racial Anglo-Saxonism* (Cambridge, Mass.: Harvard University Press, 1981), 209 (Busnell), 213 (Houston); and Bram Stoker, *A Glimpse of America* (London: Sampson Low, Marston, 1886), 47–48.

38. Quotes from Arthur Whitaker, *The United States and the Independence of Latin America, 1800–1830* (Baltimore: Johns Hopkins Press, 1941), 183 (John Randolph of Virginia), 188n (Jefferson); John Quincy Adams, *Memoirs of John Quincy Adams*, ed. Charles Francis Adams, 12 vols. (New York: AMS Press, 1970), 5:325; Horsman, *Race and Manifest Destiny*, 217, 241 (Buchanan); and Norman A. Graebner, ed., *Manifest Destiny* (Indianapolis, Ind.: Bobbs-Merrill, 1968), 208 (Whitman).

39. Quotes from Michael H. Hunt, *The Making of a Special Relationship: The United States and China to 1914* (New York: Columbia University Press, 1983), 18 (Caleb Cushing), 34 (geography of 1784).

40. Quoted in Alden T. Vaughn, "From White Man to Redskin: Changing Anglo-American Perceptions of the American Indian," *American Historical Review* 87 (October 1982): 920.

41. Quotes from Elson, *Guardians of Tradition*, 87–88, 97 (white views of 1789 and 1900); and Steven Hahn, *A Nation under Our Feet: Black Political Struggles in the Rural South from Slavery to the Great Migration* (Cambridge, Mass.: Harvard University Press, 2003), 451 (black view).

42. James Phelan quote from 1900 in Roger Daniels, *The Politics of Prejudice: The Anti-Japanese Movement in California and the Struggle for Japanese Exclusion* (Berkeley: University of California Press, 1962), 21; Roosevelt in *The Works of Theodore Roosevelt*, ed. Hermann Hagedorn (New York: C. Scribner's Sons, 1923–26), 14:245.

43. Quotes from John Higham, *Strangers in the Land: Patterns of American Nativism, 1860–1925* (New York: Atheneum, 1965), 142 (Lodge); and Matthew Frye Jacobson, *Barbarian Virtues: The United States Encounters Foreign Peoples at Home and Abroad, 1876–1917* (New York: Hill and Wang, 2000), 62, 198 (Remington, Turner, and James).

44. Thomas Paine, "Common Sense," in *Thomas Paine: Collected Writings*, ed. Eric Foner (New York: Library of America, 1995), 52.

45. Hamilton quotes from "The Federalist No. 11," 24 November 1787 (American system), and from "The Defence No. II" on the Jay treaty, 25 July 1795 (embryo), both in *The Papers of Alexander Hamilton*, ed. Harold C. Syrett et al. (New York: Columbia University Press, 1961–87), 4:346 and 18:498.

46. Thomas Jefferson, *Notes on the State of Virginia*, ed. William Peden (Chapel Hill: University of North Carolina Press, 1995), 175.

47. Madison quoted in Drew R. McCoy, *The Elusive Republic: Political Economy in Jeffersonian America* (Chapel Hill: University of North Carolina Press, 1980), 138.

48. Jefferson quoted in McCoy, *Elusive Republic*, 249.

49. For a summary treatment of Britain's pioneering role as a "military-fiscal state," see P. J. Cain and A. G. Hopkins, *British Imperialism, 1688–2000*, 2nd ed. (Harlow, U.K.: Longman, 2002), 76–81. The phrase is from the full-scale treatment: John Brewer, *The Sinews of Power: War, Money and the English State, 1688–1783* (London: Unwin Hyman, 1989).

CHAPTER 2

1. Montgomery was the chief telegraph operator and executive clerk. To the right of him are two telegraph operators.

2. Quoted in Gerald F. Linderman, *The Mirror of War: American Society and the Spanish-American War* (Ann Arbor: University of Michigan Press, 1974), 29.

3. Christopher Endy, "Travel and World Power: Americans in Europe, 1890–1917," *Diplomatic History* 22 (Fall 1998): 567 (estimates on numbers of travelers), 579 (*New York Times* quote).

4. Beveridge speech from September 1898 in his *The Meaning of the Times* (India-

napolis: Bobbs-Merrill, 1908), 47; Leonard Wood quoted in Matthew Frye Jacobson, *Barbarian Virtues: The United States Encounters Foreign Peoples at Home and Abroad, 1876–1917* (New York: Hill and Wang, 2000), 237; MacArthur comments in 1902 in *American Imperialism and the Philippine Insurrection: Testimony Taken from Hearings on Affairs in the Philippine Islands before the Senate Committee on the Philippines—1902*, ed. Henry F. Graff (Boston: Little, Brown, 1969), 139 (destiny) and 140 (plastic); Wilson writing in October 1900 in *The Papers of Woodrow Wilson*, ed. Arthur S. Link et al., 69 vols. (Princeton, N.J.: Princeton University Press, 1966–94), 12:18 (opening and transformation) and 19 (undeveloped peoples); Theodore Roosevelt in 1902 quoted in Stuart C. Miller, *"Benevolent Assimilation": The American Conquest of the Philippines, 1899–1903* (New Haven, Conn.: Yale University Press, 1982), 251.

5. Quote from *Journal of Commerce* in Walter LaFeber, *The New Empire: An Interpretation of American Expansion, 1860–1898* (Ithaca, N.Y.: Cornell University Press, 1963), 356.

6. Quote from the American Anti-Imperialist League's platform, 18 October 1899, available at Jim Zwick's excellent website titled "Anti-Imperialism in the United States, 1898–1935," <http://www.boondocksnet.com/ai/ailtexts/ailplat.html> (accessed 7 July 2004).

7. Quote from Henry Labouchère's "The Brown Man's Burden," reprinted in *Literary Digest* in February 1899, available online at Zwick's "Anti-Imperialism in the United States, 1898–1935," <http://www.boondocksnet.com//ai/kipling/labouche.html> (accessed 4 September 2004).

8. This paragraph on Twain draws from my essay titled "East Asia in Henry Luce's 'American Century,'" *Diplomatic History* 23 (Spring 1999): 349–51. Quotes from William M. Gibson, "Mark Twain and Howells: Anti-Imperialists," *New England Quarterly*, 15 (December 1947): 444 (October 1900 interview); Twain, "To the Person Sitting in Darkness," *North American Review* 172 (February 1901): 164; and "The War Prayer" in *Mark Twain's Weapons of Satire: Anti-Imperialist Writings on the Philippine-American War*, ed. Jim Zwick (Syracuse, N.Y.: Syracuse University Press, 1992), 156, 160.

9. Quoted phrase from Roosevelt to Silas McBee, 27 August 1907, in *The Letters of Theodore Roosevelt*, ed. Elting E. Morison et al., 8 vols. (Cambridge, Mass.: Harvard University Press, 1951–54), 5:776

10. Quoted in my *The Making of a Special Relationship: The United States and China to 1914* (New York: Columbia University Press, 1983), 209.

11. Quote from Louis A. Pérez Jr., *The War of 1898: The United States and Cuba in History and Historiography* (Chapel Hill: University of North Carolina Press, 1998), 122.

12. Roosevelt's annual message to Congress, 6 December 1904, in *The Works of Theodore Roosevelt: Presidential Addresses and State Papers*, pt. 3 (New York: P. F. Collier and Son, 1905), 176.

13. Quoted in David F. Schmitz, *Thank God They're on Our Side: The United States and Right-Wing Dictatorships, 1921–1965* (Chapel Hill: University of North Carolina Press, 1999), 25.

14. Data from Lance E. Davis and Robert J. Cull, "Capital Movements, Markets, and Growth, 1820–1914," in *The Cambridge Economic History of the United States*, vol. 2: *The Long Nineteenth Century*, ed. Stanley Engerman and Robert E. Gallman (Cambridge, U.K.: Cambridge University Press, 2000), 787.

15. Wilson comment to House, April 1914, quoted in Robert Quirk, *An Affair of Honor: Woodrow Wilson and the Occupation of Veracruz* (Lexington: University of Kentucky Press, 1962), 77.

16. Quotes from Link et al., *Papers of Woodrow Wilson*, 45:551, 557.

17. "American Sympathies in the War," *Literary Digest* 49 (14 November 1914): 939.

18. Quotes from Link et al., *Papers of Woodrow Wilson*, 30:462, 472; 31:458–59 (memo of a half-hour confidential interview by Herbert Bruce Brougham).

19. The phrase is Grand Admiral Alfred von Tirpitz's from *Official German Documents Relating to the World War*, comp. and trans. Carnegie Endowment for International Peace, Division of International Law, 2 vols. (New York: Oxford University Press, 1923), 2:1126.

20. The manuscript of the speech with Wilson's final editing is reproduced in Link et al., *Papers of Woodrow Wilson*, 45:506–17.

21. Wilson quote from speech in Des Moines, Iowa, 6 September 1919, in Link et al., *Papers of Woodrow Wilson*, 63:77.

22. John Maynard Keynes, *The Economic Consequences of the Peace* (New York: Harcourt, Brace and Howe, 1920), 41.

23. Quotes from Erez Manela, "The Wilsonian Moment and the Rise of Anticolonial Nationalism: The Case of Egypt," *Diplomacy and Statecraft* 12 (December 2001): 104 (Egyptian nationalist); and Douglas Little, *American Orientalism: The United States and the Middle East since 1945* (Chapel Hill: University of North Carolina Press, 2002), 160 (Lansing).

24. From the Covenant of the League of Nations, signed at Versailles, 28 June 1919, available on the website for the Avalon Project at the Yale Law School, <http://www.yale.edu/lawweb/avalon/leagcov.htm> (accessed 3 August 2004).

25. Wilson quote from Thomas J. Knock, *To End All Wars: Woodrow Wilson and the Quest for a New World Order* (Princeton, N.J.: Princeton University Press, 1992), 264.

26. Lord Robert Cecil quoted in David Dimbleby and David Reynolds, *An Ocean Apart: The Relationship between Britain and America in the Twentieth Century* (New York: Random House, 1988), 84.

27. On government employees (total and under the merit system): U.S. Bureau of the Census, *Historical Statistics of the United States: Colonial Times to 1970* (Washington, D.C.: U.S. Government Printing Office, 1975), 1102–3; and Stephen Skowronek, *Building a New American State: The Expansion of National Administrative Capacities, 1877–1920* (Cambridge, U.K.: Cambridge University Press, 1982), 49, 210. On comparative government expenditures, see Angus Maddison, *The World Economy: A Millennial Perspective* (Paris: Development Centre of the Organisation for Economic Co-operation and Development, 2001), 178, 184; U.S. Bureau of the Census, *Historical Statistics of the United States*, 1114; and B. R. Mitchell, *International Historical Statistics: Europe, 1750–2000*, 5th ed. (New York: Palgrave Macmillan, 2003), 817–21, 906–30.

28. Personnel data from State Department's Office of the Historian, available online at <http://www.state.gov/r/pa/ho/faq/#personnel> (accessed 6 January 2005).

29. Data on size of army and marines: U.S. Bureau of the Census, *Historical Statistics of the United States*, 1141–42.

30. Root quote from Richard W. Leopold, *Elihu Root and the Conservative Tradition* (Boston: Little, Brown, 1954), 41–42.

31. Skowronek, *Building a New American State*, 235–36.

32. Quoted in Robert L. Beisner, *From the Old Diplomacy to the New, 1865–1900*, 2nd ed. (Arlington Heights, Ill.: Harlan Davidson, 1986), 8.

33. Data from Lewis L. Gould, *The Modern American Presidency* (Lawrence: University Press of Kansas, 2003), 14 (McKinley), 34 (TR/Taft).

34. Wilson quoted in Gould, *Modern American Presidency*, 42.

35. McKinley quoted in Lewis L. Gould, *The Spanish-American War and President McKinley* (Lawrence: University Press of Kansas, 1982), 104, 111, 119.

CHAPTER 3

1. Figures from John Ellis and Michael Cox, eds., *The World War I Databook: The Essential Facts and Figures for All the Combatants* (London: Arum Press, 2001), 269–70; Guglielmo Ferrero from 1919 quoted in Arno J. Mayer, *Politics and Diplomacy of Peacemaking: Containment and Counterrevolution at Versailles, 1918–1919* (New York: Knopf, 1967), 6.

2. R. L. Craigie quoted in Frank Costigliola, *Awkward Dominion: American Political, Economic, and Cultural Relations with Europe, 1919–1933* (Ithaca, N.Y.: Cornell University Press, 1984), 187.

3. Data from Louis Johnston and Samuel H. Williamson, "The Annual Real and

Nominal GDP for the United States, 1789–Present," Economic History Services, March 2004, <http://www.eh.net/hmit/gdp/> (accessed 5 July 2004).

4. Mark Harrison, ed., *The Economics of World War II: Six Great Powers in International Comparison* (Cambridge, U.K.: Cambridge University Press, 1998), 10 (relative 1938 GDP).

5. J. R. McNeill, *Something New under the Sun: An Environmental History of the Twentieth-Century World* (New York: Norton, 2000), 13–16.

6. Johnston and Williamson, "Annual Real and Nominal GDP for the United States."

7. Quotes from T. Christopher Jespersen, *American Images of China, 1931–1949* (Stanford, Calif.: Stanford University Press, 1996), 22 (Andrew Kopkind on marketing voices); and Charles McGovern, "Consumption and Citizenship in the United States, 1900–1940," in *Getting and Spending: European and American Consumer Societies in the Twentieth Century*, ed. Susan Strasser, Charles McGovern, and Matthias Judt (New York: Cambridge University Press, 1998), 43 (on wealth and happiness).

8. Quoted in Lizabeth Cohen, "The New Deal State and the Making of Citizen Consumers," in Strasser, McGovern, and Judt, *Getting and Spending*, 121.

9. Data from U.S. Bureau of the Census, *Historical Statistics of the United States: Colonial Times to 1970* (Washington, D.C.: U.S. Government Printing Office, 1975), 869 (direct investment); and Barry Eichengreen, "U.S. Foreign Financial Relations in the Twentieth Century," in *The Cambridge Economic History of the United States*, vol. 3: *The Twentieth Century*, ed. Stanley L. Engerman and Robert E. Gallman (Cambridge, U.K.: Cambridge University Press, 2000), 476 (total investment).

10. Data from Jeremy Tunstall, *The Media Are American: Anglo-American Media in the World* (New York: Columbia University Press, 1977), 284, 289–92. Quotes from Victoria de Grazia, "Mass Culture and Sovereignty: The American Challenge to European Cinemas, 1920–1960," *Journal of Modern History* 61 (March 1989): 53 (London paper); and Costigliola, *Awkward Dominion*, 177 (Will H. Hays).

11. Tourist data from Costigliola, *Awkward Dominion*, 173.

12. Nolan, *Visions of Modernity*, 112 (quote), 119 (data on German workers); and Carlo Levi, *Christ Stopped at Eboli: The Story of a Year*, trans. Frances Frenaye (New York: Farrar, Straus and Giroux, 1963), a memoir of exile in impoverished rural southern Italy.

13. Quote from Nolan, *Visions of Modernity*, 111.

14. Richard F. Kuisel, *Seducing the French: The Dilemma of Americanization* (Berkeley: University of California Press, 1993), 10 (chef quote); Georges Duhamel, *America the Menace: Scenes from the Life of the Future*, trans. Charles Miner Thompson (Boston: Houghton Mifflin, 1931), 35, 199, 202, 203. Duhamel would make a second U.S. visit in 1945 that would inspire a more generous appraisal.

15. Duhamel, *America the Menace*, 211, 215; Arthur Feiler, *America Seen through German Eyes*, trans. Margaret Leland Goldsmith (New York: New Republic, 1928), 28.

16. Quote from Akio Morita, with Edwin M. Reingold and Mitsuko Shimomura, *Made in Japan: Akio Morita and Sony* (New York: E. P. Dutton, 1986), 15.

17. Hoover to Wilson, 28 March 1919, quoted at length in Mayer, *Politics and Diplomacy of Peacemaking*, 25.

18. Numbers of late nineteenth-century accords from Armand Mattelart, *Networking the World, 1794–2000*, trans. Liz Carey-Libbrecht and James A. Cohen (Minneapolis: University of Minnesota Press, 2000), 7.

19. The treaty text is available at the Avalon Project website, <http://www.yale.edu/lawweb/avalon/imt/kbpact.htm> (accessed 6 September 2004).

20. Walter Lippmann, *U.S. Foreign Policy: Shield of the Republic* (Boston, Little, Brown, 1943), 54.

21. Quoted in Melvyn P. Leffler, "Political Isolationism, Economic Expansionism, or Diplomatic Realism: American Policy toward Western Europe, 1921–1933," *Perspectives in American History* 8 (1974): 439.

22. GE investment figure and details on Lamont's career from Costigliola, *Awkward Dominion*, 151–54.

23. Coolidge quote from 1925 in Howard H. Quint and Robert H. Ferrell, eds., *The Talkative President: The Off-the-Record Press Conferences of Calvin Coolidge* (Amherst: University of Massachusetts Press, 1964), 257; Stalin quote from his "The Foundations of Leninism," April 1924, which came to serve as a party primer circulated widely in the Soviet Union as well as abroad in translation, in J. V. Stalin, *Works*, ed. Marx-Engels-Lenin Institute of the Central Committee of the Communist Party of the Soviet Union (Bolshevik), vol. 6 (Moscow: Foreign Languages Publishing House, 1953), 195.

24. Root quoted in David F. Schmitz, *Thank God They're on Our Side: The United States and Right-Wing Dictatorships, 1921–1965* (Chapel Hill: University of North Carolina Press, 1999), 45; Thomas Lamont of J. P. Morgan quoted in Costigliola, *Awkward Dominion*, 148.

25. NGO data from Akira Iriye, *Global Community: The Role of International Organizations in the Making of the Contemporary World* (Berkeley: University of California Press, 2002), 20–21.

26. League report quoted in Harold James, *The End of Globalization: Lessons from the Great Depression* (Cambridge, Mass.: Harvard University Press, 2001), 51; Ernie Pyle quoted in Marilyn Young, "The Age of Global Power," in *Rethinking American History in a Global Age*, ed. Thomas Bender (Berkeley: University of California Press, 2002), 285.

27. *Gallup Poll: Public Opinion, 1935–1997*, CD-ROM edition (Wilmington, Del.: Scholarly Resources, 2000), entries for 1937, p. 54 (on view of World War I) and p. 71 (poll of 10 October on Ludlow amendment).

28. Quoted in Robert A. Divine, *Roosevelt and World War II* (Baltimore: Johns Hopkins Press, 1969), 9.

29. The Chicago address is in Samuel I. Rosenman, ed., *The Public Papers and Addresses of Franklin D. Roosevelt, 1937* (New York: Macmillan, 1941), 407–11, while the September 1939 statement is in Samuel I. Rosenman, ed., *The Public Papers and Addresses of Franklin D. Roosevelt, 1939* (New York: Macmillan, 1941), 460–63. The diplomat is Adolf Berle, quoted in Anne Orde, *The Eclipse of Great Britain: The United States and Imperial Decline, 1895–1956* (New York: St. Martin's Press, 1996), 128.

30. Investment data from Cleona Lewis, with Karl T. Schlotterbeck, *America's Stake in International Investments* (Washington, D.C.: Brookings Institution, 1938), 606.

31. The "boa constrictor" charge quoted in Jonathan C. Brown, "Jersey Standard and the Politics of Latin American Oil Production, 1911–1930," in *Latin American Oil Companies and the Politics of Energy*, ed. John D. Wirth (Lincoln: University of Nebraska Press, 1985), 15.

32. Coolidge quote from March 1927 in Quint and Ferrell, *Talkative President*, 241.

33. Quotes from Schmitz, *Thank God They're on Our Side*, 49 (Hughes); and Robert Freeman Smith, *The United States and Revolutionary Nationalism in Mexico, 1916–1932* (Chicago: University of Chicago Press, 1972), 232 (Ambassador Sheffield).

34. Quoted in Robert Dallek, *Franklin D. Roosevelt and American Foreign Policy, 1932–1945* (New York: Oxford University Press, 1979), 176.

35. Quote from Schmitz, *Thank God They're on Our Side*, 69.

36. Investment data from Lewis, *America's Stake*, 606, 616.

37. Quotes from Schmitz, *Thank God They're on Our Side*, 78 (Welles); and Dallek, *Franklin D. Roosevelt*, 61 (Roosevelt).

38. Kellogg comment to Coolidge, quoted in Donald R. McCoy, *Calvin Coolidge: The Quiet President* (New York: Macmillan, 1967), 341.

39. The quoted phrase is Konoe Fumimaro's from 1918, in *Sources of Japanese Tradition*, vol. 2: *1600–2000*, 2nd ed., comp. Wm. Theodore de Bary et al. (New York: Columbia University Press, 2005), 985.

40. Lodge quote from August 1919 in John A. Garraty, *Henry Cabot Lodge: A Biography* (New York: Knopf, 1953), 374.

41. Entry for 9 October 1931, Henry L. Stimson diaries, vol. 18, pp. 111–12 (microfilm edition reel 3), Stimson Papers, Manuscripts and Archives, Yale University Library, New Haven, Conn.

CHAPTER 4

1. The feature article accompanying the cover, "A Dictator's Hour," *Time*, 14 April 1941, appears on pp. 26–28 (quotes from 26).

2. Quote on 1939 cover from W. A. Swanberg, *Luce and His Empire* (New York: Scribner, 1972), 160; Henry R. Luce, "The American Century," *Life* 10 (17 February 1941): 61–65.

3. Quoted in David F. Schmitz, *Thank God They're on Our Side: The United States and Right-Wing Dictatorships, 1921–1965* (Chapel Hill: University of North Carolina Press, 1999), 121–23.

4. President Roosevelt to Ambassador Grew, letter of 21 January 1941 (drafted by Stanley K. Hornbeck, the State Department's senior specialist on East Asia), in U.S. Department of State, *Foreign Relations of the United States* [hereafter *FRUS*], *1941*, vol. 4 (Washington, D.C.: U.S. Government Printing Office, 1956), 8.

5. For the quote from the Pearl Harbor address, see *The Public Papers and Addresses of Franklin D. Roosevelt*, vol. 10: *1941*, ed. Samuel I. Rosenman (New York: Harper and Brothers, 1950), 528. The Atlantic Charter, 14 August 1941, is available at the Avalon Project website, <http://www.yale.edu/lawweb/avalon/wwii/atlantic/at10.htm#1> (accessed 12 May 2002).

6. Lippmann quote from 7 April 1945, in Ronald Steel, *Walter Lippmann and the American Century* (Boston: Little, Brown, 1980), 416–17.

7. Truman quotes from Harry S. Truman, *Memoirs*, vol. 1 (Garden City, N.J.: Doubleday, 1955), 5, 19.

8. Quotes from Wilson D. Miscamble, "The Evolution of an Internationalist: Harry S. Truman and American Foreign Policy," *Australian Journal of Politics and History* 23 (August 1977): 270, 275.

9. Quotes from Robert H. Ferrell, ed., *Off the Record: The Private Papers of Harry S. Truman* (New York: Harper and Row, 1980), 80 (Truman on babying the Soviets in letter to Byrnes in January 1946); and from James Forrestal, *The Forrestal Diaries*, ed. Walter Millis (New York: Viking Press, 1951), 192 (Truman on confronting Soviet world conquest).

10. Truman, address to Congress, 12 March 1947 in *Public Papers of the Presidents* [hereafter *PPP*]: *Harry S. Truman, 1947* (Washington, D.C.: U.S. Government Printing Office, 1963), 178–79.

11. Dean Acheson, *Present at the Creation: My Years in the State Department* (New York: New American Library, 1970), 293.

12. For the meaning of totalitarianism as it was understood in the 1920s and 1930s, see Les K. Adler and Thomas G. Paterson, "Red Fascism: The Merger of Nazi Germany and Soviet Russia in the American Image of Totalitarianism, 1930's–

1950's," *American Historical Review* 75 (April 1970): 1052–55; and Abbott Gleason, *Totalitarianism: The Inner History of the Cold War* (New York: Oxford University Press, 1995), 4.

13. Truman quotes from Margaret Truman, *Harry S. Truman* (New York: Morrow, 1973), 359; and Miscamble, "Evolution of an Internationalist," 271. For other good evidence on Truman's views on the totalitarian danger going back to 1939, see Margaret Truman, *Harry S. Truman*, 141, 323, 343, 360. For the address to Congress, see *PPP: Harry S. Truman, 1947* (Washington, D.C.: U.S. Government Printing Office, 1963), 178–80.

14. The quote is from Ian Kershaw, "'Working towards the Führer': Reflections on the Nature of the Hitler Dictatorship," *Stalinism and Nazism: Dictatorships in Comparison*, ed. Kershaw and Moshe Lewin (Cambridge, U.K.: Cambridge University Press, 1997), 89. See also the discussion in Kershaw and Lewin's introduction to the volume, "The Regimes and Their Dictators: Perspectives of Comparison," 4–5.

15. The observation is Richard J. Barnet's from *Roots of War: The Men and Institutions behind U.S. Foreign Policy* (New York: Atheneum, 1972), 187.

16. Attorney General J. Howard McGrath quoted in Geoffrey S. Smith, "National Security and Personal Isolation: Sex, Gender, and Disease in the Cold-War United States," *International History Review* 14 (May 1992): 312; George Kennan memo, 17 October 1949, identifying the "maladjusted groups," in *FRUS, 1949*, vol. 1 (Washington, D.C.: Government Printing Office, 1976), 404; and Hoover testimony quoted in Ellen Schrecker, *The Age of McCarthyism: A Brief History with Documents* (Boston: Bedford Books, 1994), 120.

17. Alex Roland, *The Military-Industrial Complex* (Washington, D.C.: American Historical Association, 2001), 4. Data from Mark Harrison, ed., *The Economics of World War II: Six Great Powers in International Comparison* (Cambridge, U.K.: Cambridge University Press, 1998), 10 (comparative GDP); and Robert M. Collins, *More: The Politics of Economic Growth in Postwar America* (Oxford: Oxford University Press, 2000), 13 (U.S. output).

18. Hitler quote from Gerhard L. Weinberg, "Hitler's Image of the United States," *American Historical Review* 69 (July 1964): 1013.

19. Tojo remarks at imperial conference, 5 November 1941, in *Japan's Decision for War: Records of the 1941 Policy Conferences*, trans. and ed. Nobutaka Ike (Stanford, Calif.: Stanford University Press, 1967), 238.

20. Data on military spending from Center for Defense Information's *Military Almanac, 2001–2002*, 35 (available online, <http://www.cdi.org/products/almanac0102.pdf>); and from U.S. Bureau of the Census, *Historical Statistics of the United States:*

Colonial Times to 1970 (Washington, D.C.: U.S. Government Printing Office, 1975), 1116.

21. R&D data from David C. Mowery and Nathan Rosenberg, *Technology and the Pursuit of Economic Growth* (Cambridge, U.K.: Cambridge University Press, 1989), 161–65.

22. John W. Dower, *War without Mercy: Race and Power in the Pacific War* (New York: Pantheon, 1986), 40.

23. From the Leo Szilard petition, first version, 3 July 1945, in the Gene Dannen collection on the atomic bomb: <http://www.dannen.com/decision/45-07-03.html> (accessed 3 August 2004).

24. Truman diary entry, 25 July 1945, reflecting on news of the first successful atomic test, in "Ross" folder, Box 322, President's Secretary's Files, Papers of Harry S. Truman, Truman Library, Independence, Mo.; Truman comments at a Cabinet meeting, 10 August 1945, recorded by Secretary of Commerce Henry A. Wallace, in *The Price of Vision: The Diary of Henry A. Wallace, 1942–1946*, ed. John M. Blum (Boston: Houghton Mifflin, 1973), 474; Secretary of War Henry L. Stimson to President Truman, 11 September 1945, in *FRUS, 1945*, vol. 2 (Washington, D.C.: U.S. Government Printing Office, 1971), 42; and Truman comment from June 1948 in the midst of the Berlin crisis, quoted in Alonzo L. Hamby, *Man of the People: The Life of Harry S. Truman* (New York: Oxford University Press, 1995), 445.

25. Stalin quote from Steven J. Zaloga, *Target America: The Soviet Union and the Strategic Arms Race, 1945–1964* (Novato, Calif.: Presidio Press, 1993), 27.

26. For a graphic presentation of this point, see Robert S. McNamara, *Blundering into Disaster: Surviving the First Century of the Nuclear Age* (New York: Pantheon, 1986), 151.

27. Data from Paul Bairoch, "International Industrialization Levels from 1750 to 1980," *Journal of European Economic History* 11 (Fall 1982): 284; and Angus Maddison, *The World Economy: A Millennial Perspective* (Paris: Development Centre of the Organisation for Economic Co-operation and Development, 2001), 274–75.

28. The witticism, attributed to Lord Ismay, is quoted in Gregory F. Treverton, *America, Germany, and the Future of Europe* (Princeton, N.J.: Princeton University Press, 1992), 153. The comparative military data come from Matthew A. Evangelista, "Stalin's Postwar Army Reappraised," *International Security* 7 (Winter 1982–83): 110–38.

29. Truman remarks, 21 November 1952, in *PPP: Harry S. Truman, 1952–53* (Washington, D.C.: U.S. Government Printing Office, 1966), 1061; National Security Council report 162/2, 29 October 1953, in *FRUS, 1952–1954*, vol. 2 (Washington, D.C.: U.S. Government Printing Office, 1983), 579; Eisenhower, diary entry, 23 Janu-

ary 1956, in *The Eisenhower Diaries*, ed. Robert H. Ferrell (New York: W. W. Norton, 1981), 311; and Eisenhower's expression of fear quoted in David A. Rosenberg, "The Origins of Overkill: Nuclear Weapons and American Strategy, 1945–1960," *International Security* 7 (Spring 1983): 8.

30. Quotes from undated interview with McNamara, available on the website for the National Security Archives, <http://www.gwu.edu/nsarchiv/coldwar/interviews/episode-10/mcnamara3.html> (accessed 20 July 2004); and from President Kennedy's commencement address at the American University, 10 June 1963, in *PPP: John F. Kennedy, 1963* (Washington, D.C.: U.S. Government Printing Office, 1964), 462.

31. The phrase comes from Arthur M. Schlesinger Jr., *The Imperial Presidency* (Boston: Houghton Mifflin, 1973).

32. Lewis L. Gould, *The Modern American Presidency* (Lawrence: University Press of Kansas, 2003), 109.

33. Data from U.S. Bureau of the Census, *Historical Statistics of the United States*, 1102 (federal civilian employees), 1114 (federal expenditures), and 1141 (armed forces); and Louis Johnston and Samuel H. Williamson, "The Annual Real and Nominal GDP for the United States, 1789–Present," Economic History Services, March 2004, <http://www.eh.net/hmit/gdp/> (accessed 5 July 2004).

34. See Federation of American Scientists website for revelation about the 1955 CIA budget of $335 million (or $1.8 billion if converted to 2000 constant dollars) concealed in eleven separate Defense Department budget lines: <http://www.fas.org/irp/budget/cia1955.pdf> (accessed 25 March 2005). For CIA budgets for 1963 to 1966, see <http://www.fas.org/sgp/foia/1947/sa092704.pdf> (accessed 9 October 2004).

35. Michael J. Hogan, *A Cross of Iron: Harry S. Truman and the Origins of the National Security State, 1945–1954* (Cambridge, U.K.: Cambridge University Press, 1998), 114.

36. NSC numbers from Gould, *Modern American Presidency*, 118.

37. White House staff from Gould, *Modern American Presidency*, 138.

38. Roosevelt radio address, 27 May 1941, in *Public Papers and Addresses of Franklin D. Roosevelt*, 10:191.

39. Polls of 2, 14, and 22 November 1941, in George H. Gallup, *The Gallup Poll: Public Opinion, 1935–1971*, 3 vols. (New York: Random House, 1972), 1:304, 306, 307.

40. Gallup, *Gallup Poll*, 1:492 (poll of 11 March 1945), 565 (24 March 1946), 617 (3 January 1947), and 2:788 (4 February 1949).

41. Truman and Acheson quotes from Walter LaFeber, "American Policy-Makers,

Public Opinion, and the Outbreak of the Cold War, 1945–50," in *The Origins of the Cold War in Asia*, ed. Yōnosuke Nagai and Akira Iriye (New York: Columbia University Press, 1977), 60.

CHAPTER 5

1. Khrushchev quote from *Khrushchev Remembers: The Last Testament*, ed. and trans. Strobe Talbott (Boston: Little, Brown, 1974), 366.

2. Henry R. Luce, "The American Century," *Life* 10 (17 February 1941): 64–65.

3. Data from Paul Bairoch, "International Industrialization Levels from 1750 to 1980," *Journal of European Economic History* 11 (Fall 1982): 301.

4. Roosevelt quote from his January 1945 State of the Union address quoted in Townsend Hoopes and Douglas Brinkley, *FDR and the Creation of the U.N.* (New Haven, Conn.: Yale University Press, 1997), 172.

5. Truman quoted in Hoopes and Brinkley, *FDR and the Creation of the U.N.*, 202.

6. Quotes from *The Nuremberg War Crimes Trial, 1945–1946: A Documentary History*, comp. Michael R. Marrus (Boston: Bedford Books, 1997), 43 (Roberts), 87 (British associate Hartley Shawcross).

7. Quote from John W. Dower, *War without Mercy: Race and Power in the Pacific War* (New York: Pantheon, 1986), 37.

8. The phrase is Jeremy Bentham's and is quoted in Burns H. Weston's "Human Rights" entry in *Encyclopaedia Britannica*, 15th ed. (2002), available at the website for the University of Iowa Human Rights Center, <http://www.uiowa.edu/~uichr/publi cations/documents/HRBritannica05part1.pdf> (accessed 9 August 2006), 657.

9. A copy of the charter is available on the UN website, <http://www.un.org/aboutun/charter/> (accessed 20 July 2005).

10. A copy of the declaration is on the UN website, <http://www.un.org/rights/50/decla.htm> (accessed 24 January 2003).

11. Quote from a UNESCO memo on human rights, 27 March 1947, in Paul Gordon Lauren, *The Evolution of International Human Rights: Visions Seen* (Philadelphia: University of Pennsylvania Press, 1998), 223.

12. Quotes from Richard N. Gardner, *Sterling-Dollar Diplomacy in Current Perspective: The Origins and Prospects of Our International Economic Order*, rev. ed. (New York: Columbia University Press, 1980), xiii (Keynes); and from Elizabeth Borgwardt, *A New Deal for the World: America's Vision for Human Rights* (Cambridge, Mass.: Harvard University Press, 2005), 113 (U.S. response).

13. Quote from Keynes, "The End of Laissez-Faire," reproduced in *The Collected Works of John Maynard Keynes*, ed. Elizabeth Johnson et al., vol. 9: *Essays in Persuasion* (London: Macmillan, 1972), 288.

14. The major socialist economies taken together accounted for around 17.5 per-

cent of global GDP in both 1950 and 1973 according to Angus Maddison, *The World Economy: A Millennial Perspective* (Paris: Development Centre of the Organisation for Economic Co-operation and Development, 2001), 261.

15. The phrase comes from Geir Lundestad, "Empire by Invitation? The United States and Western Europe, 1945–1952," *Journal of Peace Research* 23 (September 1986): 263–77. For poll data, see 272–73.

16. Quote from the verbatim version of the speech Marshall delivered at Harvard University, 4 June 1947, proposing a recovery plan, available online from the George C. Marshall International Center, <http://www.georgecmarshall.org/lt/speeches/marshall_plan.cfm> (accessed 1 January 2003).

17. All figures (in contemporary dollars) from Alfred E. Eckes Jr. and Thomas W. Zeiler, *Globalization and the American Century* (Cambridge, U.K.: Cambridge University Press, 2003), 265 (direct investment); and from U.S. Bureau of the Census, *Historical Statistics of the United States: Colonial Times to 1970* (Washington, D.C.: U.S. Government Printing Office, 1975), 874 (government assistance).

18. Quote from Mario Del Pero, "The United States and 'Psychological Warfare' in Italy, 1948–1955," *Journal of American History* 87 (March 2001): 1316.

19. Roosevelt comments, 19 August 1944, recorded by Henry Morgenthau, in *From the Morgenthau Diaries: Years of War, 1941–1945*, ed. John Morton Blum (Boston: Houghton Mifflin, 1967), 342.

20. Ernest Bevin quote from Alan S. Milward, with George Brennan and Federico Romero, *The European Rescue of the Nation-State*, 2nd ed. (London: Routledge, 2000), 390.

21. Wilson quote from Wm. Roger Louis, "The Dissolution of the British Empire in the Era of Vietnam," *American Historical Review* 107 (February 2002): 4.

22. Quotes from John W. Dower, *Embracing Defeat: Japan in the Wake of World War II* (New York: W. W. Norton, 1999), 217 (*Saturday Evening Post*, 15 December 1945), 324 (MacArthur on the emperor), 550 (MacArthur on tutorial role).

23. Shiomi Kitarō letter of 18 February 1946, in Sodei Rinjirō, *Dear General MacArthur: Letters from the Japanese during the American Occupation*, ed. John Junkerman and trans. Shizue Matsuda (Lanham, Md.: Rowman and Littlefield, 2001), 22.

24. Aid figure (1946–1952) in contemporary dollars from U.S. Bureau of the Census, *Historical Statistics of the United States*, 875; Korean War spending in Japan in Dower, *Embracing Defeat*, 542.

25. Lizabeth Cohen, *A Consumer's Republic: The Politics of Mass Consumption in Postwar America* (New York: Knopf, 2003), 71 (savings data), 73 (quote). Data on income and consumer goods in this and the following paragraph come from William H. Chafe, *The Unfinished Journey: America since World War II*, 3rd ed. (New York: Oxford University Press, 1995), 111–12.

26. Data from Maddison, *World Economy*, 264–65.

27. GDP data from Maddison, *World Economy*, 126; Ike comment in National Security Council meeting, 11 March 1953, in U.S. Department of State, *Foreign Relations of the United States, 1952–1954*, vol. 8 (Washington, D.C.: Government Printing Office, 1988), 1123.

28. Woodruff quote from Frederick Allen, *Secret Formula: How Brilliant Marketing and Relentless Salesmanship Made Coca-Cola the Best-Known Product in the World* (New York: HarperCollins, 1994), 166.

29. Woodruff quotes from Constance L. Hays, *The Real Thing: Truth and Power at the Coca-Cola Company* (New York: Random House, 2004), 81.

30. Allen, *Secret Formula*, 311 (early postwar overseas presence and revenue), 343 (film), 365 (overseas presence circa 1977), 383 (1980 revenue).

31. For postwar data, see Jeremy Tunstall, *The Media Are American: Anglo-American Media in the World* (New York: Columbia University Press, 1977), 282, 289–92, 299.

32. Jean Baudrillard, *America*, trans. Chris Turner (London: Verso, 1988), 76.

33. Quote from Rob Kroes, "American Empire and Cultural Imperialism: A View from the Receiving End," in *Rethinking American History in a Global Age*, ed. Thomas Bender (Berkeley: University of California Press, 2002), 300. Other terms for this transformative process invoked by anthropologists and sociologists include "localization," "indigenization," and "hybridization."

34. These are the recollections of Reinhold Wagnleitner contained in his *Coca-Colonization and the Cold War: The Cultural Mission of the United States in Austria after the Second World War*, trans. Diana M. Wolf (Chapel Hill: University of North Carolina Press, 1994), ix–xi.

35. Bertrand Russell, "The Political and Cultural Influence," in Russell et al., *The Impact of America on European Culture* (Boston: Beacon Press, 1951), 17–19.

36. Georges Perec, *"Things: A Story of the Sixties" and "A Man Asleep"* (Boston: David R. Godine, 1990), 31, 35, 36, 41. David Bellos translated the half of this collection devoted to *Things* (*Les choses*).

37. Quotes from Richard F. Kuisel, *Seducing the French: The Dilemma of Americanization* (Berkeley: University of California Press, 1993), 55, 63.

38. Quote from Charles Ambler, "Popular Films and Colonial Audiences: The Movies in Northern Rhodesia," *American Historical Review* 106 (February 2001): 94.

39. Gradsky recollection in Timothy W. Ryback, *Rock around the Bloc: A History of Rock Music in Eastern Europe and the Soviet Union* (New York: Oxford University Press, 1990), 109.

40. Quotes from Ryback, *Rock around the Bloc*, 11 (late Stalin-era denunciation of

jazz); and William J. Tompson, *Khrushchev: A Political Life* (New York: St. Martin's Press, 1995), 257 (Khrushchev on jazz).

41. On the Plastic People and the ferment surrounding their emergence, see Jaroslav Riedel, ed., *The Plastic People of the Universe*, trans. Olga Záhorbenská (Prague: Globus Music and Mata, 1999); and Joseph Yanosik, "The Plastic People of the Universe" (March 1996), available online at <http://www.furious.com/perfect/pulnoc.html> (accessed 23 July 2005).

42. The treatment that follows draws on Nicola White, *Reconstructing Italian Fashion: America and the Development of the Italian Fashion Industry* (Oxford, U.K.: Berg, 2000); Luigi Settembrini, "From Haute Couture to Prêt-à-porter," trans. Anthony Shugaar, in *The Italian Metamorphosis, 1943–68,* ed. Germano Celant (New York: Guggenheim Museum, 1994), 482–94; the striking photos in "Italy Gets Dressed Up," *Life* 31 (20 August 1951): 104–12; Ernestine Carter, *With Tongue in Chic* (London: Michael Joseph, 1974), 133–35; Bettina Ballard, *In My Fashion* (New York: David McCay, 1960), 250–51, 254–58; Micol Fontana, *Specchio a tre luci* [A mirror for three lights] (Torino: Nuova ERI, 1991); and *Nasce Il Made in Italy: 50 anni di Moda— Abiti e documenti della Fondazione Micol Fontana* [Made in Italy is born: Fifty years of fashion—designs and documents from the Micol Fontana Foundation] (CD-ROM prepared by Massimo Bevilacqua, 2001). For hints that the postwar French garment industry also wrestled with U.S. markets, consumer preferences, and production techniques, see Nancy L. Green, *Ready-to-Wear and Ready-to-Work: A Century of Industry and Immigrants in Paris and New York* (Durham, N.C.: Duke University Press, 1997), 99–103, 110–11.

43. Marya Mannes, "Italian Fashion," *Vogue* 109 (1 January 1947): 156.

CHAPTER 6

1. Population data from Angus Maddison, *The World Economy: A Millennial Perspective* (Paris: Development Centre of the Organisation for Economic Co-operation and Development, 2001), 213, 241.

2. This last point about the three frames was suggested by Matthew Connelly, "Taking Off the Cold War Lens: Visions of North-South Conflict during the Algerian War for Independence," *American Historical Review* 105 (June 2000): 755.

3. See Wm. Roger Louis, *Imperialism at Bay: The United States and the Decolonization of the British Empire, 1941–1945* (New York: Oxford University Press, 1978), 123–24, 231.

4. *The Indian Nationalist Movement, 1885–1947: Select Documents,* ed. B. N. Pandey (London: Macmillan, 1979), 142.

5. Maddison, *World Economy,* 143.

6. Nehru quoted in Dennis Merrill, *Bread and the Ballot: The United States and India's Economic Development, 1947–1963* (Chapel Hill: University of North Carolina Press, 1990), 15.

7. Nkrumah quoted in Marika Sherwood, *Kwame Nkrumah: The Years Abroad, 1935–1947* (Legon, Accra, Ghana: Freedom Publications, 1996), 98.

8. Mao quoted in my *The Genesis of Chinese Communist Foreign Policy* (New York: Columbia University Press, 1996), 150.

9. *Selected Works of Mao Tse-tung*, vol. 5 (Beijing: Foreign Language Press, 1977), 16.

10. Arbenz quoted in Jim Handy, *Revolution in the Countryside: Rural Conflict and Agrarian Reform in Guatemala, 1944–1954* (Chapel Hill: University of North Carolina Press, 1994), 78.

11. FDR quoted in Lloyd C. Gardner, "Why We 'Lost' Vietnam, 1940–54," in *The United States and Decolonization: Power and Freedom*, ed. David Ryan and Victor Pungong (London: Macmillan, 2000), 129.

12. FDR quoted in Paul Orders, "'Adjusting to a New Period in World History': Franklin Roosevelt and European Colonialism," in Ryan and Pungong, *United States and Decolonization*, 69.

13. Quote from Louis, *Imperialism at Bay*, 533. Potsdam paper in U.S. Department of State, *Foreign Relations of the United States* [hereafter *FRUS*], *1945*, vol. 6 (Washington, D.C.: Government Printing Office, 1969), 557–58.

14. This paragraph draws at points verbatim from my *Ideology and U.S. Foreign Policy* (New Haven, Conn.: Yale University Press, 1987), 163. Truman quoted on India in Andrew J. Rotter, "Gender Relations, Foreign Relations: The United States and South Asia, 1947–1964," *Journal of American History* 81 (September 1994): 520.

15. Ike quote from Douglas Little, *American Orientalism: The United States and the Middle East since 1945* (Chapel Hill: University of North Carolina Press, 2002), 218.

16. Khrushchev report to the Twentieth Congress of the Communist Party of the Soviet Union, 14 February 1956, in *Current Digest of the Soviet Press* 8, no. 4 (23–29 January 1956): 7; Khrushchev speech at the Institute of Marxism-Leninism, 6 January 1961, in *The Foreign Policy of the Soviet Union*, ed. Alvin Z. Rubinstein, 3rd ed. (New York: Random House, 1972), 268.

17. Frantz Fanon, *The Wretched of the Earth*, trans. Constance Farrington (New York: Grove Press, 1968), 93. This was originally published in 1961 as *Les damnés de la terre*.

18. Lin Piao [Lin Biao], *Long Live the Victory of People's War!* (Peking: Foreign Languages Press, 1965), 54.

19. Che Guevara, "Message to the Tricontinental," written in 1966 and published on April 16, 1967, available online at <http://www.marxists.org/archive/guevara/works.htm> (accessed 7 January 2003).

20. Quote from Kwame Nkrumah's *The Spectre of Black Power* (1968) reprinted in his *Revolutionary Path* (New York: International Publishers, 1973), 426.

21. *Capitalism and Underdevelopment in Latin America: Historical Studies of Chile and Brazil* (New York: Monthly Review Press, 1967) by the German-born and U.S.-educated André Gunder Frank offered the boldest and best-known version of the "dependency" argument.

22. Quotes from National Security Council meeting of 7 August 1958, in *FRUS, 1958–1960*, vol. 14 (Washington, D.C.: U.S. Government Printing Office, 1992), 20 (Ike on Indians et al.); David F. Schmitz, *Thank God They're on Our Side: The United States and Right-Wing Dictatorships, 1921–1965* (Chapel Hill: University of North Carolina Press, 1999), 182 (Dulles); Blanche Wiesen Cook, *The Declassified Eisenhower: A Divided Legacy* (Garden City, N.Y.: Doubleday, 1981), 366 n. 66 (C. D. Jackson); Scott Lucas, "The Limits of Ideology: US Foreign Policy and Arab Nationalism in the Early Cold War," in Ryan and Pungong, *United States and Decolonization*, 147 (Eisenhower on Nasser), 141 (Caffrey on Nasser); and Donald Neff, *Warriors at Suez: Eisenhower Takes America into the Middle East* (New York: Simon and Schuster, 1981), 387 (Ike on the British).

23. Ike quote from Mary L. Dudziak, *Cold War Civil Rights: Race and the Image of American Democracy* (Princeton, N.J.: Princeton University Press, 2000), 130.

24. Kennedy on support for independence movements, 4 July 1962, in *Public Papers of the Presidents* [hereafter *PPP*]: *John F. Kennedy, 1962* (Washington, D.C.: U.S. Government Printing Office, 1963), 278.

25. Kennedy quote from Dudziak, *Cold War Civil Rights*, 168.

26. Kennedy quoted on Khrushchev's "clue" in Michael E. Latham, *Modernization as Ideology: American Social Science and "Nation Building" in the Kennedy Era* (Chapel Hill: University of North Carolina Press, 2000), 3; Kennedy on national wars of liberation, April 1961, in *PPP: John F. Kennedy, 1961* (Washington, D.C.: U.S. Government Printing Office, 1962), 336; and Kennedy on the Congo, quoted in Richard D. Mahoney, *JFK: Ordeal in Africa* (New York: Oxford University Press, 1983), 109.

27. Henry A. Byroade quoted in Nick Cullather, "Damming Afghanistan: Modernization in a Buffer State," *Journal of American History* 89 (September 2002), 513.

28. Rusk in *Department of State Bulletin* 44 (22 May 1961): 763.

29. Kennan quote from Schmitz, *Thank God They're on Our Side*, 151.

30. Truman quoted in Leslie Bethell and Ian Roxborough, "Latin America be-

tween the Second World War and the Cold War: Some Reflections on the 1945–8 Conjuncture," *Journal of Latin American Studies* 20 (May 1988): 186.

31. Ike quote from Richard H. Immerman, *The CIA in Guatemala: The Foreign Policy of Intervention* (Austin: University of Texas Press, 1982), 178.

32. Quotes from Schmitz, *Thank God They're on Our Side*, 217 (State Department), 218 (Dulles).

33. Quotes from Schmitz, *Thank God They're on Our Side*, 182 (Mann); and from *PPP: Lyndon Johnson, 1965* (Washington, D.C.: U.S. Government Printing Office, 1966), 471.

34. Press conference comments, 11 March 1948, in *PPP: Harry S. Truman, 1948* (Washington, D.C.: U.S. Government Printing Office, 1964), 181.

35. Truman public statement, 27 June 1950, *FRUS, 1950*, vol. 7 (Washington, D.C.: Government Printing Office, 1976), 202.

36. Early February 1951 survey in George H. Gallup, *The Gallup Poll: Public Opinion, 1935–1971*, 3 vols. (New York: Random House, 1972), 2:968.

37. Quotes from Schmitz, *Thank God They're on Our Side*, 171 (Marshall), 200 (Dulles).

38. Ike quote from Little, *American Orientalism*, 28.

39. Dulles quote from Little, *American Orientalism*, 28.

40. Quotes from Neff, *Warriors at Suez*, 293 (Dulles on Nasser); and from Anne Orde, *The Eclipse of Great Britain: The United States and Imperial Decline, 1895–1956* (New York: St. Martin's Press, 1996), 192 (Dulles on replacing Britain).

41. Ike quote from Little, *American Orientalism*, 136.

42. National Security Council report of 23 August 1957, in *FRUS, 1955–1957*, vol. 18 (Washington, D.C.: Government Printing Office, 1989), 79, 84.

43. *FRUS, 1958–1960*, 14:75.

44. *FRUS, 1961–1963*, vol. 21 (Washington, D.C.: Government Printing Office, 1995), 355, 391.

45. Quoted in Connelly, "Taking Off the Cold War Lens," 757.

46. Kennedy quoted in memo of conversation with Mobutu, 31 May 1963, in *FRUS, 1961–1963*, vol. 20 (Washington, D.C.: U.S. Government Printing Office, 1994), 861.

47. Quotes from Thomas J. Noer, *Cold War and Black Liberation: The United States and White Rule in Africa, 1948–1968* (Columbia: University of Missouri Press, 1985), 27 ("driving the natives"), 55 (Ike), 58 (State Department official).

48. For the context of this famous remark from the "Melian Dialogue," see Robert B. Strassler, ed., *The Landmark Thucydides: A Comprehensive Guide to the Peloponnesian War* (New York: Touchstone, 1996), 352.

49. Walter Lippmann, *The Cold War: A Study in U.S. Foreign Policy* (New York:

Harper and Row, 1972), 14. This volume, originally published in 1947, drew together Lippmann's contemporary newspaper columns.

CHAPTER 7

1. Data from Christopher Endy, *Cold War Holidays: American Tourism in France* (Chapel Hill: University of North Carolina Press, 2004), 8 (visits to France), 128 (transatlantic travelers), 131 (student travel).

2. Figures on nongovernmental organizations from Akira Iriye, *Global Community: The Role of International Organizations in the Making of the Contemporary World* (Berkeley: University of California Press, 2002), 55, 98, 129.

3. Data from the website of the Federation of American Scientists, <http://fas.org/nuke/guide/index.html> (accessed 16 August 2004); and Bill Keller, "South Africa Says It Built 6 Atom Bombs," *New York Times* (online edition), 25 March 1993 (accessed 19 April 2006).

4. Quotes from Iriye, *Global Community*, 70 (SANE); and from Albert Carnesale et al., *Living with Nuclear Weapons* (New York: Bantam Books, 1983), 13 (gift-giving witticism from Robert Jay Lifton).

5. Message of 12 September 1980 in *Islam and Revolution: Writings and Declarations of Imam Khomeini*, ed. and trans. Hamid Algar (Berkeley: Mizan Press, 1981), 305.

6. Quotes from *"Takin' it to the streets": A Sixties Reader*, 2nd ed., ed. Alexander Bloom and Wini Breines (New York: Oxford University Press, 2003), 56 (Port Huron), 89 (Mario Savio at Berkeley).

7. SDS president Paul Potter at the first antiwar demonstration in Washington, 17 April 1965, in Bloom and Breines, *"Takin' it to the streets"*, 176.

8. Data on output from Angus Maddison, *The World Economy: A Millennial Perspective* (Paris: Development Centre of the Organisation for Economic Co-operation and Development, 2001), 263; Galbraith quote and data on wage stagnation and job loss from Alfred E. Eckes, "Trading American Interests," *Foreign Affairs* 71 (Fall 1992): 144, 152.

9. George H. Gallup, *The Gallup Poll: Public Opinion, 1935–1971*, 3 vols. (New York: Random House, 1972), 3:2338.

10. Walter Russell Mead, "The Bush Administration and the New World Order," *World Policy Journal* 8 (Summer 1991): 418–19.

11. Paul Kennedy, *The Rise and Fall of the Great Powers: Economic Change and Military Conflict from 1500 to 2000* (New York: Random House, 1987). Rejoinders to this pessimistic appraisal came from Henry R. Nau, who had served in the Reagan White House, in *The Myth of America's Decline: Leading the World Economy into the 1990s* (New York: Oxford University Press, 1990); and from Joseph S. Nye Jr., a Harvard profes-

sor of government who would work in the Clinton Defense Department, in *Bound to Lead: The Changing Nature of American Power* (New York: Basic Books, 1990).

12. De Gaulle quote from February 1963 in Francis J. Gavin, *Gold, Dollars, and Power: The Politics of International Monetary Relations, 1958–1971* (Chapel Hill: University of North Carolina Press, 2004), 122.

13. Nixon quoted in Melvin Small, *The Presidency of Richard Nixon* (Lawrence: University Press of Kansas, 1999), 59.

14. Nixon remarks to White House staff on 19 July 1971, available at <http://www.gwu.edu/nsarchiv/NSAEBB/NSAEBB66/ch-41.pdf> (accessed 17 August 2004); speech in Kansas City, 6 July 1971, *Public Papers of the Presidents* [hereafter *PPP*]: *Richard Nixon, 1971* (Washington, D.C.: Government Printing Office, 1972), 804.

15. Entry for 21 July 1971, in H. R. Haldeman, *The Haldeman Diaries: Inside the Nixon White House* (New York: G.P. Putnam's, 1994), 326.

16. This 29 May 1972 statement is in *Department of State Bulletin* 66 (26 June 1972): 898–99.

17. Nixon speech, 30 April 1970, announcing the invasion of Cambodia, in *PPP: Richard Nixon, 1970* (Washington, D.C.: U.S. Government Printing Office, 1970), 409.

18. Entry for 27 June 1972, in Haldeman, *Haldeman Diaries*, 476.

19. Quote from Gaddis Smith, *Morality, Reason, and Power: American Diplomacy in the Carter Years* (New York: Hill and Wang, 1986), 28.

20. Quote from Carter's commencement address, Notre Dame University, 22 May 1977, in *PPP: Jimmy Carter, 1977*, vol. 1 (Washington, D.C.: Government Printing Office, 1977), 957.

21. Soviet ambassador to the United States Anatoly F. Dobrynin, secret report to Foreign Minister Gromyko, 11 July 1978, translated by Mark Doctoroff and published in *Cold War International History Project Bulletin*, issue 8–9 (Winter 1996/97), 120.

22. Quotes from Brzezinski memo for Carter, 26 December 1979, in *The Fall of Détente: Soviet-American Relations during the Carter Years*, ed. Odd Arne Westad (Oslo: Scandinavian University Press, 1997), 329; from Zbigniew Brzezinski, *Power and Principle: Memoirs of the National Security Adviser, 1977–1981* (New York: Farrar, Straus, Giroux, 1983), 436; and from Carter's State of the Union address to Congress, 23 January 1980, in *PPP: Jimmy Carter, 1980–81*, vol. 1 (Washington, D.C.: Government Printing Office, 1981), 196.

23. Norman Podhoretz, *The Present Danger* (New York: Simon and Schuster, 1980), 94.

24. Reagan address to the Republican National Convention, 17 August 1952, in *Actor, Ideologue, Politician: The Public Speeches of Ronald Reagan*, ed. Davis W. Houck

and Amos Kiewe (Westport, Conn.: Greenwood, 1993), 330–31; and 1975 radio address in *Reagan, in His Own Hand: The Writings of Ronald Reagan That Reveal His Revolutionary Vision for America*, ed. Kiron K. Skinner, Annelise Anderson, and Martin Anderson (New York: Free Press, 2001), 12.

25. Reagan remarks at the Annual Convention of the National Association of Evangelicals in Orlando, Florida, 8 March 1983, available at <http://www.reagan.utexas .edu/resource/speeches/1983/30883b.htm> (accessed 2 April 2002).

26. Reagan nationwide radio and television address, 23 March 1983, available at <http://www.reagan.utexas.edu/resource/speeches/1983/32383d.htm> (accessed 2 April 2002).

27. *Gallup Poll: Public Opinion, 1935–1997*, CD-ROM edition (Wilmington, Del.: Scholarly Resources, 2000), entries for 1984, p. 265 (December survey on Reagan heading toward war); and Jonathan Schell, *Fate of the Earth* (New York: Knopf, 1982), 182.

28. *Gallup Poll: Public Opinion, 1935–1997*, entries for 1984, p. 107.

29. Gorbachev's memoirs quoted in Matthew Evangelista, *Unarmed Forces: The Transnational Movement to End the Cold War* (Ithaca, N.Y.: Cornell University Press, 1999), 261; and Tatyana Zaslavkya interview quoted in Stephen F. Cohen and Katrina vanden Heuvel, *Voices of Glasnost: Interviews with Gorbachev's Reformers* (New York: W. W. Norton, 1989), 122.

30. Both quotes from Robert M. Collins, *More: The Politics of Economic Growth in Postwar America* (Oxford: Oxford University Press, 2000), 192.

31. All three quotes from Ronald Reagan, *An American Life* (New York: Simon and Schuster, 1990), 296 (comment to Kohl), 447 (comment to parents), 473 (retrospective comment).

32. Reagan speech, 16 January 1984, available at <http://www.reagan.utexas.edu/ archives/speeches/1984/11684a.htm> (accessed 13 April 2006); and Dana H. Allin, *Cold War Illusions: America, Europe and Soviet Power, 1969–1989* (New York: St. Martin's Press, 1995), 177.

33. Reported in Frances FitzGerald, *Way Out There in the Blue: Reagan, Star Wars, and the End of the Cold War* (New York: Simon and Schuster, 2000), 150.

34. Quoted in Paul Lewis, "Ex-Foes Trade Stories from Cold War Trenches," *New York Times* (online edition), 1 March 1993 (accessed 19 April 2006).

35. Gorbachev quoted in Don Oberdorfer, *From the Cold War to a New Era: The United States and the Soviet Union, 1983–1991*, 2nd ed. (Baltimore: Johns Hopkins University Press, 1998), 383.

36. Quoted in Archie Brown, *The Gorbachev Factor* (Oxford: Oxford University Press, 1996), 88.

CHAPTER 8

1. Francis Fukuyama, "The End of History?" *National Interest*, no. 16 (Summer 1989): 3–18 (quote from p. 4). More recent echoes of the Fukuyama thesis can be found in Michael Mandelbaum, *The Ideas That Conquered the World: Peace, Democracy, and Free Markets in the Twenty-first Century* (New York: PublicAffairs, 2002), which is rambunctiously confident in tone; and Fareed Zakaria, *The Future of Freedom: Illiberal Democracy at Home and Abroad* (New York: Norton, 2003), which is tinged with anxiety.

2. Bush addresses to Congress, 31 January 1990, 29 January 1991, and 28 January 1992, all available at the website for the George Bush Presidential Library, <http://bushlibrary.tamu.edu/research/papers/1990/90013101.html>, </1991/91012902.html>, and </1992/92012801.html> (accessed 21 August 2004).

3. Transcript of Clinton's remarks, 27 November 1995, in "Clinton's Words on Mission to Bosnia: 'The Right Thing to Do,'" *New York Times* (online edition), 28 November 1995 (accessed 19 April 2006).

4. Clinton's public remarks, 9 November 1993, available at the Government Printing Office website, <http://frwebgate4.access.gpo.gov/cgi-bin/waisgate.cgi?WAISdocID=1919013460+3+0+0&WAISaction=retrieve> (accessed 13 February 2003).

5. From Clinton's State of the Union address, 23 January 1996, available at the Government Printing Office website, <http://frwebgate4.access.gpo.gov/cgi-bin/waisgate.cgi?WAISdocID=79392810140+12+0+0&WAISaction=retrieve> (accessed 7 July 2005).

6. Quote from Thomas L. Friedman, "A Manifesto for the Fast World," *New York Times Magazine*, 28 March 1999, 42. The fuller statement is his *The Lexus and the Olive Tree* (New York: Farrar, Straus, Giroux, 1999). Friedman put out a revised edition of the book in 2000.

7. Friedman, "Manifesto for the Fast World," 43.

8. Jerry Brown quoted in Susan A. Aaronson, *Trade and the American Dream: A Social History of Postwar Trade Policy* (Lexington: University Press of Kentucky, 1996), 147. For key works reflecting the varied reaction against globalization by the late 1990s, see Patrick J. Buchanan, *The Great Betrayal: How American Sovereignty and Social Justice Are Betrayed to the Gods of the Global Economy* (Boston: Little, Brown, 1998); Benjamin R. Barber, *Jihad vs. McWorld* (New York: Times Books, 1995); and William Greider, *One World, Ready or Not: The Manic Logic of Global Capitalism* (New York: Simon and Schuster, 1997).

9. On public disquiet, see the survey data in John E. Rielly, ed., "American Public Opinion and U.S. Foreign Policy 1999," chap. 3. This study was sponsored by the Chicago Council on Foreign Relations and is available at the council's website, <http://

www.ccfr.org/publications/opinion/American%20Public%20Opinion%20Report%201999.pdf> (accessed 16 June 2005).

10. Dick Cheney, *Defense Strategy for the 1990s: The Regional Defense Strategy* ([Washington, D.C.: U.S. Department of Defense] January 1993), 27. A draft of this report appeared in the *New York Times* (online edition), 8 March 1992 (accessed 12 August 2006).

11. Quotes from Samuel Huntington, "The Clash of Civilizations?" *Foreign Affairs* 72 (Summer 1993): 40; and Huntington, "The West Unique, Not Universal," *Foreign Affairs* 75 (November/December 1996): 41. The latter essay extended his attack against an optimistic reading of globalization. Just a year after Huntington's famous essay appeared, Robert D. Kaplan offered an equally dark and widely noticed picture of a world fragmenting under mounting social, demographic, and environmental pressures. See "The Coming Anarchy," *Atlantic Monthly*, February 1994, 44–76. Kaplan gave fuller elaboration to the theme of the threatening chaos in the developing world in *The Ends of the Earth: A Journey at the Dawn of the 21st Century* (New York: Random House, 1996).

12. William Kristol and Robert Kagan, "Toward a Neo-Reaganite Foreign Policy," *Foreign Affairs* 75 (July–August 1996): 20, 23; and "Statement of Principles" issued by the Project for the New American Century, 3 June 1997, available at the Project's website, <http://www.newamericancentury.org/statementofprinciples.htm> (accessed 11 March 2006).

13. Bush quote from campaign speech at the Reagan Presidential Library, 19 November 1999, in Stefan Halper and Jonathan Clarke, *America Alone: The Neo-Conservatives and the Global Order* (Cambridge, U.K.: Cambridge University Press, 2004), 133.

14. Bush address to Congress and the nation, 20 September 2001, available online at <http://www.whitehouse.gov/news/releases/2001/09/20010920-8.html> (accessed 21 November 2001); Bush State of the Union address, 29 January 2002, available online at <http://www.whitehouse.gov/news/releases/2002/01/20020129-11.html> (accessed 11 May 2002).

15. Bush address at the U.S. Military Academy, 1 June 2002, available online at <http://www.whitehouse.gov/news/releases/2002/06/20020601-3.html> (accessed 23 July 2002). The Bush Doctrine, formally known as "The National Security Strategy of the United States of America," was released 20 September 2002 and is available at <http://www.whitehouse.gov/nsc/nss.html>. Bush comments on freedom in Iraq date from 28 March 2003 and appear in Bob Woodward, *Plan of Attack* (New York: Simon and Schuster, 2004), 405.

16. Edward W. Said, "The Clash of Ignorance," *Nation*, 22 October 2001, 12; and

Zelikow quoted in Judith Miller, "Keeping U.S. No. 1: Is It Wise? Is It New?" *New York Times* (online edition), 26 October 2002 (accessed 26 October 2002).

17. Clinton quote from remarks at Harvard University, 19 November 2001, available at <http://www.news.harvard.edu/specials/2001/clinton/clintonspeech.html> (accessed 2 July 2005); and Huntington quoted in an interview by Deborah Solomon, "Three Cheers for Assimilation," *New York Times Magazine* (online edition), 2 May 2004 (accessed 25 June 2004).

18. Military data from Clyde Prestowitz, *Rogue Nation: American Unilateralism and the Failure of Good Intentions* (New York: Basic Books, 2003), 26.

19. The term is Michael Ignatieff's and gets developed in his *Virtual War: Kosovo and Beyond* (New York: Henry Holt, 2000).

20. Anonymous interviewee, quoted in Piero Gleijeses, "Reflections on Victory: The United States and Central America," *SAIS Review* 10 (Summer–Fall 1990): 176.

21. Bush's declaration is captured in the PBS video documentary "The Gulf War" (written and produced by Eamonn Matthews; first shown 9 January 1996; 4 hours; BBC/WGBH Frontline coproduction).

22. Bush remarks, 1 March 1991, available online at <http://bushlibrary.tamu.edu/research/papers/1991/91030102.html> (accessed 21 August 2004); Jack Kelly, "Estimates of Deaths in First War Still in Dispute," *Pittsburgh Post-Gazette*, 16 February 2003; and Richard Garfield, "Morbidity and Mortality among Iraqi Children from 1990 to 1998," available at the Fourth Freedom Forum website: <http://www.fourthfreedom.org> (accessed 16 July 2006).

23. Bush comments recalled by Richard A. Clarke, *Against All Enemies: Inside America's War on Terror* (New York: Free Press, 2004), 32; Matthew Rycroft secret memo of meeting with the prime minister, 23 July 2002, available from the online edition of London's *Sunday Times* at <http://www.timesonline.co.uk/article/0,,2087-1593607,00.html> (accessed 6 May 2005); and Gen. Michael T. Moseley quoted in Michael R. Gordon and Bernard E. Trainor, *Cobra II: The Inside Story of the Invasion and Occupation of Iraq* (New York: Pantheon, 2006), 423.

24. With Iraq looming as a failure, H. R. McMaster, *Dereliction of Duty: Lyndon Johnson, Robert McNamara, the Joint Chiefs of Staff, and the Lies That Led to Vietnam* (New York: HarperCollins, 1997), became the reference point for officers looking for lessons just as they had consulted Harry G. Summers, *On Strategy: A Critical Analysis of the Vietnam War* (Novato, Calif.: Presidio Press, 1982), in the wake of the Vietnam failure. Both focused on flaws in U.S. decision making and downplayed the broader set of constraints at work on U.S. policymakers at home and internationally. The warning is Otto von Bismarck's, quoted in Walter Isaacson, *Kissinger: A Biography* (New York: Simon and Schuster, 1992), 488.

25. Madeleine Albright, with Bill Woodward, *Madam Secretary* (New York: Miramax Books, 2003), 182.

26. Aid data from United Nations Development Programme, *Human Development Report, 1991* (New York: Oxford University Press, 1991), 53; *Human Development Report, 1998* (New York: Oxford University Press, 1998), 196; *Human Development Report, 1999* (New York: Oxford University Press, 1999), 49.

27. Polling data from Edward C. Luck, *Mixed Messages: American Politics and International Organization, 1919–1999* (Washington, D.C.: Brookings Institution Press, 1999), 35–39.

28. Stanley Meisler, *United Nations: The First Fifty Years* (New York: Atlantic Monthly Press, 1995), 219 (quotes from Heritage Foundation study, Heritage Foundation vice president Burton Yale Pines, and Kirkpatrick).

29. Comment by John Bolton in 1999 quoted in David C. Hendrickson, "The Curious Case of American Hegemony: Imperial Aspirations and National Decline," *World Policy Journal* 22 (Summer 2005): 4.

30. This paragraph draws on Samantha Power, *"A Problem from Hell": America and the Age of Genocide* (New York: Basic Books, 2002). The comment is David Rieff's, quoted on p. 504.

31. Lewis L. Gould, *The Modern American Presidency* (Lawrence: University Press of Kansas, 2003), 152, 218, 275 n. 11.

32. Roy Rosenzweig and David Thelen, *The Presence of the Past: Popular Uses of History in American Life* (New York: Columbia University Press, 1998), 204.

33. William Celis, "Study Says Half of Adults in U.S. Lack Reading and Math Abilities," *New York Times* (online edition), 9 September 1993 (accessed 19 April 2006); and David Leonhardt, "More Americans Were Uninsured and Poor in 2003, Census Finds," *New York Times* (online edition), 27 August 2004 (accessed 19 April 2006).

34. Eric Monkkonen, "Homicide: Explaining America's Exceptionalism," *American Historical Review* 111 (February 2006): 78; and AP report, "Nation's Inmate Population Increased 2.3 Percent Last Year," *New York Times* (online edition), 25 April 2005 (accessed 20 April 2006).

35. Steven Kull et al., "Misperceptions, the Media and the Iraq War," 2 October 2003, available online at <http://www.worldpublicopinion.org/pipa/articles/international_security_bt/102.php?nid=&id=&pnt=102&lb=brusc> (accessed 11 March 2006); and "Opinion Leaders Turn Cautious, Public Looks Homeward," 17 November 2005, available online at <http://people-press.org/reports/display.php3?ReportID=263> (accessed 13 March 2006).

36. For evidence on the public's attitude toward the military, see Peter D. Feaver and Richard H. Kohn, eds., *Soldiers and Civilians: The Civil-Military Gap and Ameri-*

can National Security (Cambridge, Mass.: MIT Press, 2001), 134 (graph in the essay by Paul Gronke and Peter D. Feaver); and David C. King and Zachary Karabell, *The Generation of Trust: Public Confidence in the U.S. Military since Vietnam* (Washington, D.C.: AEI Press, 2003), 4, 9.

37. Peter W. Singer, *Corporate Warriors: The Rise of the Privatized Military Industry* (Ithaca, N.Y.: Cornell University Press, 2003), 15–17.

38. For critical points from Feaver and Kohn, *Soldiers and Civilians*, on which this paragraph draws, see pp. 97 (from Ole R. Holsti summary of survey findings), 436 (quote from Elliot A. Cohen's adept treatment of civil-military complexities), and 459–67 (from the Kohn-Feaver conclusion).

39. Savings rate for 2005 in "Business Digest," *New York Times* (online edition), 31 January 2006 (accessed 20 April 2006); and debt information in Congressional Budget Office, "Historical Budget Data," 26 January 2006, available online at <http://www.cbo.gov/budget/historical.pdf> (accessed 16 March 2006).

40. Prestowitz, *Rogue Nation*, 27 (on Internet communications); Torbjørn L. Knutsen, *The Rise and Fall of World Orders* (Manchester, U.K.: Manchester University Press, 1999), 291 (for top movies in 1994).

41. "Cabinet Office paper: Conditions for military action," 21 July 2002, obtained by London's *Sunday Times* and made available on 12 June 2005 at the Timesonline website, <http://www.timesonline.co.uk/article/0,,2089-1648758,00.html> (accessed 12 June 2005).

42. Quoted in Alan S. Milward, with George Brennan and Federico Romero, *European Rescue of the Nation-State*, 2nd ed. (London: Routledge, 2000), 208.

43. "Transatlantic Trends 2004" available online at <http://www.transatlantictrends.org/> (accessed 13 March 2005); and quote from Régis Debray in *Le Figaro*, September 2003, translated in "The Indispensable Nation," *Harper's Magazine*, January 2004, 18.

44. "A Year after Iraq War," 9, 21, 37. This nine-country survey was conducted in February–March 2004 by the Pew Research Center for the People and the Press, available online at <http://www.people-press.org> (accessed 7 October 2004).

45. Ishihara Shintarō and Morita Akio were the coauthors of the Japanese edition of *The Japan That Can Say No*, which enjoyed an enormous success when it appeared in 1989. Ishihara's name alone appears on the translation into English, *The Japan That Can Say No: Why Japan Will Be First among Equals* (New York: Simon and Schuster, 1991). Poll data in David Sanger, "Gloom Lifts in U.S. and Falls on Japan," *New York Times* (online edition), 29 December 1992 (accessed 20 April 2006). Perhaps the most notable example of the "say no" genre from China is the best-selling Song Qiang et al., *Zhongguo keyi shuo bu* [The China that can say no] (Hong Kong: Ming bao, 1996).

46. Polling data from the Pew Global Attitudes Project, which is available online at <http://www.people-press.org/121901que.htm> (accessed 5 January 2002); and "A Year after Iraq War," 16–21. Quotes from Anthony Shadid, "In Arab World Ally, Anti-American Feeling Runs Deep," *Boston Globe* (online edition), 14 October 2001 (accessed 10 August 2006).

CONCLUSION

1. Attributed to Camus in Armand Mattelart, *Networking the World, 1794–2000*, trans. Liz Carey-Libbrecht and James A. Cohen (Minneapolis: University of Minnesota Press, 2000), 97.

2. "Anglophone empire" is Niall Ferguson's coinage in his *Colossus: The Price of America's Empire* (New York: Penguin Press, 2004).

3. Patrick J. Buchanan, "USA Is Not Wanted in Iraq," editorial in *USA Today*, 14 November 2002, available online at <http://www.usatoday.com/news/opinion/edi torials/2002-11-14-edit-oppose_x.htm> (accessed 19 April 2006).

4. Angus Maddison, *The World Economy: A Millennial Perspective* (Paris: Development Centre of the Organisation for Economic Co-operation and Development, 2001), 263.

5. The soft-hard power distinction is Joseph S. Nye's, first elaborated in "Soft Power," *Foreign Policy* 80 (Fall 1990): 153–71, and in *Bound to Lead: The Changing Nature of American Power* (New York: Basic Books, 1990), 32. On the normative dimensions of hegemony, see the helpful discussion in Torbjørn L. Knutsen, *The Rise and Fall of World Orders* (Manchester, U.K.: Manchester University Press, 1999), 59–67.

6. See the estimates by the UN's Population Division, Department of Economic and Social Affairs, "World Population to 2300" (2004), 12, available at <http://www .un.org/esa/population/publications/longrange2/WorldPop2300final.pdf> (accessed 5 January 2006).

7. J. R. McNeill, *Something New under the Sun: An Environmental History of the Twentieth-Century World* (New York: Norton, 2000), 3.

8. Estimate from Robert D. Hershey Jr., "Counting the Wealth of Nations," *New York Times* (online edition), 19 December 1995 (accessed 12 August 2006).

9. Proliferation is tracked at the Federation of Atomic Scientists website, <http:// fas.org/nuke/guide/index.html>.

10. Quoted in David C. Hendrickson, "The Curious Case of American Hegemony: Imperial Aspirations and National Decline," *World Policy Journal* 22 (Summer 2005): 7.

11. Nick Donovan and David Halpern, "Life Satisfaction: the State of Knowledge and Implications for Government" (December 2002), available at <http://www.wcfia

.harvard.edu/conferences/socialcapital/Happiness%20Readings/DonovanHalpern.pdf> (accessed 1 January 2005). See particularly the graph at the bottom of p. 10.

12. The phrase is Emmanuel Todd's, from his *After the Empire: The Breakdown of the American Order*, trans. C. Jon Delogu (New York: Columbia University Press, 2004), 134.

A GUIDE TO THE LITERATURE

INTRODUCTION: FRAMING THE QUESTION
This volume draws heavily if selectively on an enormous body of work on U.S. foreign relations by historians but also by political scientists, sociologists, anthropologists, and journalists. (Memoirs, oral histories, and documentary collections are cited only in the notes.) Anyone wanting to go beyond the works discussed here has an abundance of resources to exploit. Two basic, comprehensive guides—both happily up to date—can be found in *American Foreign Relations since 1600: A Guide to the Literature*, 2nd ed., ed. Robert L. Beisner and Kurt W. Hanson (2 vols.; Santa Barbara, Calif.: ABC-CLIO, 2003); and in the survey of major trends in Michael J. Hogan and Thomas G. Paterson, eds., *Explaining the History of American Foreign Relations*, 2nd ed. (Cambridge, U.K.: Cambridge University Press, 2004). The latest foreign relations scholarship appears in the journals *Diplomatic History* and *International History Review*. The Foreign Policy Association offers "Editor's Picks" on its website (<http://www.fpa.org>), while *Foreign Affairs* maintains a substantial book review section. The study of the Cold War, with its long-standing controversies and intense preoccupation with the latest archival releases, is richly served by *Journal of Cold War Studies*, *Cold War History*, the Cold War International History Project (<http://wilsoncenter.org>), and the National Security Archives (<http://www.gwu.edu/~nsarchiv>).

The controversies surrounding the 9/11 attacks and operations in Afghanistan and Iraq have inspired an intensifying search for historical perspective. Historians with academic credentials have begun to bring their expertise to bear. Niall Ferguson in *Colossus: The Price of America's Empire* (New York: Penguin Press, 2004) has elaborated his earlier call (in *Empire: The Rise and Demise of the British World Order and the Lessons for Global Power* [New York: Basic Books, 2003]) for the United States to recognize its imperial past and accept its imperial destiny. Ferguson is not optimistic that Americans, who have repeatedly demonstrated "the absence of a will to power" (29), will live up to the proud, progressive tradition of Anglophone empire. Ferguson's argument suffers from its all-encompassing definition of empire and its self-confessed "freshman" command of U.S. history. In *Resurrecting Empire: Western Footprints and America's Perilous Path in the Middle East* (Boston: Beacon Press, 2004), Rhashid Khalidi warns that an imperial policy is unsustainable in light of the Middle East's long experience with and lively opposition to foreign control. The strength of the account is Khalidi's understanding of the region, not of U.S. policy. Greg Grandin, *Empire's Workshop: Latin America, the United States, and the Rise of the New Imperialism*

(New York: Metropolitan Books, 2006), offers another regional perspective with the same set of strengths and limits. John Lewis Gaddis has offered in *Surprise, Security, and the American Experience* (Cambridge, Mass: Harvard University Press, 2004), an extended essay that takes him out of the Cold War policy world that he knows well. He argues not altogether persuasively for precedents to the 9/11 attacks in the 1814 British march into Washington and the 1941 Japanese bombing of Pearl Harbor. All three, he contends, gave rise to new security doctrines that propelled the United States toward ever greater dominance in world affairs. Finally, Charles S. Maier's *Among Empires: American Ascendancy and Its Predecessors* (Cambridge, Mass.: Harvard University Press, 2006) and Bernard Porter's *Empire and Superempire: Britain, America and the World* (New Haven, Conn.: Yale University Press, 2006) measure the U.S. international role against imperial enterprises by other powers. To these contributions should be added the essays in Joanne Meyerowitz, ed., *History and September 11th* (Philadelphia: Temple University Press, 2003).

The impulse to bring the past to bear on current policy extends well beyond academic historians, though often with mixed results. See, by way of example, Walter Russell Mead, *Special Providence: American Foreign Policy and How It Changed the World* (New York: Knopf, 2001); Max Boot, *Savage Wars of Peace: Small Wars and the Rise of American Power* (New York: Basic Books, 2002); Andrew J. Bacevich, *American Empire: The Realities and Consequences of U.S. Diplomacy* (Cambridge, Mass.: Harvard University Press, 2002); Robert Kagan, *Of Paradise and Power: America and Europe in the New World Order* (New York: Knopf, 2003); Anatol Lieven's especially acute *America Right or Wrong: An Anatomy of American Nationalism* (New York: Oxford University Press, 2004); John B. Judis, *The Folly of Empire: What George W. Bush Could Learn from Theodore Roosevelt and Woodrow Wilson* (New York: Scribner, 2004); and Neil Smith, *The Endgame of Globalization* (New York: Routledge, 2005).

My perspective on current issues and their historical setting owes much to global history, which as a field has taken off over the last decade. For the best brief introductions, see Jürgen Osterhammel and Niels P. Petersson, *Globalization: A Short History*, trans. Dona Geyer (Princeton, N.J.: Princeton University Press, 2005); and A. G. Hopkins, "The History of Globalization—and the Globalization of History?" in *Globalization in World History*, ed. Hopkins (London: Pimlico, 2002), 11–46. Patrick Manning, *Navigating World History: Historians Create a Global Past* (New York: Palgrave Macmillan, 2003), offers a more elaborate introduction, surveying past initiatives and current issues critical to understanding the field. See also Michael Geyer and Charles Bright, "World History in a Global Age," *American Historical Review* 100 (October 1995): 1034–60; and Ross E. Dunn, ed., *The New World History: A Teacher's Companion* (Boston: Bedford/St. Martin's, 2000).

Global history perspectives have stimulated attempts to rethink U.S. history in general while reinforcing a trend within the U.S. foreign relations field toward a more international perspective. Good examples of this ferment include Carl J. Guarneri, "Internationalizing the United States Survey Course: American History for a Global Age," *History Teacher* 36 (November 2002): 37–64; Eric Foner, "American Freedom in a Global Age," *American Historical Review* 106 (February 2001): 1–16; Thomas Bender, ed., *Rethinking American History in a Global Age* (Berkeley: University of California Press, 2002); Thomas W. Zeiler, "Just Do It! Globalization for Diplomatic Historians," *Diplomatic History* 25 (Fall 2001): 529–51; and Michael J. Hogan, "The 'Next Big Thing': The Future of Diplomatic History in a Global Age," *Diplomatic History* 28 (January 2004): 1–21. For the first sustained attempts by diplomatic historians to go global, see David Ryan, *U.S. Foreign Policy in World History* (London: Routledge, 2000); and Alfred E. Eckes Jr. and Thomas W. Zeiler, *Globalization and the American Century* (Cambridge, U.K.: Cambridge University Press, 2003).

I. NINETEENTH-CENTURY FOUNDATIONS

For the United States as a case of settler colonialism with its attendant borderlands, indigenous resistance, and ideologies of conquest, see Michael Adas, "From Settler Colony to Global Hegemon: Integrating the Exceptionalist Narrative of the American Experience into World History," *American Historical Review* 106 (December 2001), especially 1697–1717. Philip D. Curtin discusses settler colonialism alongside other types of European overseas intrusion in *The World and the West: The European Challenge and the Overseas Response in the Age of Empire* (New York: Cambridge University Press, 2000), 1–17. Equally applicable is the concept of borderlands as zones of conflict. See the three instructive cases developed in Jeremy Adelman and Stephen Aron, "From Borderlands to Borders: Empires, Nation-States, and the Peoples in Between in North American History," *American History Review* 104 (June 1999): 814–41. Alan Taylor employs these interpretive frames in his *American Colonies* (New York: Viking, 2001), a skilled synthesis that extends to 1820 and across the Great Plains to the Pacific. Joyce E. Chaplin, "Expansion and Exceptionalism in Early American History," *Journal of American History* 89 (March 2003): 1431–55, offers a helpful field review.

For exemplary studies from a rich literature on the Native American dispossession, see Richard White, *The Middle Ground: Indians, Empire, and Republics in the Great Lakes Region, 1650–1815* (Cambridge, U.K.: Cambridge University Press, 1991); Gregory E. Dowd, *A Spirited Resistance: The North American Indian Struggle for Unity, 1745–1815* (Baltimore: Johns Hopkins University Press, 1991); Anthony F. C. Wallace, *The Long, Bitter Trail: Andrew Jackson and the Indians* (New York: Hill and Wang, 1993); and Jeffrey Ostler, *The Plains Sioux and U.S. Colonialism from Louis and Clark to Wounded Knee* (Cambridge, U.K.: Cambridge University Press, 2004).

The U.S. policy that ensured not only national survival but also the conquest of a continent is treated in Marie-Jeanne Rossignol, *The Nationalist Ferment: The Origins of U.S. Foreign Policy, 1789–1812*, trans. Lillian A. Parrott (Columbus: Ohio State University Press, 2004); Jerald A. Combs, *The Jay Treaty: Political Battleground of the Founding Fathers* (Berkeley: University of California Press, 1970); Drew R. McCoy, *The Elusive Republic: Political Economy in Jeffersonian America* (Chapel Hill: University of North Carolina Press, 1980); and Thomas R. Hietala, *Manifest Design: American Exceptionalism and Empire*, 2nd ed. (Ithaca, N.Y.: Cornell University Press, 2003). A towering figure in the U.S. national project gets fresh attention in John L. Harper's interpretively engaging *American Machiavelli: Alexander Hamilton and the Origins of U.S. Foreign Policy* (Cambridge, U.K.: Cambridge University Press, 2004); and Ron Chernow's full and fluent *Alexander Hamilton* (New York: Penguin Press, 2004).

On the nineteenth-century rise of global capitalism in which the U.S. economy figured ever more prominently, see E. J. Hobsbawm, *The Age of Capital, 1848–1875* (New York: Charles Scribner's Sons, 1975), and his *The Age of Empire, 1875–1914* (New York: Vintage, 1989), two parts of a grand, shrewd four-volume history of the modern era. On the features of this inaugural phase of globalization defined from an economic history perspective, see Kevin H. O'Rourke and Jeffrey G. Williamson, *Globalization and History: The Evolution of a Nineteenth-Century Atlantic Economy* (Cambridge, Mass.: MIT Press, 1999); O'Rourke and Williamson, "When Did Globalization Begin?" National Bureau of Economic Research Working Paper 7632, April 2000 (available online at <http://www.nber.org/papers/w7632>); Michael D. Brado et al., "Is Globalization Today Really Different from Globalization a Hundred Years Ago?" National Bureau of Economic Research Working Paper 7199, June 1999 (available online at <http://www.nber.org/papers/w7195>); and Patrick K. O'Brien and Geoffrey Allen Pigman, "Free Trade, British Hegemony and the International Economic Order in the Nineteenth Century," *Review of International Studies* 18 (April 1992): 89–113.

For the emergence of the U.S. economic powerhouse, see Stanley Engerman and Robert E. Gallman, eds., *The Cambridge Economic History of the United States*, vol. 2: *The Long Nineteenth Century* and vol. 3: *The Twentieth Century* (Cambridge, U.K.: Cambridge University Press, 2000); and Gavin Wright, "The Origins of American Industrial Success, 1879–1940," *American Economic Review* 80 (September 1990): 651–68. Angus Maddison, *The World Economy: A Millennial Perspective* (Paris: Development Centre of the Organisation for Economic Co-operation and Development, 2001); and Paul Bairoch, "International Industrialization Levels from 1750 to 1980," *Journal of European Economic History* 11 (Fall 1982): 269–333, are both invaluable for economic data. The importance of technological innovation to U.S. material wealth, national identity, and international conduct is highlighted in a pair of broadly cast works:

Thomas P. Hughes, *American Genesis: A Century of Invention and Technological Enthusiasm, 1870–1970* (Chicago: University of Chicago Press, 1989); and Michael Adas, *Dominance by Design: Technological Imperatives and America's Civilizing Mission* (Cambridge, Mass.: Harvard University Press, 2006). Alfred E. Eckes Jr., *Opening America's Market: U.S. Foreign Trade Policy since 1776* (Chapel Hill: University of North Carolina Press, 1995), is a tough-minded examination of free-trade orthodoxy pertinent to this as well as later phases of U.S. economic development.

A number of works illuminate the U.S. economy's voracious appetite for labor and its dynamic trade and capital flows: David Eltis, *Coerced and Free Migration: Global Perspectives* (Stanford, Calif.: Stanford University Press, 2002); Adam McKeown, "Global Migration, 1846–1940," *Journal of World History* 15 (June 2004): 155–89; Peter A. Coclanis, "Distant Thunder: The Creation of a World Market in Rice and the Transformation It Wrought," *American Historical Review* 98 (October 1993): 1050–78; and Sven Beckert, "Emancipation and Empire: Reconstructing the Worldwide Web of Cotton Production in the Age of the American Civil War," *American Historical Review* 109 (December 2004): 1405–38.

A rich literature on nationalism as a global-girdling ideology contains insights pertinent to the U.S. case. Begin with Benedict Anderson's seminal *Imagined Communities: Reflections on the Origin and Spread of Nationalism*, rev. ed. (London: Verso, 1991), along with the critical responses by Partha Chatterjee, "Whose Imagined Community?" in Chatterjee, *The Nation and Its Fragments: Colonial and Postcolonial Histories* (Princeton, N.J.: Princeton University Press, 1993), 3–13; and by Robert Wiebe, "*Imagined Communities*, Nationalist Experiences," *Journal of the Historical Society* 1 (Spring 2000): 33–63. Other notable works include Ernest Gellner, *Nations and Nationalism* (Ithaca, N.Y.: Cornell University Press, 1983); Anthony D. Smith, *The Ethnic Origins of Nations* (Oxford: Blackwell, 1986); Smith, *Chosen Peoples* (New York: Oxford University Press, 2003); E. J. Hobsbawm, *Nations and Nationalism since 1780: Programme, Myth, Reality*, rev. ed. (Cambridge, U.K.: Cambridge University Press, 1992); and Robert H. Wiebe, *Who We Are: A History of Popular Nationalism* (Princeton, N.J.: Princeton University Press, 2002). For good introductions, see Lloyd Kramer, "Historical Narratives and the Meaning of Nationalism," *Journal of the History of Ideas* 58 (July 1997): 525–45; Geoff Eley and Ronald Grigor Suny, eds., *Becoming National: A Reader* (New York: Oxford University Press, 1996); and John Hutchinson and Anthony D. Smith, eds., *Nationalism* (Oxford: Oxford University Press, 1994).

A robust, outward-looking U.S. nationalist construct gets broad-brush treatment in Anders Stephanson, *Manifest Destiny: American Expansion and the Empire of Right* (New York: Hill and Wang, 1995); Michael H. Hunt, *Ideology and U.S. Foreign Policy* (New Haven, Conn.: Yale University Press, 1987); and Cecilia Elizabeth O'Leary, *To*

Die For: The Paradox of American Patriotism (Princeton, N.J.: Princeton University Press, 1999). A large literature treats the racial preoccupations that shaped dominant U.S. views of the broader world. Begin with Audrey Smedley's synthetic, anthropologically informed *Race in North America: Origin and Evolution of a Worldview,* 2nd ed. (Boulder, Colo.: Westview Press, 1999); then see Winthrop D. Jordan, *The White Man's Burden: Historical Origins of Racism in the United States* (New York: Oxford University Press, 1974); Robert K. Berkhofer Jr., *The White Man's Indian: Images of the American Indian from Columbus to the Present* (New York: Knopf, 1978); Fredrick B. Pike, *The United States and Latin America: Myths and Stereotypes of Civilization and Nature* (Austin: University of Texas Press, 1992); Reginald Horsman, *Race and Manifest Destiny: The Origins of American Racial Anglo-Saxonism* (Cambridge, Mass.: Harvard University Press, 1981); Stuart Anderson, *Race and Rapprochement: Anglo-Saxonism and Anglo-American Relations, 1895–1904* (Rutherford, N.J.: Fairleigh Dickinson University Press, 1981); Matthew Frye Jacobson, *Barbarian Virtues: The United States Encounters Foreign Peoples at Home and Abroad, 1876–1917* (New York: Hill and Wang, 2000); and John Higham, *Strangers in the Land: Patterns of American Nativism, 1860–1925* (New York: Atheneum, 1965).

2. GRAND PROJECTS, 1898–1920

For help in putting the United States in the context of the imperial projects that galvanized the North Atlantic world around the turn of the century, see E. J. Hobsbawm, *The Age of Empire, 1875–1914* (New York: Vintage, 1989); Michael Adas, *Machines as the Measure of Men: Science, Technology, and Ideologies of Western Dominance* (Ithaca, N.Y.: Cornell University Press, 1989); Frederick Cooper and Ann Laura Stoler, eds., *Tensions of Empire: Colonial Cultures in a Bourgeois World* (Berkeley: University of California Press, 1997); Frederick Cooper, *Colonialism in Question: Theory, Knowledge, History* (Berkeley: University of California Press, 2005); and David Spurr, *The Rhetoric of Empire: Colonial Discourse in Journalism, Travel Writing, and Imperial Administration* (Durham, N.C.: Duke University Press, 1993).

The work on U.S. expansion that looms above all others is William Appleman Williams, *The Tragedy of American Diplomacy,* 1st ed. (Cleveland: World Publishing Company, 1959), once controversial and now a classic. Walter LaFeber has further developed Williams's notion of expansion as economically driven, first in *The New Empire: An Interpretation of American Expansion, 1860–1898* (Ithaca, N.Y.: Cornell University Press, 1963), and more recently in *The American Search for Opportunity, 1865–1913* (New York: Cambridge University Press, 1993). For alternative readings, see Robert L. Beisner, *From the Old Diplomacy to the New, 1865–1900,* 2nd ed. (Arlington Heights, Ill.: Harlan Davidson, 1986); and Robert E. Hannigan, *The New World Power: American Foreign Policy, 1898–1917* (Philadelphia: University of Pennsylvania

Press, 2002). For good guides to the literature, see Joseph A. Fry, "From Open Door to World Systems: Economic Interpretations of Late Nineteenth Century American Foreign Relations," *Pacific Historical Review* 65 (May 1996): 277–303; and Louis A. Pérez Jr., *The War of 1898: The United States and Cuba in History and Historiography* (Chapel Hill: University of North Carolina Press, 1998). Special studies of note include Lewis L. Gould, *The Spanish-American War and President McKinley* (Lawrence: University Press of Kansas, 1982); John L. Offner, *An Unwanted War: The Diplomacy of the United States and Spain over Cuba, 1895–1898* (Chapel Hill: University of North Carolina Press, 1992); Kristin L. Hoganson, *Fighting for American Manhood: How Gender Politics Provoked the Spanish-American and Philippine-American Wars* (New Haven, Conn.: Yale University Press, 1998); and Walter L. Williams, "United States Indian Policy and the Debate over Philippine Annexation: Implications for the Origins of American Imperialism," *Journal of American History* 66 (March 1980): 810–31. The diverse opponents of empire get their due in Robert L. Beisner, *Twelve against Empire: The Anti-Imperialists, 1898–1900* (Chicago: University of Chicago Press, 1968); and Eric T. L. Love, *Race over Empire: Racism and U.S. Imperialism, 1865–1900* (Chapel Hill: University of North Carolina Press, 2004). For the popular dimensions of this entanglement with the outside world, see Robert W. Rydell, *All the World's a Fair: Visions of Empire at American International Expositions, 1876–1916* (Chicago: University of Chicago Press, 1984); Christopher Endy, "Travel and World Power: Americans in Europe, 1890–1917," *Diplomatic History* 22 (Fall 1998): 565–94; and Kristin Hoganson, "Cosmopolitan Domesticity: Importing the American Dream, 1865–1920," *American Historical Review* 107 (February 2002): 55–83.

For the deepening U.S. interest in the Caribbean and the Pacific, see Emily Rosenberg, *Financial Missionaries to the World: The Politics and Culture of Dollar Diplomacy, 1900–1930* (Cambridge, Mass.: Harvard University Press, 1999); John J. Johnson, *A Hemisphere Apart: The Foundations of United States Policy toward Latin America* (Baltimore: Johns Hopkins University Press, 1990); and Nancy Mitchell, *The Danger of Dreams: German and American Imperialism in Latin America* (Chapel Hill: University of North Carolina Press, 1999), which is impressively international in its interpretation. General accounts on the U.S. role in Latin America relevant here as well as for later periods include Lars Schoultz, *Beneath the United States: A History of U.S. Policy toward Latin America* (Cambridge, Mass.: Harvard University Press, 1998), which is strong on the role of racial and nationalist ideas; Walter LaFeber, *Inevitable Revolutions: The United States in Central America*, 2nd ed. (New York: W. W. Norton, 1993), which offers an alternative economic perspective; and Louis A. Pérez Jr., *Cuba and the United States: Ties of Singular Intimacy*, 3rd ed. (Athens: University of Georgia Press, 2003), a spirited treatment of a key case. Gathering U.S. involvement in East Asia is examined by Thomas J. McCormick, *China Market: America's Quest for*

Informal Empire, 1893–1901 (Chicago: Quadrangle Books, 1967); Marilyn B. Young, *The Rhetoric of Empire: American China Policy, 1895–1901* (Cambridge, Mass.: Harvard University Press, 1968); Michael H. Hunt, *The Making of a Special Relationship: The United States and China to 1914* (New York: Columbia University Press, 1983); and Akira Iriye, *Pacific Estrangement: Japanese and American Expansion, 1897–1911* (Cambridge, Mass.: Harvard University Press, 1972).

On the Philippines, Glenn A. May, the preeminent authority, provides excellent guidance on a rich literature in "The Unfathomable Other: Historical Studies of U.S.–Philippine Relations," in *Pacific Passage: The Study of American–East Asian Relations on the Eve of the Twenty-first Century*, ed. Warren I. Cohen (New York: Columbia University Press, 1996), 279–312. His *Battle for Batangas: A Philippine Province at War* (New Haven, Conn.: Yale University Press, 1991) and *Social Engineering and the Philippines: The Aims, Execution, and Impact of American Colonial Policy, 1900–1913* (Westport: Greenwood Press, 1980) loom large in the literature along with Stuart C. Miller, *"Benevolent Assimilation": The American Conquest of the Philippines, 1899–1903* (New Haven, Conn.: Yale University Press, 1982); Richard E. Welch, Jr., *Response to Imperialism: The United States and the Philippine-American War, 1899–1902* (Chapel Hill: University of North Carolina Press, 1979); Benedict Anderson, "Cacique Democracy in the Philippines: Origins and Dreams," in *Discrepant Histories: Translocal Essays on Filipino Culture*, ed. Vicente L. Rafael (Philadelphia: Temple University Press, 1995), 3–47; Julian Go and Anne L. Foster, eds., *The American Colonial State in the Philippines: Global Perspectives* (Durham, N.C.: Duke University Press, 2003); and Paul A. Kramer, *The Blood of Government: Race, Empire, the United States, and the Philippines* (Chapel Hill: University of North Carolina Press, 2006).

For a helpful review of the Wilson literature, see David Steigerwald, "The Reclamation of Woodrow Wilson?" *Diplomatic History* 23 (Winter 1999): 79–99. Key works include Lloyd E. Ambrosius's critical appraisal in *Wilsonian Statecraft: Theory and Practice of Liberal Internationalism during World War I* (Wilmington, Del.: Scholarly Resources, 1991); John W. Coogan's authoritative reading of Wilson's policy in the context of contemporary conceptions of international law in *The End of Neutrality: The United States, Britain, and Maritime Rights, 1899–1915* (Ithaca, N.Y.: Cornell University Press, 1981); Thomas J. Knock's sympathetic *To End All Wars: Woodrow Wilson and the Quest for a New World Order* (Princeton, N.J.: Princeton University Press, 1992); Ross A. Kennedy, "Woodrow Wilson, World War I, and an American Conception of National Security," *Diplomatic History* 25 (Winter 2001): 1–31, a fresh review of Wilson's views that finds striking sophistication and coherence along with profound flaws; and John Milton Cooper Jr., *Breaking the Heart of the World: Woodrow Wilson and the Fight for the League of Nations* (Cambridge, U.K.: Cambridge University Press, 2001), which makes Wilson's troubled physical and psychological state an important part of the bitter battle over the League of Nations. Wilson's response to the Russian revolution has long been controversial. Eugene P. Trani, "Woodrow Wilson and the Decision to Intervene in Russia: A Reconsideration," *Journal of Modern History* 48 (September 1976): 440–61, makes a cogent case for Wilson's caution and moderation. On the other side, Arno J. Mayer, *Politics and Diplomacy of Peacemaking: Containment and Counterrevolution at Versailles, 1918–1919* (New York: Knopf, 1967); and Lloyd C. Gardner, *Safe for Democracy: The Anglo-American Response to Revolution, 1913–1923* (New York: Oxford University Press, 1984), see a counterrevolutionary impulse driving Wilson and his European allies. Wilson's significance in the evolution of U.S. policy is the subject of Frank Ninkovich, *The Wilsonian Century: U.S. Foreign Policy since 1900* (Chicago: University of Chicago Press, 1999), and David Steigerwald, *Wilsonian Idealism in America* (Ithaca, N.Y.: Cornell University Press, 1994). The Anglo-American "special relationship," so dramatically to the fore during World War I, is surveyed in Anne Orde, *The Eclipse of Great Britain: The United States and Imperial Decline, 1895–1956* (New York: St. Martin's Press, 1996).

My sense of the state as a concept owes a good deal to Theda Skocpol. Her "Bringing the State Back In," *Social Science Research Council Items* 36 (June 1982): 1–8, makes in brief compass the case for seeing the state not as an arena for policy conflict among social groups and economic interests but rather as a relatively autonomous entity with legal, administrative, and coercive functions sustained by regular and substantial claims on economic resources. Raymond Grew masterfully develops the point in "The Nineteenth-Century European State," in *Statemaking and Social Movements*, ed. Charles Bright and Susan Harding (Ann Arbor: University of Michigan Press, 1984), 83–120. See also Peter B. Evans, Dietrich Rueschemeyer, and Theda Skocpol, eds., *Bringing the State Back In* (New York: Cambridge University Press, 1985); James C. Scott, *Seeing Like a State: How Certain Schemes to Improve the Human Condition Have Failed* (New Haven, Conn.: Yale University Press, 1998); the set of review essays on Scott's work in *American Historical Review* 106 (February 2001): 106–29; Mark Mazower, "Violence and the State in the Twentieth Century," *American Historical Review* 107 (October 2002): 1158–78; and Christopher Pierson, *The Modern State*, 2nd ed. (London: Routledge, 2004), a clear, thoughtful primer.

On U.S. state consolidation with the presidency at the center, see Lewis L. Gould, *The Modern American Presidency* (Lawrence: University Press of Kansas, 2003); and Stephen Skowronek, *Building a New American State: The Expansion of National Administrative Capacities, 1877–1920* (Cambridge, U.K.: Cambridge University Press, 1982). For light on state mobilization of the public on matters of foreign policy at the turn of the century, see Robert C. Hilderbrand, *Power and the People: Executive Management of Public Opinion in Foreign Affairs, 1897–1921* (Chapel Hill: University of North Carolina Press, 1981); and Ernest R. May's treatment of "The Structure of Public Opinion," in his *American Imperialism: A Speculative Essay* (New York: Atheneum, 1968), chap. 2. On the elites that played a central role in state building over the first half of the twentieth century, see Priscilla Roberts, "'All the Right People': The Historiography of the American Foreign Policy Establishment," *Journal of American Studies* 26 (December 1992): 409–34; Roberts, "The Anglo-American Theme: American Visions of an Atlantic Alliance, 1914–1933," *Diplomatic History* 21 (Summer 1997): 333–64; and Eric P. Kaufmann, *The Rise and Fall of Anglo-America* (Cambridge, Mass.: Harvard University Press, 2004). The development of the instruments of state power are treated in Richard H. Werking, *The Master Architects: Building the United States Foreign Service, 1890–1913* (Lexington: University of Kentucky Press, 1977); Robert D. Schulzinger, *The Making of the Diplomatic Mind: The Training, Outlook, and Style of United States Foreign Service Officers, 1908–1931* (Middletown, Conn.: Wesleyan University Press, 1975); and Paul A. C. Koistinen, *Mobilizing for Modern War: The Political Economy of American Warfare, 1865–1919* (Lawrence: University Press of Kansas, 1997), especially the synthetic treatment of the navy and the army in chapters 3 and 4.

3. THE AMERICAN WAY IN A FRAGMENTING WORLD, 1921–1940

The global drift toward disaster figures as the essential backdrop for interwar U.S. foreign relations. For Europe's central role, begin with E. J. Hobsbawm, *The Age of Extremes, 1914–1991* (New York: Pantheon, 1995), part 1; and Charles S. Maier, *Recasting Bourgeois Europe: Stabilization in France, Germany, and Italy after World War I* (Princeton, N.J.: Princeton University Press, 1975). On the unraveling of the transatlantic economy, see Dietmar Rothermund, *The Global Impact of the Great Depression, 1929–1939* (London: Routledge, 1996), a sketch emphasizing global dimensions; Harold James, *The End of Globalization: Lessons from the Great Depression* (Cambridge, Mass.: Harvard University Press, 2001), a cautionary tale about the fragility of the global economy; and Barry Eichengreen, *Golden Fetters: The Gold Standard and the Great Depression, 1919–1939* (New York: Oxford University Press, 1992), a detailed, broadly cast analysis. More specialized studies on the troubled interwar economy include M. E. Falkus, "United States Economic Policy and the 'Dollar Gap' of the 1920's," *Economic History Review*, 2nd ser., 24 (November 1971): 599–623; William C. McNeil, *American Money and the Weimar Republic: Economics and Politics on the Eve of the Great Depression* (New York: Columbia University Press, 1986); and Stephen A. Schuker, *American "Reparations" to Germany, 1919–33: Implications for the Third-World Debt Crisis* (Princeton, N.J.: Princeton University Department of Economics, 1988). The intensifying challenge to Western dominance after World War I—a matter of concern to Americans nearly as much as to Europeans—is the subject of Michael

Adas, "Contested Hegemony: The Great War and the Afro-Asian Assault on the Civilizing Mission Ideology," *Journal of World History* 15 (March 2004): 31–63.

On the origins and workings of the U.S. consumer model that became so consequential abroad, the following are especially helpful: Olivier Zunz, *Why the American Century?* (Chicago: University of Chicago Press, 1998); Susan Strasser, *Satisfaction Guaranteed: The Making of the American Mass Market* (New York: Pantheon, 1989); Daniel Horowitz, *The Morality of Spending: Attitudes toward the Consumer Society in America, 1875–1940* (Baltimore: Johns Hopkins University Press, 1985); Richard W. Fox and T. J. Jackson Lears, eds., *The Culture of Consumption: Critical Essays in American History, 1880–1980* (New York: Pantheon, 1983); Roland Marchand, *Advertising the American Dream: Making Way for Modernity, 1920–1940* (Berkeley: University of California Press, 1985); Robert W. Rydell and Rob Kroes, *Buffalo Bill in Bologna: The Americanization of the World, 1869–1922* (Chicago: University of Chicago Press, 2005), which is more preoccupied with domestic origins and less with international reception than the title suggests; and Gary Cross, *An All-Consuming Century: Why Commercialism Won in Modern America* (New York: Columbia University Press, 2000).

The florescence of U.S. economic and cultural influence in Europe and Latin America has lately attracted scholarly attention. Victoria de Grazia, *Irresistible Empire: America's Advance through Twentieth-Century Europe* (Cambridge, Mass.: Harvard University Press, 2005), is a tour de force that is filled with revealing detail. See also de Grazia, "Mass Culture and Sovereignty: The American Challenge to European Cinemas, 1920–1960," *Journal of Modern History* 61 (March 1989): 53–87; Mary Nolan, *Visions of Modernity: American Business and the Modernization of Germany* (New York: Oxford University Press, 1994); and Gilbert M. Joseph, Catherine C. LeGrand, and Ricardo D. Salvatore, eds., *Close Encounters of Empire: Writing the Cultural History of U.S.–Latin American Relations* (Durham, N.C.: Duke University Press, 1998). For additional help in setting the U.S. model in global context, see Peter N. Stearns, *Consumerism in World History: The Global Transformation of Desire* (London: Routledge, 2001); Susan Strasser, Charles McGovern, and Matthias Judt, eds., *Getting and Spending: European and American Consumer Societies in the Twentieth Century* (New York: Cambridge University Press, 1998); and Victoria de Grazia with Ellen Furlough, eds., *The Sex of Things: Gender and Consumption in Historical Perspective* (Berkeley: University of California Press, 1996). The following provide reminders that U.S. consumer demand for agricultural products and minerals was politically, environmentally, and socially disruptive: Thomas F. O'Brien, *The Revolutionary Mission: American Enterprise in Latin America, 1900–1945* (Cambridge, U.K.: Cambridge University Press, 1996); Richard P. Tucker, *Insatiable Appetite: The United States and the Ecological Degradation of the Tropical World* (Berkeley: University of California Press, 2000);

and Steve Marquandt, "'Green Havoc': Panama Disease, Environmental Change, and Labor Process in the Central American Banana Industry," *American Historical Review* 106 (February 2001): 49–80.

The stock of postwar Republicans has risen dramatically among historians. The trailblazing studies are Emily Rosenberg, *Spreading the American Dream: American Economic and Cultural Expansion, 1890–1945* (New York: Hill and Wang, 1982); and Frank Costigliola, *Awkward Dominion: American Political, Economic, and Cultural Relations with Europe, 1919–1933* (Ithaca, N.Y.: Cornell University Press, 1984). On "corporatism," a pivotal interpretive concept in this literature, see the exchange between Michael J. Hogan and John Gaddis in *Diplomatic History* 10 (Fall 1986): 357–72. Robert David Johnson, *The Peace Progressives and American Foreign Relations* (Cambridge, Mass.: Harvard University Press, 1995), offers a fresh examination of the critics of Republican orthodoxy. Franklin Roosevelt's foreign policy is well handled in Robert Dallek, *Franklin D. Roosevelt and American Foreign Policy, 1932–1945* (New York: Oxford University Press, 1979); and Robert A. Divine, *Roosevelt and World War II* (Baltimore: Johns Hopkins Press, 1969).

For recent work that highlights the globalizing trends in which the Republicans participated, see Francis Anthony Boyle, *Foundations of World Order: The Legalist Approach to International Relations (1898–1922)* (Durham, N.C.: Duke University Press, 1999); Akira Iriye, *Global Community: The Role of International Organizations in the Making of the Contemporary World* (Berkeley: University of California Press, 2002); Leila J. Rupp, *Worlds of Women: The Making of an International Women's Movement* (Princeton, N.J.: Princeton University Press, 1997); Daniel T. Rodgers, *Atlantic Crossings: Social Politics in a Progressive Age* (Cambridge, Mass.: Harvard University Press, 1998); Alan Dawley, *Changing the World: American Progressives in War and Revolution* (Princeton, N.J.: Princeton University Press, 2003); Robert A. McCaughey, "Four Academic Ambassadors: International Studies and the American University before the Second World War," *Perspectives in American History* 12 (1979): 563–607; and Robert D. Schulzinger, *The Wise Men of Foreign Affairs: The History of the Council on Foreign Relations* (New York: Columbia University Press, 1984).

The troubled interwar U.S. encounter with nationalism and Bolshevism in the hemisphere and Europe is treated in David F. Schmitz, *Thank God They're on Our Side: The United States and Right-wing Dictatorships, 1921–1965* (Chapel Hill: University of North Carolina Press, 1999); Lars Schoultz, *Beneath the United States: A History of U.S. Policy toward Latin America* (Cambridge, Mass.: Harvard University Press, 1998); Walter LaFeber, *Inevitable Revolutions: The United States in Central America*, 2nd ed. (New York: W. W. Norton, 1993); and Louis A. Pérez Jr., *Cuba and the United States: Ties of Singular Intimacy*, 3rd ed. (Athens: University of Georgia Press, 2003). The Mexican case is nicely covered from several angles by Daniela Spenser, *The Im-*

possible Triangle: Mexico, Soviet Russia, and the United States in the 1920s (Durham, N.C.: Duke University Press, 1999); John A. Britton, *Revolution and Ideology: Images of the Mexican Revolution in the United States* (Lexington: University Press of Kentucky, 1995); and Jürgen Buchenau, *In the Shadow of the Giant: The Making of Mexico's Central America Policy, 1876–1930* (Tuscaloosa: University of Alabama Press, 1996), particularly chaps. 5–7. For rising radicalism in China, see Edmund S. K. Fung, "The Chinese Nationalists and the Unequal Treaties 1924–1931," *Modern Asian Studies* 21 (October 1987): 793–819; P. Cavendish, "Anti-imperialism in the Kuomintang, 1923–8," in *Studies in the Social History of China and South-east Asia*, ed. Jerome Ch'en and Nicholas Tarling (Cambridge, U.K.: Cambridge University Press, 1970), 23–56; and Michael H. Hunt, *The Genesis of Chinese Communist Foreign Policy* (New York: Columbia University Press, 1996).

4. REACHING FOR GEOPOLITICAL DOMINANCE, 1941–1968

Images of the enemy, critical to understanding the U.S. response to aggressor states at midcentury, is the subject of the pioneering work by Les K. Adler and Thomas G. Paterson, "Red Fascism: The Merger of Nazi Germany and Soviet Russia in the American Image of Totalitarianism, 1930's–1950's," *American Historical Review* 75 (April 1970): 1046–64. More recent works that fill out the picture include Abbott Gleason, *Totalitarianism: The Inner History of the Cold War* (New York: Oxford University Press, 1995); Michaela Hoenicke Moore, "American Interpretations of National Socialism, 1933–1945," in *The Impact of Nazism: New Perspectives on the Third Reich and Its Legacy*, ed. Alan E. Steinweis and Daniel E. Rogers (Lincoln: University of Nebraska Press, 2003), 1–18; John L. Harper, *American Visions of Europe: Franklin D. Roosevelt, George F. Kennan, and Dean G. Acheson* (Cambridge, U.K.: Cambridge University Press, 1994); John W. Dower, *War without Mercy: Race and Power in the Pacific War* (New York: Pantheon, 1986); and Eduard Marks, "October or Thermidor? Interpretations of Stalinism and the Perception of Soviet Foreign Policy in the United States, 1927–1947," *American Historical Review* 94 (October 1989): 937–62. For critical appraisals of the Cold War equation of the German and Soviet regimes, see Ian Kershaw and Moshe Lewin, eds., *Stalinism and Nazism: Dictatorships in Comparison* (Cambridge, U.K.: Cambridge University Press, 1997); and the discussion continued in Henry Rousso and Richard J. Golsan, eds., *Stalinism and Nazism: History and Memory Compared*, trans. Lucy B. Golsan et al. (Lincoln: University of Nebraska Press, 2004).

Leading works on Roosevelt's foreign policy include Robert Dallek, *Franklin D. Roosevelt and American Foreign Policy, 1932–1945* (New York: Oxford University Press, 1979); Robert A. Divine, *Roosevelt and World War II* (Baltimore: Johns Hopkins Press, 1969); Waldo Heinrichs, *Threshold of War: Franklin D. Roosevelt and American Entry into World War II* (New York: Oxford University Press, 1988); David Reynolds, *From Munich to Pearl Harbor: Roosevelt's America and the Origins of the Second World War* (Chicago: Ivan R. Dee, 2001), a fresh, crisp synthesis; Warren F. Kimball, *Forged in War: Roosevelt, Churchill, and the Second World War* (New York: William Morrow, 1997); and David S. Wyman, *The Abandonment of the Jews: America and the Holocaust, 1941–1945* (New York: Pantheon, 1984). Anyone wishing to put Roosevelt in the overall context of World War II can consult a pair of authoritative overviews: Gerhard L. Weinberg, *A World at Arms: A Global History of World War II*, 2nd ed. (Cambridge, U.K.: Cambridge University Press, 2005); and Richard Overy, *Why the Allies Won* (London: Jonathan Cape, 1995). On the popular and professional geographical interests that informed U.S. foreign policy through the first half of the twentieth century, see Susan Schulten, *The Geographical Imagination in America, 1880–1950* (Chicago: University of Chicago Press, 2001); and Neil Smith, *American Empire: Roosevelt's Geographer and the Prelude to Globalization* (Berkeley: University of California Press, 2003).

The long-running controversy over Cold War origins has of late focused on how much in fact U.S. policymakers followed a containment strategy. Sarah-Jane Corke, "History, Historians and the Naming of Foreign Policy: A Postmodern Reflection on American Strategic Thinking during the Truman Administration," *Intelligence and National Security* 16 (Autumn 2001): 146–63, lays out the issues. The view that a defensive containment guided U.S. policy has long been associated with the work of John Gaddis, initially in *The United States and the Origins of the Cold War, 1941–1947* (New York: Columbia University Press, 1972); then in a broader treatment, *Strategies of Containment: A Critical Appraisal of Postwar American National Security Policy* (New York: Oxford University Press, 1982); and once again in *We Now Know: Rethinking Cold War History* (New York: Oxford University Press, 1997). An equally impressive case for a defensive, containment-driven U.S. policy emerges from Melvyn P. Leffler, *A Preponderance of Power: National Security, the Truman Administration, and the Cold War* (Stanford, Calif.: Stanford University Press, 1992), rendered in a more interpretively explicit and tightly argued version in Leffler, *The Specter of Communism: The United States and the Origins of the Cold War, 1917–1953* (New York: Hill and Wang, 1994). For the recent interpretive challenge giving prominence to a more aggressive rollback or liberation strategy pursued through covert operations and political warfare, see Walter L. Hixson, *Parting the Curtain: Propaganda, Culture, and the Cold War, 1945–1961* (New York: St. Martin's, 1997); Scott Lucas, *Freedom's War: The American Crusade against the Soviet Union* (New York: New York University Press, 1999); Gregory Mitrovich, *Undermining the Kremlin: America's Strategy to Subvert the Soviet Bloc, 1947–1956* (Ithaca, N.Y.: Cornell University Press, 2000); Peter Grose, *Operation Rollback: America's Secret War behind the Iron Curtain* (Boston: Houghton

Mifflin, 2000); Jeffrey Burds, *The Early Cold War in Soviet West Ukraine, 1944–1948* (Pittsburgh: University of Pittsburgh Center for Russian and East European Studies, 2001); and Arnold A. Offner, *Another Such Victory: President Truman and the Cold War, 1945–1953* (Stanford, Calif.: Stanford University Press, 2002).

The impact of World War II and the Cold War on American society and culture is the subject of Michael S. Sherry, *In the Shadow of War: The United States since the 1930s* (New Haven, Conn.: Yale University Press, 1995); Stephen J. Whitfield, *The Culture of the Cold War*, 2nd ed. (Baltimore: Johns Hopkins University Press, 1996); John Fousek, *To Lead the Free World: American Nationalism and the Cultural Roots of the Cold War* (Chapel Hill: University of North Carolina Press, 2000); Ellen Schrecker, *The Age of McCarthyism: A Brief History with Documents*, 2nd ed. (Boston: Bedford/ St. Martin's, 2002); Schrecker's fuller account, *Many Are the Crimes: McCarthyism in America* (Boston: Little, Brown, 1998); and Richard M. Fried, *Nightmare in Red: The McCarthy Era in Perspective* (New York: Oxford University Press, 1990). Machismo was a defining feature of early Cold War America, as becomes clear in Geoffrey S. Smith, "National Security and Personal Isolation: Sex, Gender, and Disease in the Cold-War United States," *International History Review* 14 (May 1992): 307–37; K. A. Cuordileone, "'Politics in an Age of Anxiety': Cold War Political Culture and the Crisis in American Masculinity, 1949–1960," *Journal of American History* 87 (September 2000): 515–45; and Robert D. Dean, *Imperial Brotherhood: Gender and the Making of Cold War Foreign Policy* (Amherst: University of Massachusetts Press, 2001). Luce gets his due as popularizer as well as proponent of an activist global outlook in Robert E. Herzstein, *Henry R. Luce: A Political Portrait of the Man Who Created the American Century* (New York: C. Scribner's Sons, 1994), which stops in the mid-1940s; Herzstein, *Henry R. Luce, Time, and the American Crusade in Asia* (Cambridge, U.K.: Cambridge University Press, 2005), which deals with postwar developments; and W. A. Swanberg, *Luce and His Empire* (New York: Scribner, 1972), a full-scale, spirited, sharply critical study.

To understand the amazing inventiveness and productivity that benefited the U.S. military at midcentury, begin with Alex Roland's brief but perceptive treatment in *The Military-Industrial Complex* (Washington, D.C.: American Historical Association, 2001); then continue with Paul A. C. Koistinen, *Planning War, Pursuing Peace: The Political Economy of American Warfare, 1920–1939* (Lawrence: University Press of Kansas, 1998); Koistinen, *Arsenal of World War II: The Political Economy of American Warfare, 1940–1945* (Lawrence: University Press of Kansas, 2004); Roger W. Lotchin, *Fortress California, 1910–1961: From Warfare to Welfare* (New York: Oxford University Press, 1992); Ann Markusen et al., *The Rise of the Gunbelt: The Military Remapping of Industrial America* (New York: Oxford University Press, 1991); Aaron L. Friedberg, *In the Shadow of the Garrison State: America's Anti-Statism and Its Cold War Grand*

Strategy (Princeton, N.J.: Princeton University Press, 2000); Stuart W. Leslie, *The Cold War and American Science: The Military-Industrial Complex at MIT and Stanford* (New York: Columbia University Press, 1993); and Rebecca S. Lowen, *Creating the Cold War University: The Transformation of Stanford* (Berkeley: University of California Press, 1997).

The U.S. military's frightening capacity to annihilate is treated in Russell F. Weigley's classic *The American Way of War: A History of the United States Military Strategy and Policy* (New York: Macmillan, 1973); and by Marek Thee's provocative but neglected *Military Technology, Military Strategy, and the Arms Race* (London: Croom Helm, 1986). For Brian M. Linn's critique of Weigley with a response, see "The American Way of War Revisited," *Journal of Military History* 66 (April 2002): 501–33. On the growing acceptance of indiscriminate attacks on cities, see Tami Davis Biddle, *Rhetoric and Reality in Air Warfare: The Evolution of British and American Ideas about Strategic Bombing, 1914–1945* (Princeton, N.J.: Princeton University Press, 2002). For the dawn of the nuclear age, turn to J. Samuel Walker, *Prompt and Utter Destruction: Truman and the Use of Atomic Bombs against Japan*, 2nd ed. (Chapel Hill: University of North Carolina Press, 2004), a calm, concise, up-to-date introduction to a contentious topic; Martin J. Sherwin, *A World Destroyed: Hiroshima and Its Legacies*, 3rd ed. (Stanford, Calif.: Stanford University Press, 2003); and David Holloway, *Stalin and the Bomb: The Soviet Union and Atomic Energy, 1939–1956* (New Haven, Conn.: Yale University Press, 1994). U.S. nuclear policy over its first two decades is the subject of a pair of foundational studies by David A. Rosenberg: "American Atomic Strategy and the Hydrogen Bomb Decision," *Journal of American History* 71 (June 1979): 62–87; and "The Origins of Overkill: Nuclear Weapons and American Strategy, 1945–1960," *International Security* 7 (Spring 1983): 3–71. Gerard J. DeGroot, *The Bomb: A Life* (Cambridge, Mass.: Harvard University Press, 2005), emphasizes the lasting importance of developments from the 1940s to the early 1960s.

For the constraints nuclear weapons imposed on the Soviet-American rivalry, see Vladislav Zubok and Constantine Pleshakov, *Inside the Kremlin's Cold War: From Stalin to Khrushchev* (Cambridge, Mass.: Harvard University Press, 1996); Vojtech Mastny, *The Cold War and Soviet Insecurity: The Stalin Years* (New York: Oxford University Press, 1996); Campbell Craig, *Destroying the Village: Eisenhower and Thermonuclear War* (New York: Columbia University Press, 1998); Robert R. Bowie and Richard H. Immerman, *Waging Peace: How Eisenhower Shaped an Enduring Cold War Strategy* (New York: Oxford University Press, 1998); Aleksandr Fursenko and Timothy Naftali, *"One Hell of a Gamble": Khrushchev, Castro, and Kennedy, 1958–1964* (New York: W. W. Norton, 1997); Michael R. Beschloss, *The Crisis Years: Kennedy and Khrushchev, 1960–1963* (New York: Edward Burlingame Books, 1991); Lawrence Freedman, *Kennedy's Wars: Berlin, Cuba, Laos, and Vietnam* (New York: Oxford University Press,

2000); and Matthew Evangelista, *Unarmed Forces: The Transnational Movement to End the Cold War* (Ithaca, N.Y.: Cornell University Press, 1999).

The notion of a midcentury transformation of the U.S. state originated with the work of Richard J. Barnet, who broached the theme of the "National Security Managers" in *Intervention and Revolution: America's Confrontation with Insurgent Movements Around the World* (New York: Meridian Books, 1968) and elaborated on it in *Roots of War: The Men and Institutions behind U.S. Foreign Policy* (New York: Atheneum, 1972). The best brief treatment of the expanding Cold War bureaucracy is Charles Neu, "The Rise of the National Security Bureaucracy," in *The New American State: Bureaucracies and Policies since World War II*, ed. Louis Galambos (Baltimore: Johns Hopkins University Press, 1987), 85–108, while Michael J. Hogan, *A Cross of Iron: Harry S. Truman and the Origins of the National Security State, 1945–1954* (Cambridge, U.K.: Cambridge University Press, 1998), develops in detail the tension between midcentury state builders and those fearful of a garrison state inimical to American values. John Prados, *Keepers of the Keys: A History of the National Security Council from Truman to Bush* (New York: William Morrow, 1991), surveys a key institution over the course of the Cold War. Particularly suggestive works on the president's increasingly potent power to persuade are Mark L. Chadwin, *The Warhawks: American Interventionists before Pearl Harbor* (originally published in 1968 as *The Hawks of World War II*; New York: Norton, 1970); Wayne S. Cole, *Roosevelt and the Isolationists, 1932–45* (Lincoln: University of Nebraska Press, 1983); and Walter LaFeber, "American Policy-Makers, Public Opinion, and the Outbreak of the Cold War, 1945–50," in *The Origins of the Cold War in Asia*, ed. Yonosuke Nagai and Akira Iriye (New York: Columbia University Press, 1977), 43–65. The proponents of a more cautious policy get their due in Justus D. Doenecke, *Storm on the Horizon: The Challenge to American Intervention, 1939–1941* (Lanham, Md.: Rowman and Littlefield, 2000); and in Thomas G. Paterson, ed., *Cold War Critics: Alternatives to American Foreign Policy in the Truman Years* (Chicago: Quadrangle Books, 1971).

5. IN THE AMERICAN IMAGE, 1941–1968

The U.S. design for postwar global governance has been drawing considerable scholarly attention of late. The United Nations, the cornerstone of that design, is treated by Stanley Meisler, *United Nations: The First Fifty Years* (New York: Atlantic Monthly Press, 1995); and Townsend Hoopes and Douglas Brinkley, *FDR and the Creation of the U.N.* (New Haven, Conn.: Yale University Press, 1997). For the precedent-setting trials of Axis leaders, see the compact, clear-headed introduction by Michael R. Marrus, ed., *The Nuremberg War Crimes Trial, 1945–1946: A Documentary History* (Boston: Bedford Books, 1997); and the pioneering study by Richard H. Minear, *Victors' Justice: The Tokyo War Crimes Trial* (Princeton, N.J.: Princeton University Press, 1971).

For the rise of a human rights agenda—both the U.S. role and the broad context—see Elizabeth Borgwardt, *A New Deal for the World: America's Vision for Human Rights* (Cambridge, Mass.: Harvard University Press, 2005); Paul Gordon Lauren, *The Evolution of International Human Rights: Visions Seen* (Philadelphia: University of Pennsylvania Press, 1998), as well as Lauren's companion study, *Power and Prejudice: The Politics and Diplomacy of Racial Discrimination*, 2nd ed. (Boulder, Colo.: Westview Press, 1996); Micheline R. Ishay, *The History of Human Rights: From Ancient Times to the Globalization Era* (Berkeley: University of California Press, 2004); Burns H. Weston's fine entry for "Human Rights" in *Encyclopaedia Britannica*, 15th ed. (2002), available at the website for the University of Iowa Human Rights Center, <http://www.uiowa.edu/~uichr/publications/documents/HRBritannica05part1.pdf> and <HRBritannica05part2.pdf>; Jan Herman Burgers, "The Road to San Francisco: The Revival of the Human Rights Idea in the Twentieth Century," *Human Rights Quarterly* 14 (November 1992): 447–77; and Mary Ann Glendon, *A World Made New: Eleanor Roosevelt and the Universal Declaration of Human Rights* (New York: Random House, 2001). Kenneth Cmiel, "The Recent History of Human Rights," *American Historical Review* 109 (February 2004): 117–35, surveys an expanding body of literature. The excesses that made limiting state sovereignty seem such a pressing matter from midcentury onward are recounted in Jonathan Glover, *Humanity: A Moral History of the Twentieth Century* (New Haven, Conn.: Yale University Press, 2000); and Eric D. Weitz, *A Century of Genocide: Utopias of Race and Nation* (Princeton, N.J.: Princeton University Press, 2003).

For an introduction to the postwar international economy that American leaders put in place, turn to Daniel A. Yergin and Joseph Stanislaw's sprightly *The Commanding Heights: The Battle for the World Economy*, rev. ed. (New York: Simon and Schuster, 2002). Other broad treatments also spanning the postwar period include Diane B. Kunz, *Butter and Guns: America's Cold War Economic Diplomacy* (New York: Free Press, 1997), which follows the role of U.S. policymakers within that economy; and Harold James, *International Monetary Cooperation since Bretton Woods* (Washington, D.C.: International Monetary Fund and New York: Oxford University Press, 1996), a commissioned history of a key institution. Thomas W. Zeiler, *Free Trade, Free World: The Advent of GATT* (Chapel Hill: University of North Carolina Press, 1999), treats the troubled early efforts to create a liberal free-trade regime. The economist who exercised an outsized influence over postwar economics has attracted two masterful biographers; their findings are distilled in D. E. Moggridge, *Keynes*, 3rd ed. (Toronto: University of Toronto Press, 1993); and Robert J. A. Skidelsky, *Keynes* (Oxford: Oxford University Press, 1996). Peter A. Hall, ed., *The Political Power of Economic Ideas: Keynesianism across Nations* (Princeton, N.J.: Princeton University Press, 1989), considers Keynes's worldwide impact.

Western Europe's recovery under U.S. auspices is dealt with in broad terms in David W. Ellwood, *Rebuilding Europe: Western Europe, America, and Postwar Reconstruction* (London: Longman, 1992); Alan S. Milward with George Brennan and Federico Romero, *The European Rescue of the Nation-State*, 2nd ed. (London: Routledge, 2000); Michael J. Hogan, *The Marshall Plan: America, Britain, and the Reconstruction of Western Europe, 1947–1952* (Cambridge, U.K.: Cambridge University Press, 1987); Geir Lundestad, "Empire by Invitation? The United States and Western Europe, 1945–1952," *Journal of Peace Research* 23 (September 1986): 263–77; Marc Trachtenberg, *A Constructed Peace: The Making of the European Settlement, 1945–1963* (Princeton, N.J.: Princeton University Press, 1999); and John McCormick, *Understanding the European Union: A Concise Introduction*, 3rd ed. (New York: Palgrave, 2005). Notable country studies include Irwin M. Wall, *The United States and the Making of Postwar France, 1945–1954* (Cambridge, U.K.: Cambridge University Press, 1991); John L. Harper, *America and the Reconstruction of Italy, 1945–1948* (Cambridge, U.K.: Cambridge University Press, 1986); Chiarella Esposito, *America's Feeble Weapon: Funding the Marshall Plan in France and Italy, 1948–1950* (Westport, Conn.: Greenwood Press, 1994); Federico Romero, *The United States and the European Trade Union Movement, 1944–1951*, trans. Harvey Fergusson II (Chapel Hill: University of North Carolina Press, 1992); Ronald L. Filippelli, *American Labor and Postwar Italy, 1943–1953: A Study of Cold War Politics* (Stanford, Calif.: Stanford University Press, 1989); Thomas Alan Schwartz, *America's Germany: John J. McCloy and the Federal Republic of Germany* (Cambridge, Mass.: Harvard University Press, 1991); Petra Goedde, *GIs and Germans: Culture, Gender, and Foreign Relations, 1945–1949* (New Haven, Conn.: Yale University Press, 2003); and Charles S. Maier and Günter Bischof, eds., *The Marshall Plan and Germany: West German Development within the Framework of the European Recovery Program* (New York: Berg, 1990).

On Japan's recovery beginning with the U.S. occupation, see John W. Dower, *Embracing Defeat: Japan in the Wake of World War II* (New York: W. W. Norton, 1999), the product of a lifetime of research; and Andrew Gordon, ed., *Postwar Japan as History* (Berkeley: University of California Press, 1993). Insight on the Japanese growth strategy can be found in Shigeto Tsuru, *Japan's Capitalism: Creative Defeat and Beyond* (Cambridge, U.K.: Cambridge University Press, 1993); Yutaka Kosai, "The Postwar Japanese Economy, 1945–1973" (trans. Andrew Goble), in *The Cambridge History of Japan*, vol. 6: *The Twentieth Century*, ed. Peter Duus (Cambridge, U.K.: Cambridge University Press, 1988), 494–537; and Chalmers Johnson, *MITI and the Japanese Miracle: The Growth of Industrial Policy, 1925–1975* (Stanford, Calif.: Stanford University Press, 1982). For important aspects of the early postwar U.S.–Japan relationship, see Yukiko Koshiro, *Trans-Pacific Racisms and the U.S. Occupation of Japan* (New York: Columbia University Press, 1999); and Sayuri Shimizu, *Creating People of Plenty: The*

United States and Japan's Economic Alternatives, 1950–1960 (Kent, Ohio: Kent State University Press, 2001).

For general works on postwar consumer trends, see Robert M. Collins, *More: The Politics of Economic Growth in Postwar America* (Oxford: Oxford University Press, 2000); Lizabeth Cohen, *A Consumer's Republic: The Politics of Mass Consumption in Postwar America* (New York: Knopf, 2003); Gary Cross, *An All-Consuming Century: Why Commercialism Won in Modern America* (New York: Columbia University Press, 2000); Heide Fehrenbach and Uta G. Poiger, eds., *Transactions, Transgressions, Transformations: American Culture in Western Europe and Japan* (New York: Berghahn Books, 2000); Reinhold Wagnleitner and Elaine Tyler May, eds., *"Here, There, and Everywhere": The Foreign Politics of American Popular Culture* (Hanover, N.H.: University Press of New England, 2000); and Jessica C. E. Gienow-Hecht, "Shame on US? Academics, Cultural Transfer, and the Cold War—A Critical Review," *Diplomatic History* 24 (Summer 2000): 465–94.

The U.S. cultural impact overseas after 1945 has been an active area of scholarship. Notable works on western Europe include Victoria de Grazia, *Irresistible Empire: America's Advance through Twentieth-Century Europe* (Cambridge, Mass.: Harvard University Press, 2005); Richard Pells, *Not Like Us: How Europeans Have Loved, Hated, and Transformed American Culture since World War II* (New York: Basic Books, 1997); Richard F. Kuisel, *Seducing the French: The Dilemma of Americanization* (Berkeley: University of California Press, 1993); Christopher Endy, *Cold War Holidays: American Tourism in France* (Chapel Hill: University of North Carolina Press, 2004); Maria Höhn, *GIs and Fräuleins: The German-American Encounter in 1950s West Germany* (Chapel Hill: University of North Carolina Press, 2002); Jessica C. E. Gienow-Hecht, *Transmission Impossible: American Journalism as Cultural Diplomacy in Postwar Germany, 1945–1955* (Baton Rouge: Louisiana State University Press, 1999); Uta G. Poiger, *Jazz, Rock, and Rebels: Cold War Politics and American Culture in a Divided Germany* (Berkeley: University of California Press, 2000); and Reinhold Wagnleitner, *Coca-Colonization and the Cold War: The Cultural Mission of the United States in Austria after the Second World War*, trans. Diana M. Wolf (Chapel Hill: University of North Carolina Press, 1994). For the rising appeal of consumer culture outside western Europe, see Timothy W. Ryback, *Rock around the Bloc: A History of Rock Music in Eastern Europe and the Soviet Union* (New York: Oxford University Press, 1990); Walter L. Hixson, *Parting the Curtain: Propaganda, Culture, and the Cold War, 1945–1961* (New York: St. Martin's, 1997); and Joseph J. Tobin, ed., *Re-made in Japan: Everyday Life and Consumer Taste in a Changing Society* (New Haven, Conn.: Yale University Press, 1992).

Firms associated with signature U.S. cultural exports have garnered some attention. Scattered insights on Coke can be found in Frederick Allen, *Secret Formula:*

How Brilliant Marketing and Relentless Salesmanship Made Coca-Cola the Best-Known Product in the World (New York: HarperCollins, 1994); Constance L. Hays, *The Real Thing: Truth and Power at the Coca-Cola Company* (New York: Random House, 2004); and Mark Pendergrast, *For God, Country, and Coca-Cola: The Definitive History of the World's Most Popular Soft Drink*, rev. ed. (London: Orion Business Books, 2000). The Mexico initiatives of J. Walter Thompson in advertising and Sears in retail sales are examined in Julio Moreno, *Yankee Don't Go Home! Mexican Nationalism, American Business Culture, and the Shaping of Modern Mexico, 1920–1950* (Chapel Hill: University of North Carolina Press, 2003), chaps. 5 and 6.

6. THE THIRD-WORLD CHALLENGE, 1941–1968

On the origins of the idea of a third world, see Carl Pletsch, "The Three Worlds, or the Division of Social Scientific Labor, circa 1950–1975," *Comparative Studies in Society and History* 23 (October 1981): 565–90. For thoughtful discussions of geographical constructs, see Martin W. Lewis and Kären E. Wigen, *The Myth of Continents: A Critique of Metageography* (Berkeley: University of California Press, 1997); Edward W. Said, *Orientalism* (first published 1978; new edition with added afterword, New York: Vintage Books, 1994); and Catherine A. Lutz and Jane L. Collins, *Reading National Geographic* (Chicago: University of Chicago Press, 1993).

Diverse perspectives on the postwar radicalism that so bedeviled U.S. policymakers emerge from Theodore Hamerow, *From the Finland Station: The Graying of Revolution in the Twentieth Century* (New York: Basic Books, 1990); Forrest D. Colburn, *The Vogue of Revolution in Poor Countries* (Princeton: Princeton University Press, 1994); L. S. Stavrianos, *Global Rift: The Third World Comes of Age* (New York: Morrow, 1981); Theodore H. Von Laue, *The World Revolution of Westernization: The Twentieth Century in Global Perspective* (New York: Oxford University Press, 1987); and Nigel Harris, *The End of the Third World: Newly Industrializing Countries and the End of an Ideology* (London: Tauris, 1986). For an introduction to a recent interpretive trend, see Gyan Prakash, "Subaltern Studies as Postcolonial Criticism," *American Historical Review* 99 (December 1994): 1475–90.

Sampling from an enormous body of regional literature provides a sense of the radical vogue at midcentury. For an African perspective, see Basil Davidson, *Black Star: A View of the Life and Times of Kwame Nkrumah* (New York: Praeger, 1974), along with the update by Marika Sherwood, *Kwame Nkrumah: The Years Abroad, 1935–1947* (Legon, Accra, Ghana: Freedom Publications, 1996). On the China case, see Odd Arne Westad, *Decisive Encounters: The Chinese Civil War, 1946–1950* (Stanford, Calif.: Stanford University Press, 2003); and Chen Jian, *Mao's China and the Cold War* (Chapel Hill: University of North Carolina Press, 2001). Revealing studies on Latin America include Leslie Bethell and Ian Roxborough, "Latin America between the Second World War and the Cold War: Some Reflections on the 1945–8 Conjuncture," *Journal of Latin American Studies* 20 (May 1988): 167–89; Cristóbal Kay, *Latin American Theories of Development and Underdevelopment* (London: Routledge, 1989); Joseph L. Love, "Economic Ideas and Ideologies in Latin America since 1930," in *The Cambridge History of Latin America*, ed. Leslie Bethell, vol. 6, pt. 1 (Cambridge, U.K.: Cambridge University Press, 1994), chap. 7; Jim Handy, *Revolution in the Countryside: Rural Conflict and Agrarian Reform in Guatemala, 1944–1954* (Chapel Hill: University of North Carolina Press, 1994); Tad Szulc, *Fidel: A Critical Portrait* (New York: Morrow, 1987); and Peter G. Bourne, *Fidel: A Biography of Fidel Castro* (New York: Dodd, Mead, 1986). For a sense of the intense political and social change gripping North Africa, see P. J. Vatikiotis, *Nasser and His Generation* (London: C. Helm, 1978); Peter Woodward, *Nasser* (London: Longman, 1992); and Matthew Connelly, *A Diplomatic Revolution: Algeria's Fight for Independence and the Origins of the Post–Cold War Era* (New York: Oxford University Press, 2002).

The importance of incorporating the local dynamic into any study of great-power control comes across clearly in Ronald Robinson's classic "Non-European Foundations of European Imperialism: Sketch for a Theory of Collaboration," in *Studies in the Theory of Imperialism*, ed. Roger Owen and Bob Sutcliffe (London: Longman, 1972), 117–40. The point is further developed and applied to the Cold War by Odd Arne Westad, *The Global Cold War: Third World Interventions and the Making of Our Time* (Cambridge, U.K.: Cambridge University Press, 2005); and by Michael H. Hunt and Steven I. Levine, "The Revolutionary Challenge to Early U.S. Cold War Policy in Asia," in *The Great Powers in East Asia, 1953–1960*, ed. Warren I. Cohen and Akira Iriye (New York: Columbia University Press, 1990), 13–34.

For overviews on the U.S. policy toward the third world, see David Ryan and Victor Pungong, eds., *The United States and Decolonization: Power and Freedom* (London: Macmillan, 2000); and David F. Schmitz, *Thank God They're on Our Side: The United States and Right-wing Dictatorships, 1921–1965* (Chapel Hill: University of North Carolina Press, 1999), which is especially helpful in highlighting the continuity between the Cold War and earlier periods. For thoughtful treatments of interpretive approaches, see David S. Painter, "Explaining U.S. Relations with the Third World," *Diplomatic History* 19 (Summer 1995): 525–48; and Robert J. McMahon, "Eisenhower and Third World Nationalism: A Critique of the Revisionists," *Political Science Quarterly* 101 (Fall 1986): 453–73.

Historians have treated U.S. perceptions of the third world from a rich variety of directions. On the influence of the social science idea of modernization, see Michael E. Latham, *Modernization as Ideology: American Social Science and "Nation Building" in the Kennedy Era* (Chapel Hill: University of North Carolina Press, 2000); David C. Engerman et al., eds., *Staging Growth: Modernization, Development, and the*

Global Cold War (Amherst, Mass.: University of Massachusetts Press, 2003); Nick Cullather, "Damming Afghanistan: Modernization in a Buffer State," *Journal of American History* 89 (September 2002): 512–37; Suzanne M. Moon, "Takeoff or Self-Sufficiency? Ideologies of Development in Indonesia, 1957–1961," *Technology and Culture* 39 (April 1998): 187–212; and Gilbert Rist, *The History of Development: From Western Origins to Global Faith*, trans. Patrick Camiller, 2nd ed. (London: Zed Books, 2002). On the impact of racial concerns, see Thomas Borstelmann, *The Cold War and the Color Line: American Race Relations in the Global Arena* (Cambridge, Mass.: Harvard University Press, 2001); Penny M. Von Eschen, *Race against Empire: Black Americans and Anticolonialism, 1937–1957* (Ithaca: Cornell University Press, 1997); and Mary L. Dudziak, *Cold War Civil Rights: Race and the Image of American Democracy* (Princeton, N.J.: Princeton University Press, 2000). On gender as a prism for U.S. perspectives, see Andrew J. Rotter, "Gender Relations, Foreign Relations: The United States and South Asia, 1947–1964," *Journal of American History* 81 (September 1994): 518–42. On the application of "orientalism," see Andrew J. Rotter, "Saidism without Said: *Orientalism* and U.S. Diplomatic History," *American Historical Review* 105 (October 2000): 1205–17.

Each contested third-world region can boast a strong set of studies emphasizing the interplay between U.S. Cold War policy and the challenges it faced. For the persistence of old patterns in the Latin American sphere, see Piero Gleijeses, *Shattered Hope: The Guatemalan Revolution and the United States, 1944–1954* (Princeton, N.J.: Princeton University Press, 1991); Greg Grandin, *The Blood of Guatemala: A History of Race and Nation* (Durham, N.C.: Duke University Press, 2000); Grandin, *The Last Colonial Massacre: Latin America in the Cold War* (Chicago: University of Chicago Press, 2004); Alan McPherson, *Yankee No! Anti-Americanism in U.S.–Latin American Relations* (Cambridge, Mass.: Harvard University Press, 2003); and Stephen G. Rabe, *The Most Dangerous Area in the World: John F. Kennedy Confronts Communist Revolution in Latin America* (Chapel Hill: University of North Carolina Press, 1999); as well as the general treatments listed in the discussion of the literature related to chapter 2. For the last phase of the U.S. crusade along the western Pacific rim, see Bruce Cumings, *The Origins of the Korean War*, 2 vols. (Princeton, N.J.: Princeton University Press, 1981–90); William Stueck, *Rethinking the Korean War: A New Diplomatic and Strategic History* (Princeton, N.J.: Princeton University Press, 2002); George C. Herring, *The Longest War: The United States and Vietnam, 1950–1975*, 4th ed. (Boston: McGraw-Hill, 2002); Marilyn B. Young, *The Vietnam Wars, 1945–1990* (New York: HarperCollins, 1991); Robert J. McMahon, *The Limits of Empire: The United States and Southeast Asia since World War II* (New York: Columbia University Press, 1999); Nick Cullather, "'Fuel for the Good Dragon': The United States and Industrial Policy in Taiwan, 1950–1965," *Diplomatic History* 20 (Winter 1996): 1–25; and

Cullather, *Illusions of Influence: The Political Economy of United States–Philippines Relations, 1942–1960* (Stanford, Calif.: Stanford University Press, 1994). Key works on the rising commitment in the Middle East include Douglas Little, *American Orientalism: The United States and the Middle East since 1945* (Chapel Hill: University of North Carolina Press, 2002); H. W. Brands, *Into the Labyrinth: The United States and the Middle East, 1945–1993* (New York: McGraw-Hill, 1994); Melani McAlister, *Epic Encounters: Culture, Media, and U.S. Interests in the Middle East since 1945*, 2nd ed. (Berkeley: University of California Press, 2005); Rhashid Khalidi, *Resurrecting Empire: Western Footprints and America's Perilous Path in the Middle East* (Boston: Beacon Press, 2004); James A. Bill, *The Eagle and the Lion: The Tragedy of American-Iranian Relations* (New Haven, Conn.: Yale University Press, 1988); and Richard W. Cottam, *Iran and the United States: A Cold War Case Study* (Pittsburgh, Pa.: University of Pittsburgh Press, 1988). On sub-Saharan Africa, Piero Gleijeses, *Conflicting Missions: Havana, Washington, and Africa, 1959–1976* (Chapel Hill: University of North Carolina Press, 2002); and Thomas Borstelmann, *Apartheid's Reluctant Uncle: The United States and Southern Africa in the Early Cold War* (New York: Oxford University Press, 1993), are especially valuable.

7. DISORIENTED GIANT, 1968–1991

For guidance on U.S. policy during the final phase of the Cold War, turn to the authoritative and suitably critical two-volume account by a U.S. policy insider and Soviet specialist: Raymond L. Garthoff, *Détente and Confrontation: American-Soviet Relations from Nixon to Reagan*, 2nd ed. (Washington, D.C.: Brookings Institution, 1994), and *The Great Transition: American-Soviet Relations at the End of the Cold War* (Washington, D.C.: Brookings Institution, 1994). See also H. W. Brands, *Since Vietnam: The United States in World Affairs, 1973–1995* (New York: McGraw-Hill, 1996), which is brief and lively; Wilfried Loth, *Overcoming the Cold War: A History of Détente, 1950–1991*, trans. Robert F. Hogg (Houndmills, Basingstoke, Hampshire, U.K.: Palgrave, 2002), which highlights the Soviet and European contributions to ending the Cold War; and Michael J. Hogan, ed., *The End of the Cold War: Its Meaning and Implications* (Cambridge, U.K.: Cambridge University Press, 1992), which brings together reflections by historians.

The domestic discontents so disruptive of U.S. policy get their due in Mark H. Lytle, *America's Uncivil Wars: The Sixties Era from Elvis to the Fall of Richard Nixon* (New York: Oxford University Press, 2006); and Terry H. Anderson, *The Movement and the Sixties: Protest in America from Greensboro to Wounded Knee* (New York: Oxford University Press, 1995). Treatment of important social and political discontents can be found in Allan M. Winkler, *Life under a Cloud: American Anxiety about the Atom* (New York: Oxford University Press, 1993); Elizabeth Cobbs Hoffman, *All You Need*

Is Love: The Peace Corps and the Spirit of the 1960s (Cambridge, Mass.: Harvard University Press, 1998); Rhodri Jeffreys-Jones, Peace Now! American Society and the Ending of the Vietnam War (New Haven, Conn.: Yale University Press, 1999); David W. Levy, The Debate over Vietnam, 2nd ed. (Baltimore: Johns Hopkins University Press, 1996); Kirkpatrick Sale, The Green Revolution: The American Environmental Movement, 1962–1992 (New York: Hill and Wang, 1993); Daniel Horowitz, The Anxieties of Affluence: Critiques of American Consumer Culture, 1939–1979 (Amherst: University of Massachusetts Press, 2004); and Christian Smith, Resisting Reagan: The U.S. Central America Peace Movement (Chicago: University of Chicago Press, 1996). The degree to which U.S. unrest was part of a global phenomenon becomes apparent in Arthur Marwick, The Sixties: Cultural Revolution in Britain, France, Italy, and the United States, c.1958–c.1974 (Oxford: Oxford University Press, 1998); Robert V. Daniels, Year of the Heroic Guerrilla: World Revolution and Counterrevolution in 1968 (New York: Basic Books, 1989); Jeremi Suri, Power and Protest: Global Revolution and the Rise of Detente (Cambridge, Mass.: Harvard University Press, 2003); Thomas R. H. Havens, Fire across the Sea: The Vietnam War and Japan, 1965–1975 (Princeton, N.J.: Princeton University Press, 1987); and John McCormick, Reclaiming Paradise: The Global Environmental Movement (Bloomington: Indiana University Press, 1989).

Good places to start on the troubled Nixon and Carter administrations are Melvin Small, The Presidency of Richard Nixon (Lawrence: University Press of Kansas, 1999); Walter Isaacson, Kissinger: A Biography (New York: Simon and Schuster, 1992); Robert D. Schulzinger, Henry Kissinger: Doctor of Diplomacy (New York: Columbia University Press, 1989); David Skidmore, "Carter and Foreign Policy Reform," Political Science Quarterly 108 (Winter 1993–94): 699–729; Gaddis Smith, Morality, Reason, and Power: American Diplomacy in the Carter Years (New York: Hill and Wang, 1986); Odd Arne Westad, ed., The Fall of Détente: Soviet-American Relations during the Carter Years (Oslo: Scandinavian University Press, 1997); and David Farber, Taken Hostage: The Iran Hostage Crisis and America's First Encounter with Radical Islam (Princeton, N.J.: Princeton University Press, 2005). For the gathering interest in human rights that influenced Carter, see Kenneth Cmiel, "The Emergence of Human Rights in the United States," Journal of American History 86 (December 1999): 1231–50; Ann Marie Clark, Diplomacy of Conscience: Amnesty International and Changing Human Rights Norms (Princeton, N.J.: Princeton University Press, 2001); and Judith P. Zinsser, "From Mexico to Nairobi: The United Nations Decade for Women, 1975–1985," Journal of World History 13 (Spring 2002): 139–68.

On Reagan-Bush policy through the final phase of the Cold War, see Frances FitzGerald's pungent Way Out There in the Blue: Reagan, Star Wars, and the End of the Cold War (New York: Simon and Schuster, 2000); Lou Cannon, President Reagan: The Role of a Lifetime (New York: Simon and Schuster, 1991); and Don Oberdorfer, From *the Cold War to a New Era: The United States and the Soviet Union, 1983–1991*, 2nd ed. (Baltimore: Johns Hopkins University Press, 1998). The political and intellectual trends that shaped the Reagan years and beyond are the subject of John Ehrman, *The Rise of Neoconservatism: Intellectuals and Foreign Affairs, 1945–1994* (New Haven, Conn.: Yale University Press, 1995); William C. Berman, *America's Right Turn: From Nixon to Clinton*, 2nd ed. (Baltimore: Johns Hopkins University Press, 1998); John Micklethwait and Adrian Wooldridge, *The Right Nation: Conservative Power in America* (New York: Penguin Press, 2004), a thoughtful treatment by a pair of British journalists who bring a comparative perspective; and Stefan Halper and Jonathan Clarke, *America Alone: The Neo-conservatives and the Global Order* (Cambridge, U.K.: Cambridge University Press, 2004). On Reagan's indispensable Soviet partner and the concerns guiding the Soviet side, see Archie Brown's judicious assessment, *The Gorbachev Factor* (Oxford: Oxford University Press, 1996); Moshe Lewin, *The Gorbachev Phenomenon: A Historical Interpretation*, 2nd ed. (Berkeley: University of California Press, 1991); Robert D. English, *Russia and the Idea of the West: Gorbachev, Intellectuals, and the End of the Cold War* (New York: Columbia University Press, 2000); and Matthew Evangelista, *Unarmed Forces: The Transnational Movement to End the Cold War* (Ithaca, N.Y.: Cornell University Press, 1999).

For the regional problems that bedeviled late Cold War presidents, see generally Odd Arne Westad, *The Global Cold War: Third World Interventions and the Making of Our Time* (Cambridge, U.K.: Cambridge University Press, 2005). More focused works include William M. LeoGrande, *Our Own Backyard: The United States in Central America, 1977–1992* (Chapel Hill: University of North Carolina Press, 1998); Fawaz A. Gerges, *America and Political Islam: A Clash of Cultures or Clash of Interests?* (Cambridge, U.K.: Cambridge University Press, 1999); David W. Lesch, *1979: The Year That Shaped the Modern Middle East* (Boulder, Colo.: Westview Press, 2001); Nikki R. Keddie, with Yann Richard, *Modern Iran: Roots and Results of Revolution* (New Haven, Conn.: Yale University Press, 2003); and Charles Kurzman, *The Unthinkable Revolution in Iran*, 2nd ed. (Cambridge, Mass.: Harvard University Press, 2004).

8. THE NEOLIBERAL TRIUMPH, 1991–

Journalists and other observers have unleashed a flood of works that seek to make sense of developments over the last decade and a half. Particularly helpful general accounts include Charles A. Kupchan, *The End of the American Era: U.S. Foreign Policy and the Geopolitics of the Twenty-first Century* (New York: Knopf, 2002); Joseph S. Nye Jr., *The Paradox of American Power: Why the World's Only Superpower Can't Go It Alone* (New York: Oxford University Press, 2002); Clyde Prestowitz, *Rogue Nation: American Unilateralism and the Failure of Good Intentions* (New York: Basic Books, 2003); Benjamin R. Barber, *Fear's Empire: War, Terrorism, and Democracy* (New

York: W. W. Norton, 2003); Emmanuel Todd, *After the Empire: The Breakdown of the American Order*, trans. C. Jon Delogu (New York: Columbia University Press, 2004); Andrew J. Bacevich, *The New American Militarism: How Americans Are Seduced by War* (New York: Oxford University Press, 2005); Bacevich, *American Empire: The Realities and Consequences of U.S. Diplomacy* (Cambridge, Mass.: Harvard University Press, 2002); and Anatol Lieven, *America Right or Wrong: An Anatomy of American Nationalism* (New York: Oxford University Press, 2004).

The recent exercise of U.S. military power has attracted considerable attention, much of it dealing with the war on terrorism and the invasion of Iraq. Works that serve especially well as first-cut history include Lawrence Freedman and Efraim Karsh, *The Gulf Conflict, 1990–1991: Diplomacy and War in the New World Order* (Princeton, N.J.: Princeton University Press, 1993); Steven L. Burg and Paul S. Shoup, *The War in Bosnia-Herzegovina: Ethnic Conflict and International Intervention* (Armonk, N.Y.: M. E. Sharpe, 1999); James Mann, *Rise of the Vulcans: The History of Bush's War Cabinet* (New York: Viking Press, 2004), an engaging group biography; Michael R. Gordon and Bernard E. Trainor, *Cobra II: The Inside Story of the Invasion and Occupation of Iraq* (New York: Pantheon, 2006), an impressively detailed reconstruction; and George Packer, *The Assassins' Gate: America in Iraq* (New York: Farrar, Straus and Giroux, 2005), tracing the stunning string of mistakes attending the U.S. occupation. For revealing works on the Islamist challenge against which U.S. policy is arrayed, see Gilles Kepel, *Jihad: The Trail of Political Islam*, trans. Anthony F. Roberts (Cambridge, Mass.: Harvard University Press, 2002); and Fawaz A. Gerges, *The Far Enemy: Why Jihad Went Global* (New York: Cambridge University Press, 2005).

The recent U.S.–influenced global regime has received some helpful scholarly attention. On the freeing of international finance from the 1960s onward, see Eric Helleiner, *States and the Reemergence of Global Finance: From Bretton Woods to the 1990s* (Ithaca, N.Y.: Cornell University Press, 1994); and Robert Solomon, *The Transformation of the World Economy*, 2nd ed. (New York: St. Martin's Press, 1999), a compact insider account. For critical examinations of the neoliberal program, see Susan George and Fabrizio Sabelli, *Faith and Credit: The World Bank's Secular Empire* (Boulder, Colo.: Westview, 1994); Joseph E. Stiglitz, *Globalization and Its Discontents* (New York: W. W. Norton, 2002); Ha-Joon Chang, *Kicking Away the Ladder: Development Strategy in Historical Perspective* (London: Anthem Press, 2002); and Andrew Ross, *Low Pay, High Profile: The Global Push for Fair Labor* (New York: New Press, 2004). Samantha Power, *"A Problem from Hell": America and the Age of Genocide* (New York: Basic Books, 2002), underlines the U.S. reluctance to act against gross human cruelty across the twentieth century. For a critical look at the awkward U.S. relationship to the human rights regime, see Julie A. Mertus, *Bait and Switch: Human Rights and U.S. Foreign Policy* (New York: Routledge, 2004). A wide-ranging, no-nonsense survey of pressing environmental issues can be found in Lorraine Elliott, *The Global Politics of the Environment*, 2nd ed. (New York: New York University Press, 2004).

For insights on the varied consequences of neoliberalism for American society, see Kevin Phillips, *Wealth and Democracy: A Political History of the American Rich* (New York: Broadway Books, 2002); Studs Terkel, *The Great Divide: Second Thoughts on the American Dream* (New York: Pantheon, 1988); Peter D. Feaver and Richard H. Kohn, eds., *Soldiers and Civilians: The Civil-Military Gap and American National Security* (Cambridge, Mass.: MIT Press, 2001); Peter W. Singer, *Corporate Warriors: The Rise of the Privatized Military Industry* (Ithaca, N.Y.: Cornell University Press, 2003); and Michael S. Sherry, *In the Shadow of War: The United States since the 1930s* (New Haven, Conn.: Yale University Press, 1995). For help in understanding the currently turbulent U.S. views on international commitments and organizations, see Steven Kull and I. M. Destler, *Misreading the Public: The Myth of a New Isolationism* (Washington, D.C.: Brookings Institution Press, 1999); and Edward C. Luck, *Mixed Messages: American Politics and International Organization, 1919–1999* (Washington, D.C.: Brookings Institution Press, 1999). For a pair of engaging case studies that explore the continuing appeal and cultural complexity of U.S. exports and the U.S. model, see James L. Watson, ed., *Golden Arches East: McDonald's in East Asia* (Stanford, Calif.: Stanford University Press, 1997); and Yvette Djachechi Monga, "Dollars and Lipstick: The United States through the Eyes of African Women," *Africa* 70 (Spring 2000): 192–208. Barry Rubin and Judith Colp Rubin, *Hating America: A History* (Oxford: Oxford University Press, 2004), helpfully shows that the current antipathy has an old intellectual pedigree but also manages to dismiss what it ostensibly seeks to understand.

CONCLUSION: HEGEMONY IN QUESTION

The U.S. imperial role has of late been both a controversial and a slippery issue. For forceful statements in favor of empire, see Max Boot, *Savage Wars of Peace: Small Wars and the Rise of American Power* (New York: Basic Books, 2002); and Niall Ferguson, *Colossus: The Price of America's Empire* (New York: Penguin Press, 2004). Hostility to empire on ideological or practical grounds is a prominent theme in Patrick J. Buchanan, *A Republic, Not an Empire: Reclaiming America's Destiny* (Washington, D.C.: Regnery, 1999); Chalmers A. Johnson, *Blowback: The Costs and Consequences of American Empire* (New York: Metropolitan Books, 2000); Johnson, *The Sorrows of Empire: Militarism, Secrecy, and the End of the Republic* (New York: Metropolitan Books, 2004); and Michael Mann, *Incoherent Empire* (London: Verso, 2003). See also Rashid Khalidi, *Resurrecting Empire: Western Footprints and America's Perilous Path in the Middle East* (Boston: Beacon Press, 2004); Greg Grandin, *Empire's Workshop: Latin America, the United States, and the Rise of the New Imperialism* (New York:

Metropolitan Books, 2006); John B. Judis, *The Folly of Empire: What George W. Bush Could Learn from Theodore Roosevelt and Woodrow Wilson* (New York: Scribner, 2004); Andrew J. Bacevich, *American Empire: The Realities and Consequences of U.S. Diplomacy* (Cambridge, Mass.: Harvard University Press, 2002); Bacevich, *The New American Militarism: How Americans Are Seduced by War* (New York: Oxford University Press, 2005); Clyde Prestowitz, *Rogue Nation: American Unilateralism and the Failure of Good Intentions* (New York: Basic Books, 2003); and Charles S. Maier, *Among Empires: American Ascendancy and Its Predecessors* (Cambridge, Mass.: Harvard University Press, 2006).

The distinction between British and American dominance is the subject of Bernard Porter, *Empire and Superempire: Britain, America and the World* (New Haven, Conn.: Yale University Press, 2006); Patrick Karl O'Brien, "The Pax Britannica and American Hegemony: Precedent, Antecedent or Just Another History?" and John M. Hobson, "Two Hegemonies or One? A Historical-Sociological Critique of Hegemonic Stability Theory," both in *Two Hegemonies: Britain 1846–1914 and the United States 1941–2001*, ed. Patrick Karl O'Brien and Armand Clesse (Aldershot, U.K.: Ashgate, 2002), 3–64 and 305–25. For a response to *Two Hegemonies*, see Niall Ferguson, "Hegemony or Empire?" *Foreign Affairs* 82 (September/October 2003): 154–61. For additional discussions that are helpfully critical, see John Agnew, *Hegemony: The New Shape of Global Power* (Philadelphia: Temple University Press, 2005); and David C. Hendrickson, "The Curious Case of American Hegemony: Imperial Aspirations and National Decline," *World Policy Journal* 22 (Summer 2005): 1–22.

ACKNOWLEDGMENTS

I owe a major debt to the University of North Carolina at Chapel Hill, which gave me time and opportunity to think through the issues critical to this volume. In particular I am grateful for support from the William N. Reynolds fund, the Everett H. Emerson Professorship fund, the Institute for Arts and Humanities, Peter Coclanis as chair of the Department of History, and his successor, Lloyd Kramer.

At the top of the list of colleagues abetting me in this project is Charles Grench of the University of North Carolina Press. He brought to bear those essential traits of a good editor—trust, enthusiasm, and critical detachment—familiar from earlier collaborations. Paul Betz's careful, critical scrutiny did much to improve my manuscript. Rich Hendel, Katy O'Brien, and Amanda McMillan were also part of the skilled team that combined to magically convert a clutter of paper into the book now in your hands. Christopher Endy generously provided a quick, discerning reading of the entire manuscript at a critical point. Michaela Hoenecke Moore during the fall 2002 term and Jerma Jackson during the fall 2005 term taught with me in courses that both sharpened and expanded my understanding of many of the topics treated here. My thanks to both. Working with students in those courses as well as in other global history and foreign relations courses that I taught between 1999 and 2003 guided me to insights richer than I could have possibly conveyed to them. Two of those students—Rosalie Genova and Heeyong Jang—deserve a special nod for critically engaging the argument of this study. Thanks to Sydney Conrad, Luke Farley, Nathaniel Smith, and Jacqueline Whitt for research assistance. Notable among generous friends and colleagues willing to provide special guidance were William Barney, Magnus Bernhardsson, Chad Bryant, Kathleen DuVal, Curtis Jones, Charles Kurzman, Timothy McKeown, Theda Perdue, Tom Rand, Sarah Shields, and Deborah Weissman. I am grateful to Marilyn Young and Piero Gleijesis for helpful reviews of the initial proposal to UNC Press as well as of the final manuscript. Young and Endy generously took time to help me think through my concluding reflections on how the past might bear on the future.

I ask indulgence if some of the formulations developed in previously published works of mine have found their way into this account. I learned a great deal about some of the issues that inform this study in working with the fine staff at Bedford/ St. Martin's, above all Louise Townsend, as we developed the text *The World Transformed: 1945 to the Present* (2003) and its companion reader. Portions of chapters 1 and 2 draw from "Traditions of American diplomacy: from colony to great power," in *American Foreign Relations Reconsidered, 1890–1993*, ed. Gordon Martel (London: Routledge, 1994), 1–20; and from *Ideology and U.S. Foreign Policy* (Yale University Press, 1987). Chapter 2 incorporates elements from "1898: The Onset of America's Troubled Asian Century," *OAH Magazine of History* 12 (Spring 1998): 30–36. Chapter 6 developed out of "The Decolonization Puzzle in US Policy: Promise versus Performance," in *The United States and Decolonization: Power and Freedom*, ed. David Ryan and Victor Pungong (London: Macmillan, 2000), 207–29. Chapter 8 develops insights first tried out in "In the Wake of September 11: The Clash of What?" *Journal of American History* 89 (September 2002): 416–25 (reprinted in *History and September 11th*, ed. Joanne Meyerowitz [Philadelphia: Temple University Press, 2003], 8–21). For several chapters I have borrowed from "East Asia in Henry Luce's 'American Century'," *Diplomatic History* 23 (Spring 1999): 321–53 (reprinted in *The Ambiguous Legacy: U.S. Foreign Relations in the "American Century"*, ed. Michael J. Hogan [Cambridge, U.K.: Cambridge University Press, 1999], 232–78).

Corporatism, 96–98, 99

Council on Foreign Relations, 91–93

Creel, George, 74, 77

Cuba: and Spain, 20; independence movement in, 45, 46; U.S. occupation of, 50, 55, 56, 71, 72; U.S. investments in, 51, 56; and Spanish-American War, 57; and McKinley, 75; and Franklin Roosevelt, 104; and Hughes, 107; and communism, 109, 208, 270; and economic development, 201–2; and revolutionary movements, 204, 231; and Soviet Union, 212, 263; and Reagan, 256; U.S. impact on, 312

Cuban missile crisis, 138, 145, 157, 230

Cuban Revolution, 188, 203

Czechoslovakia, 115, 118

De Gaulle, Charles, 198, 239, 302

Democracy: and neoliberalism, 9, 271, 289, 296; U.S. as model for, 42; and Fourteen Points, 61, 62, 63; European view of, 87; and Japan, 111, 174, 175, 235, 304; and totalitarianism, 124, 125; and China, 270; and globalization, 275; and Middle East, 279, 280; and Iraq war, 280; and Afghanistan, 286; and East Asia, 304; and imperial presidency, 322–23

Democratic Party: and manifest destiny, 34; restrictive position on immigration, 38; and Philippines, 52, 310; and Cuba, 55; and Paris peace treaty, 66; and interwar period, 91; and Latin America, 107–8; and Cold War policy, 128; and nuclear weapons, 138; and civil rights movement, 207; and Korean War, 214; and militant

cold warriors, 253; and neoliberalism, 268; and NAFTA, 272

Dominican Republic, 56, 57, 107, 211, 213, 291

Duhamel, Georges, 88–89, 130, 333 (n. 14)

Dulles, Allen, 142, 144, 212

Dulles, John Foster, 143–44, 154, 197, 202, 206, 216–17, 219

East Asia: and U.S. economic model, 25; and racial hierarchy, 36–37; and McKinley, 48; and Fourteen Points, 61; U.S. influence in, 81, 190; and interwar period, 105, 106, 110–13, 172; economy of, 175, 269, 272, 291, 304, 315; and liberation movements, 195; and U.S. intervention, 213–17, 309; and Nixon, 242; and George W. Bush, 278; U.S. reputation in, 304; and nuclear weapons, 319

Eastern Europe: immigrants from, 39; and Soviet Union, 122, 125, 202; and human rights, 161, 245, 247; economy of, 165, 177, 272, 302; and Marshall Plan, 167; and consumer society, 184–85; and West Germany, 239; and Gorbachev, 257; collapse of socialism in, 261, 263, 270, 284

Economic growth: and U.S. dominance, 2, 3, 26–33, 51, 78, 326 (n. 20); and globalization, 6, 272; in nineteenth century, 11, 23–33; and slavery, 38; and consumer society, 81, 85, 176; and interwar period, 82; challenges to, 234–38, 239, 241, 268, 317; and public opinion, 297

Economic policies: and consumer society, 85, 151, 153, 297; in inter-

129–30; and totalitarianism, 124–26; and nuclear weapons, 135; division of, 170; reunification of, 261, 272

Ghana, 192, 193–94, 201, 221

Global history, 3, 6, 7, 12

Globalization: features of, 4; effect on modern state, 5–6, 274; post–World War II phase of, 31; and technology, 48, 269, 274; Wilson's insight on, 68–69; and Bretton Woods, 165; and neoliberalism, 270–72, 274–76; and Clinton, 272–73, 280; opposition to, 275–77, 351 (n. 11)

GNP. *See* Gross national product

Good neighbor policy, 107–9, 196, 211–13

Gorbachev, Mikhail, 251, 257–64, 284

Great Depression, 81–82, 85–86, 89, 91, 98, 101, 107, 140, 164

Greece, 115, 123, 124, 137, 171, 218

Gross domestic product (GDP): as measure of economic growth, 23, 24, 327 (n. 27); total world GDP, 26, 165, 340–41 (n. 14); federal government's share of, 70, 73, 140; and Great Depression, 81–82; and military-industrial complex, 129, 131–32, 263; U.S.–Soviet Union comparison, 136; after World War II, 176–77; and economic aid, 290; Britain's percentage of global GDP, 311. *See also* Per capita GDP; Social GDP

Gross national product (GNP), 29, 290, 327 (n. 27)

Group of Seven (G-7), 244, 261

Group of 77, 205, 275

Guam Doctrine, 242–43

Guatemala, 142, 192, 196, 212, 223, 231, 319

Gulf War, 270, 271, 284–85, 293, 299, 305

Haiti, 57, 107, 276, 282–83

Hamilton, Alexander, 40–43, 62

Harding, Warren G., 67, 91, 92, 94, 96, 146

Hay, John, 47, 48, 55, 74

Hegemony: empire vs. hegemony debate, 1, 9, 308–14; and Cold War militants, 277; British attitudes toward U.S. hegemon, 301–2; and American legitimacy, 312, 313, 316, 320; prospects for U.S., 314–24

Hitler, Adolf, 102, 115, 118, 123–26, 130–31, 151, 252

Holocaust, 118, 160, 252, 294

Hoover, Herbert, 63, 91, 92, 98–99, 102, 107, 109, 113

Hoover, J. Edgar, 67, 128, 148

Hughes, Charles Evans, 91, 94, 97, 107, 108

Hull, Cordell, 104, 107, 109, 113, 143, 148, 154, 158, 162, 170

Human rights: and United Nations, 153, 160–61; and international law, 159–61; and East Asia, 160, 242, 304; U.S. policy on, 160, 313, 323; controversy over, 162, 251, 252; and Carter, 245–47, 249, 250; and neoliberalism, 276; and European Union, 303

Huntington, Samuel, 276–79

Hussein, Saddam, 279, 283–84, 286–87, 294, 299

Immigrants and immigration, 38–40, 51, 67, 75, 128

Imperial presidency: formation of, 69, 117; and bureaucratic capacity, 140–

policy compared to, 46; and China, 54–55, 102–5, 110–13, 118, 172, 194; and Russia, 58; and World War I, 63, 64; U.S. bargains with, 75, 94; and economic output, 82, 177, 235, 269, 271; film market in, 86; and modernity, 90, 111; and economic policies, 104, 235; and democracy, 111, 174, 175, 235, 304; and World War II, 117, 119–21, 130, 148, 172; and Cold War policy, 127, 174; nuclear weapons used against, 131, 133, 134, 135, 172; U.S. occupation of, 144, 173–74; and post–World War II recovery, 165, 172–75, 289, 313, 324; and consumer society, 177, 322; and American film industry, 180; and decolonization, 191, 192; and Vietnam, 216; and nongovernmental organizations, 228; and anti-Americanism, 239; as great power center, 241; and international economy, 244; and Gulf War, 299; U.S. reputation in, 304–5

Jefferson, Thomas, 15, 36, 41–43, 62, 279, 310

Johnson, Lyndon: and Vietnam War, 8, 146, 217, 230, 236, 238, 243, 299; and nuclear nonproliferation, 139; and CIA, 142; and National Security Council, 145; and third world, 201, 213; and civil rights movement, 207, 209; and Israel, 220; Great Society programs of, 227, 236; and trade, 235

Kellogg-Briand Pact, 95, 158

Kennedy, John F.: and nuclear weapons, 138–39, 230; and CIA, 142; and National Security Council, 145; public persona of, 146; and United

Nations, 157; and GATT, 165; and containment policy, 201; and third world, 207–8, 212–13; and Vietnam, 217, 225, 299; and Israel, 220; and Africa, 221, 222

Keynes, John Maynard, 85, 99, 163, 164, 266, 268

Khrushchev, Nikita, 137, 138, 151, 178, 184, 203, 264

Kirkpatrick, Jeanne, 252, 254, 293

Kissinger, Henry, 238–39, 240, 241, 242, 245, 256, 281

Knox, Philander C., 55, 66, 71, 74, 111–12

Korea: and U.S. naval expeditions, 48, 52; and Japan, 112; and U.S. Cold War policy, 127, 131; division of, 214–15. *See also* North Korea; South Korea

Korean War, 144–46, 149, 170–71, 174, 199, 200, 210, 214–15, 236, 298–99

Kosovo, 276, 287, 293, 295

Labor force, 13, 17, 28, 30–33, 38–40, 83, 130, 165, 235, 275

Labor unions, 67, 81, 118, 128, 196, 297

Lansing, Robert, 57, 65, 66, 74

Latin America: Spain's colonies in, 20, 22; and U.S. exports, 30; and racial hierarchy, 36; and Monroe Doctrine, 51; and Fourteen Points, 61; U.S. influence in, 81, 113, 190, 321; nationalism in, 100, 101, 106, 206, 211; and interwar period, 105, 106–9, 110, 113; and liberation movements, 191, 195, 200, 203; and U.S. Cold War intervention, 211–13, 309; and Soviet Union, 253; and Reagan, 282; and structural adjustment programs, 290

League of Nations, 61, 65–67, 77, 93–96, 102, 121, 153

Lebanon, 219, 256, 259, 283, 305

Liang Qichao, 25, 110

Lippmann, Walter, 95, 122, 154, 223–24

Lodge, Henry Cabot, 39, 62, 64, 66, 91–92, 112

Luce, Henry, 115, 117–18, 120, 125, 128, 151, 153, 275, 321

MacArthur, Douglas, 144, 173–74, 214, 216

Mao Zedong, 65, 194–95, 203–4, 215–16, 223, 231, 242

Marshall, George C., 143–45, 167, 216, 280

Marshall Plan, 166–67

Marxism, 193, 195, 203, 232, 250–51

McCarthy, Joseph, 128, 220, 240

McKinley, William: and U.S. dominance, 7; and presidential powers, 7, 74, 75, 140, 143; war room of, 45, 48, 70, 145; Caribbean initiatives of, 45, 55–56, 57, 76; imperial impulse of, 46–57, 69, 76, 227, 310; Pacific initiatives of, 52, 54, 57, 75; and Root, 71; and public opinion, 76, 77; and Republican Party, 92; and international arbitration, 94

McNamara, Robert, 139, 145, 225

Mexican War (1840s), 42, 75, 310

Mexico: creole society of, 12; independence of, 20; and France, 22; and U.S. direct investments, 32; and racial hierarchy, 36; and Wilson, 56–57, 108; and American films, 86, 180; and debt crisis, 291

Middle East: and European imperialism, 51, 81; and Paris peace conference, 65; and U.S. Cold War policy, 124, 217–20, 231–32, 244; and liberation movements, 191, 200, 203; and oil industry, 217–18, 232, 237, 283, 305; and Carter, 248; and George W. Bush, 278–79, 305–6; and U.S. as global policeman, 283–85; U.S. reputation in, 305–6; and nuclear weapons, 319; U.S. influence in, 321

Military-industrial complex, 129–33, 233, 234, 281–88

Military technology: state's embrace of, 6; and Native Americans, 14, 16; costs of, 48, 322; and imperialism, 50; and military-industrial complex, 130–31; and arms race, 139, 229, 244; and Reagan, 255; and U.S. as global policeman, 282; and empire vs. hegemony debate, 311. *See also* Arms race; Military-industrial complex; Nuclear weapons; Technowar

Milosevic, Slobodan, 261–62, 287–88

Modernity: U.S. as leading indicator of, 6, 82–85, 90–91, 301, 308, 312; U.S. exporting of, 85–91, 180; European view of, 87–89, 180–81; and Japan, 90, 111; and totalitarianism, 124, 126

Modernization theory, 208–9, 213

Monroe Doctrine, 22, 51, 56, 65, 66, 107, 211

Morgan, J. P., 79, 98, 100

Morgenthau, Henry, 108, 143, 158, 162, 170

Mussolini, Benito, 100, 118, 124, 126

Nasser, Gamal Abdul, 202, 206, 218–19

National identity, 11, 40, 69, 85, 181, 298, 315

Nationalism (U.S.): and U.S. domi-

Roosevelt, Franklin D.: and U.S. dominance, 7; as vice-presidential candidate, 67, 102; and economic policies, 85, 102–4; and interwar policy, 91, 102–5, 107–8, 113; and Republican Party, 91, 92; and Wilson, 102, 105, 107, 118–21, 123, 153; and World War II, 117, 118–22, 153, 240; and presidential powers, 117, 120, 143, 146–48; and United Nations, 121, 153–56; and totalitarianism, 125; and nuclear weapons, 131, 134, 135; and Office of Strategic Services, 141; and press, 146; and human rights, 160; and reform of Germany, 170; and decolonization, 197–98

Roosevelt, Theodore, 39, 50, 54–56, 58, 73–75, 93, 102, 107

Root, Elihu, 56, 63, 66, 70–72, 74, 91, 92, 94

Rostow, Walt, 145, 209, 252

Rubin, Robert, 273, 281

Rumsfeld, Donald, 278, 281, 286

Rusk, Dean, 144, 145, 210

Russia: and Alaska, 20; and Japan, 58; and World War I, 59, 62, 63; and Fourteen Points, 61; Bolshevik regime in, 81; and nuclear weapons, 262; and post-Soviet developments, 271, 276, 291–92, 303–4, 311; and United Nations, 293. *See also* Soviet Union

Russo-Japanese War, 112

Rwanda, 276, 288, 294, 295

Saudi Arabia, 161, 237, 285, 305

Schuman, Robert, 166, 168–69

Scowcroft, Brent, 262, 280, 281

Self-determination: and Fourteen Points, 61, 62, 65; European view of, 87; and decolonization, 191, 192, 193–94; and Atlantic Charter, 191–92, 194, 198, 220; U.S. doubts about, 196–200, 234, 322; and Kennedy, 207; and empire vs. hegemony debate, 309, 310

Settler colonialism/settler society: U.S. case, 4, 12–18, 26, 308; defined, 12; and U.S. nationalism, 33–34, 37; in Hawaii, 47; in third world, 201; and racial hierarchy, 190, 210; in Africa, 221–22

Shultz, George, 259–60, 281

Singapore, 12, 175, 305

Social GDP, 318, 322

Somalia, 156, 250, 276, 285, 288, 293

Somoza, Anastasio, 108–9, 211, 231, 250

South Africa, 12, 26, 29, 43, 161, 201, 222–23, 229, 232, 244

South Korea, 157, 175, 197, 214–15, 291

South Vietnam, 213, 216, 243

Soviet Union: U.S. rivalry with, 8, 199; economy of, 82, 136, 165, 177, 263–64; and Franklin Roosevelt, 104, 121, 125; and third world, 105, 190, 192, 200–201, 202–3, 207, 250, 256; and World War II, 115, 120–21, 130, 136, 195; and Truman, 117, 122–23, 134–35; and China, 123, 136, 195, 203, 242, 254; and totalitarianism, 124–26; and nuclear weapons, 127, 135–39, 149, 228, 320; and consumer society, 151, 184, 263; and United Nations, 154–55; and Nuremberg war crimes trial, 159; and human rights, 160, 161, 245, 246; and Marshall Plan, 167; and Afghanistan, 203, 231, 249–51, 253, 256–57, 263, 283, 285;

and Cuba, 212, 263; and Middle East, 218, 219; collapse of, 227, 236, 251, 257, 261, 262–63, 265, 269, 271, 284, 303, 306; and Nixon, 240–42, 247, 251–53; and Carter, 247–48, 249, 250–51; and Reagan, 254, 255–60, 263; and George H. W. Bush, 261–62. *See also* Russia

Spain, 4, 13–14, 20, 36, 45–47, 55, 100, 103, 126

Spanish-American War (1898), 42, 45, 47–49, 71, 73, 75, 81

Stalin, Joseph, 10, 104, 118, 121–22, 125–26, 135–37, 149, 155–56, 170, 184, 200–203, 264

State building: significance of, 2, 69; U.S. case, 3, 4–5, 45, 69–73. *See also* Imperial presidency; Presidential powers

Stimson, Henry L., 91, 92, 108–9, 112–13, 134–35, 143–44, 157–58, 170

Strategic Arms Limitations Treaty (SALT), 242, 247, 249, 294

Strategic Arms Reduction Talks (START), 260, 262

Strategic Defense Initiative (SDI/Star Wars), 255, 257, 259

Structural adjustment programs (SAPS), 290

Sub-Saharan Africa, 183–84, 191, 200–201, 206, 232, 253, 290, 317

Sudan, 14, 286, 288

Syria, 200, 219, 253, 284

Taft, William Howard, 54–56, 62, 66, 74, 92, 96, 111–12

Taiwan, 175, 214–16, 231, 242, 247, 305

Technology: and U.S. dominance, 6, 8, 16, 48–49, 311; and U.S. economy, 25, 26–29, 48, 82–83, 86, 87–88, 89–90, 98; and state building, 45, 69; and globalization, 48, 269, 274; and U.S. armed forces, 51, 95; and geopolitics, 119, 124. *See also* Military technology

Technowar, 129, 133–34, 139–40, 282, 286

Thatcher, Margaret, 259–60, 289

Third world/global periphery: challenges from, 7, 105, 187–88, 190–96, 199–205, 230–32; U.S. impact on, 8, 223–24, 311–12; and U.S. interwar policy, 105–14; and Truman administration, 127, 198–200; and U.S. Cold War interventions, 142, 210–23; and American film industry, 180; definition of, 188, 190; and U.S. Cold War views, 190–91, 205–10, 213, 220–21, 252; and Roosevelt administration, 196–98; and international economy, 237, 275, 290, 291, 319; and Carter, 248, 250; and post–Cold War U.S. policy, 281, 290; and United Nations, 292. *See also* Africa; East Asia; Latin America; Middle East

Tokyo war crimes trial, 159

Totalitarianism, 124–26, 129, 140, 153, 225, 252, 256

Truman, Harry S.: and phrase "American ascendancy," 1; and U.S. dominance, 7, 321; and Soviet Union, 117, 122–23, 134–35; and presidential powers, 117, 146; and Wilson, 122, 123, 155; and Cold War policy, 122–29; and nuclear weapons, 134–35, 137–38, 171; and CIA, 141; and State Department, 143; and National

and Roosevelt, 197; and Truman administration, 200, 216–17; and China, 195, 231; and Carter, 250; and Soviet Union, 263. *See also* South Vietnam

Vietnam War: and U.S. policy, 142, 146, 217, 225, 230–31, 243, 245, 281; costs of, 223–24; opposition to, 233–34, 235, 239, 252, 298–99, 300, 310

Voice of America, 123, 143, 184

Wallace, Henry, 128, 149

War crimes, 293–94

War on terrorism, 1, 266, 270, 286, 287, 294, 305, 306

Washington consensus, 289–93

Western Europe: and post–World War II recovery, 165, 166–70, 235–36, 244, 289, 312; regional integration of, 168–69, 313; and consumer society, 176, 177, 322; and decolonization, 196–97, 200; and Cold War, 239, 241, 255, 257, 302; tensions with U.S., 302, 315, 321

West Germany, 137, 166, 169–71, 177, 239, 248, 253, 324. *See also* Germany

Wilson, Woodrow: and World War I, 3, 45, 55, 57–60, 63–64, 77, 92; and U.S. dominance, 7, 321; and Philippines, 55; and Latin America, 56–57, 106, 107, 108; and foreign policy ideology, 57, 68–69, 78, 93, 128,

129, 153; and international reform, 57–69; and Paris peace treaty, 65–67, 75, 77, 92, 103, 313; significance of, 67–69, 78; and strong executive, 73–74, 75, 76, 77; and radio industry, 97; and Franklin Roosevelt, 102; and Truman, 122, 123, 155; and Reagan, 254; and empire vs. hegemony debate, 310. *See also* Fourteen Points

Wolfowitz, Paul, 276, 278

Woodruff, Robert, 178–80

World Bank, 163, 210, 244, 313, 317

World Trade Organization (WTO), 5, 275, 289, 292

World War I: and Wilson, 3, 45, 57–60, 63–64, 77, 92; and U.S. Army, 72; and presidential power, 73–74, 77; casualties of, 79, 89; and U.S. public opinion, 93, 103–5, 310; debt from, 97–99, 103

World War II: and Anglo-American relations, 68; damage done by, 81, 102, 113, 121, 133, 136; and Luce, 115, 117; and Franklin Roosevelt, 117, 118–22, 153; and U.S. military role, 129–30, 140, 141; and Soviet Union, 136; impact in third world, 191–92, 194–96

Yugoslavia, 115, 136, 263. *See also* Former Yugoslavia

Zhou Enlai, 202, 242

H. EUGENE AND LILLIAN YOUNGS LEHMAN SERIES

Lamar Cecil, *Wilhelm II: Prince and Emperor, 1859–1900* (1989).

Carolyn Merchant, *Ecological Revolutions: Nature, Gender, and Science in New England* (1989).

Gladys Engel Lang and Kurt Lang, *Etched in Memory: The Building and Survival of Artistic Reputation* (1990).

Howard Jones, *Union in Peril: The Crisis over British Intervention in the Civil War* (1992).

Robert L. Dorman, *Revolt of the Provinces: The Regionalist Movement in America* (1993).

Peter N. Stearns, *Meaning Over Memory: Recasting the Teaching of Culture and History* (1993).

Thomas Wolfe, *The Good Child's River*, edited with an introduction by Suzanne Stutman (1994).

Warren A. Nord, *Religion and American Education: Rethinking a National Dilemma* (1995).

David E. Whisnant, *Rascally Signs in Sacred Places: The Politics of Culture in Nicaragua* (1995).

Lamar Cecil, *Wilhelm II: Emperor and Exile, 1900–1941* (1996).

Jonathan Hartlyn, *The Struggle for Democratic Politics in the Dominican Republic* (1998).

Louis A. Pérez Jr., *On Becoming Cuban: Identity, Nationality, and Culture* (1999).

Yaakov Ariel, *Evangelizing the Chosen People: Missions to the Jews in America, 1880–2000* (2000).

Philip F. Gura, *C. F. Martin and His Guitars, 1796–1873* (2003).

Louis A. Pérez Jr., *To Die in Cuba: Suicide and Society* (2005).

Peter Filene, *The Joy of Teaching: A Practical Guide for New College Instructors* (2005).

John Charles Boger and Gary Orfield, eds., *School Resegregation: Must the South Turn Back?* (2005).

Jock Lauterer, *Community Journalism: Relentlessly Local* (2006).

Michael Hunt, *The American Ascendancy: How the United States Gained and Wielded Global Dominance* (2007).